BIRDS
of the World

BIRDS
of the World

p

This is a Parragon Publishing book
First published in 2005

Parragon Publishing
Queen Street House
4 Queen Street, Bath
BA1 IHE, UK

All photographs © OSF/Photolibrary.com and Ardea (see page 319 for details)
Text © Parragon
Produced by Atlantic Publishing

ISBN 1-40545-052-5
Printed in China

Contents

Passerines 180

Introduction

Birds have been a source of fascination for humans throughout the world, and throughout time. The ability of most birds to fly and escape the confines of the earth has provided a powerful symbol for numerous religious beliefs. The Ancient Egyptians held the Sacred Ibis to be one of the forms of the god Thoth, scribe to the gods of Egypt. In Christianity the most well-known bird is the Dove which symbolizes the Holy Spirit. For the Native Americans the Eagle is symbolic of the Divine Spirit and protection from evil, and significantly, the Eagle has become the emblem of the United States.

There is still much to learn about birds, their life cycles and interaction with their habitats and, most intriguingly, particularly in birds that migrate seasonally, how they navigate. Nevertheless, some mysteries have been clarified. We know a great deal about bird anatomy, how flight is achieved and the way in which birds have developed from their shared ancestry with the reptiles. We have also devised ways of grouping species, recognizing similarities between what can seem quite unrelated birds.

Birds of the World is organized using this conventional classification system. There is a major division between the "passerines" which generally includes the smaller, perching birds, and the "non-passerines", a category for the most part comprising larger birds. Within these two large subsections the birds are arranged according to their scientific classification as a species, or "kind" of bird. Species are grouped together in families, with closely related species being placed near one another. Thus, the Great Horned Owl (*Bubo virginianus*) of the Americas is placed next to the Eurasian Eagle Owl (*Bubo bubo*) as they are closely related members of the Strigidae family which falls within the non-passerine category.

The magnificent and splendidly detailed photographs in this book illustrate in striking detail the rich variety of world bird life, from the beautifully marked, tiny Striated Pardalote of the eucalyptus forests of Australia to the gigantic, night-feeding Wandering Albatross of the southern oceans, seen here with a chick in its snowbound nest. In between these two extremes are the common birds that, if we take a moment to look, we can see every day in our locality; birds whose songs and silhouettes in flight we often take for granted. But you will also find, photographed close-up with stunning clarity, occasional visitors to these shores, together with images of birds from all over the world. *Birds of the World* offers a window on the world, and the life, of more than 400 species.

A highly informative text educates by providing details of each individual bird's size, habitat and habits, as well as explaining breeding and nesting patterns. There is also information about the threats to individual species. There are many ways in which human activity impinges on the world of birds. The flightless Greater Rhea, the largest bird in South America, is at direct risk from man, as it is hunted for food and to protect the yields of the crops on which it is an unwelcome feeder. Under a less overt threat from man, but nonetheless suffering severe decline, is the Crested Caracara which suffers depredation from its habit of feeding on roadkill, as well as the encroachment of man on its habitat. But *Birds of the World* also notes man's success stories, where endangered species have been supported to increase in numbers by human intervention. The re-introduction of the Red Kite to Britain has seen a steady increase in its population and the process of designating the Chough a protected species in the UK has had positive effects on its numbers, particularly in the south-west of England.

In a world in which many individual bird species are endangered, or threatened with extinction, education is the starting point in a process to ensure we keep the rich and abundant variety of bird life throughout the world.

NON-PASSERINES

Ostrich

SCIENTIFIC NAME:	*Struthio camelus*
FAMILY:	Struthionidae
LENGTH:	250cm (98in)
HABITAT:	Desert, arid grassland
DISTRIBUTION:	Across Africa, from Senegal to Somalia, south into Tanzania with a separate population present in South Africa
IDENTIFICATION:	Very tall, long necked and long legged. Black body feathers, white, downy feathers on wings and tail. Bald head and neck, two toes on each foot

The Ostrich is the largest living bird species, attaining an average height of almost 2.5 meters, or around eight feet, and is also the fastest biped on Earth. As with its close relatives it is unable to fly, but has extremely large, powerful legs and when running it may attain speeds of over 60km/h (37m.p.h.), a feat which may be sustained for around 30 minutes. Living in open habitats, the ability to run at such speed protects this bird from potential predators such as big cats (although it is capable of inflicting fatal wounds with its huge feet), and also enables it to move swiftly between food supplies. The Ostrich is nomadic and well adapted to desert life, having keen eyesight and the ability to go without water for long periods, absorbing moisture from the plant matter that comprises most of its diet. However, it will also consume small vertebrates. When breeding, males attract females by sitting on the ground and ruffling their downy wing plumes. Although this species will typically pair, the male may mate with several females that will lay their eggs in a communal scrape. The dominant female usually removes several of these from the nest and it has been observed that they have a remarkable ability to recognize their own eggs. Both birds take part in incubation and the rearing of their young.

GREATER RHEA

SCIENTIFIC NAME:	*Rhea americana*
FAMILY:	Rheidae
LENGTH:	135cm (53in)
HABITAT:	Open grassland, semiwooded areas
DISTRIBUTION:	Eastern and central South America, from Brazil, south to parts of Argentina
IDENTIFICATION:	Tall, long-necked and long-legged with a shaggy appearance. Gray-brown in color, three toes on each foot

The largest bird found in South America, the Common or Greater Rhea belongs to a group of flightless birds known as ratites, which includes species such as the Ostrich, Cassowary and Emu. They are also closely related to the tinamous. Being flightless, rheas rely on their size and strong legs to avoid predation. They are excellent runners and can also deliver a powerful kick, and are most aggressive during the breeding season when males may fight in order to dominate rivals or to protect their young. At this time the Greater Rhea will even charge at humans. Males tend to form "harems" when breeding, creating a scrape on the ground and mating with several females that will each lay around 20 to 30 eggs in this nest, following which the male will incubate them alone. The Greater Rhea is omnivorous, feeding on vegetation, insects and even small vertebrates. Wild populations are at threat from man as they are hunted for food and to protect crops, but this species is also commercially farmed.

EMU

SCIENTIFIC NAME:	*Dromaius novaehollandiae*
FAMILY:	Dromaiidae
LENGTH:	200cm (79in)
HABITAT:	Arid grassland, desert, and open woodland
DISTRIBUTION:	Throughout most of Australia
IDENTIFICATION:	Very large, tall bird. Shaggy appearance, brown overall with black feathers on head and neck, bare patches on neck reveal blue skin

After the closely related Ostrich, the Emu is the second largest living bird, and as with other ratites, it has greatly reduced wings, lacks long flight feathers and has a shaggy appearance. It is a nomadic, wandering bird with a walking stride of over two meters (eight or nine feet) and a running speed of around 48km/h (30m.p.h.). For these reasons, it is able to range over huge distances. It is found in pairs or small groups across most of Australia in a range of habitats, but generally avoids the more inhospitable barren desert areas where food is most scarce, as well as dense forest and populated regions. The Emu feeds mainly on grasses and other plant material, but is omnivorous, supplementing its intake with insects, small vertebrates and carrion. Breeding takes place during the dry season between March and October, with the female depositing 5 to 20 eggs in a shallow depression, often lined with leaves, grass and bark. The male incubates the eggs alone for around eight weeks, and does not eat during this time, losing considerable weight as a result. After hatching the male will care for the chicks for up to 18 months.

SOUTHERN/DOUBLE-WATTLED CASSOWARY ◀

SCIENTIFIC NAME:	*Casuarius casuarius*
FAMILY:	Casuaridae
LENGTH:	180cm (71in)
HABITAT:	Rainforest
DISTRIBUTION:	Parts of northeastern Australia and much of New Guinea
IDENTIFICATION:	Tall and thickset, mainly black with a bald, blue head and neck, two red neck wattles, horny casque on head and powerful, scaly feet

A striking bird, the Southern or Double-wattled Cassowary has perhaps the most unusual appearance of any of the large flightless species, with its vivid skin coloration and large, bony crest. The intensity of its blue and red head and neck is also known to vary according to mood, becoming brighter during periods of agitation or excitement. Found in northeastern Australia and much of New Guinea, it usually inhabits quite densely vegetated areas of rainforest, and being a rare species it is infrequently encountered by man. However, it may wander onto farmland or beaches at times, and should not be approached as it can be aggressive and is capable of inflicting fatal injuries with its powerful legs and very sharp claws. Despite its endangered status, the Southern Cassowary is regarded as highly important to the ecology of its habitat, encouraging the growth of many plant species by disseminating seeds in its droppings. It feeds on plants, fruits, and occasionally small vertebrates. Generally solitary, cassowaries come together to breed, with the male being left to incubate around four large, green eggs and rear the chicks alone. The young remain with the parent bird for up to a year and are born striped, becoming black after about three years.

UNDULATED TINAMOU

SCIENTIFIC NAME:	*Crypturellus undulates*
FAMILY:	Tinamidae
LENGTH:	30cm (12in)
HABITAT:	Forest and scrubland
DISTRIBUTION:	Much of South America, most common in the Amazon Basin
IDENTIFICATION:	Plump, with reddish-brown plumage, patterned with darker, wavy markings. Underside lighter

The Undulated Tinamou is quite common throughout its range but like other tinamous it is highly secretive and is rarely encountered. It is mainly an inhabitant of dense rainforest where it is camouflaged by its plumage and, being a ground dwelling species, it is also necessarily cautious in order to avoid predation. However, it may be identified by its high pitched call. This species tends to be either solitary or found in pairs, but small family groups are not unknown as the young tend to remain with parent birds following hatching. It is the male bird that typically constructs a shallow nest on the ground and incubates the eggs alone, often having mated with several females which will all lay their eggs in his single nest. The Undulated Tinamou is omnivorous, feeding on both vegetable matter and invertebrates.

Brown Kiwi

SCIENTIFIC NAME:	*Apteryx australis*
FAMILY:	Apterygidae
LENGTH:	65cm (25in)
HABITAT:	Woodland
DISTRIBUTION:	Both islands of New Zealand
IDENTIFICATION:	Squat, with reddish-brown, hairlike plumage and thick, powerful legs. The beak is long with bristles at the base

The Brown Kiwi and its subspecies are the smallest of the ratites, a group of flightless birds that includes the Ostrich and Emu, which lack a keeled breastbone capable of supporting wing muscles. Kiwis are found only on the two islands of New Zealand where they inhabit woodland, and are almost exclusively nocturnal, dwelling amongst vegetation on the forest floor or in burrows during the day, emerging to forage for food at night. Using its long bill, tipped with highly sensitive nostrils, and equipped with sensitive whiskers or bristles, the Brown Kiwi probes for invertebrates in the soil. It feeds mainly on worms and insects although, being omnivorous, it will eat vegetation such as leaves, seeds, and berries. Often found close to water, the Brown Kiwi will also take small crustaceans and amphibians. They are usually found living in breeding pairs. The female lays one or two eggs in a burrow or hollow log, and produces the largest eggs relative to body size of any bird. The incubation period is also the longest, at around 80 days, the task being performed solely by the male bird.

Elegant Tinamou

SCIENTIFIC NAME:	*Eudromia elegans*
FAMILY:	Tinamidae
LENGTH:	40cm (16in)
HABITAT:	Grassland, forest, and scrub
DISTRIBUTION:	Southern parts of South America
IDENTIFICATION:	Plump, heavy-bodied with mottled, gray-brown plumage, a small head and slender neck. A narrow, curving crest extends up and backwards from the head

Although related to the flightless ratites, tinamous are capable of flight, but are mainly ground dwelling birds. Most species live in dense forests, but the Elegant Tinamou usually inhabits open grassland, where its mottled plumage provides good camouflage from potential predators. The Elegant Tinamou may run or fly short distances when startled, but it is more likely to remain motionless hidden amongst vegetation. Occasionally solitary, this species pairs to mate, but it is also amongst the most sociable of the tinamous and may be found in groups of 50 or more birds, particularly outside of the breeding season. When breeding, nesting occurs on the ground, with around ten eggs being laid in a shallow scrape, often beneath or close to a low shrub. Incubation is performed by the male bird and the young are active almost immediately after hatching. The male continues to look after the young for some weeks, and they develop rapidly, being more likely to fly than adults. The Elegant Tinamou is an omnivorous species, feeding on low vegetation, seeds, berries, and small invertebrates.

PENGUINS

Penguins belong to the order Sphenisciformes, and the family Spheniscidae which is comprised of 17 distinct species that together make up the largest group of flightless birds. This is also the only order of birds that are both flightless and aquatic. Penguins are highly adapted for a pelagic existence, being well streamlined and possessing long flat wings which are used to "fly" underwater. It is this development of stiff, flipper-like wings that precludes penguins from flight, but has enabled them to exploit the vast supply of fish and crustaceans found in the southern oceans.

Penguins are almost exclusively confined to the Southern Hemisphere, and are thought of as only dwelling in the frozen Antarctic, but they occur on most southern islands and around the coasts, being found in warmer waters around Australasia, South Africa, and South America, and in the case of the **Galapagos Penguin** (*Spheniscus mendiculus*) north as far as the Galapagos Islands which straddle the equator. Although fossil records are somewhat sparse, it is generally agreed that early penguins evolved from birds that could fly, but also swam strongly underwater, much like auks and puffins. Today, their closest relatives are believed to be the Albatross and Petrels in the family Procellaridae and the divers of the family Gaviidae.

Penguins also have several other adaptations that set them apart from most other birds. Their bones are solid rather than hollow, enabling them to remain submerged with ease, and their feathers are short and dense with a downy under-layer that helps them to stay warm and dry. Some penguins, notably those that that dwell in the coldest Antarctic regions, such as the **Emperor Penguin** (*Aptenodytes forsteri*) and **Adelie Penguin** (*Pygoscelis adeliae*) also have a thick insulating layer of fat. The webbed feet, which act as rudders, are set well back on the body, giving penguins an upright posture, but their

Emperor Penguin

short legs insure a rather shuffling gait on land. Those penguins found in snowy and icy habitats sometimes move around by sliding on their bellies, whilst some small penguins are able to hop from place to place.

Most penguins breed every year, with the exception of the **King Penguin** (*Aptenodytes patagonicus*) which is usually only capable of raising two chicks in a three-year period due to an extended breeding cycle. The King Penguin and Emperor Penguin are the largest of their kind, reaching lengths of around 90 and 115 centimeters (35 and 45 inches) respectively. Like most penguins, they have black backs and white fronts, and both these species also have an orange-yellow breast patch. They can usually be told apart by the color of their ear patches since those of King Penguins are orange as opposed to yellow. Their ranges are also different, with Emperor Penguins found only on and around Antarctica, whilst King Penguins are usually found farther

north on sub-Antarctic islands. In fact, the Emperor Penguin is the only species never found on solid land, living its entire life on and around the pack-ice. Like other penguins it breeds in large colonies, but whereas many penguins share incubation, the male Emperor Penguin is left alone throughout the harsh winter to incubate the single egg on its feet. The females return around two months later to help raise the young, at which time the males return to the sea for some weeks in order to feed.

Adelie Penguins (*Pygoscelis adeliae*) build nests of pebbles, whilst Galapagos Penguins nest in burrows. As with all species, the young hatch with a downy layer and are tended to by their parents until they have undergone a molt and are able to enter the sea. Adult Adelie Penguins grow to around 70 centimeters (28 inches), whilst Galapagos Penguins are much smaller, reaching a height of about 40 centimeters (16 inches).

Adelie Penguin

COMMON LOON/GREAT NORTHERN ▲ DIVER

SCIENTIFIC NAME:	*Gavia immer*
FAMILY:	Gaviidae
LENGTH:	90cm (35in)
HABITAT:	Lakes and coastlines
DISTRIBUTION:	From North America, across Greenland and Iceland to Britain and northern Europe
IDENTIFICATION:	Fairly large waterbird with a dark head, neck and back, white underside, and barring on neck and throat. In summer, the back is marked with white spots

The Common Loon is highly aquatic and spends most of its time in water, being poorly equipped for life on land, with heavy bones, and feet which are set very far back on its body. However, it is in its element underwater, and these characteristics are positive assets for a diving species. It is also well streamlined with keen eyesight, enabling it to out-maneuver the small fish for which it hunts. Relying on its eyesight, this species typically hunts in relatively clear, shallow water, but it has been known to dive to depths of up to 60 meters (200 feet) and may remain submerged for over a minute at a time. In addition to fish, the Common Loon feeds on amphibians, mollusks, crustaceans and other invertebrates. During the breeding season, a nest of vegetation is formed close to the water's edge, often on an island, and following mating the female will typically produce two eggs. These are incubated by both parents, and the family will remain together throughout the summer. In winter they may migrate to coastal waters, but will often stay on large inland lakes that remain free of ice.

LITTLE GREBE ▼

SCIENTIFIC NAME:	*Tachybaptus ruficollis*
FAMILY:	Podicipedidae
LENGTH:	25cm (10in)
HABITAT:	Vegetated ponds, lakes, and rivers; also coastal waters in winter
DISTRIBUTION:	Much of Europe, North Africa, and the Middle East
IDENTIFICATION:	Smallest grebe. Dark brown above, reddish below, with a chestnut face and neck. Neck relatively short. Much paler overall in winter

Sometimes also known as the Dabchick, the Little Grebe is the smallest member of the grebe family, but it is much like other grebes in terms of behavior. It is an aquatic, diving bird, which seldom comes ashore except to breed, finding movement on land difficult. It may be found in a variety of vegetated lowland waters, but given its size and diet of small prey, it may be found on smaller bodies of water than other grebes. The Little Grebe feeds on small fish, amphibians, and aquatic invertebrates. A shy bird, this species has a tendency to hide amongst reeds, and during the breeding season in spring, it forms a nest of flattened vegetation, often a floating structure secured to submerged plants. Two to five eggs are usually laid in the nest, and these are incubated by both parents. As with most grebes, the young are striped, and may be carried on their parents' backs soon after hatching.

GREAT CRESTED GREBE

SCIENTIFIC NAME:	*Podiceps cristatus*
FAMILY:	Podicipedidae
LENGTH:	50cm (20in)
HABITAT:	Reedy lakes and rivers, often moving to coastlines in winter
DISTRIBUTION:	From Britain, across Europe and Asia to China. Also south through Africa and to Australasia
IDENTIFICATION:	Largest grebe. Gray-brown above, white below, with distinctive black eartufts and chestnut cheek-ruffs or tippets, although these are absent in winter

Amongst the largest of grebes, the Great Crested Grebe is mainly aquatic, and is highly elegant when on or below the water. However, having its feet set well back on its elongated body makes this a clumsy bird on land. It also has relatively small wings and will tend to dive rather than fly if threatened. Being streamlined, with powerful, although only partially webbed feet, this species swims well underwater, and dives to catch small fish, amphibians, and invertebrates. Grebes are well known for their courtship displays, and that of the Great Crested Grebe is particularly elaborate. Males and females begin to pair up in winter and display by rearing up face to face in the water with weed in their bills, shaking their heads from side to side. The nest is a platform made of flattened vegetation, usually secluded amongst bankside reeds. Around four or five eggs are laid, and these are incubated for about four weeks by both parents. Following hatching, the adult birds carry the chicks on their backs.

WANDERING ALBATROSS

SCIENTIFIC NAME:	*Diomedea exulans*
FAMILY:	Diomedeidae
LENGTH:	135cm (53in)
HABITAT:	Open oceans, nesting in coastal regions
DISTRIBUTION:	Oceans, islands, and coastlines around Antarctica, South America, South Africa, and Australasia
IDENTIFICATION:	Huge seabird with long, narrow wings. Mainly white, black areas on back of wings, pinkish feet and bill, bill-tip yellow

A huge bird, the Wandering Albatross is amongst the largest living avian species, and in fact has the greatest wingspan, sometimes measuring almost four meters (12 feet). It is a bird of the open oceans, spending most of its life on the wing, landing only to feed and breed. Able to lock its wings in position, it takes advantage of strong winds to glide effortlessly, sometimes for hours at a time between wing beats, and may cover distances of hundreds of miles in a matter of days, commonly following fishing boats in search of scraps. However, the Wandering Albatross feeds mainly on squid and fish taken from the water's surface, usually at night. Breeding adults tend to pair for life, with mating occurring once every two years as it may take up to ten months for a chick to leave the nest. The adult birds form a cylindrical nest-mound of mud and vegetation on an exposed island slope into which a single egg is laid. Incubation lasts around two months, and is undertaken by both parents.

WILSON'S STORM-PETREL

SCIENTIFIC NAME:	*Oceanites oceanicus*
FAMILY:	Hydrobatidae
LENGTH:	18cm (7in)
HABITAT:	Open oceans and coastal areas
DISTRIBUTION:	Throughout southern waters, venturing north into the Atlantic
IDENTIFICATION:	Small, dark brown seabird with white rump and long legs which trail in flight

This little seabird is one of the most abundant of all birds, nesting in colonies of millions across a vast expanse of ocean in the Southern Hemisphere. However, only a single egg is laid at a time, which both parent birds incubate in a burrow or crevice. Breeding takes place on the Antarctic coast and southern oceanic islands, north as far as the Falkland Islands. During the summer it migrates into the open oceans of the Northern Hemisphere, particularly into the North Atlantic. Whilst nesting, this species tends to be nocturnal, becoming active by day outside of the breeding season when it is generally pelagic, although it may sometimes be seen close to the shore. Wilson's Storm-Petrel has a distinctive fluttering flight, trailing its legs behind, and as it feeds on plankton and small fish it patters the water's surface with its feet.

SOUTHERN GIANT PETREL

SCIENTIFIC NAME:	*Macronectes giganteus*
FAMILY:	Procellariidae
LENGTH:	99cm (39in)
HABITAT:	Open oceans and coastlines
DISTRIBUTION:	Southern oceans, from Antarctica to southern continental coastlines and islands
IDENTIFICATION:	Large, heavy bodied seabird. Mottled gray-brown plumage, pale head and neck, yellow bill

Due to its large size and habit of following ships, the Southern Giant Petrel may sometimes be confused with an albatross, but it has shorter wings and something of a humpbacked shape. It is also more commonly seen feeding on shorelines where it scavenges for carrion such as the carcasses of penguins and seals. It is also known to attack smaller birds, particularly chicks, and to hunt at sea for fish and squid. Like the albatrosses, this species spends much of its time flying over the open ocean, covering considerable distances in search of food. Breeding takes place on southern islands and mainland shores in loose colonies, sometimes numbering over 200 pairs. Nests are made on the ground, and usually consist of a scrape surrounded by stones or vegetation. A single egg is laid and is incubated for around two months, with the chick being fully fledged about four months later.

(Northern) Fulmar ▲

Scientific name:	*Fulmarus glacialis*
Family:	Procellariidae
Length:	45cm (18in)
Habitat:	Open oceans and coastal cliffs
Distribution:	Northern waters, nesting on both North Atlantic and North Pacific coastlines
Identification:	Gull-like petrel, gray above, white below, with white head and dark trailing wing edges. Northernmost (Arctic) individuals usually darker overall

Somewhat more gull-like in appearance than other petrels, the Fulmar can however be distinguished from most gulls by its stiff winged, gliding flight, more reminiscent of that of an albatross. It spends a great deal of time over the open ocean, flying long distances in search of food. It feeds on fish, squid, and other marine invertebrates, often diving short distances below the surface, also consuming refuse thrown from fishing vessels which it sometimes follows. It breeds high up on rocky cliffs in large, noisy colonies often numbering several thousand birds. The Fulmar typically does not construct a nest, but lays a single egg in a depression on a bare rocky ledge, sometimes lined with a small amount of grass. Both parents incubate the egg for about two months and the young leave the nest around two months after hatching.

Fairy Prion

Scientific name:	*Pachyptila turtur*
Family:	Procellariidae
Length:	28cm (11in)
Habitat:	Open oceans and coastal areas
Distribution:	Distinct colonies in the southern oceans around Australasia, South Africa, and South America
Identification:	Small petrel, gray above with black wing markings and tail tip, white underparts

A small southern petrel, the Fairy Prion is pelagic, spending most of its life on the open oceans. It has a tendency to form flocks, feeding at night at the water's surface on planktonic crustaceans and other tiny creatures, filtering them from the water with tiny plates in the bill known as lamellae. The Fairy Prion will also follow fishing vessels in pursuit of discarded scraps. A highly colonial bird, breeding takes place in large numbers on southern islands and continental coastlines, with eggs being laid in burrows dug on grassy cliff tops or placed between rocks. Incubation lasts for around 55 days, after which the parents feed their chick for about a further 50 days. Rather vulnerable on land, Fairy Prions, and particularly their chicks, are preyed upon by small mammals such as rats, but perhaps the greatest threat comes from skuas.

MANX SHEARWATER

SCIENTIFIC NAME:	*Puffinus puffinus*
FAMILY:	Procellariidae
LENGTH:	35cm (14in)
HABITAT:	Open oceans and sandy or rocky coastlines
DISTRIBUTION:	Throughout the North Atlantic, from North America to northern Europe, south as far as South America and South Africa, also occurring in Australia
IDENTIFICATION:	Medium sized seabird, black above with white underparts and narrow black bill

The Manx Shearwater flies low over the ocean's surface on long, straight wings, occasionally banking or "shearing" to glide along the troughs of waves as it searches for food. Its diet consists of small fish such as herrings and sardines, and also small crustaceans such as shrimp. As with many pelagic species, the Manx Shearwater winters out on the open oceans, before coming ashore to breed in summer, when conditions are more favorable. It breeds in large colonies which may number hundreds of thousands of pairs, and prefers to nest on offshore islands in order to minimize predation by mammals such as rats or foxes. At night, thousands of these birds may gather in the sea before coming inland to their nesting sites. A single egg is laid in a burrow and is incubated by both parents. Although breeding typically takes place in northern parts of its range, this species then tends to head toward warmer waters off South America and South Africa in winter.

BROWN PELICAN ▼

SCIENTIFIC NAME:	*Pelecanus occidentalis*
FAMILY:	Pelecanidae
LENGTH:	127cm (50in)
HABITAT:	Coastal areas and estuaries, rare inland
DISTRIBUTION:	Along both the Atlantic and Pacific coasts of North America, south to Peru and Brazil
IDENTIFICATION:	Large waterbird, mainly gray-brown, with white or yellowish head and neck. Breeding adult develops brown neck with yellow patch at base of throat

Like the American White Pelican, the Brown Pelican is highly sociable, forming large colonies throughout the year. However, it is rarely found far inland, preferring coastal habitats, with breeding colonies established on offshore islands. When breeding, the male will usually select a nesting site, either on the ground or in a bush or tree, and will perform a display of head movements in order to attract a mate. Nests on the ground usually consist of a feather-lined scrape, whilst those in trees tend to be quite bulky constructions of sticks, reeds, and grasses. Brown Pelicans generally lay two or three eggs, which are incubated for about 30 days. Following hatching, the young may wander from ground nests after around 30 days, but those in trees will not attempt to fly until they are about 2^1/$_2$ months old. The Brown Pelican feeds almost exclusively on fish which it captures by means of spectacular plunge-dives.

WHITE-TAILED TROPICBIRD ▲

SCIENTIFIC NAME:	*Phaethon lepturus*
FAMILY:	Phaethontidae
LENGTH:	80cm (31in)
HABITAT:	Open oceans; breeding occurs on tropical island coasts
DISTRIBUTION:	Tropical waters across the Pacific, Atlantic and Indian Oceans, occasionally as far north as North Carolina in the US
IDENTIFICATION:	White tropical seabird with very long black-tipped wings, black stripe on upper wing, long tail streamers and yellow bill

Although not a large species, the length of the White-tailed Tropicbird is doubled by its extended tail feathers or streamers, and for a bird of its size it has very long wings. It is also highly streamlined, creating a very graceful appearance. It is pelagic, spending most of its time in the open oceans, only coming ashore to breed. Generally solitary, this species begins to breed at about four years of age, when pairs will display by flying together in parallel. Mating occurs year round, but is less common in winter, despite their tropical habitat. Breeding takes place on islands, where a single egg is produced, and laid either on bare ground or in a hollow, often amongst tree roots or rocks. Both adults participate in incubation, which lasts around 40 days. The White-tailed Tropicbird feeds on fish and marine invertebrates, often plunge-diving to catch its prey.

(AMERICAN) WHITE PELICAN

SCIENTIFIC NAME:	*Pelecanus erythrorhynchos*
FAMILY:	Pelecanidae
LENGTH:	170cm (67in)
HABITAT:	Large lakes and coastal areas
DISTRIBUTION:	Much of North America, most common in southern states, also Mexico and Central America
IDENTIFICATION:	Large waterbird with huge wingspan, white overall with black wingtips, orange-yellow, pouched bill. Breeding adult develops pale yellow crest and ridge on bill

The American White Pelican is amongst the largest of the waterbirds, with a huge pouched beak and a wingspan of almost three meters (nine feet). It is a highly gregarious species, forming large colonies on lakes and coastal shorelines, and it is one of the few bird species that feeds cooperatively. Several individuals will encircle a group of fish and force them into shallow water before scooping them up and swallowing them whole. In addition to fish, they will also consume amphibians and crustaceans such as crayfish. During the breeding season populations in northern parts may migrate southward over land in large numbers, but southerly colonies tend to be non-migratory. Nesting takes place on the ground, with the parents forming a mound of earth into which two or three eggs are usually laid. These are incubated for about 30 days and the chicks are fully fledged around 70 days after hatching.

BLUE-FOOTED BOOBY ▼

SCIENTIFIC NAME:	*Sula nebouxii*
FAMILY:	Sulidae
LENGTH:	89cm (35in)
HABITAT:	Coastal waters and offshore islands, rarely venturing far into open waters
DISTRIBUTION:	Along the Pacific coast from Mexico, south to the Galapagos Islands and Peru
IDENTIFICATION:	Gannet-like, but darker overall with a brown back and mottled gray-brown head. Off-white below with blue feet

The name "booby" is derived from "bobo," the Spanish word for stupid, on account of the supposed stupidity of these birds; for they are quite fearless of man and relatively clumsy on land. However, they fly well, being highly streamlined, and are capable of swimming underwater in search of prey. Feeding almost exclusively on fish, the Blue-footed Booby typically plunge-dives from heights of up to 25 meters (80 feet), but it is also capable of diving from a resting position on the water's surface, and is in fact the only booby which does so. Breeding takes place throughout the year, and begins with an elaborate courtship display in which the male birds show off their feet, both in flight, and on land with high-stepping walks. Nesting usually occurs on bare earth, with a typical clutch consisting of two or three eggs. Both parents incubate the eggs, keeping them warm with their feet. When hatching begins, the eggs are transferred to the top of the feet, and the young remain supported in this way for the first month of their lives.

(NORTHERN) GANNET ▲

SCIENTIFIC NAME:	*Morus bassanus*
FAMILY:	Sulidae
LENGTH:	89cm (35in)
HABITAT:	Open waters, breeding on ledges on rocky coastlines
DISTRIBUTION:	North Atlantic from North America to Greenland and northern Europe, south as far as the Gulf of Mexico and North Africa when breeding
IDENTIFICATION:	Fairly large seabird, streamlined, white overall with long, black-tipped wings and a yellowish head

A fairly large seabird, the Gannet is nevertheless highly streamlined, an adaptation which allows it to make spectacular plunge-dives in order to catch fish, often from heights of over 30 meters (100 feet). It feeds on fairly small prey such as mackerel and herring, locating shoals with its keen eyesight. Gannets are quite sociable and may be observed flying in flocks at sea, often in single file, sometimes following boats. They also breed in large colonies, nesting together on cliffs, and breeding pairs indulge in quite elaborate courtship displays; greeting their mate with bill tapping, bowing and mutual preening. However, pairs tend to be aggressive toward neighboring birds at this time. Gannets construct their nests from seaweed and various other plant materials, cemented together with droppings. A single egg is laid and incubated by both parent birds for around 40 days.

MASKED/BLUE-FACED BOOBY

SCIENTIFIC NAME:	*Sula dactylatra*
FAMILY:	Sulidae
LENGTH:	86cm (34in)
HABITAT:	Mainly tropical waters, in open sea, breeding on tropical islands
DISTRIBUTION:	Ranges widely in tropical areas in the Atlantic, Pacific, and Indian Oceans, south to Australia, South America, and South Africa. Sometimes found north to Gulf of Mexico, the southeastern US and, rarely, western Europe
IDENTIFICATION:	Gannet-like, white overall with black edges on wings, black tail, dark face-mask and large, pointed, yellow bill

Very similar in appearance to a Gannet, the Masked or Blue-faced Booby may be distinguished by its white, rather than yellow head, and although there is some overlap in range, it is resident in warmer waters throughout the year. Pelagic, the Masked Booby spends most of its time over the open ocean, tending to come ashore on islands in order to rest and breed. Nesting takes place in large colonies, with one or two eggs generally being laid on bare ground. These are incubated by both parent birds, and warmed with their large webbed feet. Hatching occurs after about 40 days; however, where two eggs have been laid, one will typically not hatch. In cases where both eggs do hatch, one chick tends to emerge several days earlier and will then often force the other from the nest. As with other boobies, this species feeds mainly on fish, but also consumes some crustaceans such as shrimp.

DOUBLE-CRESTED CORMORANT

SCIENTIFIC NAME:	*Phalacrocorax auritus*
FAMILY:	Phalacrocoracidae
LENGTH:	82cm (32in)
HABITAT:	Coastal areas and large inland waters
DISTRIBUTION:	Throughout much of North America, occasionally straying across the Atlantic to Britain
IDENTIFICATION:	Black waterbird with a double crest of feathers on the back of the head, long neck, yellow-orange face and small throat pouch, and large, hooked bill

Although the Double-crested Cormorant is a waterbird, it spends a great deal of time out of water, resting in elevated sites such as in trees, on cliffs, or on buoys and bridges, often with its wings outstretched. When feeding, however, the cormorant dives for its food from the water's surface and swims strongly underwater, sometimes remaining submerged for over a minute in pursuit of fish. In addition, it will also consume amphibians and invertebrates, typically surfacing before swallowing its prey. Usually found in small groups, large colonies are established during the breeding season, sometimes numbering several thousand birds. Males attract mates with courtship dances and by presenting females with nesting materials, and nests may be placed either on the ground or in trees. Clutches usually number around four eggs, with incubation and care of the young being performed by both parents.

GREAT CORMORANT

SCIENTIFIC NAME:	*Phalacrocorax carbo*
FAMILY:	Phalacrocoracidae
LENGTH:	91cm (36in)
HABITAT:	Coasts, estuaries, and inland waters
DISTRIBUTION:	Eastern North America, most of Europe, Asia, and parts of Africa and Australasia
IDENTIFICATION:	Large, black, long-necked waterbird with white chin and cheeks, and a yellow-orange throat pouch. Breeding adult has white patch on each thigh and wispy plumes on head

The most widespread member of the cormorant family, the Great Cormorant is also the largest, with a wingspan reaching around 160 cm (63 inches). Like most cormorants it is quite gregarious and usually occurs in small flocks outside of the breeding season, forming large colonies when nesting. Common on large bodies of freshwater, the Great Cormorant is also found along coastlines and estuaries, and is an excellent swimmer, diving for up to a minute in search of prey. In fact, Japanese fishermen have trained and used these cormorants for over 1,000 years. They feed primarily on fish, supplementing their diet with invertebrates, and in freshwater, amphibians. Depending on food supply, breeding may occur throughout the year in much of their range, with both parent birds cooperating in nest-building, incubation, and the care of young. The nest, which is usually a large structure made of sticks, may be positioned in a tree, on the ground, or on a ledge, and a typical brood will consist of four or five chicks.

ANHINGA

SCIENTIFIC NAME:	*Anhinga anhinga*
FAMILY:	Anhingidae
LENGTH:	90cm (35in)
HABITAT:	Swamps, marshland, and coastal areas
DISTRIBUTION:	From the southeast US through Central America, south to Argentina
IDENTIFICATION:	Cormorant-like, but black, with white markings on back and wings, a longer neck and tail, and a long, sharply pointed (rather than hooked) bill

Closely related to the cormorants, the Anhinga is similar in appearance, but may be distinguished by its white markings, proportionally longer neck, narrow head, and more slender, tapering bill. It is also less commonly associated with coastal habitats, preferring to inhabit swamps and marshland where trees provide cover, nesting sites, and places for these birds to sun themselves after hunting. It feeds mainly on fish (but its diet also includes amphibians and aquatic invertebrates), spearing its prey with its daggerlike bill. Usually solitary, the Anhinga breeds in loose colonies throughout the year, sometimes with birds such as herons or egrets, and pairs may maintain a bond for life. Following mating, around four eggs are laid in a treetop nest to be incubated for around a month. The young are fully fledged around six weeks after hatching, but remain with their parents for several more weeks before becoming independent.

EUROPEAN SHAG ▼

SCIENTIFIC NAME:	*Phalacrocorax aristotelis*
FAMILY:	Phalacrocoracidae
LENGTH:	72cm (28in)
HABITAT:	Coastal waters, cliffs, and rocky shorelines
DISTRIBUTION:	From Iceland, across Britain and much of Europe, beyond into Russia, the Mediterranean, and Africa. Mediterranean and African examples are generally regarded as subspecies, however (*P.a. desmarestii* and *P.a. riggenbachi* respectively)
IDENTIFICATION:	All black, but with a greenish, iridescent sheen and narrow yellow bill. Breeding adult develops tuft on crown

A fairly small member of the cormorant family, the European Shag is more of a seabird than most of its close relatives, rarely venturing far inland, although in stormy weather, young birds particularly may be forced inland; an event known as a "wreck." Shags tend to inhabit rocky coastlines, nesting on cliffs during the breeding season, and preferring sheltered ledges, crevices, and caves, often on offshore islands. The nest is made mainly of seaweed and other vegetation, lined with feathers and grass, and is constructed by both parent birds. A pair will often maintain a bond over successive seasons, especially if breeding is successful, and both birds will incubate the eggs and care for the young. Incubation lasts for around one month, and the young will typically remain with their parents for two months after hatching. Shags feed mainly on fish, diving from the surface to catch their prey underwater.

GREAT FRIGATEBIRD/GREATER FRIGATEBIRD ▲

SCIENTIFIC NAME:	*Fregata minor*
FAMILY:	Fregatidae
LENGTH:	100cm (39in)
HABITAT:	Open oceans, coastlines, and mangrove thickets
DISTRIBUTION:	In the Pacific from Central America to southeast Asia and Australia, west to East Africa. Also islands in the Southern Atlantic and off Brazil
IDENTIFICATION:	Large black seabird with a long forked tail and large hooked beak. Males have red throat sac, whilst females have a white throat and chest

The Great Frigatebird is a large seabird, found mainly in the Pacific, where it typically inhabits island territories. It feeds mainly on fish and squid which are scooped from the ocean's surface in flight, but it is something of an opportunist, and obtains much of its food by means of harassing smaller birds, such as boobies, into dropping their catches. Other food includes carrion and turtle hatchlings taken from beaches. Great Frigatebirds develop slowly, with chicks relying on parent birds for up to a year and a half after hatching, limiting the breeding rate of females. It is thought that males may often breed with a second female later in the year, although they share incubation duties. Males attract females by inflating their throat pouches, spreading their wings, and shaking their heads, and following mating, a single egg is laid on a platform of twigs located in a bush or tree. Incubation lasts for around 55 days.

(GREAT) BITTERN

SCIENTIFIC NAME:	*Botaurus stellaris*
FAMILY:	Ardeidae
LENGTH:	75cm (30in)
HABITAT:	Reedbeds, swamps, and marshes, lakes and ponds
DISTRIBUTION:	From Britain, throughout most of Europe, beyond into parts of Asia and Africa
IDENTIFICATION:	Fairly large, heron-like waterbird with mottled and barred brown plumage, black crown, short green legs, and large feet

A scarce and highly secretive bird, the Bittern is very rarely seen, being more likely to be heard emitting a low, booming call during the breeding season, which may carry for a distance of around two kilometers (1.2 miles). Highly camouflaged, this species also adopts an unusual posture when disturbed; stretching its neck vertically to aid concealment amongst reeds and rushes. When breeding, males will often mate with several females that will usually each go on to lay four or five eggs in March or April. Nests take the form of platforms of flattened reeds and the female takes sole responsibility for incubating the eggs and caring for the young; hatchlings tend to leave the nest quite quickly, becoming independent after around two weeks. Hunting in fairly shallow waters with slow, deliberate movements, the Bittern feeds on fish, particularly eels, amphibians, invertebrates, and even small mammals such as rodents.

AMERICAN BITTERN

SCIENTIFIC NAME:	*Botaurus lentiginosus*
FAMILY:	Ardeidae
LENGTH:	71cm (28in)
HABITAT:	Marshland and vegetated shores
DISTRIBUTION:	Throughout most of North America, south to Mexico. Rare vagrant to Britain and Western Europe
IDENTIFICATION:	Fairly large, short legged, heron-like waterbird. Mottled brown with dark barring, black wingtips and markings on neck

Like its Eurasian counterpart, the American Bittern is highly secretive, and is rarely seen, particularly when on the ground, as it tends to remain hidden amongst dense vegetation. It may sometimes be spotted in flight, but its presence is most likely to be announced by the males' vocalizations. It is mainly active at dawn and dusk, when it hunts for prey such as fish, amphibians, reptiles, small mammals, and invertebrates, moving slowly through shoreline vegetation, or remaining motionless before ambushing prey. Breeding tends to begin in early summer, with pairs forming from May, but following mating, incubation and rearing duties are performed solely by the female. A typical clutch will consist of four or five eggs which hatch after around 30 days, and although the young often leave the nest after about two weeks, the female may continue to feed them for a further month.

HERONS

The Herons are long legged and generally long necked wading birds that belong to the family Ardeidae, which also includes egrets and bitterns. They range in size from around 40 centimeters to over 140 centimeters (16 to 55 inches) and are all carnivorous, preying on fish, amphibians, reptiles, and invertebrates. Larger species may also consume prey such as small mammals, nestlings, and eggs. Herons usually forage in or near water, across a range of wetland habitats, from rivers to lakes and in both saltwater and freshwater marshes. They are typically solitary birds and will defend feeding territories, although a few species do feed in flocks. Most species have long, pointed bills which they use to spear their prey, and they hunt in the shallows, often amongst reedbeds or other vegetation, employing a variety of hunting methods; sometimes standing still and waiting patiently for a potential meal, or at other times disturbing prey as they wade, flushing small animals from their hiding places by stirring the water with their feet.

The **Green Heron** (*Butorides virescens*), sometimes also known as the Green-backed Heron, a fairly small short necked species which is found across much of the US and Central America, also utilizes the rather unusual technique of "bait fishing"; dropping invertebrates or small pieces of vegetation onto the water's surface in order to attract fish. Very few bird species appear to display learned behavior of this kind, and along with members of the crow family and parrots, the Green Heron is believed to be amongst the most intelligent of birds. It occurs in both freshwater and coastal wetlands, preferring timbered habitats, and it frequently perches in trees. It also tends to nest above the ground, although it will sometimes lay its eggs on a platform of sticks amongst reeds or mangrove roots. As with most herons, this species is monogamous, forming pairs in order to breed and raise their young. Between four and five eggs are usual, incubated by both parents for around three weeks. The adult birds may be recognized by a greenish-gray crown and wings, purplish head, neck, and breast, and white belly. They grow to around 46 centimeters (18 inches) long.

Green Heron pairs often nest alone, or in quite loose groups, but generally it is more common for herons to nest in large colonies, sometimes with other waders.

The **Great Blue Heron** (*Ardea herodias*) which is another common North American species, and the largest in its range at around 127 centimeters (50 inches) long, may breed in groups of up to 50 pairs, usually in treetops over water. This species builds bulky stick nests, where it lays three to five eggs, which are incubated for about 28 days. Easily recognized by its size, other distinguishing features include its mainly blue-gray plumage, with a buff neck, black crest and shoulder patch, and very long neck and legs. In the south-eastern US, a pure white form, long thought to be a separate species, also occurs and it is known as the Great White Heron.

The **Gray Heron** (*Ardea cinerea*), common throughout much of Europe, Asia, and Africa, is almost identical to the Great Blue Heron, although it is slightly smaller, at around 96 centimeters (38 inches) in length. It occurs throughout a variety of habitats, often visiting suburban garden ponds to prey on fish, and it will also hunt on land for rodents. It too tends to nest in colonies, sharing breeding habits with its American counterpart.

The **Black-crowned Night-Heron** (*Nycticorax nycticorax*) also breeds in colonies, but it tends to be quite social throughout the year, usually roosting with others of its kind. It probably has the widest distribution of any heron species in the world, being found throughout most of the Americas, Africa, and much of Europe and Asia, although it is absent from more northerly parts. It is medium sized, about 65 centimeters (26 inches) long, and quite stocky, with a short neck and legs, giving it a rather squat appearance. It has a gray tail and wings, white underparts, and a black crown and back. When breeding, it develops a pair of long plumes at the back of its crown. It nests in trees, laying two to five eggs, which are incubated for about 25 days. As with other herons, the young tend to leave the nest and begin climbing amongst the branches before they are fledged.

◀ *Gray Heron*

Great Blue Heron ▼

CATTLE EGRET

SCIENTIFIC NAME:	*Bubulcus ibis*
FAMILY:	Ardeidae
LENGTH:	50cm (20in)
HABITAT:	Marshland, swamps, and grasslands close to water
DISTRIBUTION:	Widely distributed throughout the Americas, Europe, Africa, Asia, and Australasia, but rare in much of Canada, Britain, and northwestern Europe
IDENTIFICATION:	Fairly small, long legged wading bird, white overall, with yellow bill. When breeding, crown, back, and chest acquire yellowish hue, bill becomes more red

The most terrestrial heron, the Cattle Egret often occurs close to water, or in marshy areas, but unusually, it does not wade in water when searching for food, instead feeding on the ground. As its name might suggest, this species is often associated with cattle, and indeed it may be found with many other large mammals, sometimes perching on their backs as they graze, preying on insects that are disturbed from the grass. Prey includes worms, spiders, crickets, and moths, but the Cattle Egret will also consume small vertebrates. A sociable bird, the Cattle Egret often feeds in quite large flocks, and roosts in large colonies, often alongside other heron species. When breeding, both males and females participate in nest-building, incubation and care of the young, with clutches averaging three or four eggs. Incubation lasts for around 24 days, with the young becoming independent at around two months old.

SNOWY EGRET

SCIENTIFIC NAME:	*Egretta thula*
FAMILY:	Ardeidae
LENGTH:	60cm (24in)
HABITAT:	Marshes, mangroves, lakes, and ponds
DISTRIBUTION:	Throughout most of the Americas, but absent from northernmost parts
IDENTIFICATION:	Medium sized, long legged wader. White plumage, with small plumes on head, and, when breeding, long wispy plumes on back. Legs and bill black, feet yellow

A medium sized member of the heron family, the Snowy Egret is quite elegant, with a very slender bill and delicate build. A crepuscular species, it is most active at dawn and dusk when it will forage for food, preferring to rest for much of the day. Its diet is highly varied and consists of insects, crustaceans, fish, reptiles, amphibians, and small mammals, and it will often travel some distance from a roost in order to search for prey. Breeding typically begins in late March or April and is accompanied by the changing of foot color from yellow to orange, the growth of fine plumes, and increased vocalization. Female egrets usually build the nest, forming a platform of twigs, sometimes on the ground or amongst reeds, but usually quite high in a tree. Between two to six eggs are typically produced, to be incubated for around 24 days by both parents.

SHOEBILL

SCIENTIFIC NAME:	*Balaeniceps rex*
FAMILY:	Balaenicipitidae
LENGTH:	120cm (47in)
HABITAT:	Marshland, densely vegetated lakes and rivers
DISTRIBUTION:	Central Africa
IDENTIFICATION:	Large, long legged waterbird, with a very large head and bill. Color is gray-brown overall, often darkest on the back and wings

Thought to be closely related to herons and storks, the Shoebill is highly distinctive due to its extraordinary shoe-shaped bill, with its hooked tip; an adaptation no doubt useful in securing the lungfish, catfish, amphibians, and aquatic reptiles upon which it preys. It hunts by means of slow stalking or by waiting motionlessly before lunging and falling upon its prey, often grabbing large amounts of vegetation in the process, which it will release before swallowing its catch. Typically monogamous, the Shoebill is nevertheless highly solitary, and even breeding pairs that share a territory will tend to hunt alone. When breeding however, both parents participate in nest-building, incubation, and the rearing of young. Nests are large platforms of trampled vegetation into which two eggs are normally laid, although only one chick will usually survive. Incubation lasts for around a month, during which time the parents will scoop water onto the eggs to keep them cool, and the young develop slowly, being cared for for around four months after hatching.

WHITE STORK

SCIENTIFIC NAME:	*Ciconia ciconia*
FAMILY:	Ciconiidae
LENGTH:	112cm (44in)
HABITAT:	Shallow wetland and damp grassland, often close to human habitations
DISTRIBUTION:	Much of continental Europe, parts of Africa and the Near East, beyond into parts of Asia. Rare visitor to Britain
IDENTIFICATION:	Tall, long legged, long necked waterbird. Predominantly white, with black primary and secondary flight feathers, red legs and beak

Whilst the White Stork breeds in pairs or small groups in parts of Europe during the summer, it overwinters in large numbers in Africa, and migrating flocks are an impressive sight. Tending to soar at height, with wings, legs, and neck extended, these storks migrate overland as far as possible in order to take advantage of thermal currents, returning to the same nesting sites year after year via regular routes. It is perhaps this behavior that gives rise to the birds' status as an omen of good luck, and association with spring births. Nests are often located in urban areas and positioned on rooftops, chimneys, and telegraph poles, but may also be found in trees or on cliff ledges. They are constructed from sticks and breeding pairs will add new material each year, resulting in large platforms. Clutches number up to around six or seven eggs, which both parents take turns to incubate. The White Stork feeds on fish, amphibians, invertebrates, and small mammals.

WOOD STORK ▲

SCIENTIFIC NAME:	*Mycteria Americana*
FAMILY:	Ciconiidae
LENGTH:	105cm (41in)
HABITAT:	Marshes, moist grassland, lakes, ponds, and shallow coastal waters
DISTRIBUTION:	Throughout much of the Americas, but absent or rare in parts of the far north and also parts of the west coast of South America
IDENTIFICATION:	Large, ibis-like stork, mainly white, with black wing edges. Head is bare with relatively large downcurved bill

The Wood Stork is the only stork native to America and tends to be found in freshwater marshes, but it also frequents the more brackish waters of mangrove swamps. It has a somewhat vulturine appearance with a bald head and neck, which allows it to feed in muddy water without spoiling its plumage, and it also has a large downcurved bill with which it probes for prey. It feeds on a range of small creatures including invertebrates, fish, small mammals, and reptiles including juvenile alligators. Highly gregarious, this species often occurs in flocks, and breeds in large colonies, often with other storks. Pairs will often mate for life and nesting takes place in waterside trees, with around four eggs being laid on a platform of sticks. Incubation lasts for about 30 days, with juveniles being fully fledged about two months later.

MARABOU STORK

SCIENTIFIC NAME:	*Leptoptilos crumeniferus*
FAMILY:	Ciconiidae
LENGTH:	150cm (59in)
HABITAT:	Grassland and marshes, sometimes near to human settlements
DISTRIBUTION:	Much of sub-Saharan Africa, occasionally also being found in parts of Asia and Mediterranean Europe
IDENTIFICATION:	Very large stork, with a bare head and neck, large throat wattle, and massive, powerful bill. Dark back and wings, with visible white-edged secondary feathers and white underside

A huge, striking looking bird, the Marabou Stork is mainly a scavenger and will glide at great heights in search of food, often landing to feed at carcasses in competition with vultures. However, it has a voracious appetite and will eat almost anything, hunting for invertebrates, fish, reptiles, amphibians, small birds, and mammals. In addition, it frequents rubbish tips close to human settlements to feed on scraps. In fact, the expansion of towns and villages has encouraged the growth of Marabou Stork populations, to the point that they are considered a pest in some areas. Highly social, this species is almost never seen alone, and breeds in colonies, usually pairing for life. Nests are made of sticks, and are usually positioned on cliff ledges or in trees. A typical clutch will number two or three eggs, with parenting duties performed by both birds.

IBISES

Within the order Ciconiiformes, which is composed mainly of large, long legged wading birds such as storks, herons, and flamingos, the ibises and spoonbills form the family Threskiornithidae, which is then divided into two subfamilies: Plateinae, or the spoonbills, and Threskionithinae, the ibises. There are some 25 species of ibis, found across much of the world, but they are most common in tropical regions, in a range of freshwater and brackish habitats. Almost all ibises inhabit wetlands such as marshes, mudflats, lakes, and river edges, sometimes also occurring on drier, adjacent land such as grassland, cultivated fields, and dumps near human settlements. Two species however, are unusual in their preference for dry habitats. The

Wattled Ibis (*Bostrychia carunculata*) is found only in the Ethiopian highlands, where it lives on moorland and rocky cliffs, whilst the **African Green Ibis**, or **Olive Ibis** (*Bostrychia olivacea*), is found in mountainous woodlands.

Most species are highly gregarious, feeding, roosting, and nesting together, often also in the company of other large waders such as herons. They are diurnal, foraging by day for aquatic and terrestrial invertebrates, and other small animals, including fish, amphibians, and reptiles. Some species will also feed on small birds, particularly nestlings, and small mammals. Ibises range from about 50 to 100 centimeters (20–39 inches) in length, with quite elongated bodies,

Scarlet Ibis

long legs and necks, and distinctive, long, downcurved bills, which are used to probe for food. They also tend to have bare, or partially bare heads, and partially webbed feet.

The adult **Scarlet Ibis** (*Eudocimus ruber*) is perhaps the most striking species, being almost completely red. It has scarlet plumage, except for its black wingtips, and an orange-red bill and legs. The juveniles, however, are a rather dull gray-brown overall, with white underparts. They are helpless upon hatching, but are tended by both parent birds and develop quite rapidly, usually fledging at between three and five weeks old, and attaining an adult length of around 60 centimeters (24 inches). Breeding takes place in large, noisy colonies, with nests being located close together in trees, often overhanging water. Flocking in this way no doubt offers an increased degree of protection, although the mortality rate amongst the young may be as high as 50 percent, with birds of prey and big cats being major threats. The Scarlet Ibis is found in tropical swamps, mangroves, and estuaries in northern parts of South America.

The **Glossy Ibis** (*Plegadis falcinellus*) is the most widespread ibis species, being found throughout much of Europe, Asia, Africa, and Central America, and also north into the US. It grows to around the same size as the Scarlet Ibis, but its plumage is a rich brown overall, with iridescent green wings. It occurs in a variety of habitats, from coastal lagoons, bays, and mudflats, to inland marshes and moist fields, tending to migrate seasonally. Like other ibises, it nests colonially, frequently with herons, making its platform nest in trees, although it will sometimes nest on the ground amongst reeds. It produces a clutch of three to four eggs, which are incubated for around three weeks. It feeds mainly on aquatic invertebrates, including crabs and crayfish, but it will also forage for snakes, lizards, and other vertebrates.

The **Sacred Ibis** (*Threskiornis aethiopicus*) is a larger species, growing to about 75 centimeters (30 inches) in length, and it is more of a generalist in terms of feeding. It forages in marshy habitats, probing with its bill for aquatic invertebrates, amphibians, and other small animals, but it also frequently hunts in grassland and agricultural fields, and is a visitor to dumps near towns, where it will feed on carrion. It has a largely bare, black head and neck, and black plumes across the back and tail. The remaining plumage is white. It is highly sociable, and nests in large colonies, often in association with other large waders. Its breeding season tends to coincide with the rainy season, at which time it will tend to migrate north to moist grasslands, returning to coastal regions and large, permanent bodies of water in the dry season. Its nest may be positioned in a tree, shrub, or on the ground, and a clutch typically consists of two to five eggs, with incubation lasting around four weeks. Both parent birds assist with incubation and the care of their young. This species obtains its common name through being highly revered by the ancient Egyptians, who worshiped an ibis-headed god, Thoth. Now rare in Egypt, the Sacred Ibis is found mainly throughout sub-Saharan Africa, but also occurs in parts of the Middle East and southern Asia.

Glossy Ibis

GREATER FLAMINGO

SCIENTIFIC NAME:	*Phoenicopterus ruber*
FAMILY:	Phoenicopteridae
LENGTH:	145cm (57in)
HABITAT:	Lakes, lagoons, and coastal shallows
DISTRIBUTION:	Parts of Africa, southern Europe, and Asia. Those found in the Caribbean, Mexico, and Galapagos Islands and referred to as American Flamingos are sometimes regarded as a subspecies
IDENTIFICATION:	Tall and very slender waterbird with long legs and neck. Plumage is pinkish-red. Bill is distinctively angled, and pink with a black tip

Amongst the most instantly recognizable of birds, on account of its intense coloration, the Greater Flamingo is also well known for its unusual bill. Short and straight in young birds, the bill becomes distinctively hooked as the bird matures, and contains several rows of fine plates, or lamellae, enabling this species to feed in quite an unusual manner. Flamingos filter-feed in the shallows, drawing water into their upturned bills in order to trap tiny organisms such as shrimps and algae, and perhaps somewhat strangely, it is their diet that provides their vivid coloration. Highly sociable, flamingos form breeding colonies of many thousands of individuals, and long term bonds are established between breeding adults. Nest mounds are constructed from mud, and following mating, the female will produce a single egg which both parents will incubate for around a month. The downy young are initially gray, molting through brown some weeks later, before obtaining their adult plumage.

(Eurasian) Spoonbill

Scientific name:	*Platalea leucorodia*
Family:	Threskiornithidae
Length:	88cm (35in)
Habitat:	Reedbeds, shallow lakes, marshes, and lagoons
Distribution:	Parts of North Africa, Asia, and Europe, although rare in Britain
Identification:	Fairly large wader, long legs and neck. Plumage mainly white with a hanging, yellowish crest. During breeding chest becomes orange-yellow. Bill is long with a distinctive spoon shaped tip

The adult Eurasian Spoonbill is easily identified by its broad-ended, yellow-tipped bill, although juveniles lack this pronounced feature, having a lighter-colored, narrower bill that lacks the spoonlike tip. This species spends most of its time feeding in quite shallow water, sweeping its head back and forth whilst wading, in order to catch reptiles, fish, amphibians, and invertebrates, also consuming some plant material. Quite gregarious, the Eurasian Spoonbill may be seen flying in straight-line formations, often feeds in flocks, and nests in large colonies, but it tends to avoid mixing with other waterbirds. Nesting colonies are normally established amongst reeds, bushes, or trees, where stick platforms are formed, and breeding adults tend to mate for life. A typical clutch consists of three or four eggs, with incubation lasting around three weeks.

MUTE SWAN

SCIENTIFIC NAME:	*Cygnus olor*
FAMILY:	Anatidae
LENGTH:	152cm (60in)
HABITAT:	Large stretches of still or slow-moving inland waters, smaller ponds and lakes, and estuaries
DISTRIBUTION:	Native populations in Britain, Europe, and parts of Asia, also introduced in North America, South Africa, and Australasia
IDENTIFICATION:	Large, heavy waterfowl with a long neck, typically held in an S-curve. Plumage white, bill orange with a black knob at base, tail quite long and pointed

The stockiest and heaviest of the swans, the Mute Swan is also the most common swan species in its native range, but tends only to form large groups outside of the breeding season in winter. It is also at this time that Mute Swans are most likely to be encountered at estuaries or in inshore waters. At other times of the year this species is usually seen in pairs on ponds and lakes, often in urban parkland. They graze out of water, but most feeding occurs from the water's surface, with their long necks being used to reach underwater in search of aquatic vegetation. In addition, their diet is supplemented by aquatic invertebrates and some small fish and amphibians. Pairs will usually remain together throughout a season, and may mate for life, although, in some cases, Mute Swans will mate with several partners. Nesting occurs in spring, with a large mound of vegetation being constructed amongst a reedbed or in a sheltered bankside location. Clutches usually number around six eggs, which are incubated for about 35 days by both parent birds. Following hatching, the cygnets leave the nest after just one day, but the adults continue to care for their offspring until the following spring.

WHOOPER SWAN ▼

SCIENTIFIC NAME:	*Cygnus cygnus*
FAMILY:	Anatidae
LENGTH:	152cm (60in)
HABITAT:	Marshland, tundra, ponds, and lakes, often close to woodland
DISTRIBUTION:	From Iceland across much of Europe, east to Siberia. Winters in southern Europe and parts of Asia
IDENTIFICATION:	Large waterfowl, white plumage, long neck, usually held erect. Fairly flat head, long bill with yellow base, relatively short, blunt tail

Found mainly in Iceland and the far north of Europe, where some populations remain resident throughout the year, many of these swans do however undertake migrations to parts of Britain, southern Europe, and Asia during the winter months. At this time, the Whooper Swan can often be found grazing along coastlines or lakes in large numbers, but may also congregate in agricultural areas where it has been known to cause damage to crops. Generally, however, its diet consists of aquatic vegetation and some invertebrates. During the breeding season, the Whooper Swan is far less sociable and also far less bold, tending to nest in isolated pairs, shunning more open habitats in favor of remaining hidden amongst dense reedbeds. Pairs may mate for life and although both birds care for their cygnets, only the female bird incubates the clutch of between five and seven eggs, a process that takes around 35 days.

BEWICK'S SWAN

SCIENTIFIC NAME:	*Cygnus columbianus (bewickii)*
FAMILY:	Anatidae
LENGTH:	125cm (49in)
HABITAT:	Arctic tundra, marshland, lakes, rivers, and coastal bays
DISTRIBUTION:	From Siberia to Alaska, along the Arctic coast to Hudson Bay, wintering south to Britain and North America. *C.c. bewickii* is often considered a subspecies, found from Finland through Russia, east to Siberia
IDENTIFICATION:	Goose-like swan, very similar to Whooper Swan, but proportionately smaller, with round head, shorter neck and bill, with small yellow patch at base

Also known as the Tundra Swan, Bewick's Swan nests on marshy tundra across Alaska, Canada, and sub-Arctic Eurasia, forming monogamous pairs. Nesting takes place from spring to summer, with around three to six eggs in a typical clutch, and the female takes most of the responsibility for incubation, rarely leaving the nest. However, the male is often in attendance. The young usually hatch by late June and migrate with their parents to warmer climes as winter approaches. Family groups may then remain together until the young become sexually mature around a year later. Like other swans Bewick's Swan feeds mainly on aquatic vegetation, but also takes invertebrates such as mollusks and will graze on shoots and seeds on land. Less common than other swans throughout much of its range, this species may be mistaken for the Whooper Swan, although it is relatively small with a more goose-like appearance.

TRUE GEESE

The True Geese are medium-sized, long-necked waterfowl that belong to the same family as ducks and swans, Anatidae, but they are often further classified in the subfamily Anserinae, and the tribe Anserini, in which there are two main genera, Anser and Branta. Several other species named as geese, including the Andean Goose (*Chloephaga melanoptera*) and Egyptian Goose (*Alopochen aegyptiacus*), are more closely related to the shelducks, whilst the Magpie Goose (*Anseranas semipalmata*) is in its own family, Anseranatidae.

True Geese share several characteristics: they are all herbivorous, feeding mainly on land by grazing; most are migratory, although there are resident feral populations in many areas; and all tend to be similar in their breeding habits, being ground-nesting and monogamous, pairing for life and sharing parental duties. Furthermore, the sexes are usually outwardly alike, and their plumage is typically some combination of grays, browns, black, and white. The species belonging to the genus Anser are more commonly referred to as "gray geese." However, this is not strictly accurate. They tend to be quite uniformly colored overall, but are often barred, and are usually more brown than gray. There are also white forms, or morphs, of many species. Perhaps more distinctively, the bills and legs of these species

are pink, orange, or yellow. The **Greylag Goose** (*Anser anser*) is amongst the most common and widespread of the "gray geese," occurring from Iceland across most of Europe and Asia. It is also the only goose indigenous to Britain, although it now only breeds in the United Kingdom in small numbers. At one time it was far more numerous, having been domesticated hundreds of years ago, and it is the ancestor of most domesticated geese in the western world. It is a large goose, around 90 centimeters (35 inches) long, gray-brown overall, with darker wings and a paler breast. Its bill is almost triangular, and is orange-pink in color, as are its legs. It lays four to six eggs in a depression on the ground, lined with vegetation and down, incubating them for around 28 days.

The **Pink-footed Goose** (*Anser brachyrhynchus*) is somewhat smaller at around 65 centimeters (26 inches), and more slender. It is similar in color to the Greylag, but its legs and feet are typically a brighter pink, and its bill is pink in the middle and dark at both the base and tip. It breeds in Greenland, Iceland, and Norway, wintering in northwestern Europe, particularly in Britain, where it is often found at estuaries, tending to feed in adjacent farmland. It is also found in North America as a vagrant from Greenland.

Conversely, the **Snow Goose** (*Anser caerulescens*) is essentially a

Canada Goose

Snow Goose

North American species that sometimes wanders to parts of Britain. It breeds on the tundra in Canada, Greenland, and Siberia, wintering south in the US and Mexico. It grows to around 70 centimeters (28 inches) in length, and occurs in two color forms, or morphs; blue and white. The blue form has a white head, brown back, and a blue-gray body and wings, whilst the white form is white overall, with black primaries. Snow Geese lay three to five eggs, which are incubated for around 25 days. Some taxonomists place this species in the genus Chen, rather than Anser. Just as Anser geese are not all gray, those of the genus Branta, also known as the "black geese," are typically not black, but the legs and bills of these birds always are. In terms of plumage, most display some black or dark brown, usually boldly contrasting with areas of white.

The **Canada Goose** (*Branta canadensis*) is amongst the most familiar, and is a large species, often exceeding 110 centimeters (43 inches) in length. It is easily recognized, with a black head and neck, white throat patch, gray-brown body and brown wings. It occurs throughout North America, migrating south to New Mexico, but it is also widespread as an introduced species in much of northwest Europe, where it is frequently found in urban parks. It often gathers in large, noisy flocks, and is sometimes regarded as a pest. It usually nests close to water, laying five or six eggs in a down-lined hollow amongst vegetation. Known in North America as the **Brant**, the **Brent Goose** (*Branta bernicla*) is a small, dark species, usually encountered in coastal habitats, both on the tundra where it breeds, and around estuaries and bays in winter. It is rarely found inland except during migration, on its way south to North American and European coasts. During the breeding season, this species typically produces three to five eggs, which are incubated for around 25 days. As with other geese, shortly after hatching the young are led to feeding areas to begin grazing. Geese will eat other vegetation as well as grass, and are sometimes destructive to cultivated crops.

Greylag Goose

MALLARD ▼

SCIENTIFIC NAME:	*Anas platyrhynchos*
FAMILY:	Anatidae
LENGTH:	60cm (24in)
HABITAT:	Ponds, lakes, rivers, and canals, often in urban areas
DISTRIBUTION:	Widespread throughout the Northern Hemisphere in Britain, western Europe, and North America, south to North Africa, southeast Asia, and Mexico in winter
IDENTIFICATION:	Large dabbling duck, male has green head, white collar, brown chest, gray underparts, black rump, and yellow bill. Female is mottled brown with orange bill. Both have brownish wings with blue and white markings

Amongst the most common and widespread of ducks, the Mallard is a familiar bird, frequently found living in close proximity to man; inhabiting ponds and lakes in rural areas and urban parks. In some areas they are hunted as a game bird, but this species is so numerous and seemingly adaptable that human intervention appears to have little impact upon their populations. Fairly sociable birds, mallards often occur in large groups during the winter, tending to pair up in order to mate in spring. However, once a female has laid her eggs, males often form small groups and may attempt to seek further females in order to mate again. The females lay around 12 eggs in a nest of vegetation and feathers, usually on the ground, but sometimes positioned in a hollow tree or on a rooftop, incubating the eggs for around 28 days. The female will then lead her offspring to water. Mallards are "dabbling ducks," feeding at the surface or up-ending to search for vegetation and invertebrates; they will also graze. Where food is plentiful, resident populations are common, although some will migrate south to warmer areas in winter.

(NORTHERN) PINTAIL ▲

SCIENTIFIC NAME:	*Anas acuta*
FAMILY:	Anatidae
LENGTH:	65cm (26in)
HABITAT:	Lakes, marshes, lagoons, and estuaries
DISTRIBUTION:	Throughout Eurasia and North America, migrating to Central America, Africa, and India in winter
IDENTIFICATION:	Slender dabbling duck, male has dark brown head, white stripes on neck extend to breast, gray flanks, dark wing stripes and long dark tail feathers. Female mottled gray-brown with white-edged wings

Named after the long, tapering tail feathers, which are most exaggerated in the male during the breeding season, the Pintail is common in much of the Northern Hemisphere throughout the breeding season, migrating south to warmer climates in winter. Breeding usually takes place in early summer, when males will attempt to attract a mate by swimming alongside a female with the tail held aloft. Mating then typically occurs in the water, after which the female will produce a clutch of around eight eggs which she incubates alone for around three weeks in a shallow, feather-lined nest. The chicks follow the mother to water to begin feeding soon after hatching, taking vegetable matter and invertebrates at the surface. Like other dabbling ducks, this species also feeds by up-ending and has a relatively long neck, useful in seeking food at greater depths.

(COMMON) TEAL

SCIENTIFIC NAME:	*Anas crecca*
FAMILY:	Anatidae
LENGTH:	38cm (15in)
HABITAT:	Marshes, woodland, vegetated ponds, and streams. Also estuaries at times
DISTRIBUTION:	Found across most of North America and Eurasia, overwinters in Central America, North Africa, India and southeast Asia
IDENTIFICATION:	Small dabbling duck, brown overall, with black, white, and green wing patches. Male has a chestnut head with green patch over eye

Amongst the smallest of the surface-feeding or dabbling ducks, the Common Teal tends to be found in fairly small, vegetated bodies of water, but occurs in a range of habitats, and will often be found on larger bodies of water outside of the breeding season, sometimes migrating to coastal areas. Courtship begins in the fall, with pairs forming over the winter, although mating will not typically occur until late spring or early summer. The female undertakes nest-building, forming a depression amongst reeds or other waterside vegetation, which she lines with dry plant material and down from her breast. Following mating she will produce a clutch of around six eggs. These are incubated solely by the female for around three weeks, during which time she will leave the nest only for short periods in order to feed. Teals feed on a range of aquatic vegetation and invertebrates.

GOOSANDER/COMMON MERGANSER ▼

SCIENTIFIC NAME:	*Mergus merganser*
FAMILY:	Anatidae
LENGTH:	65cm (26in)
HABITAT:	Lakes, reservoirs, and rivers, often near woodland, occasionally also in estuaries and on sheltered coastlines
DISTRIBUTION:	Most of Eurasia and North America, wintering farther south
IDENTIFICATION:	Large diver. Male mainly white with a black back, green head, and long, hooked, red bill. Female gray-brown, mottled breast, white throat and reddish head

The Goosander or Common Merganser is a large diving duck, typically found on fairly large bodies of water where trees are present, as this species tends to spend much of its time perching. Trees, rock faces, and buildings are also favored nesting locations, although roosts and nests are sometimes established on the ground. Breeding pairs form in winter, with eggs being laid from spring to early summer, and clutches number around ten eggs, which are incubated by the female. The young feed mainly on aquatic insects, but the adult birds feed almost exclusively on fish and are highly adapted to the task, being well streamlined with a hooked, serrated bill. The Goosander usually associates in pairs or groups of up to about 20, but outside of the breeding season much larger single-sex flocks may group together at locations such as estuaries or on reservoirs.

WOOD DUCK ▲

SCIENTIFIC NAME:	*Aix sponsa*
FAMILY:	Anatidae
LENGTH:	45cm (18in)
HABITAT:	Woodland ponds, lakes, and rivers
DISTRIBUTION:	Throughout most of North America except for arid south-western regions. Also found in Cuba
IDENTIFICATION:	Male has iridescent purple and green head with white markings and a long crest, red bill, chestnut breast, tawny flanks, dark back, and blue-green iridescent wing feathers. Female gray-brown with white eye-patch

As with many bird species in which only the female undertakes the incubation of eggs, there is a marked difference in appearance between the sexes. The male Wood Duck is amongst the most striking of American ducks, whilst the female's plumage is much duller, providing camouflage during the nesting period. Interestingly, however, this species does not nest on the ground as most ducks do, preferring to nest in tree cavities or nesting boxes where provided, and it may be observed perching in trees, sometimes at a considerable distance from water. Pairs tend to form in winter, with breeding taking place from spring, and in the south of its range the Wood Duck may produce two clutches of eggs in a year. Clutches usually number between six and twelve eggs, but where several birds nest in close proximity, communal nests are not uncommon and may contain up to 40 eggs or more. Following hatching the young drop from the tree and head toward water, encouraged by calls from the females. Wood Ducks feed on acorns, seeds, and other plant matter as well as invertebrates.

MANDARIN DUCK

SCIENTIFIC NAME:	*Aix galericulata*
FAMILY:	Anatidae
LENGTH:	45cm (18in)
HABITAT:	Woodland ponds, lakes, and streams
DISTRIBUTION:	Eastern Asia, south to China in winter, with feral populations in the UK
IDENTIFICATION:	Male has a bushy brown crest and cheek ruffs, large white eye-patches, dark neck and back with black and white markings, greenish flanks, and large, bronze, swept-back inner wing feathers. Female mainly gray-brown

Closely related to the Wood Duck of North America, the Mandarin Duck favors wooded watercourses and spends much of its time perching and nesting in trees, feeding at dawn and dusk. It also shares a similar diet, preferring deciduous woodland where acorns and seeds are plentiful, supplemented with terrestrial insects and small aquatic animals such as mollusks and even small fish. Although somewhat different in coloration, the species are also similar in that the males possess striking plumage whilst the females are quite drab. Pairing occurs in winter, with breeding usually taking place from April. Nests are made in abandoned woodpecker holes or similar cavities, into which around ten eggs are laid. These are incubated solely by the female for around 30 days. Upon hatching, the mother calls to the chicks which then drop to the ground and head toward water to begin feeding.

KING EIDER ▲

SCIENTIFIC NAME:	*Somateria spectabilis*
FAMILY:	Anatidae
LENGTH:	55cm (22in)
HABITAT:	Tundra, rocky islands, and coastlines
DISTRIBUTION:	Northern Alaska, Canada, Greenland, and Eurasia, occasionally farther south
IDENTIFICATION:	Male has white neck, breast, and shoulders, black belly, rump and back. Crown blue-gray, cheeks pale green, bill reddish with large orange forehead shield. Female mottled brown with dark bill

The King Eider is a sea duck, which inhabits harsh, cold waters in the far north, even wintering at sea on the southern edge of the pack ice. It requires a thick layer of downy insulating feathers for much of the year, and during the breeding season, when this bird comes ashore, the female plucks this down from her breast in order to line her nest. The eiderdown collected by humans for lining clothing, pillows, and suchlike usually comes from the Common Eider (*Somateria mollissima*), however. Pairs tend to nest in the summer near tundra ponds, where the female lays and incubates four or five eggs in a shallow scrape. Incubation lasts around three weeks, during which time the female will often not eat. Shortly after hatching, some females may return to the sea, whilst others remain with the juveniles, which will flock together, foraging for vegetation and insects. The adults feed by diving, sometimes to depths of 50m (150ft), preying on mollusks, crustaceans, echinoderms, and small fish.

CANVASBACK

SCIENTIFIC NAME:	*Aythya valisineria*
FAMILY:	Anatidae
LENGTH:	53cm (21in)
HABITAT:	Lakes, rivers, estuaries, and bays
DISTRIBUTION:	Much of North America, wintering as far south as Mexico
IDENTIFICATION:	Large diving duck. Male has rust-colored head and neck, black breast and rump, and pale gray flanks. The female is mottled gray with a brown head, neck and rump

The Canvasback is a large diving duck, notable for the long sloping profile of its head and bill. Being quite large, it may dive to greater depths than some other species, but it is often found on small inland waters when breeding, frequently in marshland, where it nests amongst reeds or similar vegetation, either on the ground or sometimes on a floating raft at the water's edge. Following mating the female produces an average clutch of around ten eggs, which she incubates alone for three to four weeks. The young are quite well developed and are able to follow their mother into the water soon after hatching to begin foraging for food. The Canvasback uses its long, sloping bill to dig around on the lake or river bottom, and it feeds mainly on the submerged roots of aquatic plants such as wild celery, also consuming invertebrates and other small aquatic creatures. Following the breeding season, this species migrates to large inland lakes, estuaries, or sheltered bays for the winter, typically moving south as far as the Gulf Coast and Mexico.

TUFTED DUCK ▼

SCIENTIFIC NAME:	*Aythya fuligula*
FAMILY:	Anatidae
LENGTH:	43cm (17in)
HABITAT:	Lakes, ponds, and rivers, often in urban parks. Also occasionally on the sea
DISTRIBUTION:	Throughout most of Eurasia, wintering south to parts of Africa and India
IDENTIFICATION:	Male is black with white flanks, female dull brown with paler flanks. Both have bright yellow eyes and crest at the back of head, longer in male

Like other freshwater diving ducks, the Tufted Duck belongs to the tribe Aythyini, or diving ducks, distinct from the sawbills such as the mergansers, and sea ducks like the eiders, although they are also accomplished divers. The Aythyini are much like the dabbling ducks in general appearance, but tend to have somewhat shorter legs, set farther back on the body, which are used for propulsion as they forage underwater. They feed mainly on aquatic invertebrates such as snails, insects, and worms, but are capable of catching small fish, and they also consume some vegetation. As well as hunting below the surface, these ducks will tend to submerge if alarmed, rather than fleeing on land or flying. The Tufted Duck is amongst the most common of the diving ducks throughout much of its range, and is quite sociable, sometimes breeding in loose colonies. It nests on the ground, usually amongst vegetation, where it lays a clutch of around nine eggs.

POCHARD

SCIENTIFIC NAME:	*Aythya ferina*
FAMILY:	Anatidae
LENGTH:	46cm (18in)
HABITAT:	Marshes, lakes, gravel pits, and occasionally estuaries
DISTRIBUTION:	Throughout much of Europe, Asia, and North Africa, occasionally straying to Alaska and the western US
IDENTIFICATION:	Stout diving duck with high forehead and sloping bill. Male is gray with rusty head and neck, black breast and tail. Female is blotchy brown with a darker head and gray throat. Both have gray bar across black bill

The Pochard is a fairly common diving duck, which is much like the larger North American Canvasback in appearance. It has been threatened by hunting, habitat destruction, and pollution in parts of its range, but in some areas, notably in the United Kingdom, its numbers are increasing somewhat, perhaps mainly due to its exploitation of reservoirs and flooded gravel pits, although breeding numbers remain fairly small. It is far more abundant in winter, being joined in Britain by populations from northern Europe, and at such times it may be found in more open habitats such as marshes and estuaries. It feeds on aquatic vegetation, insects and other invertebrates, and small fish, being most active in the early morning and evening, and tending to rest on land by day. However, like other diving ducks, it is rather clumsy on land due to the position of its short legs. It nests amongst vegetation, producing a clutch of around nine or ten eggs, which are incubated for about four weeks.

CALIFORNIA CONDOR

SCIENTIFIC NAME:	*Gymnogyps californianus*
FAMILY:	Cathartidae
LENGTH:	120cm (47in)
HABITAT:	Open, rocky, lightly wooded, and semidesert terrain
DISTRIBUTION:	Southern California and parts of Arizona
IDENTIFICATION:	Huge carrion eater. Predominantly black, with white wing markings and a naked, orange-pink head

The California Condor is a huge bird with a wingspan measuring around 3 meters (almost 10 feet), yet it is scarcely seen in the wild, being amongst the rarest of all bird species. Years of persecution and the Condor's slow breeding rate saw numbers dwindle to fewer than 20 wild specimens by the mid-1980s. However, captive breeding and reintroduction programs have had some success in recent years. A carrion feeder, the California Condor ranges over huge distances in search of food, gliding on thermals at altitudes of over 450 meters (1,500 feet), sometimes covering distances of around 160 kilometers (100 miles) in a day. Typically alighting to feed at large carcasses such as those of cattle and other livestock, these birds will also feed on smaller animals such as rabbits and ground squirrels. When not feeding, much of the Condor's time is spent preening or basking in the sun, wings outstretched. Sexual maturity is reached at around seven years, and the California Condor tends to pair for life, breeding in spring to produce a single egg that is laid on the bare ground of a cave or ledge. Incubation may take almost 60 days, after which the juvenile may remain with its parents for about a year, although its first flights occur at around six months.

ANDEAN CONDOR ▲

SCIENTIFIC NAME:	*Vultur gryphus*
FAMILY:	Cathartidae
LENGTH:	130cm (51in)
HABITAT:	Open, mountainous areas
DISTRIBUTION:	Throughout the length of the Andean mountain range
IDENTIFICATION:	Huge, vulture-like carrion eater. Predominantly black, with white wing feathers and a white neck-ruff. Bald head is pink in males, with a distinctive comb, and black in females

The largest of the birds of prey, the Andean Condor has a wingspan of over 3 meters (10 feet) and may weigh in excess of 13 kilos (30 pounds). It is also amongst the most long-lived of bird species, commonly reaching 50 years old. However, being such a large, slow-developing bird, its reproductive cycle is also slow, with sexual maturity reached at about eight years, and chicks typically produced every other year. Correspondingly, population numbers are slow to recover when threatened by man. Breeding usually takes place in spring, with a single egg being laid on a rocky ledge, sometimes surrounded by a few twigs. Both parents incubate the egg and care for their offspring and although the young may fly at around six months, it will remain with the parents for up to two years. The Andean Condor feeds almost exclusively on carrion, occasionally taking live prey such as small rodents and reptiles, or newborn and dying animals. It will also consume the eggs of other birds, particularly those of seabirds where large breeding colonies tend to provide a plentiful supply.

EGYPTIAN VULTURE

SCIENTIFIC NAME:	*Neophron percnopterus*
FAMILY:	Accipitridae
LENGTH:	65cm (26in)
HABITAT:	Open, arid plains and semidesert regions
DISTRIBUTION:	From the Mediterranean into parts of Asia and Africa
IDENTIFICATION:	Pale or off-white, with brown flight feathers, a ruff around the throat and face, which are bare and yellow. Bill is hooked with a black tip

Despite its name, the Egyptian Vulture occurs throughout most of Africa, the Middle East, India, and southern Europe, and it is the smallest and most common vulture to occur in Europe. As such it is often driven away from carcasses by larger carrion feeders, but due to its size it has the advantage of being less reliant on thermal currents to attain height, and therefore tends to begin searching for food earlier in the day than its competitors. In addition to feeding on carrion, the Egyptian Vulture also preys on invertebrates and may eat fruit and other vegetable matter, but it is perhaps best known for eating the eggs of other birds, specifically because of the methods that it employs in order to do so. Unusually amongst birds, this species is a tool-user, cracking large eggs, such as those of Ostriches, with stones. Smaller eggs are lifted from the ground and dropped. This species also displays quite unusual courtship behavior for a vulture, including mid-air grappling. Both birds take parental responsibility; from nest construction, through incubation, to rearing their young.

TURKEY VULTURE

SCIENTIFIC NAME:	*Cathartes aura*
FAMILY:	Cathartidae
LENGTH:	72cm (28in)
HABITAT:	Woodland, farmland, and open country
DISTRIBUTION:	Throughout much of the Americas, from southern Canada to the Falkland Islands
IDENTIFICATION:	Large carrion eater, gray-black plumage with lighter wing edges, naked red head and white bill

Amongst the largest of America's predatory birds, the Turkey Vulture may prey on young or injured animals, small rodents, reptiles, and the hatchlings of other birds, but like its close relatives, it is predominantly a carrion feeder. It has an acute sense of smell and may soar at great heights, enabling it to locate animal carcasses from some distance, and has a characteristically bald head, which prevents its feathers from becoming soiled when feeding. Like other vultures it also has a sophisticated immune system that allows it to consume badly decaying meat. The Turkey Vulture breeds from March to June, producing a single clutch of up to three eggs each year. These are laid in caves, on cliff ledges or amongst rocks on the ground, and are incubated by both parents for about 40 days. The young are usually then cared for for a further ten weeks as they learn to fly and hunt. In warmer areas the Turkey Vulture may be a year-round resident, but it will tend to migrate south from the northern parts of its range in winter.

LAMMERGEIER/BEARDED VULTURE

SCIENTIFIC NAME:	*Gypaetus barbatus*
FAMILY:	Accipitridae
LENGTH:	110cm (43in)
HABITAT:	Remote mountainous regions
DISTRIBUTION:	Southern Europe around the Mediterranean, the Middle East, Central Asia, and parts of Africa
IDENTIFICATION:	Large vulture with dark back and wings, tawny head, neck, underside, and heavily feathered legs. Wings long and pointed, tail diamond shaped. Tuft hangs below bill

Although mainly an inhabitant of remote mountain areas, the Lammergeier or Bearded Vulture also frequents the edges of human settlements in areas where it is most numerous, scavenging for carrion and invertebrates amongst human refuse and agricultural waste. Additionally, a large part of its diet consists of bones and bone marrow, which it extracts with its specially shaped tongue. It also has a unique habit of dropping bones from great heights in order to break them open. Breeding usually takes place in February and begins with courtship displays much like that of the Egyptian Vulture, involving the touching of talons whilst in flight. Nests are positioned on rocky crags and are formed of various materials including sticks, fur, and dung, and are usually scattered with skulls and other bones. One or two eggs are laid which are incubated solely by the female for around 50 days; both parents bring food to the fledglings until they are old enough to seek food independently around 16 to 20 weeks later.

GRIFFON VULTURE

SCIENTIFIC NAME:	*Gyps fulvus*
FAMILY:	Accipitridae
LENGTH:	100cm (39in)
HABITAT:	Mountainous regions
DISTRIBUTION:	From Spain and North Africa across southern Europe to Asia and the Middle East
IDENTIFICATION:	Large vulture, mostly light brown with darker tail and wing edges, white head, neck, and collar

The Griffon Vulture is usually seen soaring over open country in mountainous regions, but relies upon rocky cliff faces for roosting and nesting. A sociable bird, this species feeds and nests communally, sometimes forming colonies of over 100 pairs; however, congregations this large are uncommon, with groups usually consisting of fewer than 20 pairs. Breeding takes place between winter and early summer, depending upon conditions such as climate and altitude, with a single egg being laid in a loose nest of sticks positioned on a rocky crag. Incubation lasts around 50 days, and the young are fledged after about six months. When not roosting or nesting, the Griffon Vulture spends around eight hours each day searching for food, soaring on thermals until carrion is located. Once a food source has been found, several vultures will rapidly assemble and may chase smaller scavengers from a carcass. They rely on larger birds or mammals to expose flesh before they can feed, and will often have to wait their turn at a kill.

OSPREY

SCIENTIFIC NAME:	*Pandion haliaetus*
FAMILY:	Pandionidae
LENGTH:	55cm (22in)
HABITAT:	Woodland, open country or rocky cliffs close to lakes, rivers, or the coast
DISTRIBUTION:	Almost global, with the exception of polar regions
IDENTIFICATION:	Fairly large predatory bird. Brown above and white below with brown markings. Dark stripes run across yellow eyes, down the neck to the back

The only species in its family, the Osprey is regarded as a fish-hawk, and is unusual amongst birds of prey, or raptors, in feeding almost exclusively on fish. This trait has enabled the Osprey to establish itself in a range of habitats wherever food is plentiful, from lakes and rivers to marshes and coastlines. In fact, it is one of the most widely distributed of bird species, occurring on every continent with the exception of Antarctica. Fish are taken at the water's surface in the Osprey's talons, and it is capable of catching quite large prey; sometimes up to a kilo (2.2lbs) or more. The food is then taken to a nearby perch to be eaten. During the breeding season, a catch will typically be taken back to the nest, or at least close to it. Nesting occurs from spring to summer when migrants return from wintering in the more southerly parts of their range. The nests are usually positioned in trees and are quite bulky constructions made of sticks and other found materials. Breeding pairs may use the same nest year after year, adding new material each season. Clutches usually number two or three eggs, which are incubated by the female for almost 40 days, and whilst the male supplies nearly all of the food for the chicks, the female tends to remain with them and feed them directly.

RED KITE ▲

SCIENTIFIC NAME:	*Milvus milvus*
FAMILY:	Accipitridae
LENGTH:	65cm (26in)
HABITAT:	Wooded, sometimes mountainous or hilly areas, often close to water
DISTRIBUTION:	Much of Europe, into Asia, the Middle East, and parts of North Africa
IDENTIFICATION:	Large, streamlined bird of prey with a deeply forked tail. Mainly rusty-red, with a gray face. Large white sections visible under wings when in flight

Although easily recognized by its long, deeply forked tail, the Red Kite was at one time a much more familiar sight throughout much of its range than it is today, particularly in Britain and northern Europe where it is now relatively scarce. Highly valued as a scavenger several hundred years ago, the Red Kite became so numerous in places as to be regarded as vermin and it was relentlessly persecuted by man up until the 20th century. By the time conservation efforts began to be made, this bird had to contend with habitat destruction and poisoning by pesticides. However, recent years have seen a slow increase in its numbers, in parts of Britain for example, where it was once almost extinct. In addition to scavenging for carrion, the Red Kite feeds on insects and other invertebrates, and hunts for small mammals up to the size of rabbits. Both parent birds care for their young during the breeding season, with the female spending most of her time at the nest and the male providing food for her and the young during incubation and fledging, as is typical of many raptors.

BLACK KITE

SCIENTIFIC NAME:	*Milvus migrans*
FAMILY:	Accipitridae
LENGTH:	60cm (24in)
HABITAT:	Open country, marsh and farmland, urban areas
DISTRIBUTION:	Much of Eurasia, south to parts of Africa and Australia
IDENTIFICATION:	Usually uniformly dark brown, although some populations (non-European), have noticeably pale underwing sections. Tail is shorter and less deeply forked than that of Red Kite

Similar in overall appearance to the Red Kite, the Black Kite differs somewhat in its behavior, being a far more sociable bird, notably gathering in vast colonies in parts of Australia. It is also far more tolerant of human presence and will scavenge amongst refuse in human settlements and even steal food from markets if the opportunity arises. In addition to feeding on scraps and carrion, the Black Kite also consumes invertebrates, amphibians, reptiles, fish, small birds, and mammals. A partial migrant, northern populations tend to head south for the winter following breeding, but this species may reproduce at almost any time of year if conditions allow. Loose nesting colonies are typically established in woodland, often close to water, with nests being placed in trees; the Black Kite is also known to build its nests on buildings. The female produces and incubates one to three eggs whilst the male provides food. The young hatch after about a month, leaving the nest around 40 days later.

(Western) Marsh Harrier/ ▲ Swamp Harrier

Scientific name:	*Circus aeruginosus*
Family:	Accipitridae
Length:	56cm (22in)
Habitat:	Marshes, moist open meadows, and farmland
Distribution:	Widespread across Europe, Africa, Asia, and Pacific islands close to Australia
Identification:	Typically brown overall, with varying amounts of gray on wings and tail. Underside rusty, buff, or, in females, more yellowish

The largest of the harriers, the Marsh or Swamp Harrier, as its name would suggest, is typically encountered in wetlands, and is also increasingly common in areas such as farmland, favoring open country where there is sufficient ground cover for nesting and to provide habitats for the range of small animals that make up its diet. These include invertebrates, reptiles, small birds, and mammals. Much of its diet consists of frogs, and it is rarely found far from water; even avoiding drier regions when migrating to wintering grounds, preferring to follow the courses of rivers or streams. Breeding typically begins in spring, with females making their nests in April or May. As with other harriers, the Marsh Harrier usually constructs its nest on the ground or in low vegetation, with reedbeds being a favored location of this species. The female produces and incubates a clutch of around four or five eggs, which hatch after about 35 days. The male, meanwhile, provides both her and the young with food. The chicks leave the nest after a further 40 days or so.

Hen/Northern Harrier

Scientific name:	*Circus cyaneus*
Family:	Accipitridae
Length:	50cm (20in)
Habitat:	Open meadows, moorland, and marshland
Distribution:	Throughout North America and Eurasia, migrating south to Central America, North Africa, and southeast Asia
Identification:	Male pale gray with black wing tips, white rump and underside. Female brown above, streaked with white below

Although diurnal, that is, active by day, the Hen Harrier has a small but distinct facial disk similar to that of owls, which is thought to enhance its hearing as it flies low over the ground in search of prey such as small mammals, amphibians, and invertebrates. However, this species is also known to take game birds such as grouse, a habit which has seen it suffer persecution from man, particularly in the upland areas where it may reside for much of the year. In winter, though, Hen Harriers are more likely to be encountered in low-lying marshes or coastal regions. Breeding typically occurs in spring, at which time pairs perform aerial displays, including spectacular dives and the presentation of talons. Nesting takes place on the ground, often amongst heather or similarly dense ground cover, where the female will lay and incubate up to four eggs. The male will provide most of the food throughout the incubation and fledging period which lasts for a total of 10 to 12 weeks, with the young becoming fully independent a few weeks later.

MONTAGU'S HARRIER

SCIENTIFIC NAME:	*Circus pygargus*
FAMILY:	Accipitridae
LENGTH:	45cm (18in)
HABITAT:	Coastal marshes, open grassy fields and slopes
DISTRIBUTION:	Much of Europe, Africa, and Asia
IDENTIFICATION:	Male dark gray with black wing bars and tips, pale belly, streaked with brown. Female brown above, streaked with white below and narrow, white patch on rump and toward rear of eye

Like other harriers, Montagu's Harrier prefers quite open habitats with sufficient ground cover to provide for its dietary and nesting needs, and flies quite low and slowly over such areas in search of prey. This species is perhaps the most slender and agile of its group, displaying a particularly buoyant flight, which many observers have described as tern-like. It preys on small mammals, especially mice and voles, small birds, amphibians, and invertebrates, but will also feed on carrion when other food sources are scarce. It nests on the ground amongst tall grasses or other vegetation, with a clutch of three to five eggs being laid in early summer. These are incubated solely by the female for around four weeks, with the male providing food for her, and for the chicks once hatching has occurred. As with other harriers, males of this species are generally monogamous but may sometimes mate with two females and support both of their broods.

HAWKS

The term "hawk" is sometimes used loosely to refer to almost any of the raptors, or birds of prey, and particularly to describe birds of the family Accipitridae, which includes Old World vultures, eagles, buzzards and kites. More specifically, it is assigned to members of the subfamily Accipitrinae, regarded as the True Hawks. Many other species named as hawks, including Harris' Hawk (*Parabuteo unicinctus*) and the Red-tailed Hawk (*Buteo jamaicensis*), are usually assigned to the subfamily Buteoninae, which includes the buzzards and eagles. The True Hawks are mainly comprised of birds of the genus Accipiter, the largest genus not only in birds of prey, but of all birds, with a total of 49 species. They are sometimes known as "bird hawks," and are mainly woodland predators that specialize in ambushing smaller birds in flight. Typical characteristics include broad, rounded wings, long tails which are used to brake and steer, and quite large eyes, which are often yellow or orange in color. The large goshawks possess strong legs and large powerful feet, whilst the smaller sparrowhawks tend to have much thinner legs, long grasping

toes and needle-like talons. They usually nest in trees, forming quite loose platform nests of sticks and twigs, which they line with bark and feathers. As with most birds of prey the females are often somewhat larger than the males.

The **Eurasian Sparrowhawk** (*Accipiter nisus*) is amongst the smallest raptors within its range, which extends from Britain, throughout most of Europe and Asia, south into North Africa, northern India, and southern China. The male is blue-gray above and white below, with close orange barring, and grows to around 28 centimeters (11 inches), whilst the female is brown above with dark barring below and reaches lengths of up to 38 centimeters (15 inches). It usually nests in coniferous forests, but is also found in deciduous woodland, and even urban parks and gardens. The female incubates the clutch of around five eggs for up to 42 days, but both parents feed the young. The Eurasian Sparrowhawk may be seen soaring, but it flies fast and low when hunting for small birds. Its counterpart in North America is the **Sharp-shinned Hawk** (*Accipiter striatus*), which

(Eurasian) Sparrowhawk

is of almost identical appearance and habit. It is widely distributed throughout North America, wintering south to Costa Rica.

The **Northern Goshawk** (*Accipiter gentilis*) is quite similar in appearance, being gray-brown above, with dark barring on its pale underside, but it is larger, with males and females reaching 48 and 58 centimeters (19 and 23 inches) in length respectively. It has distinctive white eyebrows and the male has dark patches behind his eyes. This species is found in a wide band across much of the Northern Hemisphere, although it is absent from the far north. It is found in various woodland habitats, but prefers to avoid areas of human habitation. It preys on fairly large birds, including Wood Pigeons and Common Pheasants, also taking amphibians, reptiles, and mammals as large as rabbits from the ground. When breeding, the male constructs the nest, but the female incubates their clutch of up to five eggs alone. Incubation lasts for around 36 days, after which the male will bring food for the chicks, but the female tends to actually feed them.

Harris' Hawk is a heavily built species, which hunts in both lightly wooded and more open habitats, being found in semidesert and scrub from the southern US, throughout much of South America. It makes most of its kills on the ground, preying on mammals such as

rodents and rabbits, but also feeds on reptiles and birds. It is unusual in that it often hunts cooperatively, with up to five birds, usually led by a female, assuming different roles in order to secure a catch, with one or more flushing out an animal from a hiding place, whilst the others wait to give chase. Nesting females are also frequently fed by groups of males, which will then share in the care of her brood. A typical clutch consists of between two and four eggs, and a female may produce up to three clutches in a year. Harris' Hawks are dark brown overall, with reddish-brown patches on the wings, and have yellow black-tipped bills and yellow feet. Males reach about 44 centimeters (17 inches) in length, and females 58 centimeters (23 inches).

The **Red-tailed Hawk** is another large, heavily built species, with males growing to about 50 centimeters (20 inches) and females up to 63 centimeters (25 inches). It is brown above, with dark streaking, and pale and mottled below. As its name suggests it has a rufous tail. It hunts mainly in open habitats, from lightly wooded areas to grasslands and semidesert, typically soaring, or utilizing high perches to spot its prey, which includes invertebrates, reptiles, birds, and mammals. It is found throughout most of North and Central America and the Caribbean. The Red-tailed Hawk creates a bulky nest in which both sexes incubate up to five eggs for around a month.

(Northern) Goshawk

Harris' Hawk

COMMON BUZZARD

SCIENTIFIC NAME:	*Buteo buteo*
FAMILY:	Accipitridae
LENGTH:	50cm (20in)
HABITAT:	Hills, meadows, remote coastlines, and forested areas
DISTRIBUTION:	Throughout Europe and much of Asia, wintering south throughout Africa, India, and southeast Asia
IDENTIFICATION:	Broad-winged, thickset bird of prey. Predominantly brown with light band on breast and barred tail

Probably the most common medium sized raptor to be encountered in much of Europe, and particularly in the United Kingdom, the Common Buzzard thrives in a variety of habitats and is often found close to farmland in rural areas, either soaring at length or perched on fence posts, telegraph poles, and pylons, keeping a watchful eye for the movement of potential prey. It feeds on creatures as small as insects, sometimes also hunting on the ground, but much of its diet consists of small mammals, with rabbits being a staple throughout much of its range. Additionally, carrion may be consumed when the opportunity arises. Common Buzzards form monogamous breeding pairs usually mating for life, and, where resident, they may defend a territory throughout the year. Nests are built by both birds and used in successive years, sometimes becoming bulky constructions of sticks over one meter (three feet) across. Clutches typically number two to four eggs, with incubation and rearing being performed by both parent birds.

ROUGH-LEGGED BUZZARD/HAWK

SCIENTIFIC NAME:	*Buteo lagopus*
FAMILY:	Accipitridae
LENGTH:	55cm (22in)
HABITAT:	Mountains, woodland, and open terrain
DISTRIBUTION:	Throughout the Northern Hemisphere, those in North America often regarded as a subspecies, *B. l. sanctijohannis*
IDENTIFICATION:	Mainly brown, with whitish underwings, dark throat and belly, and white, black-tipped tail

Fairly common throughout much of its range, the Rough-legged Buzzard, or Rough-legged Hawk as it is known in North America, is a fairly large raptor that favors open, often quite mountainous terrain. Like the Common Buzzard, it has a tendency to perch on high vantage points such as telegraph poles, or may be seen soaring on thermals in order to spot its prey, but it will also often fly low to the ground in much the same way as a harrier. This species is notable, too, for its habit of hovering. It feeds on small birds, invertebrates, and some carrion, but mammals, particularly rodents such as lemmings and voles, constitute most of its diet. Breeding typically occurs during spring and summer, with quite dense nests of vegetation being constructed on rocky ledges, although trees are often also used, particularly in southern parts of the breeding range. A clutch of around three or four eggs is laid, with the female taking most of the responsibility for incubation and rearing the young, and the male supplying food to the nest. In winter, this species tends to migrate south from northern breeding grounds, often in large flocks.

BALD EAGLE

SCIENTIFIC NAME:	*Haliaeetus leucocephalus*
FAMILY:	Accipitridae
LENGTH:	75–105cm (30–41in) Male smaller than female
HABITAT:	Close to large rivers, lakes and also coastlines
DISTRIBUTION:	Throughout most of North America, south to Mexico, but absent from parts of the far north. Occasionally also strays into Russia and parts of northern Europe
IDENTIFICATION:	Large eagle, predominantly brown plumage with distinctive white head, neck, and tail. Bill and talons yellow

Instantly recognizable to many as the national emblem of the United States of America, this species occurs throughout the region, but is most abundant in the far north, in Alaska and much of Canada, where its habitat has been less disturbed by the activities of man. However, its habitats are diverse, and northern populations tend to migrate in winter from the frozen tundra to Mexico. It is seldom encountered far from water, however, relying chiefly on fish and other aquatic animals for its prey. It feeds upon fish as large as salmon and may kill and eat quite large waterfowl such as geese. It also preys upon mammals, including rodents, rabbits, and even young sea otters. In addition to hunting for its food, the Bald Eagle will consume carrion and is also known to harass other birds of prey such as the Osprey, forcing them to release a catch. When breeding, a mating pair will often reuse and add to their nest year after year, resulting in a massive structure of sticks. In fact, the Bald Eagle is known to construct the largest nest of any arboreal-nesting species. One to three eggs are laid, with both adult birds incubating them for up to six weeks and participating in the care of the eaglets.

GOLDEN EAGLE

SCIENTIFIC NAME:	*Aquila chrysaetos*
FAMILY:	Accipitridae
LENGTH:	75–95cm (30–37in) Male smaller than female
HABITAT:	Mountainous, often forested areas, rugged open country
DISTRIBUTION:	Much of North America, Europe, and North Africa east to Asia
IDENTIFICATION:	Large bird of prey, dark brown with light brown or yellowish plumage around the head onto the back. Talons and bill yellow with black tips

A large, powerful bird of prey that tends to hunt in rugged, isolated areas, the Golden Eagle is a skillful flier that may dive onto its prey from a height at speeds of up to 320 km/h (200 m.p.h.), although it will also hunt close to the ground at times, in much the same way as a harrier. It feeds mainly on small animals such as reptiles and mammals, particularly rabbits and rodents, but is capable of tackling larger prey. However, reports of attacks on livestock have been greatly exaggerated, and Golden Eagles feeding on such animals are almost certainly feeding on carrion. In addition, this species will prey upon other birds, both on the ground and on the wing. It tends to breed from early spring to late summer, with pairs commonly mating for life and reusing nesting sites. The nest itself is typically positioned high on a crag or tree, overlooking open ground where prey may be readily hunted. Two eggs are usually produced, although a clutch may number up to four, and these are usually incubated mainly by the female alone, for a period of around 40 days. The male will remain close to the nest, providing much of the food for the family, with the young eaglets becoming self-sufficient around four months after hatching.

HARPY EAGLE ▼

SCIENTIFIC NAME:	*Harpia harpyja*
FAMILY:	Accipitridae
LENGTH:	90–100cm (35–39in) Male smaller than female
HABITAT:	Rainforest canopy
DISTRIBUTION:	From parts of Mexico south to northern Argentina
IDENTIFICATION:	Huge bird of prey with massive talons and a powerful, hooked bill. Upperparts are gray-black, head slightly lighter with dark crest, underparts white

The Harpy Eagle is amongst the largest and most powerful of the birds of prey, with an average wingspan of around 2 meters (6½ feet), and massive talons, which are used for grasping its often large prey. It feeds on a variety of birds, reptiles, and mammals, including large snakes and lizards, monkeys, sloths, and opossums, with most food being captured in trees rather than from the forest floor. It is thought to have excellent hearing and vision, probably enhanced by its owl-like facial disk. Its avian prey includes macaws, for which it has sometimes been persecuted by parrot trappers, and indigenous people sometimes hunt it for food and feathers, but the greatest threat to the Harpy Eagle probably comes from habitat destruction, and it is currently classed as an endangered species. This species is also slow to recover from population damage as it has a long breeding cycle; only one chick is raised every two or three years and sexual maturity is not reached until the age of around four or five years. As with most eagles, the Harpy Eagle is monogamous and tends to mate for life. It nests high in the forest canopy or on a cliff ledge, and although it may produce two eggs, only the first to hatch will survive. Incubation lasts around 55 days, and the chick usually remains dependent on its parents for a further ten months or more.

CRESTED CARACARA

SCIENTIFIC NAME:	*Caracara plancus*
FAMILY:	Falconidae
LENGTH:	55–60cm (22–24in) Male smaller than female
HABITAT:	Open prairie, agricultural land and scrub, often close to water
DISTRIBUTION:	Southern US, particularly Texas, beyond throughout Central and South America
IDENTIFICATION:	Large, long legged falcon with a large head and bill. Brown overall with white neck, black crown, and bare red skin on face. Breast, primary wing feathers and tail prominently barred with black and white

The Crested Caracara is the most terrestrial of the falcons, and is well adapted for spending time on the ground, having long legs and toes for walking, running, and grasping prey when hunting in the open habitats which it prefers. It is a capable predator, and its live prey includes invertebrates, reptiles, amphibians, and some small birds and mammals. It is something of an opportunistic feeder and consumes mainly carrion, sometimes associating with vultures at larger carcasses. Unfortunately, its habit of feeding on roadkill has led to several deaths, and coupled with man's encroachment upon its favored habitats, has led to a severe decline in its numbers. The relatively long fledging period of this species at around two months may also be a factor in this decline, although two broods of young each year is not uncommon. The nesting habits of the Crested Caracara are unusual amongst falcons in that it actually builds a nest, rather than using the disused nest of another species, and it often constructs its nest on the ground, building a rather large, ragged structure of sticks and vines. Up to three eggs are produced, which are incubated for about a month, and following fledging the young may continue to rely on the parents for food for several months.

SECRETARY BIRD

SCIENTIFIC NAME:	*Sagittarius serpentarius*
FAMILY:	Sagittariidae
LENGTH:	150cm (59in)
HABITAT:	Open grassland and scrub
DISTRIBUTION:	Sub-Saharan Africa
IDENTIFICATION:	Very tall, ground-hunting bird of prey. Slender, with a fairly long neck, long legs, wings, and tail. Plumage gray with black flight feathers, tail tip and crest. Red eye-patch

Named after its crest, reminiscent of a secretary's quill, the Secretary Bird is unusual amongst birds of prey in that it hunts on the ground for its food, rarely flying other than to roost or nest in trees. As such, it has a number of adaptations that provide it with a rather unusual appearance. It has long, powerful legs, ideal for walking and running in the open grassland where it hunts, and small feet, as it does not need to grasp its prey in flight. It retains long wings, however, which are used primarily for balance when running. It feeds on a variety of small animals, including large invertebrates, frogs, lizards, and rodents, but it is perhaps best known for preying on snakes, and its legs are heavily scaled to protect against bites. The Secretary Bird will often stamp repeatedly on its prey in order to make a kill, or may stun an animal with a swift kick, before dispatching it with a stab from its bill. When hunting snakes, it has also been observed that this species will spread its wings, a tactic thought to break up its outline and prevent the snake from striking. Breeding tends to occur when food is most abundant, at which time a breeding pair will nest in a tree or bush, often reusing a nest year after year, and like many raptors, the Secretary Bird often pairs for life. An average of two eggs are laid, which are incubated for around 45 days.

(COMMON) KESTREL

SCIENTIFIC NAME:	*Falco tinnunculus*
FAMILY:	Falconidae
LENGTH:	30–38cm (12–15in) Male smaller than female
HABITAT:	Open country; meadows, moorland, and marshes, often close to lightly wooded areas. Also occurs in towns and cities
DISTRIBUTION:	Throughout most of Europe, Africa, and Asia
IDENTIFICATION:	Rusty brown above, buff below, darkly spotted overall except for dusky outer wings. Tail barred in female, male has gray tail, rump, and head. Both have broad, dark band near tail tip

Very common throughout much of its range, the Kestrel is familiar to many due to its habit of hovering when searching for prey, and it is often observed doing so near roadsides in open country. However, it may also perch for long periods on telegraph poles or in trees whilst scanning the ground for food. It feeds mainly on small mammals such as voles, shrews, and mice, but will also consume reptiles, amphibians, and invertebrates such as large beetles. In urban areas Kestrels tend to prey more heavily on small birds. Usually breeding from March to June, this species nests in a variety of locations according to habitat, using ledges on cliffs or buildings, holes in trees, or the disused nests of other birds such as crows. Rarely, it has also been known to nest on the ground. A typical clutch consists of between three and six eggs, which are incubated for around a month, with the chicks fledged a month after hatching. They will continue to be fed by the parent birds for some weeks whilst they learn to hunt for themselves.

(EURASIAN) HOBBY ▼

SCIENTIFIC NAME:	*Falco subbuteo*
FAMILY:	Falconidae
LENGTH:	30–36 cm (12–14in) Male smaller than female
HABITAT:	Open lowland areas; grassland, scrub, woodland edges, and farmland
DISTRIBUTION:	Much of Europe, Asia, and parts of North Africa, wintering south to southern Africa, India, and China
IDENTIFICATION:	Gray above with a black crown, pale cheeks and throat. Dark facial markings give mustachioed appearance. Underside buff with dark streaking. Thighs and undertail rufous

A small falcon, the Hobby is a fast, elegant, and acrobatic flier with excellent vision, enabling it to hunt for small, fast-flying birds such as swifts and martins. However, it is chiefly insectivorous, catching dragonflies and large moths on the wing. Often hunting at dusk, this species has a tendency to target birds which are gathering in order to roost, but it is also known to prey on bats. It frequently feeds on the wing, transferring food caught in its talons to its bill. The aerial courtship displays of the Hobby are also particularly impressive, involving loops, steep dives, and the passing of food from the talons of males to females whilst in flight. Breeding usually occurs in early summer, and following mating the female will produce a clutch of around three eggs which are frequently laid in the abandoned nest of a crow, magpie, or even squirrel. These are incubated for around a month, with the chicks being fully fledged around a month after hatching. The parent birds will initially continue to feed the young Hobbies, but they soon begin to target slow-flying insects, progressing to more rapid quarry as they grow in size and confidence.

MERLIN

SCIENTIFIC NAME:	*Falco columbarius*
FAMILY:	Falconidae
LENGTH:	25–30cm (10–12in) Male smaller than female
HABITAT:	Open grassland, moorland, marshes, and coastal regions. Sometimes breeds in coniferous woodland
DISTRIBUTION:	Occurs throughout much of the Northern Hemisphere, from North America, across Europe and Asia, wintering in northern parts of South America, Africa, and India
IDENTIFICATION:	Small falcon, buff below with dark streaking and a barred, white-tipped tail. Female is dark brown above, male is blue-gray

Amongst the smallest of all raptors, the Merlin is nevertheless a skilled and aggressive hunter, catching most of its prey on the wing following rapid chases, which usually take place quite close to the ground. It feeds mainly on small birds, but will also take large invertebrates such as dragonflies, and preys on small mammals up to the size of rabbits, spending much of its time perching on rocks, posts, or stumps watching for a potential meal. Breeding pairs have also been known to hunt cooperatively, and become highly territorial when nesting, chasing crows and even large raptors from their nest sites. In wooded areas, this species will often lay its eggs in the disused nest of another bird, but it tends to nest on the ground in more open country, laying around four eggs in a shallow scrape amongst vegetation. Both parents incubate the eggs and care for their chicks, but the male generally spends more time hunting and defending the nest.

LANNER FALCON

SCIENTIFIC NAME:	*Falco biarmicus*
FAMILY:	Falconidae
LENGTH:	35–50cm (14–20in) Male smaller than female
HABITAT:	Desert and semidesert areas, inland or coastal cliffs, savannah and open woodland
DISTRIBUTION:	Throughout much of Africa, parts of southern Europe and the Middle East
IDENTIFICATION:	Medium sized falcon, slate gray above, buff or reddish-brown below, with gray streaking. Some northern birds black-spotted below, whilst some southern individuals lack spots. Head is reddish-brown or buff with a black mustache. Females often darker than males

The Lanner Falcon occurs widely in Africa, but it is somewhat more scarce in the rest of its range, and in Europe is mainly confined to Italy and Greece. It tends to inhabit arid, rocky areas which provide good nesting and vantage points, but is also found in open woodland. Like all birds of prey, it relies mainly on sight when hunting, and will often see a potential meal from a distant perch or from the air, before making a steep dive to seize its prey. Smaller birds, which are mainly caught in flight, constitute the majority of its diet, but it will also take bats and large flying insects, and attack animals on the ground, including reptiles and small mammals. Occasionally it will also knock a bird from the sky, rather than secure it in flight, before diving onto it on the ground. The Lanner Falcon is generally solitary outside of the breeding season, but at times a pair may be observed hunting cooperatively to catch larger prey. It is a monogamous bird, and mating is preceded by aerial displays and loud calls, following which a nest will be established in a tree, on a cliff ledge or building, or in the abandoned nest of another raptor or other large bird. In treeless desert areas, it may also nest on the ground. An average clutch will consist of three or four eggs, which will be incubated by both adult birds for around 30 days. Following hatching, most of the food is initially provided by the male, but the female will join in hunting as the nestlings grow. Fledging usually occurs at between 35 to 45 days. This species does not migrate, but will range nomadically over wide areas in search of food.

PEREGRINE (FALCON)

SCIENTIFIC NAME:	*Falco peregrinus*
FAMILY:	Falconidae
LENGTH:	40–50cm (16–20in) Male smaller than female
HABITAT:	Open country; tundra, savannah, mountains, moors, marshes, estuaries, and rocky shorelines. Also occurs in urban areas
DISTRIBUTION:	Occurs worldwide in suitable habitats, but avoids rainforest and coldest parts of polar regions
IDENTIFICATION:	Slate-gray above, with black crown and "mustache", white cheek patches and breast. Underside white, closely barred with gray. Tail gray with dark barring

A large, powerful falcon, the Peregrine is renowned for the incredible speeds which it attains when diving toward its quarry. It feeds mainly on birds such as pigeons and waterfowl, but it is capable of tackling prey as large as herons. It often launches surprise attacks from above, entering a stoop that can see it achieve speeds of well over 200 km/h (125m.p.h.), fast enough to frequently kill its prey outright as it strikes. However, it may also take perching or grounded birds, as well as small mammals, reptiles, amphibians, and large invertebrates. Although widespread, and quite common throughout much of its range, this species suffered heavily as a result of indirect poisoning by insecticides in some areas including the United Kingdom, but numbers are slowly on the rise and some breeding pairs are now established in urban areas, nesting on buildings. Natural nest sites include cliff faces, or amongst rocks in mountainous regions, where the female usually makes a small scrape. It is also known to use the abandoned nests of other birds. A clutch consists of three or four eggs which are incubated for around 30 days. The female tends to the hatchlings whilst the male provides food, but she will join in the hunting after two to three weeks. The young fledge at around 40 days, becoming independent after a further two months.

MALLEEFOWL ▲

SCIENTIFIC NAME:	*Leipoa ocellata*
FAMILY:	Megapodiidae
LENGTH:	60cm (24in)
HABITAT:	Mallee, or eucalyptus scrub
DISTRIBUTION:	Parts of southern Australia, although absent from parts of the southeast
IDENTIFICATION:	Fairly large ground dwelling bird, buff-gray head and neck, mottled or barred brown, black and white above, gray below with a black line running down breast

Once widespread, the Malleefowl is currently considered to be amongst the most endangered of Australia's birds, and is now restricted to parts of the mallee eucalypt scrub of southern regions. Being a ground dwelling and nesting species, it has suffered from predation by introduced animals such as cats and foxes, but also from habitat destruction, particularly the clearance of scrub areas by fire. Perhaps the most remarkable aspect of the Malleefowl's behavior are its nesting habits; it creates a large nest mound in which to incubate its eggs. Firstly the male excavates a pit, often one meter (three feet) deep, into which a considerable amount of leaves and other vegetation is deposited and allowed to decompose. This is then covered in loose, sandy soil, resulting in a mound of around five meters (16 feet) in diameter, although it can be much larger. The female lays up to 30 eggs within the mound, often several days apart, and then the male oversees incubation by regulating their temperature, uncovering and re-covering the eggs accordingly. The eggs hatch between 50 and 100 days later, after which the hatchlings are left to fend for themselves. Although able to run within hours and to fly after about a day, many suffer from predation.

AUSTRALIAN BRUSH-TURKEY ▼

SCIENTIFIC NAME:	*Alectura lathami*
FAMILY:	Megapodiidae
LENGTH:	70cm (28in)
HABITAT:	Rainforests and scrub, usually at higher altitudes in northern parts of its range, but found in both mountainous and lowland areas in the south
DISTRIBUTION:	Along eastern Australia, from Queensland, south almost as far as Sydney
IDENTIFICATION:	Fairly large, fowl-type bird with long legs. Black overall, with a naked red head, yellow throat wattle, and a laterally flattened tail

Despite its name and appearance, the Australian Brush-Turkey is more closely related to the Malleefowl than the Wild Turkey of North America, and belongs to the family Megapodidae, also known as mound building birds. It shares similar nesting habits, constructing a mound of vegetation in which to incubate its eggs, but is typically found in areas of denser cover, forming its nest mound of leaf litter on the forest floor. The male constructs the nest, raking up litter with his feet to form a structure up to a meter (three feet) high and perhaps four meters (13 feet) across, into which the females' eggs are deposited, with a nest often being shared by several female birds. A nest may contain up to 50 eggs, which are tended by the male, who regularly checks the mound by probing with his bill. Material is then added or removed in order to regulate its temperature. Upon hatching, the young are left to fend for themselves, being able to run and fly within hours. Many, however, fall prey to predators such as lizards and snakes. The Brush-Turkey feeds on a variety of seeds, fruits, and invertebrates.

PLAIN CHACHALACA

SCIENTIFIC NAME:	*Ortalis vetula*
FAMILY:	Cracidae
LENGTH:	60cm (24in)
HABITAT:	Forests, chaparral thickets, and scrub
DISTRIBUTION:	Along the Rio Grande, from southern Texas, through Mexico to Nicaragua
IDENTIFICATION:	Fairly large, with long legs, neck, and tail, and short, rounded wings. Plumage is olive-brown above, more buff below. Tail is dark green with a white tip. Gray patch of exposed skin on throat becomes red in breeding male

Although belonging to the scientific order Galliformes, which is largely composed of ground dwelling game birds, the Plain Chachalaca prefers to spend most of its time in trees, and it is sometimes referred to as the Mexican Tree Pheasant. It usually occurs in small groups of up to five individuals, wandering amongst branches in thickets in search of seeds, berries, buds, and leaves. Its feet are well adapted to grasping, and it may even be observed hanging upside down at times in order to reach its food. It will also feed on the ground occasionally, particularly when insects are numerous or in areas such as nature reserves where it is fed by man. Under such circumstances it may become quite tame. A noisy bird, the Chachalaca is named after its call, and it is most vocal during the breeding season in early spring. Its nest is a small platform of twigs, often positioned in the fork of a tree, into which around three eggs are laid. Incubation lasts for up to 30 days, and although the young are able to climb almost immediately and fly within a week, they are not fledged until around three weeks old.

WILD TURKEY

SCIENTIFIC NAME:	*Meleagris gallopavo*
FAMILY:	Phasianidae
LENGTH:	90–20cm (35–47in) Male larger than female
HABITAT:	Open woodland
DISTRIBUTION:	Scattered populations throughout North America, from southern Canada to Mexico
IDENTIFICATION:	Very large, ground dwelling game-bird. Male has coppery, iridescent plumage, white barring on wingtips, and dark breast tuft. Exposed head is blue and red with red throat wattles. Large spurs present on the legs. Female is much duller and usually lacks tuft

Once severely threatened due to overhunting and habitat destruction, the Wild Turkey is now recovering in much of its range, although populations remain quite patchy in terms of distribution, which has led to the development of various local subspecies. The most common of these is the Eastern Wild Turkey, *M.g. silvestris*, which ranges throughout much of the eastern US. All are generally similar in terms of habit and appearance, however. Wild Turkeys favor a mixed habitat of woodland and open meadows, and they tend to feed in the open by day, roosting in trees at night. They consume a wide range of vegetation and small animals, and their diet includes seeds, nuts, fruits, flowers, invertebrates, small reptiles, and amphibians. For much of the year these birds remain in single-sex groups; however, males will form harems in early spring, attracting females by producing a gobbling sound and displaying their tail feathers. Following mating, the females nest in shallow depressions on the ground, laying around ten eggs, which will be incubated for about a month. After hatching, the young will follow their mother, and small flocks are re-established.

BLACK GROUSE ▼

SCIENTIFIC NAME:	*Tetrao tetrix*
FAMILY:	Phasianidae
LENGTH:	41–55cm (16–22in) Male larger than female
HABITAT:	Moors, marshland, and meadows, often close to forest edges
DISTRIBUTION:	From Britain across Europe and northern Asia to Siberia
IDENTIFICATION:	Large, black game-bird with white wing bars, long, white undertail feathers, red combs above the eyes, and a distinctive lyre-shaped tail. Female is mottled brown with black barring

The Black Grouse was once far more common than it is today, enjoying a wider range of habitats, including lowland heaths. Due to infringement upon such sites, however, it is now found almost exclusively in remote, upland moors, farmland, and forests. Despite a continued population decline, efforts are being made to provide better managed and more integrated environments, as this species requires both woodland and open areas in order to thrive. It is essentially a ground dwelling bird, and benefits from ground cover such as heather in the open areas where it nests and feeds for much of the year. However, it often roosts in trees, and seeks shelter in woodland during the winter months, when snow can preclude feeding in the open. It tends to feed on insects, buds, shoots, and grasses during the spring and summer, consuming more seeds and berries in winter, with food availability being particularly important during the breeding season. This begins in early summer with impressive communal displays known as lekking, during which males make whirring jumps and bubbling sounds in order to attract females. Following mating, the females nest alone, laying around nine eggs in a shallow depression on the ground. These are incubated for around 25 days, and shortly after hatching, the females and their young tend to group together with others to form small flocks.

SAGE GROUSE ▲

SCIENTIFIC NAME:	*Centrocercus urophasianus*
FAMILY:	Phasianidae
LENGTH:	55–75cm (22–30in) Male larger than female
HABITAT:	Sagebrush plains and foothills
DISTRIBUTION:	Parts of western North America
IDENTIFICATION:	Large, ground dwelling game-bird with rounded wings and long, pointed tail feathers. Both sexes mottled gray-brown and white with dark underparts, but male has black throat, white breast-ruff, and yellow eye-combs

As its name would suggest, the Sage Grouse is an inhabitant of sagebrush areas, which it relies on both for cover and for food, and although generally sedentary, it will move around whilst foraging, tending to be found on the plains in winter and in the foothills in summer. Throughout the winter months Sage Grouse are often found in single-sex flocks, with breeding adults coming together to mate in spring at sites known as leks. Here, the male birds establish territories and perform ostentatious displays in order to attract females. Their behavior typically consists of strutting, fanning of the tail and flight feathers, and the rapid inflating and deflating of air sacs on their breasts, coupled with bubbling and plopping sounds. A female will select a male, mate, and then leave to nest alone. Nesting occurs on the ground in a shallow scrape, into which around eight eggs are usually deposited. The eggs are incubated for around 40 days; soon after hatching the young will follow their mother to forage for insects. The adult birds are primarily herbivorous and feed mainly on sagebrush leaves, other vegetation such as grasses, and some invertebrates.

ROCK PTARMIGAN

SCIENTIFIC NAME:	*Lagopus mutus*
FAMILY:	Phasianidae
LENGTH:	36cm (14in)
HABITAT:	Rocky mountainous areas and tundra
DISTRIBUTION:	Occurs in the Northern Hemisphere in Canada, Greenland, Iceland, and northern Eurasia
IDENTIFICATION:	Fairly small alpine grouse with black tail and red combs above eyes. In summer, plumage mottled brown above, wings and underside mainly white, becoming increasingly white overall in the fall, retaining mottled head and neck. Winter plumage white overall with black tail

Living primarily on the Arctic tundra and on alpine slopes where plant cover is minimal, the Rock Ptarmigan undergoes a dramatic change of plumage throughout the year, becoming white in winter in order to camouflage itself against the snow. Single-sex flocks are typical during the winter, but these break up in spring prior to breeding. Unlike some grouse species, males do not display communally in order to attract mates, but establish quite large territories that are vigorously defended, and courtship displays involve tail-fanning and the rather unusual practice of circling a female whilst dragging one wing on the ground. Following mating, the female will nest on the ground, laying up to ten eggs in a shallow depression, often close to the cover of rocks. Incubation lasts around three weeks, after which the chicks may leave the nest almost immediately to begin feeding. However they will usually remain with their mother for about ten weeks. The young mainly consume invertebrates, eating more plant material such as leaves, buds, and berries as they grow.

CAPERCAILLIE

SCIENTIFIC NAME:	*Tetrao urogallus*
FAMILY:	Phasianidae
LENGTH:	80–110cm (31–43in) Male larger than female
HABITAT:	Coniferous forests and scrub, particularly in hilly or mountainous areas
DISTRIBUTION:	From Scotland, across western Europe, particularly in the north, into northern Asia
IDENTIFICATION:	Very large grouse, male dark gray to black overall, with brown wings, greenish breast, white bars on tail and underside, and red combs above eyes. Female mottled brown above, paler below, with reddish breast

The Capercaillie is the largest of the grouse species, and the male is highly distinctive, but this species has become increasingly uncommon throughout its range, mainly due to loss of habitat. The Capercaillie was in fact made extinct in Britain in the 18th century, but was reintroduced, and continues to survive in fairly small numbers in some remote parts of Scotland. Like the Black Grouse, it requires both wooded areas and more open boggy terrain, which is particularly important for breeding and providing a source of insect prey for its young. The breeding habits of the Capercaillie are also similar to those of the Black Grouse in that they are one of only a few birds within their range to mate at a lek, where the males perform courtship displays at a communal site in order to attract females. The Capercaillies' display involves strutting, tail-fanning, and various vocalizations, including bubbling and popping sounds. Fighting between males is also not uncommon at these times, and can result in injury or even death. Following mating, the females will establish nests on the ground, laying around ten eggs in a shallow scrape. Incubation lasts around four weeks, with the young able to fly about two weeks after hatching. However, they will usually remain with their mother throughout the summer before joining larger flocks.

QUAILS

Although sometimes grouped together within the family Phasianidae, which includes pheasants, turkeys, grouse, and their allies, a distinction is often made between quails of the Old World, that is Europe, North Africa, and Asia, and New World quails, or quails that are endemic or native only to the Americas. These include the **Common** or **Northern Bobwhite** (*Colinus virginianus*) and **California Quail** (*Callipepla californica*). Such birds are frequently placed in their own family, Odontophoridae, particularly by American taxonomists. However, in many ways these birds are quite similar to Old World quails, such as the **Common Quail** (*Coturnix coturnix*), in both appearance and habit.

Quails are typically fairly small to medium sized, rotund, short legged, ground dwelling birds, which inhabit quite open habitats such as grasslands and cultivated fields, usually where there is also somewhat denser cover, in the form of thickets, scrub vegetation, or sparse woodland. They forage for seeds, shoots, other plant material, and small invertebrates, nest on the ground in shallow scrapes or natural depressions, and most have mottled plumage that provides them with camouflage. The two groups also differ in various ways,

however. New World quails are generally slightly larger, more boldly patterned, and many are crested. They also tend to be more sociable, and are sedentary whereas, despite their small size, most Old World quails are strongly migratory.

The **Common Quail** is a small species that grows to around 18 centimeters (7 inches) long. It is mottled brown, with a buff underside and facial markings. The male has a well defined black and white throat, whilst the female's is duller and more spotted below. It is reasonably abundant in much of its range, which extends from Europe, throughout most of central Asia, the Middle East, and Africa. However, its numbers have declined significantly in some areas, including Britain. Like most quails, it has a habit of running into cover rather than taking flight when alarmed, but it flies well, and birds from Europe undertake migrations as far south as India and Central Africa. It nests on the ground amongst dense vegetation, producing a large clutch, containing up to 12 eggs. These are incubated solely by the female for around 18 days, and although the young may be fledged within a further 18 days, they will usually remain as a group for over a month.

Common Quail

The **Northern Bobwhite** is perhaps the best-known New World quail, and is amongst North America's most important game-birds. It is widely distributed throughout the eastern US to Central America in grassland, scrub, and open forests, and has also been introduced in the northwest. It grows to around 24 centimeters (9 inches) long, and is mottled brown, with a paler underside. As with most quails, the male is more boldly marked than the female, and has a white throat and eye-stripe. Sociable outside of the breeding season, this species is often encountered in small groups known as coveys that feed and roost together, and which may be heard before being seen, identifiable by the whistled "bob-white" call from which they get their name. When nesting, Northern Bobwhites frequently produce clutches of around 12 eggs, which may be incubated by either parent bird, with females sometimes leaving a nest to produce a further brood. The young are able to leave the nest almost immediately after hatching, and become independent at about two weeks old.

A high reproductive rate is typical of quails, which produce some of the largest clutch sizes of any birds. However, they are also very short-lived, and most die within their first year of life.

Most common along the Pacific coast, from Baja California, north to southern Oregon, the **California Quail** is an attractive species which has been widely bred and introduced outside of its natural range as a decorative bird, but it is also hunted for food and sport. It is usually most sociable outside of the breeding season, but in some cases, this species has been observed nesting communally, which seems to result in more successful brooding and lower adult mortality rates. The California Quail grows to around 26 centimeters (10 inches), is usually plump, gray-brown with white streaks or scaling on the lower breast and abdomen, and a distinctive teardrop-shaped plume or top-knot. Males have a longer crest, a black throat, and white facial markings. With a tendency to live in more arid habitats than many quails, which may obtain much of their water from dew, this species is sometimes found close to streams or other sources of water. It has been successfully introduced in parts of South America and in New Zealand.

Northern Bobwhite

COMMON/GRAY PARTRIDGE

SCIENTIFIC NAME:	*Perdix perdix*
FAMILY:	Phasianidae
LENGTH:	30cm (12in)
HABITAT:	Open meadows, dunes, farmland, and hedgerows
DISTRIBUTION:	Across central Europe and Asia, also introduced in parts of the US
IDENTIFICATION:	Gray-brown ground dwelling bird, with chestnut patch on belly and barring on flanks. Small head, orange face

At one time the Common or Gray partridge was amongst the most numerous game-birds throughout its range but numbers have declined somewhat in recent years, particularly in Britain. This is due to habitat loss, overhunting, and the scarcity of insect food because of the use of pesticides. It is also a secretive bird, preferring to remain hidden amongst crops, in hedgerows, or in similar undergrowth when alarmed, tending to fly from potential danger only when directly approached. It feeds and nests on the ground, foraging for seeds, shoots, and insects, although the latter only constitute a large part of its diet when young or when breeding. The breeding season may last from spring through to early fall, during which time it is usually found in pairs. Following this, it tends to form small flocks known as coveys. Its nest consists of a shallow scrape lined with vegetation, into which as many as 20 eggs may be laid. If a clutch is lost another is sometimes produced. Incubation usually lasts a little over three weeks, and is performed by the female, but both parent birds often remain with their chicks until the following spring.

TEMMINCK'S TRAGOPAN ▲

SCIENTIFIC NAME:	*Tragopan temminckii*
FAMILY:	Phasianidae
LENGTH:	60cm (24in)
HABITAT:	Mixed forest and rainforest, often in mountainous areas
DISTRIBUTION:	Central and southern Asia, including India, Myanmar, Tibet, Vietnam, and China
IDENTIFICATION:	Stout, short-tailed pheasant. Male is strikingly colored, with reddish-brown plumage covered with gray eye-spots, vivid orange crest, neck, and breast, bright blue face and biblike wattle

The male Temminck's Tragopan is perhaps one of the most striking of pheasants, and this species is also the most widespread of the tragopans, although it favors remote habitats, usually at quite high altitudes. As such, it is rarely encountered, but is often fearless in man's presence. It prefers shady rainforest environments, being averse to excessive heat, and is fairly arboreal for a pheasant, nesting in bushes or the lower branches of trees rather than on the ground, sometimes taking over the abandoned nest of another species. Usually solitary, the males attract a mate during the breeding season with an impressive display; puffing out their feathers, inflating the throat wattles, and raising their hornlike crests. This is usually accompanied by a great deal of head-shaking and vocalization. Following mating, the female produces between two and four eggs which she incubates for around four weeks. The chicks hatch with well developed wings and are able to fly within a few days. They feed almost exclusively on invertebrates for around the first two weeks of life, adopting a more vegetarian diet as they grow.

COMMON PHEASANT

SCIENTIFIC NAME:	*Phasianus colchicus*
FAMILY:	Phasianidae
LENGTH:	60–90cm (24–35in) Male larger than female
HABITAT:	Farmland, woodland, and marshes
DISTRIBUTION:	Throughout most of Europe and beyond, across Asia to China. Also introduced in parts of North America and Australasia
IDENTIFICATION:	Brown, with dark mottling and a long barred tail. Male has iridescent dark green head and neck, with red facial wattles and often a white collar

Although common throughout Britain and much of Europe, and to a lesser extent in North America and Australasia, the Common Pheasant is actually native to Asia, and was introduced elsewhere as a game-bird, bred in large numbers for food and sport. Despite being common this species is quite secretive, favoring countryside where there is plenty of cover in the form of crops, hedgerows, and woodland edges. It spends most of its time on the ground, foraging for food, although it is occasionally seen in trees. It has a varied diet, feeding on vegetable matter such as seeds, berries, grain, and shoots, also consuming worms and other invertebrates. Often found in small flocks for much of the year, Common Pheasants may be observed in pairs during the breeding season but males may alternately be accompanied by a harem of several females, which will go on to nest alone following mating. Nesting occurs on the ground, in a scrape amongst vegetation, and up to 15 eggs may be produced. These are incubated for about four weeks and the young are fledged around two weeks after hatching.

BLUE PEAFOWL/PEACOCK

SCIENTIFIC NAME:	*Pavo cristatus*
FAMILY:	Phasianidae
LENGTH:	85–210cm (33–83in) Male larger than female
HABITAT:	Dense tropical forests, often in hilly areas close to water
DISTRIBUTION:	India, Sri Lanka, and Pakistan
IDENTIFICATION:	Large pheasant. Male is mottled blue, with royal-blue neck and breast, white face, fan-shaped crest and long, ornate train feathers covered with eye-spots. Female is much duller, gray-brown overall, with white throat, greenish breast and neck

More commonly known simply as the Peacock, the Blue Peafowl is familiar to many as a semidomesticated or feral species in many parts of the world, even as a pest in some areas. However, it is native to parts of Asia where its natural habitat is deciduous tropical forest. It is capable of flight and often roosts in trees, but it spends most of its time on the forest floor, in clearings or adjacent open ground where it forages for food. Its diet is quite varied, consisting of vegetation such as fruit, seeds, and green plants, but it also consumes small animals such as invertebrates, reptiles, and even rodents. Usually solitary or found in small groups of up to around six individuals, male Peafowl congregate at leks, or communal breeding sites, during the mating season, establishing small territories in order to display to females, which they attract with loud, eerie calls. Displays then involve a great deal of strutting and the fanning of the impressive "tail" feathers, which are actually coverts that protrude from the lower back. A male may mate with several females that then leave to nest alone, digging a shallow scrape on the ground into which about six eggs are laid. These are incubated for about four weeks. Following hatching, the chicks will remain with their mother for around ten weeks.

IMPEYAN MONAL/HIMALAYAN MONAL

SCIENTIFIC NAME:	*Lophophorus impejanus*
FAMILY:	Phasianidae
LENGTH:	55–65cm (22–26in) Male larger than female
HABITAT:	Meadows, rocky areas, and forests in mountainous regions
DISTRIBUTION:	Through the Himalayas, in Afghanistan, Tibet, India and Pakistan
IDENTIFICATION:	Short tailed pheasant. Male iridescent green, purple, red, and blue with white rump patch, copper tail, black underparts, and peacock-like crest. Female mottled brown overall, with black, buff, and white markings, white throat and small crest. Both have blue patch around eyes

Generally a ground dwelling bird, the Impeyan or Himalayan Monal inhabits mountainous regions where there are features such as rocky crags and woodland which provide cover, roosting and nesting sites, and an adequate supply of food. It feeds on vegetation such as roots, tubers, shoots, acorns, and berries, as well as terrestrial and subterranean insects and their larvae, with much of its foraging involving digging into the ground with its shovel-like bill. This species often forages in small, single-sex groups and is quite gregarious at times, although larger flocks are often fairly loose, and are most common in winter, when habitats are more restricted. The breeding season typically lasts from spring to early summer, with males becoming more solitary and aggressive toward each other as they begin to call loudly to attract females. They then perform elaborate displays, fluffing out their feathers, strutting, and circling potential mates with one wing on the ground. The male may also offer stones or food to the female. After mating, a pair will remain together until the female begins to incubate her eggs, with the male sometimes then going on to mate again. The female nests alone, usually in woodland, where a scrape is made in a sheltered spot. Four or five eggs are laid and are incubated for about 28 days. ▼

RED JUNGLEFOWL ▲

SCIENTIFIC NAME:	*Gallus gallus*
FAMILY:	Phasianidae
LENGTH:	40–55cm (16–22in) Male larger than female
HABITAT:	Forest, scrub, and fields
DISTRIBUTION:	Throughout most of southeast Asia, including Pakistan, India, southern China, Sumatra, and Indonesia. The domesticated form is found worldwide
IDENTIFICATION:	Male generally has blackish or dark green underside, long black tail feathers, golden or orange-red head and neck, with variable amounts of red, maroon, orange, and brown on back and wings. Large, red comb on crown, red throat wattle and small white patch on each side of head. Female is duller, buff above and russet below

The Red Junglefowl is the ancestor of the domesticated chicken, and is thought to have originated in southeast Asia, perhaps in northern India, or the region of Thailand and Vietnam, where it was most likely first caught and bred for fighting and for food. The wild form is still believed to be common in such places, but in many cases it has interbred with feral chickens, and so population levels are somewhat difficult to gauge. A shy bird, the Red Junglefowl is encountered in or close to forests where there is good cover, into which it will disappear if approached. It can therefore be hard to spot, but its presence is often made known by the loud crowing of the male. It tends to live in small groups, and the males are polygamous, attracting harems of females during the breeding season. As with other members of the pheasant family, the males take no part in nest-building, incubation, or the care of the young following mating. The females lay their eggs in a depression on the ground, usually amongst dense vegetation, producing a clutch of five or six eggs, which are incubated for up to three weeks. It feeds on a variety of seeds, buds, fruit, and insects, foraging on the ground by scratching with its feet.

CRANES

Although quite similar in appearance to herons, cranes are not closely related to them, belonging instead to the order Gruiformes which includes the rails, crakes, and their allies. There are some 15 extant species of crane which make up the family Gruidae, and these can be further divided into two subfamilies: Balearicinae, also known as the crowned cranes, the two species of which are found only in Africa; and the modern, or typical cranes of the subfamily Gruinae, which are represented on most continents.

Cranes are long legged, long necked birds, with fairly large, pointed bills, and most species spend the majority of their lives in wetlands such as swamps, marshes, and reedbeds, although many also spend at least some of their time in drier habitats, like grasslands and cultivated fields. Cranes are omnivorous, consuming a wide variety of vegetation, such as seeds, roots, buds, and leaves, and also small animals, including terrestrial and aquatic invertebrates, amphibians, reptiles, fish, and small mammals. Cranes are well known for their dances, which involve jumping, flapping, and spreading their wings, and such behavior is employed particularly during the breeding season in order to establish and maintain pair bonds, and also in defending their territories, with most species becoming aggressive at this time. They are also highly vocal, able to emit loud, far-carrying calls. They breed at various times of the year, depending on species and location, usually constructing a mound of vegetation amongst reeds. A clutch of two eggs is normally incubated by both parents and the hatchlings are able to leave the nest within just days of hatching, following their parents in order to begin feeding. Cranes are strong fliers, and some species undertake massive migrations between breeding and wintering grounds.

The **Common** or **Eurasian Crane** (*Grus grus*) is a long distance migrant, moving between northern and western parts of Eurasia, to North Africa, India, and China, and it is sometimes found in Britain in summer during migration. Long extinct as a breeding species in the United Kingdom, very small numbers have begun to re-establish themselves. It grows to around 110 centimeters (43 inches), and is white overall, with a black throat and face, and white stripes extending from behind each eye to the nape. It also has a small red patch at the rear of its crown, and large, drooping tail plumes which can be raised during displays.

Japanese Crane

The **Sandhill Crane** (*Grus canadensis*) is similar in appearance, but slightly smaller at around 105 centimeters (41 inches) in length. It is also more gray than white, and its crown is mainly red. It breeds in marshes and on tundra in Canada, Alaska, and Siberia, making huge migrations south to Mexico in winter. There are also resident populations along the Gulf of Mexico.

The **Japanese Crane** (*Grus japonensis*), also known as the **Red-crowned Crane,** is amongst the largest and rarest crane species in the world. It grows to around 140 centimeters (55 inches) in length, and is exceptionally tall and graceful. It is mainly white with black legs and tail plumes, and in males, the face, throat, and neck are also black, whilst in females these parts are gray. As with many cranes, it has a bright red patch of bare skin on the crown. The Japanese Crane occurs in two main populations, a resident population on the Island of Hokkaido in northern Japan, and a population that breeds in parts of northern China, Russia, and Mongolia, and which overwinters in eastern China and both North and South Korea. Despite not having webbed feet, cranes swim well, and this species is highly aquatic, able to feed in much deeper water than other cranes on account of its extremely long legs. However, it tends to spend the summer in drier meadows, wintering in marshes and rice fields. It breeds in marshes in spring, and like other cranes, lays two eggs which are incubated for around 30 days, although usually only one chick will be successfully reared. Almost hunted to extinction in Japan at the end of the 19th century, this species is now protected, but habitat loss continues to remain a threat, and it is thought that there are only around 2,000 of these birds left in the wild.

Far more numerous, and no less beautiful, the **Gray-crowned Crane** (*Balearica regulorum*) is the most abundant African crane. It occurs from Uganda, where it is the national bird, to parts of South Africa. It is unusual among cranes due to its habit of roosting in trees, a characteristic shared only with the **Black-crowned Crane** (*Balearica pavonia*), with which it is sometimes confused. Both are around 105 centimeters (41 inches) in length, mainly dark, with broad white wing patches, long plumes on the neck and breast, and a large, spiky yellow crest. However, the Gray-crowned Crane has a significantly lighter neck than that of the Black-crowned Crane, and large white cheek patches.

Gray-crowned Crane

LIMPKIN

SCIENTIFIC NAME:	*Aramus guarauna*
FAMILY:	Aramidae
LENGTH:	66cm (26in)
HABITAT:	Swamps and wooded marshland
DISTRIBUTION:	From Florida, and occasionally in surrounding states, through the Caribbean and much of South America
IDENTIFICATION:	Fairly large wader, with long legs, neck and bill. Plumage brown to gray-green overall, with white markings. Wings small and rounded

A large wading bird of swamps and marshes, the Limpkin looks somewhat like a cross between a crane and a rail, and although it shares certain characteristics with these birds, and also with some species of stork, it has no close relatives, being the only member of the family Aramidae. Perhaps its most distinguishing feature is its long, downcurved bill, which is flattened at the sides, has a small gap behind the tip, and often also curves slightly to the right. All these features are adaptations to its highly specialized diet, enabling it to find, manipulate, and extract the large apple snails which constitute the majority of its food. It also feeds on other snails and mollusks, crustaceans, worms, amphibians and reptiles, probing amongst mud and vegetation with its bill as it wades or swims. The Limpkin is mainly nocturnal, becoming active at dusk, and its eerie, wailing calls may often be heard throughout the night. The nesting habits of this species are quite variable; it may nest on the ground, amongst reeds just above water, or in bushes and trees, constructing a platform of sticks, reeds, and grasses, lined with finer material. A clutch consists of four to eight eggs, which are incubated by both parent birds. The young begin to forage independently after about ten weeks, leaving their parents about two weeks later.

CORNCRAKE

SCIENTIFIC NAME:	*Crex crex*
FAMILY:	Rallidae
LENGTH:	26cm (10in)
HABITAT:	Moist meadows and cultivated fields
DISTRIBUTION:	Found in Ireland, Scotland, and across Europe into Central Asia, wintering in the Mediterranean and Africa
IDENTIFICATION:	Slender, with tawny upper plumage, marked with black spots, gray face, throat, and breast, barred flanks and chestnut wings. Bill and legs, short and dusky pink

The Corncrake looks superficially similar to the Common Partridge, but may be distinguished by its slightly smaller size, and its plumage, particularly by its spotted back and chestnut wings. Although a member of the family Rallidae, which is mainly comprised of marshland birds such as rails, coots, and moorhens, the Corncrake is not considered to be a waterbird, being an inhabitant of grasslands and crop-fields. However it is also found in moist habitats and has suffered somewhat due to the drainage of fields for agricultural purposes. In fact, this, and other practices, such as mechanized mowing and general habitat loss, have brought the species close to extinction in much of its natural breeding range, although efforts are now being made to protect it. During the breeding season males will call to attract females to mate, and then continue to call in order to breed again. The females nest alone, building a small cup-shaped nest on the ground into which they lay up to 12 eggs. The chicks leave the nest a few days after hatching, and often only remain with their mother for around two weeks. She may then go on to breed again and produce a second clutch.

WATER RAIL ▲

SCIENTIFIC NAME:	*Rallus aquaticus*
FAMILY:	Rallidae
LENGTH:	26cm (10in)
HABITAT:	Reedbeds or other dense vegetation by ponds and rivers or in marshland
DISTRIBUTION:	Across much of Europe, from Iceland eastwards, through the Middle East and Asia. Also North Africa
IDENTIFICATION:	Small wading bird, brown, spotted with black from crown, along back to tail. Face, breast, and underside gray, with black and white barring on flanks. Bill long and red with black tip

The Water Rail is a slender marshland bird that spends most of its time moving cautiously amongst dense reedbeds in search of food, rarely venturing into the open during the day. However, although it is rarely encountered, its presence is often betrayed by its loud, high pitched calls, which have been likened to the squeals of pigs. It is mainly active at night, foraging amongst vegetation for food, and it is known to eat some plant material, but preys chiefly on invertebrates such as worms, snails, and insect larvae. However, it is capable of killing and eating larger animals, including amphibians, nestlings and rodents such as shrews and mice. Mainly sedentary, some populations undertake migrations to the more southerly parts of their range following the breeding season. The Water Rail typically nests from April to June, constructing a woven cup-shaped nest from grasses, which it builds amongst dense reedbeds. It lays between five and 15 eggs that hatch after around three weeks. Both parent birds incubate their clutch and take care of their chicks.

WEKA/WOODHEN

SCIENTIFIC NAME:	*Gallirallus australis*
FAMILY:	Rallidae
LENGTH:	50cm (20in)
HABITAT:	Scrub, woodland edges, and grassland
DISTRIBUTION:	New Zealand
IDENTIFICATION:	Large ground dwelling rail. Brown overall with dark streaks, grayish face and underparts, very small wings, and short, sturdy legs

The Weka or Woodhen is found only in New Zealand, where it was once common on both the North and South Islands. Today, however, the North Island subspecies, *G.a. greyi*, is becoming increasingly rare and is quite timid. However, those on the South Island remain somewhat more established and are quite bold at times, sometimes approaching people for food. A flightless species, the Weka spends its time foraging on the ground and is capable of running quite quickly when necessary and it is also a good swimmer. It is omnivorous, feeding on plant material such as seeds and fruit, birds' eggs, invertebrates, carrion, and small vertebrates including birds, reptiles, and rodents. Breeding may occur throughout the year, with as many as four clutches being produced, but the peak season is typically between August and January. The nest takes the form of a shallow cup, usually placed amongst vegetation, and both parent birds incubate the clutch of up to six eggs.

TAKAHE

SCIENTIFIC NAME:	*Porphyrio mantelli*
FAMILY:	Rallidae
LENGTH:	60cm (24in)
HABITAT:	Grassland and forest in mountainous areas
DISTRIBUTION:	The South Island of New Zealand
IDENTIFICATION:	Very large ground dwelling rail. Heavily built, with short, sturdy legs, a large powerful bill, and tiny wings. Back is green, underside blue

A flightless bird, the Takahe was thought to have become extinct by 1900 due to introduced predators and grazing competitors until a small population was discovered in a remote valley in Fiordland on New Zealand's South Island in 1948. Measures were immediately put in place to protect them. The decline has been halted with the aid of captive breeding programs, and their introduction to small, predator-free islands, but this species currently remains endangered. It spends much of the year living in alpine grassland, grazing on the seeds and bases of tussock grass, typically descending into forested valleys in winter where it feeds on ferns. Takahe usually pair for life and live in small family groups, with breeding taking place around October or November. Up to three eggs are laid, either in a grass-lined hollow or cup-shaped nest amongst the tussock grass, and are incubated by both parent birds for about 30 days. Following hatching, the young are fed by their parents for around three months before they begin to graze for themselves.

(Common) Moorhen

Scientific name:	*Gallinula chloropus*
Family:	Rallidae
Length:	33cm (13in)
Habitat:	Marshland, streams, ponds, and lakes, often in urban areas
Distribution:	Found in Britain, throughout Europe, much of Africa, southeast Asia and large parts of the Americas
Identification:	Gray-black overall, with white streak on flanks and around tail. Red bill and forehead "shield." Long legs, large feet and bill-tip yellow or greenish

A very common species throughout most of its range, the Moorhen occurs in almost any freshwater habitat, from small ponds and streams to rivers and reservoirs, and it will also live in more brackish habitats in some areas. However, it prefers stretches of water with quite dense vegetation that provides cover and food. It forages both on land and in the water, and may be observed grazing, swimming, and diving, or walking across floating plant matter, spreading its weight on its very long toes. Omnivorous and opportunistic in its feeding habits, the Moorhen's diet consists mainly of aquatic plants, seeds, grasses, and invertebrates such as snails and worms, but it will also eat small fish, amphibians, and carrion. Essentially ground dwelling, this species sometimes roosts in the lower branches of trees or bushes, but nesting tends to take place either on the ground amongst bankside vegetation or just above the water's surface on a platform of reeds. The breeding habits of the Moorhen are quite unusual in that females typically compete for males, although both sexes indulge in display behaviors. Following mating, 6 to 12 eggs are produced, which are incubated by both parent birds for around three weeks.

PURPLE GALLINULE

SCIENTIFIC NAME:	*Porphyrula martinica*
FAMILY:	Rallidae
LENGTH:	33cm (13in)
HABITAT:	Vegetated lakes, lagoons, swamps, and marshes
DISTRIBUTION:	Southeastern US, through Central America, south to Argentina. Also around the Mediterranean, and rarely in Britain and parts of Africa
IDENTIFICATION:	Purple-blue plumage with green back and wings. Bill is red with yellow tip, forehead "shield" blue, and legs long and yellow

Although similar in appearance and habit to the Moorhen, and often sharing the same habitats, the Purple Gallinule is a far more striking bird with its colorful plumage and longer legs. It inhabits swamps and marshes with dense vegetation, foraging for food by wading amongst water plants in the shallows, striding across lily pads, or climbing amongst the branches of overhanging bushes. It remains in cover for much of the time, but will also feed in more open habitats such as flooded meadows and rice fields. Its diet consists of aquatic vegetation, seeds, berries, invertebrates, and amphibians. The Purple Gallinule is rather a weak flier, but it will do so if suddenly disturbed, and northern populations also tend to undertake southerly migrations following the breeding season. It nests between spring and fall, constructing a cup-shaped nest amongst reeds, or floating vegetation. A typical clutch consists of around eight eggs, which are incubated for around three weeks. As with Moorhens, this species tends to live in small family groups, and non-breeding birds may help with nest-building and care of the chicks.

(Eurasian) Coot

Scientific name:	*Fulica atra*
Family:	Rallidae
Length:	36cm (14in)
Habitat:	Reedy ponds, lakes, and rivers, often in urban areas. Also estuaries in winter
Distribution:	Throughout Britain and most of Europe, although absent from northernmost areas, south to North Africa, and throughout much of Asia to Australasia. Rarely also strays to parts of North America
Identification:	Plump, with a rounded, black head, dark gray body, with a white bill and forehead "shield"

The Coot is amongst the largest of the rails, and is easily recognized by its overall dark plumage, white bill and "shield." It also has large, lobed toes. It occurs in a variety of freshwater habitats, from large lakes and rivers to small ponds in urban parks, but tends to be found on larger bodies of water in winter, when smaller pools may freeze over. At this time it can also be found in estuaries or sheltered coastal bays, often in quite large numbers. During the breeding season, however, paired birds become territorial and may be highly aggressive to others of their species, including chicks. Nesting begins in spring, at which time a large nest mound of reeds is constructed in vegetation, on or close to the water's edge. Up to 15 eggs are laid, which are incubated by both parents for around three weeks, with a second clutch usually being produced later in the year. Coots are omnivorous, feeding on aquatic vegetation, grazing out of water, or diving for invertebrates and occasionally small fish. The American Coot, *F. Americana,* is virtually identical, but usually slightly smaller and lighter in color.

AFRICAN FINFOOT

SCIENTIFIC NAME:	*Podica senegalensis*
FAMILY:	Heliornithidae
LENGTH:	55cm (22in)
HABITAT:	Woodland streams
DISTRIBUTION:	Sub-Saharan Africa
IDENTIFICATION:	Fairly large, semiaquatic bird. Brown crown, neck, back, and wings, mottled with white, mottled buff below. White eye stripe extends down long neck. Pointed orange bill and lobed orange toes

Generally thought to be quite rare, the African Finfoot may in fact be more common than many records suggest, due to its highly secretive nature. It occurs mainly along secluded, wooded stretches of water, particularly where there is plenty of plant cover, preferring to live amongst vegetation near clear, slow-moving rivers or still water. It is somewhat like a large rail or grebe, with a streamlined body and coot-like, lobed feet, and it forages for food both in the water and out of it; swimming and diving well, and also climbing amongst the branches of overhanging trees. It feeds mainly on insects and other invertebrates, including dragonflies, beetles, snails, and shrimps, but also takes larger prey such as frogs, snakes, and fish. The African Finfoot typically breeds from September to April, nesting amongst vegetation on the ground, in reeds at the water's edge, or in the lower branches of shrubs and trees. Clutch size varies between one and three eggs, with two being most common. These are thought to be incubated by both the male and female bird for at least three weeks. The hatchlings are quite well developed, and able to swim with their parents after a matter of days.

SUNBITTERN

SCIENTIFIC NAME:	*Eurypyga helias*
FAMILY:	Eurypygidae
LENGTH:	46cm (18in)
HABITAT:	Forest streams and wooded swamps
DISTRIBUTION:	Throughout the Amazon Basin, north into Central America
IDENTIFICATION:	Fairly large, semiaquatic bird. Brown back and wings with pale barring, underside paler. Neck, breast, and forepart of wings tawny, with large, dark eye-spots visible in flight. Long, narrow, pointed bill

Despite its name, the Sunbittern is not closely related to the bitterns, but is the sole member of the family Eurypygidae, allied with the rails, cranes, and species such as the Limpkin and African Finfoot, as part of the order Gruiformes. It is however somewhat similar in appearance to a bittern or small heron, although it has a more horizontal posture and more vivid plumage, with large, sunlike eye-spots on each wing which are used in defensive displays. Usually occurring singly or in pairs, this species is quite common throughout much of its range, inhabiting swamps and other watercourses in dense forest or jungle areas, where it forages in shallow water or along river banks, feeding on insects, crustaceans, and small fish, spearing its prey with its slender, pointed bill. It nests either in trees or on the ground, building a fairly large nest of grass, mud and moss, into which two eggs are typically laid. Both parent birds share in nest-building, incubation, and the care of their young, with one bird usually gathering food whilst the other cares for the nestlings.

RED-LEGGED SERIEMA

SCIENTIFIC NAME:	*Cariama cristata*
FAMILY:	Cariamidae
LENGTH:	75cm (30in)
HABITAT:	Lightly wooded areas, grasslands, and scrub
DISTRIBUTION:	Eastern parts of South America, from Brazil to Argentina
IDENTIFICATION:	Tall, with a long neck, long red legs and a long neck. Gray-brown overall, paler beneath. Large tuft of feathers at base of bill

Mainly found in the grassy habitats of central Brazil, the Red-legged Seriema also occurs in more wooded areas, particularly in the south of its range, and is a ground dwelling species, rarely flying, but running well on its long legs as it forages in the open. It is omnivorous, although the majority of its diet consists of small animals such as insects, rodents, reptiles, amphibians, and birds, supplemented by leaves, seeds, fruit, and grain. Smaller prey tends to be consumed whole, head first, whilst larger animals are torn apart with its sharp claws. Breeding mainly takes place during the rainy months from May to September and is initiated by the male's courtship display which involves strutting, fanning the flight feathers, and raising the crest. Both sexes are involved in nest-building, constructing a cup of twigs and branches lined with mud and leaves, which is positioned in a tree or large bush. A typical clutch consists of two eggs, with incubation being carried out by both sexes for up to 30 days. The chicks are cared for by both parents and are able to leave the nest after about two weeks to begin following their parents around on the ground, becoming fledged around one month after hatching. Amongst the Red-legged Seriema's most distinctive features is its yelping call.

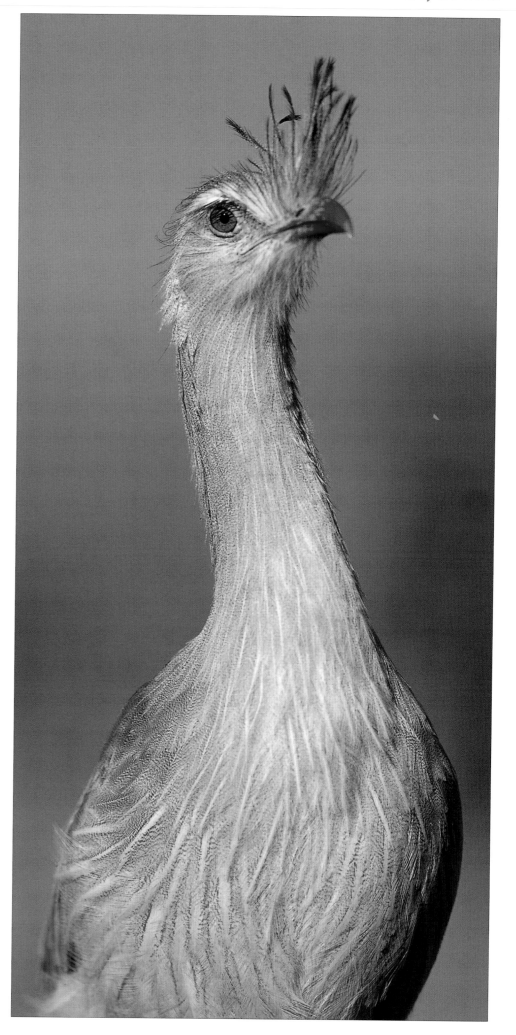

PHEASANT-TAILED JACANA ▲

SCIENTIFIC NAME:	*Hydrophasianus chirurgus*
FAMILY:	Jacanidae
LENGTH:	30cm (12in)
HABITAT:	Ponds, lakes, and marshes
DISTRIBUTION:	From India, eastward through much of southeast Asia
IDENTIFICATION:	Plumage is mainly blackish-brown, but wings, face, and throat are white, and nape of the neck is yellow. Legs and feet are gray, with extremely long toes. During the breeding season the male has a long pheasant-like tail

As its name might suggest, for much of the year the Pheasant-tailed Jacana sports long, pheasant-like tail feathers, but these are absent outside of the breeding season. This usually lasts from April until October throughout much of its range, with the peak nesting period probably occurring between May and July. Pheasant-tailed Jacanas practise polyandry, the females mating with up to around five males, producing a clutch of two to six eggs in the nest of each. The males are then responsible for incubation and caring for the nestlings. Most male birds will hatch one brood per season; however, it is not unknown for them to successfully rear two. Quite a shy bird, the Pheasant-tailed Jacana prefers undisturbed ponds, lakes, and marshlands where there is abundant vegetation, such as lily, lotus, and water hyacinth. Like other jacanas, this species has very long legs, toes, and claws, which distribute its body weight, allowing it to walk across floating plant material. In China, where this bird is often found in water chestnut fields, its elegant appearance and habits have given rise to a nickname that translates as "fairies walking over ripples." Its diet is varied, ranging from planktonic life-forms to larger invertebrates, amphibians, and small fish.

GREAT BUSTARD ▼

SCIENTIFIC NAME:	*Otis tarda*
FAMILY:	Otididae
LENGTH:	80–100cm (31–39in) Male larger than female
HABITAT:	Open grassland
DISTRIBUTION:	Parts of southern and eastern Europe, through Russia to central and eastern Asia
IDENTIFICATION:	Large grassland bird, with long neck and legs. Rufous above with dark barring. Wings and underside mainly white. Head and neck gray. Male has rufous band at base of neck and mustache-like bristles when breeding

A large bird that may stand over a meter tall, the Great Bustard is in fact the heaviest bird that is capable of flight, with males frequently weighing up to 20kg (44lbs); however, it is a ground dwelling species that rarely flies. It lives in open grassland, often close to cultivated fields, but is probably most common in the more isolated, uninhabited parts of the Eurasian steppes, its numbers having declined throughout much of its range due to habitat destruction and hunting. Once common in parts of Britain, the Great Bustard last nested in England in 1832; it has very recently been reintroduced, with around 30 chicks having been brought from Russia to be released in the southwest of England. As with some species of grouse and pheasant, breeding adults come together to breed communally at leks, where males display together as they compete for the attention of female birds. The displays are quite flamboyant, involving twisting the wings and puffing out the throat sac to present as much of its white plumage as possible. Following mating, the female nests alone on the ground, often amongst crops, laying between two and four eggs. The Great Bustard is omnivorous, feeding on a variety of vegetation, invertebrates and small vertebrates, such as voles and mice.

NORTHERN JACANA

SCIENTIFIC NAME:	*Jacana spinosa*
FAMILY:	Jacanidae
LENGTH:	23cm (9in)
HABITAT:	Ponds and marshes, usually with floating vegetation
DISTRIBUTION:	Mexico and Central America, occasionally venturing to Texas and Arizona
IDENTIFICATION:	Small, dark marsh bird with black head and neck. Upper wings and back dark rufous. Underside of wings pale green or yellow. Bill and forehead "shield" yellow. Long, gray legs and toes

Although far more restricted in terms of its range, the Northern Jacana is similar to the Moorhen in appearance and habit, although it is a more curious looking species, possessing the longest toes of any bird relative to its body size. Sometimes known as the lily-trotter, it uses its huge feet to spread its weight as it traverses floating vegetation in search of food, using its relatively long bill to pick up insects, snails, and other small invertebrates as it goes. It spends much of its time out of water in this way, preferring to do so rather than to swim, although it may also be observed wading in the shallows. It flies only occasionally, trailing its legs behind it as it does so and revealing vivid yellow patches below each wing. These are also exposed during courtship displays, which are performed by both males and females. Rather unusually, the female of this species maintains quite a large territory during the breeding season, encompassing the smaller territories and nests of several males with whom she will mate. The males will then incubate the eggs and care for the young. Rather than abandon previous mates, the female will continue to maintain bonds with each of them, a practice known as simultaneous polyandry.

(Eurasian) Oystercatcher

Scientific name:	*Haematopus ostralegus*
Family:	Haematopodidae
Length:	43cm (17in)
Habitat:	Shores, estuaries, and mudflats. Also inland in meadows and moorland in some areas
Distribution:	Found around Britain and much of Europe, into central Asia, wintering south as far as Africa and India
Identification:	Large wader, head and upperparts black, white below. Fairly large orange bill, reddish eye, and short reddish legs

A familiar saltwater wader, the Oystercatcher has increasingly colonized inland waters in parts of its range, to inhabit marshes and the banks of lakes, reservoirs, and gravel pits. At times it is also found in drier habitats such as meadows and moorland, but in winter particularly it remains more strictly coastal. It is a distinctive species, on account of its large size and bold coloration, but its presence is often first announced by its loud call. When feeding, the Oystercatcher uses its bill to probe amongst mud, or prise its prey off rocks and groynes, tending to feed mainly on earthworms further inland, consuming various mollusks such as limpets, cockles and mussels, as well as lugworms and crabs on coastal shores. Despite its name and powerful bill, however, it is not thought that oysters form a large part of its diet. In fact there is evidence to suggest that it would have difficulty in breaking open a well-developed specimen. Frequently solitary for much of the year, the Oystercatcher may be found in very large numbers in winter, when resident populations are joined by birds migrating from the northernmost parts of its range, or in pairs during the spring and summer when breeding occurs. It nests on the ground, typically producing a clutch of three eggs, which are incubated by both parent birds.

RINGED PLOVER ▼

SCIENTIFIC NAME:	*Charadrius hiaticula*
FAMILY:	Charadriidae
LENGTH:	18cm (7in)
HABITAT:	Beaches, sand dunes, estuaries, and tundra. May also be found on shores of inland waters, particularly during migration
DISTRIBUTION:	Arctic tundra from northeast Canada and Greenland to Siberia, south through Eurasia. Winters throughout much of Africa
IDENTIFICATION:	Small shorebird, gray-brown above, white below, with short orange legs. Distinctive white collar and forehead, black eye, head, and breast bands. Short bill, orange-yellow with black tip

A small, short legged, rather plump wader, some Ringed Plovers nevertheless undertake extensive migrations from their northerly breeding grounds in order to winter in warmer climes. There are resident populations in Britain which are joined in winter by birds from northern Europe, but more notably, populations from Canada and Greenland often pass through during late summer on their way to Africa. Mainly a coastal bird of sand and shingle beaches, during migration the Ringed Plover may be quite abundant at inland waters such as disused gravel pits. It is quite a gregarious species, often found in flocks of 50 or more, and it also associates with other plovers or similar species such as the Dunlin. It may be active by day or night, particularly in nontidal habitats, foraging in the fashion typical of coastal waders: darting around at the water's edge before stopping abruptly to search for food. It feeds on insects, spiders, and marine invertebrates, and may be observed vibrating its feet in soft mud to stir up its prey. It breeds on the tundra in the far north of its range, or on beaches farther south, nesting in a bare scrape on the ground. Clutches usually number two to four eggs, which are incubated equally by both parent birds for about 25 days.

(NORTHERN) LAPWING ▲

SCIENTIFIC NAME:	*Vanellus vanellus*
FAMILY:	Charadriidae
LENGTH:	30cm (12in)
HABITAT:	Meadows, farmland, and marshes. Also estuaries, particularly in winter
DISTRIBUTION:	Throughout Eurasia, from Britain to the Far East, wintering in the south of this range and in North Africa
IDENTIFICATION:	Greenish-black above, white below, with rufous rump patch. Black breast, black and white face, black crown and long black crest

Sometimes known as the Peewit on account of its call, the Lapwing is essentially a large plover, but can be easily distinguished from similar species by its crest. It is also more often encountered inland, dwelling for much of the year in habitats such as short-grass meadows, marshes, and plowed fields, where it forages for insects, worms, and other invertebrates, often at night under the cover of darkness. It may also be found on the coast and at estuaries, particularly in winter, when it may congregate in large numbers. These winter flocks typically start to disperse in February, as the birds begin to return to their breeding grounds. The Lapwing tends to nest in loose groups, usually on open ground where potential predators may be easily spotted, laying three or four eggs in a scrape lined with nearby vegetation. Both parents incubate the clutch and care for their chicks, usually leading them to moist, adjacent feeding grounds shortly after hatching, where they will remain as a family group until the young are able to fly, around six weeks later. During this time, whilst the young remain vulnerable, adult Lapwings may exhibit a rather unusual display, sometimes feigning injury in order to lure potential predators away from their brood.

KILLDEER

SCIENTIFIC NAME:	*Charadrius vociferus*
FAMILY:	Charadriidae
LENGTH:	26cm (10in)
HABITAT:	Inland on pastures, farmland, and marshes, also on coasts at estuaries and mudflats
DISTRIBUTION:	Throughout North and Central America, and northern parts of South America. Vagrant to parts of Europe
IDENTIFICATION:	Large plover, gray-brown above with rufous rump and distinctive double black breast band. Underparts and neck white

Similar in appearance to the Ringed Plover, the Killdeer may however be distinguished by its larger size, double breast band, and to an extent its habitat, for although it is classed as a shorebird, it is sometimes regarded as the American counterpart to the Lapwing, being common inland, particularly in cultivated fields. This species also shares the defensive posturing of the Lapwing when nesting or with its young, feigning injury by hobbling away and dragging one or both wings on the ground at the approach of a predator. Once sufficiently far from its clutch or brood, the Killdeer will suddenly take flight. It usually nests in a shallow depression on the ground, which may be bare, or sometimes lined with small pebbles, but it has also been known to nest on flat rooftops in more urban areas. An average clutch contains four eggs, which are incubated by both the male and female for up to four weeks. The chicks are precocial, that is, well developed upon hatching, emerging with downy feathers and open eyes, and they are able to run and feed themselves within a matter of hours. However, they remain reliant upon their parents at least until they can fly. Killdeers are considered to be omnivorous as they are known to consume vegetation such as berries, but the majority of their diet consists of invertebrates.

DUNLIN

SCIENTIFIC NAME:	*Calidris alpina*
FAMILY:	Scolopacidae
LENGTH:	18cm (7in)
HABITAT:	Tundra and moorland pools, reservoirs, marshland, shores, and estuaries
DISTRIBUTION:	Widely distributed throughout the Northern Hemisphere, breeding across the Arctic and wintering south in Europe, North America, and the Far East
IDENTIFICATION:	Gray-brown above, white below, fairly long, downcurved bill. Breeding adult has rufous crown and back, and black belly

A rather small and indistinctive wader, the Dunlin is amongst the most common and numerous of shorebirds throughout much of its range, sometimes congregating in flocks of thousands on coastal shores and estuaries, particularly in winter. It is also found somewhat further inland at times, and during the breeding season it tends to nest in marshes and moist grasslands, usually on the Arctic tundra in the far north of its range. There are resident breeding populations in northern Europe and in Britain which occur as far south as the hills of Dartmoor and South Wales. The name Dunlin is derived from the old English word "dun," meaning dull, but during the summer breeding season, the Dunlin takes on a reddish tint to its upperparts and develops a black patch on its belly, making it more easily distinguishable from other species of small sandpiper. Whilst its breeding plumage is certainly not as dull as its winter plumage, it does not serve to make the Dunlin more conspicuous but rather provides good camouflage against the rocks, mosses, and lichens of its preferred nesting habitats. It nests in the open, on the ground, laying a clutch of around four eggs. Dunlins feed on insects, mollusks, crustaceans, and worms, foraging by probing soft mud with their slightly downcurved bills.

CURLEW

SCIENTIFIC NAME:	*Numenius arquata*
FAMILY:	Scolopacidae
LENGTH:	57cm (22in)
HABITAT:	Marshland, moorland, sand dunes, mudflats, and estuaries
DISTRIBUTION:	Resident in Britain and northern Europe. Also throughout most of Eurasia, migrating to North Africa and southern Asia
IDENTIFICATION:	Large wader, mottled gray-brown with darker areas on wings. Breast more buff, rump white. Very long, downcurved bill

The largest of the European waders, the Curlew is also distinctive due to its exceptionally long, narrow, downcurved bill, and the loud, far-carrying cry from which it gets its name. In spring and summer when breeding occurs, it may be found in grassy upland habitats, bogs, moorland, and some lower-lying marshes or agricultural areas, preferring coastal habitats such as estuarine mudflats and salt-marshes in winter, when it may be found in quite large numbers. It nests on the ground in a shallow depression lined with nearby plant material, usually situated amongst low-lying vegetation such as heather. The peak laying season typically lasts from April to June, but may be longer in warmer parts of its range such as southern Europe and Asia. An average clutch consists of three to six eggs, which are incubated for about a month before hatching. In Britain, there has been something of a decline in the number of breeding birds, which is thought to relate primarily to loss of habitat; however, there are indications that the breeding success rate has improved slightly, and the number of birds wintering on British shores has also increased. Curlews feed on invertebrates such as insects, mollusks, crustaceans, and worms, using their long bills to probe for their prey.

GREATER YELLOWLEGS ▼

SCIENTIFIC NAME:	*Tringa melanoleuca*
FAMILY:	Scolopacidae
LENGTH:	36cm (14in)
HABITAT:	Marshes, swamps, forest edges, lakeshores, and mudflats
DISTRIBUTION:	Throughout North America, wintering in Central and South America. Occasional visitor to Britain and northern Europe
IDENTIFICATION:	Mottled gray-brown above, paler below, with long orange or yellow legs, and long bill. More heavily patterned in breeding plumage, with darker patches on back and spotted underside

Somewhat less sociable than other waders, the Greater Yellowlegs tends to be quite solitary. However, it does form flocks when migrating between its breeding and wintering grounds. During the breeding season, it is typically found in the north of its range, occupying a variety of mainly inland habitats such as marshes, tundra, scrub, and coniferous forests, usually close to small lakes and ponds. In the winter months it may occur in a variety of wetlands, both inland and along the coast, being more commonly found by the sea at this time of year than at any other. Here, it may be observed on mudflats, lagoons, and sometimes offshore on rocky islands, particularly when roosting. Inland it may inhabit lakeshores, flooded meadows, and in the southern US and beyond it may also be found in rice fields. It feeds mainly on invertebrates, small fish, and amphibians, but also consumes some vegetation such as berries. It may be active by day or night, feeding at low tide in coastal areas, foraging by sight or probing with its bill. It nests on the ground, often at the base of a tree or shrub, laying three to four eggs in a shallow scrape, often lined with moss or other plant material.

SNIPE ▲

SCIENTIFIC NAME:	*Gallinago gallinago*
FAMILY:	Scolopacidae
LENGTH:	26cm (10in)
HABITAT:	Marshland, damp heaths, and grassland
DISTRIBUTION:	Throughout Eurasia and North America, wintering in parts of Central Africa, southeast Asia, and South America
IDENTIFICATION:	Mottled brown above, white below, with white stripes along wings and brown and buff striped head. Bill is proportionately longer than that of other waders

A compact, short legged wader, the Snipe may sometimes be found in wetlands in coastal areas, particularly close to estuaries, but is not commonly found on the shore, preferring moist pastures and marshes with plenty of vegetation for cover. They are shy birds, often feeding at night, foraging in the shallows of ponds and streams for small invertebrates such as insects, worms, mollusks, and crustaceans. It may also eat small fish from time to time, and some vegetation such as grass seeds and berries. The Snipe takes food from the ground or water's surface, but most commonly probes with its bill, which is in fact the longest in relation to body size of any wader, and has a highly flexible tip that enables it to catch and consume its prey whilst the bill is submerged in soft mud. This species typically breeds in the north of its range in spring and summer, migrating south in winter. At the start of the breeding season, males attempt to attract a mate by producing drumming sounds, beating their wings slowly whilst descending at speed. Early in the season a female may mate with several males before settling to nest. The Snipe nests on the ground, producing a clutch of about four eggs. The chicks are cared for by both parent birds until they fledge.

Ruff

SCIENTIFIC NAME:	*Philomachus pugnax*
FAMILY:	Scolopacidae
LENGTH:	25–30 cm (10–12in) Male larger than female
HABITAT:	Tundra, marshland, moist grassland
DISTRIBUTION:	Breeds in northern Europe, Siberia, and occasionally Alaska. Winters south into Africa, Asia, and Australia
IDENTIFICATION:	Female mottled brown with white underside. Male highly variable plumage of black, white, brown, and orange with black belly. Large tufts on head and ruff around neck when breeding. Legs orange, bill dark, downcurved, often with an orange base, or entirely orange in males

The Ruff is a medium sized wader that takes its name from the dramatic breeding plumage of the male that includes a large feathery ruff and ear tufts which are used in combination with the ruffling of their wing feathers and various posturing, including crouching and jumping, in order to attract a mate. These displays take place at communal sites, or leks, with marshes and wet meadows being the favored breeding habitats. Following mating, the female nests alone on the ground in a depression, usually amongst rushes or other vegetation that will provide sufficient cover. A typical clutch consists of three or four eggs, with incubation lasting about four weeks. At the end of the breeding season the Ruff usually migrates from its northerly breeding sites to winter in warmer climes in the Southern Hemisphere, although there are resident populations in Britain and other parts of Europe. During the winter, the Ruff is often found closer to large bodies of water such as lakes than at other times of the year, and may also occur at brackish coastal lagoons. At this time, it is also highly gregarious, with over one million individual birds estimated to frequent Lake Chad in Africa. The Ruff forages in grassland and soft mud, probing, or picking up food by sight, with its diet consisting mainly of insects, worms, small fish, and amphibians.

BLACK-WINGED STILT

SCIENTIFIC NAME:	*Himantopus himantopus*
FAMILY:	Recurvirostridae
LENGTH:	38cm (15in)
HABITAT:	Shorelines, lagoons, freshwater and salt-marshes, and flooded meadows
DISTRIBUTION:	Occurs mainly around the Mediterranean, sometimes north to Britain and parts of northern Europe. Overwinters in Africa
IDENTIFICATION:	Slender wader, with incredibly long, red legs and dark, narrow bill. Plumage black above, including crown and nape, and white below

A widespread and fairly common wader, the Black-winged Stilt is closely related and similar in appearance to the Avocet. However, it can be distinguished by its smaller build, straight rather than upcurved bill, and its incredibly long legs. In fact, this species has the longest legs in relation to its body of any bird, accounting for up to 60 percent of its height. This enables it to run quickly and to feed farther from the shore than many waders. It usually takes food from the surface of the water, but also submerges its head in order to feed in the soft mud at the bottom, sometimes sweeping with its bill in much the same way as an Avocet. Its diet consists mainly of insects and other invertebrates, small amphibians, fish, and their eggs. The Black-winged Stilt may be found singly or in small groups, but often roosts communally in the open as a defense against predation. During the breeding season, small colonies are usually established on mudflats close to water, with nests varying from a bare scrape, to mounds of mud and vegetation. A typical clutch consists of between two and five eggs, which are incubated by both parent birds for about 25 days. Following hatching, the chicks usually leave the nest within 24 hours and are able to feed themselves and to swim well.

(Pied) Avocet

Scientific name:	*Recurvirostra avosetta*
Family:	Recurvirostridae
Length:	43cm (17in)
Habitat:	Estuaries, mudflats, sandbanks, and lagoons
Distribution:	From Britain and most of Europe, in a band across Asia to the Far East. Overwinters south to much of Africa, Pakistan, and China
Identification:	Elegant, long-legged wader with distinctive, long, upcurved bill. Mainly white, with black crown, nape, and wing bars. Feet are webbed

The Avocet is a highly elegant, but unusual looking wader, instantly recognizable by its plumage, long, upturned bill, and webbed feet. It wades in the shallows or walks across tidal mudflats, foraging either by picking small aquatic invertebrates from the surface, or by sweeping its bill through the water, often with its head submerged. At other times, when feeding in deeper water, it may up-end from a swimming position, much like a duck. Mollusks and crustaceans are favored prey, although at inland waters, insects make up much of its diet. Gregarious for much of the year, flocks usually consist of up to 30 birds, but where food is plentiful, several hundred may gather. Prior to the breeding season, these flocks disperse and pairing begins in late winter. Loose breeding colonies are established in spring. Breeding pairs cooperate in nest-building and incubation, placing vegetation in a shallow scrape on the ground, where a clutch of three or four eggs will be laid. The young hatch after just over three weeks and although they are able to run and feed themselves within hours, the parents may continue to care for them after they have fledged at about 40 days, being highly aggressive and protective of their offspring throughout the breeding season. Avocet populations declined in much of Europe during the 19th century, ceasing to breed in Britain in 1842. However, during the Second World War, the flooding of land by the military created perfect habitats for Avocets, and breeding populations were re-established.

(Eurasian) Woodcock

Scientific name:	*Scolopax rusticola*
Family:	Scolopacidae
Length:	35cm (14in)
Habitat:	Moist woodland and marshes
Distribution:	From Britain, east across most of Eurasia, wintering south as far as North Africa and southeast Asia
Identification:	Stocky, short legged wader with very long, straight bill. Plumage is buff, mottled and barred with rufous, brown and black

As its name suggests, the Woodcock is primarily a woodland bird, but it has a particular preference for moist forests, or marshy habitats with some trees. It is essentially ground dwelling, spending much of its time at rest amongst dense undergrowth and leaf-litter upon the woodland floor, where it is excellently camouflaged by its mottled plumage. As an added defense, it has large eyes, which are set high up on its rather narrow head, providing it with almost 360-degree vision. It is mainly crepuscular, that is, active at dawn and dusk, but it may also forage throughout the night. It feeds chiefly on insects and other invertebrates, probing amongst mud, vegetation, or soil, locating its prey with its highly sensitive bill-tip. In spring, as the breeding season begins, males may be seen and heard making their display flights at dawn and dusk, a behavior known as "roding." They fly low over the treetops, emitting both croaking and high-pitched calls in order to attract the attention of potential mates. Following mating, the female will nest alone, whilst the male will continue to search for further females. Nesting takes place on the ground, with around four eggs being incubated for about three weeks. The young are able to fly two or three weeks after hatching.

GREAT SKUA

SCIENTIFIC NAME:	*Catharacta skua*
FAMILY:	Stercorariidae
LENGTH:	58cm (23in)
HABITAT:	Open oceans, breeding on rocky coasts and moorland
DISTRIBUTION:	Occurs in the northeast Atlantic, wintering south off the North African coast. Sometimes wanders toward North America, but usually well offshore
IDENTIFICATION:	Gull-like but large and stocky with broader wings. Plumage dark brown overall with lighter streaking. White bar present at base of primary feathers. Bill large and hooked

As its name might suggest, the Great Skua is the largest member of the Skua family, and it is a powerful predatory bird. It is highly pelagic, ranging over the open sea for much of the time, where it feeds mainly on fish, making its own catches or frequently harassing smaller seabirds for theirs. It is something of an opportunistic feeder, particularly during the breeding season when it spends more of its time on land, where there is a greater variety of food. It preys on smaller birds, such as gulls and puffins, takes the eggs and nestlings of other species, and also eats carrion, rodents, and some vegetation, usually berries. It typically breeds from April to August, nesting in colonies on coastal moors, rocky shores, and islands, laying its eggs on the ground in a shallow depression lined with surrounding vegetation; often moss or heather. It usually lays two eggs, incubating them for about a month. Following hatching, the young are reliant on their parents for food until they fledge at between 40 and 50 days old. Whilst nesting, the Great Skua is highly aggressive, and will readily attack intruders to the nesting site, including humans, by dive-bombing.

LONG-TAILED SKUA/JAEGER ▼

SCIENTIFIC NAME:	*Stercorarius longicaudus*
FAMILY:	Stercorariidae
LENGTH:	55cm (22in)
HABITAT:	Pelagic, breeding on Arctic tundra and upland heaths
DISTRIBUTION:	Circumpolar in the high Arctic when breeding, wintering in the Southern Hemisphere
IDENTIFICATION:	Slender and slightly built. Breeding adult: gray above with darker flight feathers and crown, white head and underparts, yellow neck, and long central tail feathers. Nonbreeding adult has gray flecked crown, and underparts barred with brown and white. Lacks long central tail feathers

The Long-tailed Skua or Jaeger is the most pelagic of its kind, spending most of the year on the open ocean, usually at least 16km (10 miles) offshore. It is generally solitary, but may also group together in small flocks, particularly where food is abundant. It sometimes congregates close to commercial fishing vessels in search of scraps, or where schools of small fish, crustaceans, or squid are present, feeding mainly by taking its food close to the surface. Highly agile, at other times it may chase terns and other small seabirds, forcing them to drop fish that they have caught, but it does this less frequently than most other Skuas and Jaegers. During the breeding season when it returns to land, its diet and feeding methods are more varied, and in addition to hunting at sea, it is known to scavenge from feeding seals, and to prey on small rodents such as lemmings and voles. Lemmings are of particular importance, and in years when their populations are low, the Long-tailed Skua tends to breed less successfully. It will often leave the breeding grounds of the Arctic tundra much earlier than usual, and at times may not breed at all. It nests on the ground, in a shallow depression, with both parent birds incubating their clutch of two eggs for just over three weeks. Fledging occurs at 22–27 days, but the young often remain with their parents for one to three weeks longer.

ARCTIC SKUA/PARASITIC JAEGER ▲

SCIENTIFIC NAME:	*Stercorarius parasiticus*
FAMILY:	Stercorariidae
LENGTH:	46cm (18in)
HABITAT:	Pelagic, but breeds on coastal moors and tundra
DISTRIBUTION:	Breeding range circumpolar in the Northern Hemisphere, from the Arctic to more temperate waters. Winters to the tip of South America and off South Africa
IDENTIFICATION:	Medium sized gull-like bird with long, pointed wings. Light morph is brown above, with darker cap, white collar and underparts, yellowish neck. Often has dark breast band. Dark morph has brown underparts and head. Both have white patch on underwing and tail streamers that extend beyond the rest of the tail

In North America particularly, the Arctic Skua is known by the far more descriptive name, the Parasitic Jaeger, referring to its two main methods of obtaining food. The term "Parasitic" relates to its favored strategy of harassing smaller seabirds such as gulls and terns into giving up their catches of fish (a practice known as kleptoparasitism), whilst "Jaeger" comes from the German for hunter, indicating that this species also has a predatory nature. Spending much of its time at sea, this bird tends to follow the migratory movements of terns and gulls to ensure a regular supply of food, also finding easy pickings at their breeding colonies. However, when breeding itself, the Arctic Skua or Parasitic Jaeger often becomes more predatory, feeding on birds and their eggs, invertebrates, and small mammals such as rodents. It nests in a shallow depression on the ground, sometimes lined with grasses and moss, and both parent birds share the incubation of their two eggs for around four weeks. The young typically leave the nest a few days after hatching, but remain with their parents for some weeks after fledging, which usually occurs at about four weeks.

GULLS

Gulls belong to the family Laridae, within the suborder Lari, which includes the terns, skuas, and skimmers, and makes up the second largest group of seabirds after the waders, within the order Charadriiformes. They are widely distributed around the world, in a variety of coastal habitats, but apart from the kittiwakes, they are not truly pelagic, usually remaining in inshore waters. In many cases they have now colonized inland areas, being common in rural areas on cultivated land, and in towns and cities where their numbers, and particularly their noisiness and boldness, sometimes cause them to be regarded as a nuisance. They are highly gregarious birds, usually roosting and feeding in groups, and they often nest in large colonies, frequently alongside other, smaller seabirds, whose eggs and young are then sometimes preyed upon. Most gulls are omnivorous and opportunistic feeders, foraging for aquatic and terrestrial invertebrates, fish, and other small vertebrates such as rodents, a range of vegetation including grain and berries, as well as carrion and scraps from refuse tips or urban streets. At times when food is scarce during breeding, many species will also become cannibalistic, taking eggs and nestlings from within their own colonies. Gulls are typically ground nesting birds, positioning their nests on grass, or amongst reedbeds and rocks, although in towns and cities they will often nest on buildings, whilst kittiwakes establish their colonies on rocky cliffs. Gulls tend to undergo several plumage changes before reaching sexual maturity, which often takes between two and four years, but generally they are gray or white, often with darker plumage on the head and wings, sometimes also varying seasonally. They are medium sized to large birds with quite stout bills, short legs and webbed feet.

The **Common Gull** (*Larus canus*), usually known as the **Mew Gull** in North America, is widespread in the Northern Hemisphere, and found in Europe, Asia, North Africa, and North America along coastlines, estuaries, inland lakes, and marshland. It is rarely found far out at sea and will come ashore in large numbers in bad weather, or further inland in order to visit newly plowed fields in search of invertebrates. It is a medium sized gull, around

Common Gull

40 centimeters (16 inches) long, with a gray back, white head, and white underside. The legs and bill are yellow-green. Juveniles are brown with pale spots. This species breeds mainly in spring, producing clutches of two to five eggs, which are incubated by both parent birds for three to four weeks. The young will then be tended to for several weeks, often not becoming independent until of almost adult size. Due to high incidences of cannibalism by both siblings and adults, and predation by mammals, often only one hatchling per clutch will reach adulthood.

The **Herring Gull** (*Larus argentatus*) is also found in the Northern Hemisphere, but has an even wider distribution, being found both farther north and south than the Common Gull. It is very similar in appearance, but adults are typically much larger, up to 60 centimeters (24 inches) in length. They may also be distinguished by a heavier, more hooked bill that is marked with a red spot on the lower mandible, and pink legs. This species tends to breed in coastal areas, but may also be found inland throughout the year, generally in larger

numbers in winter when it is often found scavenging in urban areas. It nests in spring on grassy cliffs, buildings or in fields, producing two to four eggs, which are placed in a cup of plant material. The **Kittiwake**, or **Black-legged Kittiwake** (*Rissa tridactyla*), is pelagic during the winter, and nests on inaccessible rocky cliffs during the breeding season, never venturing far inland. It may however be seen from the shore, or in coastal towns at times. It is a medium-sized gull, reaching about 40 centimeters (16 inches), but is rather slender in appearance, with a gray back, black wingtips and legs, and a white underside. Spending much of its time at sea, it feeds heavily on fish and aquatic invertebrates, and is less inclined to scavenge than other gulls. It makes its nest on a ledge, forming a cylindrical mound of mud and vegetation, into which two or three eggs are laid. This species is found at sea and on coasts throughout the Northern Hemisphere, also wintering south into warmer waters.

Black-legged Kittiwake

BLACK SKIMMER

SCIENTIFIC NAME:	*Rhynchops niger*
FAMILY:	Rynchopidae
LENGTH:	46cm (18in)
HABITAT:	Coastal and estuarine beaches, tidal creeks, inlets, rivers, and offshore islands
DISTRIBUTION:	Along the eastern US coast and southern California, to southern parts of South America
IDENTIFICATION:	Gull-like, but with a large head and long, red, black-tipped bill in which lower mandible extends beyond upper. Plumage dark brown or black above, including crown. White forehead, underparts and trailing edge of wing

The three species of skimmer, the Black, African, and Indian, are highly distinctive, being the only birds in which the lower mandible is longer than the upper, an adaptation that enables them to feed in a unique way. They fly low over water with the lower mandible partially submerged, skimming the surface for prey. When a fish is detected by touch, the bird then snaps its bill shut to secure its meal. The Black Skimmer is found along North America's eastern coast and along both coasts in South America, with the most northerly populations typically migrating south in winter. It may also occasionally be found inland, particularly during stormy weather in summer, but it is most common along coastal beaches and bays. It breeds in colonies on beaches and islands, sometimes alongside other seabirds such as terns and gulls. Its nest is a simple scrape in the sand, where it lays three to five eggs, which hatch about three weeks later. Both parents incubate the clutch and care for the young, feeding them regurgitated fish and crustaceans until they are large enough to consume whole fish. The mandibles of the bill are of approximately equal length in young birds, and the lower does not begin to elongate until they are almost fully grown.

AFRICAN SKIMMER

Scientific name:	*Rynchops flavirostris*
Family:	Rynchopidae
Length:	40cm (16in)
Habitat:	Coasts, lakes, and rivers
Distribution:	Throughout most of sub-Saharan Africa
Identification:	Gull-like, but with a large head and long, red bill in which lower mandible extends beyond upper. Plumage dark brown or black above, including crown. White forehead, underparts, and trailing edge of wing

As with other skimmers, the African Skimmer feeds by plowing the elongated lower part of its bill through the surface of water as it flies or glides in order to catch small fish. It spends most of the day roosting, preening, and bathing, being more active from dusk until dawn when it is cooler, although the adults will tolerate high temperatures without seeking shade. By feeding at night, it also avoids competition from other birds and from gulls which may attempt to steal its catches. Pairs sometimes nest alone, but breeding typically occurs in small colonies of up to about 20 pairs, providing better protection from birds of prey and other predators, which they will deter by mobbing. Perhaps somewhat surprisingly, this behavior even extends to crocodiles! As a further defense, the adults will sometimes distract predators away from their brood by feigning injury, limping along the sand whilst dragging their wings. Two to four eggs are usually laid, with incubation lasting around three weeks. During this time, the adults may cool the eggs by wetting their bellies before settling on the nest. The chicks leave the nest one or two days after hatching, and are brooded by the parents for several weeks, being fed, shaded, and led to water.

TERNS

The terns belong to a group known as Sternidae, which is usually regarded as a distinct family, although it is sometimes considered as a subfamily of Laridae, the gulls. In any event, the two groups are certainly closely related, although there are a number of important differences. Terns probably differ most notably in being far more streamlined and elegant in appearance, with long, slender wings and forked tails. For this reason, they are sometimes referred to as "sea swallows." Most have brilliant white or grayish plumage, and often develop a black crown during the breeding season. They are found throughout the world, and many species are more pelagic than gulls, with some species that breed in temperate parts of the Northern Hemisphere undertaking extensive migrations to warmer, southern coastal waters in order to overwinter. Unlike gulls, terns are rarely encountered in urban habitats, and do not often walk on land, having very short legs, also swimming less adeptly. However, many species do frequent inland waters such as gravel pits, reservoirs, and large lakes and rivers, particularly where there are gravel bars or shingle banks and beaches. There are also species regarded as "marsh terns," which, as this collective term suggests, spend much of their time in marshland. These birds tend to be more heavily built, with shorter, more rounded wings, and whereas most terns feed mainly by plunge-diving for small fish or crustaceans such as shrimp, they take their insect prey from the water's surface.

When breeding, most terns nest in dense colonies on the ground, usually in open habitats such as tundra or beaches, and social structures are fairly complex, with elaborate aerial courtship displays between pairs, often involving the passing of food, and colonies acting cooperatively to defend nest sites if they are threatened. Terns will even attack unwary humans that stray too near. Tern nests may consist of a simple scrape or depression, or a more complicated structure of twigs, grass, and other materials such as shells. Marsh terns will often nest amongst reeds, whilst others may use cliff ledges or occasionally trees. Terns nesting in tropical regions frequently produce only a single egg, whilst those which breed in more northerly habitats will often lay a clutch of three, or more rarely four. Both adult birds share responsibility for incubation, which commonly lasts for between three and four weeks, and will care for their chicks more or less equally. Reproductive maturity is usually reached at around three years of age, although nonbreeding juveniles may return to their breeding colonies before such time. Some terns however may spend almost all their time on the wing until they are ready to breed.

Terns tend to be quite long lived, reaching ages of over 30 years,

Caspian Tern

and may even continue to breed at over 20 years of age. The largest of all terns is the **Caspian Tern** (*Sterna caspia*), at around 56 centimeters (22 inches). It has a powerful bill and tends to be more predatory than other terns, for in addition to plunge-diving for fish and invertebrates, it will sometimes steal food from other birds and may take the nestlings and eggs of other species. It is also less gregarious than many terns, and although it will nest in small colonies, single pairs may also nest alone or associate loosely with colonies of gulls. It breeds on large lakes or along coastlines across much of North America, Eurasia, Africa, and Australasia, typically wintering south of the northernmost parts of its range. It nests in a shallow depression on the ground, sometimes amongst rocks or other debris, which it lines with seaweed and other plant material. Two to three eggs are usually laid, to be incubated for around three weeks. The young fledge at about 30 to 40 days, but may continue to be fed for up to a further seven months; the longest period of any tern.

The **Arctic Tern** (*Sterna paradisaea*) is a far more sociable bird, nesting in large colonies on coastlines high in the Northern Hemisphere, with a circumpolar distribution across Arctic and sub-Arctic regions, although it is found south to Britain and northern France, and south to Massachusetts in the US. It prefers to nest on sandy or rocky shores, but is also found inland in tundra areas. Two to four eggs are incubated in a depression on the ground for about three weeks, with the young fledging around a further three weeks later. Following the breeding season, this bird undertakes a massive migration of over 19,000 kilometers (12,000 miles) in order to spend the winter in Antarctic waters; in doing so, it is thought that this species experiences more daylight than any other creature on Earth. The Arctic Tern is medium sized, attaining an adult length of around 35 centimeters (14 inches).

The **Black Tern** (*Childonias niger*) is regarded as a marsh tern, and is a small and distinctive species, being around only 25 centimeters (10 inches) long. The breeding adult birds have a dark gray back, black head, neck, and belly, with a gray tail, short dark legs and a short black bill. Outside of the breeding season they are greyer overall, with the exception of the crown. When nesting, this species is found across much of North America, Europe, and parts of Asia, where it breeds in marshlands, flooded meadows, and lakes, usually nesting amongst reeds close to the water's edge, or on floating vegetation, where a clutch of two to four eggs is usually laid. Black Terns tend to overwinter in the Southern Hemisphere, around the coasts of northern South America and Africa. This species does not dive for fish, but may pick them from the surface in flight; it feeds mainly on insects, caught on the wing at or near the water's surface.

Common Tern

RAZORBILL ▼

SCIENTIFIC NAME:	*Alca torda*
FAMILY:	Alcidae
LENGTH:	43cm (17in)
HABITAT:	Rocky cliffs on mainland coasts and offshore islands, pelagic in winter
DISTRIBUTION:	Throughout the North Atlantic
IDENTIFICATION:	Stocky, with a thick neck, large head, and heavy black bill with white bar. Plumage black above, white below, including underwings

During the winter, the Razorbill is pelagic, living on the open ocean, and is rarely encountered in inshore waters. However, it comes ashore during spring and summer to breed, nesting on rocky coastlines in quite large colonies. Egg-laying largely occurs in May, with the female producing a single egg, which is laid in a crevice or on a ledge, usually amongst the cover of boulders. The egg is often laid on bare rock, but some birds collect surrounding pebbles, lichen, or other vegetation with which to line the nest. Although the Razorbill forms pairs, prior to nesting, many females will leave their mate to copulate with other males, and may continue to do so whilst their partner is incubating. Razorbills feed mainly on schooling fish such as herring, sprat, and young cod, but also prey on crustaceans, diving from the surface to catch their prey. They are highly skilled, agile divers, using their wings like flippers to swim underwater, diving to depths of between 25 and 35 meters (82–115 feet), remaining submerged for around 30 seconds at a time.

LITTLE AUK ▲

SCIENTIFIC NAME:	*Alle alle*
FAMILY:	Alcidae
LENGTH:	20cm (8in)
HABITAT:	Rocky coastlines, inland cliffs, and the open ocean
DISTRIBUTION:	Circumpolar on Arctic coasts, wintering south in the North Atlantic
IDENTIFICATION:	Small and squat, with short legs, tail, neck, and bill. Plumage black above, white below

The Little Auk is an incredibly abundant seabird, and is in fact amongst the most numerous of all birds. During the summer months it breeds in rocky Arctic habitats, nesting in vast colonies, numbering tens of thousands of individuals. It nests on coastal or inland cliffs in a burrow or crevice amongst the rocks, where it lays a single egg that is incubated for about a month. During the winter it is pelagic, but avoids the frozen Arctic, migrating south into the open waters of the North Atlantic Ocean and around the United Kingdom in the North Sea. The Little Auk usually dwells quite far offshore, but may be seen from the coast, encountered on beaches, or even seen inland, particularly during bad weather. It typically flies low over the water's surface with rapid, whirring wingbeats, but feeds by diving from the surface, swimming underwater by using its wings like flippers. It may remain submerged for long periods, feeding on small fish and tiny planktonic crustaceans known as copepods.

GUILLEMOT

SCIENTIFIC NAME:	*Uria aalge*
FAMILY:	Alcidae
LENGTH:	43cm (17in)
HABITAT:	Rocky cliffs on mainland coasts and offshore islands, pelagic in winter
DISTRIBUTION:	Circumpolar, occurring in the North Atlantic and North Pacific
IDENTIFICATION:	Rather penguin-like, black above, white below, with long, slender bill

A common Auk throughout much of its range, and the most common off British shores, the Guillemot is a medium-sized seabird, that like its close relatives is pelagic in winter, coming ashore on rocky coasts and cliffs to breed in spring and summer. During the breeding season it establishes large colonies, numbering thousands of birds, usually on vertical cliff faces where predation is more difficult. From May to July, the females lay a single egg directly onto a bare ledge, where it is prevented from rolling off by its rather conical shape. The egg is incubated for around 30 days, and around two or three weeks after hatching, the chick leaves the ledge, plunging into the sea to be looked after by the male parent. At this stage the young Guillemot is still incapable of flight, usually becoming fledged about six weeks later. Once the adult birds have left the breeding colony they undergo a molt, becoming flightless for several weeks, before dispersing more widely throughout the winter. Like other auks, Guillemots feed by diving from the surface, swimming underwater in search of small fish, mollusks, crustaceans, and other marine invertebrates.

COMMON/ATLANTIC PUFFIN

SCIENTIFIC NAME:	*Fratercula arctica*
FAMILY:	Alcidae
LENGTH:	30cm (12in)
HABITAT:	Breeds on rocky shores, overwintering far out at sea
DISTRIBUTION:	Northern Atlantic; Greenland, Canada, Iceland, northern Scandinavia, Russia, Ireland and the north-west of France
IDENTIFICATION:	Short and stocky, black above with white undersides and white cheeks. Bill is large, triangular and parrot-like, bright orange with blue patch bordered with yellow when breeding. Bill and face darker in winter

The Common or Atlantic Puffin spends the winter months at sea, where it dives from the air or the water's surface, to swim underwater in order to catch mollusks, crustaceans, and small fish such as sand-eels. They usually swallow their food underwater unless they have young to feed, at which time they may carry as many as 20 or 30 fish back to their nests at a time in their bills. During the breeding season in spring and summer these puffins come ashore to nest in large colonies on rocky shores. Puffins walk erect on land, and tend to be inquisitive and rather tame, traits which sometimes leave them vulnerable to predation by large gulls, foxes, and even man. The Common Puffin nests in a burrow, excavated mainly by the male, where the female will usually lay a single egg. Both parent birds share responsibility for incubation, which takes around 40 days. The parents return to the sea about a further 40 days later, leaving the young, which will enter the water to begin feeding after a week or so, usually just before they are able to fly.

TUFTED PUFFIN

SCIENTIFIC NAME:	*Fratercula cirrhata*
FAMILY:	Alcidae
LENGTH:	38cm (15in)
HABITAT:	Breeds on grassy coastal slopes and rocky cliffs, overwintering at sea
DISTRIBUTION:	Northern Pacific; from California to Alaska and Japan to northeastern Asia
IDENTIFICATION:	Short and stocky, brownish-black overall, with white underwing patches, white face, and yellow plumes extending back from the eyes. Bill is large and parrot-like, mainly red, with yellow or greenish markings. After breeding, plumes are lost, bill duller and belly lightly speckled.

As with other puffins, the Tufted Puffin spends much of the year on the open ocean, coming ashore to nest on grassy or rocky coastlines in large colonies in spring and summer. The nests take the form of burrows, amongst rocks or on grassy slopes, where a single egg will be laid. Both parent birds incubate the egg for some 40 or 50 days, and will then feed the nestling until it is fledged 45 to 55 days later. The young bird will then enter the sea, and may not return to land for up to two years, when it will usually go back to the breeding colony from which it originated. The adult birds tend to disperse whilst at sea, but may be found in groups of around twenty individuals. The Tufted Puffin feeds mainly on small fish, but will also consume crustaceans, mollusks, and other marine invertebrates. It swims underwater to forage, usually diving below the surface from a low flight. Once hunted extensively for food, the Tufted Puffin is now protected throughout most of its range, and today its major predators are large birds of prey and Arctic Foxes.

LICHTENSTEIN'S SANDGROUSE ▲

SCIENTIFIC NAME:	*Pterocles lichtensteinii*
FAMILY:	Pteroclidae
LENGTH:	24cm (10in)
HABITAT:	Semidesert, rocky hillsides, and scrub
DISTRIBUTION:	Scattered distribution in parts of North and East Africa, the Middle East, Pakistan, and Afghanistan
IDENTIFICATION:	Fairly small, with long wings and short tail. Sandy plumage, heavily barred with black and white, buff breast with black bands

There has been much discussion concerning the classification of sandgrouse species, as they appear to share many characteristics of both the Columbiformes, that is, pigeons and doves, and the Charadriiformes, shorebirds such as plovers. Sometimes assigned to either of these groups, they are now usually placed in their own order, Pteroclidiformes, considered to be somewhere between the two. Although the smallest of its kind within its range, Lichtenstein's Sandgrouse is a fairly typical species, being a somewhat partridge-like, ground dwelling bird that inhabits arid, stony, or sandy terrain. Its habitat typically necessitates long daily flights to water, usually in large, noisy flocks. These journeys are undertaken every morning, and sometimes again in the evening in particularly hot weather. Whilst nesting, males will also collect water in their breast feathers for their young. Nesting takes place on the ground, where two or three eggs are laid in a bare scrape. These are incubated by both the male and female for up to four weeks. Following hatching, the young are able to begin foraging for food almost immediately, feeding on seeds, berries, and insects.

PIN-TAILED SANDGROUSE ▼

SCIENTIFIC NAME:	*Pterocles alchata*
FAMILY:	Pteroclidae
LENGTH:	32cm (13in)
HABITAT:	Semidesert and savannah, often close to cereal crops
DISTRIBUTION:	From Portugal, Spain, and North Africa, across the Mediterranean to central Asia, as far east as northwest India
IDENTIFICATION:	Sandy above with black and gray barring, white below with brown breast edged in black, black eye-stripe. Central tail feathers taper. Breeding male develops greenish tint and more rufous breast

As with other sandgrouse, the Pin-Tailed is well camouflaged by its patterned plumage and may be difficult to spot on the ground amongst rocks and vegetation; however, it has a distinctive white underside and white, black-tipped underwings which are more easily seen in flight. Its tail is also quite distinctive, with two elongated central feathers. Pallas's Sandgrouse, *Syrrhaptes paradoxus*, has a similar tail, but may be distinguished by its elongated primaries and black belly patch. Favoring dry habitats, the Pin-tailed Sandgrouse makes daily trips to water in order to drink, sometimes traveling many kilometers to do so, and during the breeding season males will collect water in the feathers of their breasts and bellies for their unfledged young. This species nests in a scrape on the ground, producing a clutch of around three eggs, which are incubated mainly by the male. The Pin-tailed Sandgrouse is quite gregarious, usually nesting in loose colonies; in winter and early spring it may be found in large flocks of several thousand birds, congregating on wheat and barley fields after planting. It feeds mainly on seeds, grain, leaves, and shoots.

BLACK-BELLIED SANDGROUSE

SCIENTIFIC NAME:	*Pterocles orientalis*
FAMILY:	Pteroclidae
LENGTH:	33cm (13in)
HABITAT:	Dry steppes, often close to cereal crops
DISTRIBUTION:	Southwest Europe and North Africa, across the Mediterranean to central Asia, as far east as northwest India and Nepal
IDENTIFICATION:	Stocky, male gray above, with buff and rufous markings, gray head and neck, chestnut throat with black patch, black band above buff breast, black below. Female more heavily streaked and spotted, including head and neck

The Black-bellied Sandgrouse is amongst the largest in its range and is quite rotund, with a rounded breast and belly. Like other sandgrouse it is a ground dwelling species that inhabits dry regions, but it tends to avoid areas of open desert, being more common on plains, often near to cultivated land. Feeding primarily on seeds and grain, it is frequently found where cereal crops are grown, although somewhat ironically, intensive farming methods have led to a reduction in its preferred habitat, and consequently to a decline in its numbers. It also faces threats from hunting in parts of its range. Flocks of Black-bellied Sandgrouse make flights to ponds or streams each day in order to drink, and during the breeding season the adult birds, usually the males, collect water in specially adapted feathers on their bellies, carrying it back to the nesting site for their chicks. Nesting takes place on the ground, with an average of three eggs being laid in a bare scrape. These are incubated for between three and four weeks, with both parent birds involved in caring for the eggs and chicks.

ROCK DOVE ▲

SCIENTIFIC NAME:	*Columba livia*
FAMILY:	Columbidae
LENGTH:	33cm (13in)
HABITAT:	Rocky mountainous slopes, coastal cliffs, and adjacent fields
DISTRIBUTION:	Western Europe and North Africa, across the Mediterranean and Middle East to India
IDENTIFICATION:	Light gray above, with black wing bars, white rump and underwings. Head and underside blue-gray, neck iridescent green and purple

The Rock Dove is the wild ancestor of domestic birds such as racing pigeons, messenger pigeons, fancy varieties that are often bred for shows, and also the feral pigeons which are common in rural and urban habitats throughout the world. In its wild state, however, the Rock Dove tends to inhabit fairly remote areas, typically dwelling on cliff faces by the sea. It is a gregarious species, often nesting, roosting, and feeding in quite large flocks, but when breeding, both sexes are often aggressive toward others of their kind. Mating may occur at any time of the year, and is preceded by display behavior by the males, which strut, fluff up their neck feathers, and drag their tails on the ground whilst cooing loudly. The males are responsible for choosing nest sites and undertake most of the nest construction, building a shallow, often quite untidy structure of sticks, usually positioned on a rocky ledge. The female lays one or two eggs and performs most of the incubation, which lasts for a little under three weeks. Hatchlings, or squabs, are fed with a substance called "pigeon milk" that is produced in the crops of both parents. The young leave the nest at four to six weeks of age, and a further clutch is sometimes produced before the first young are fledged. Adult birds feed mainly on seeds, also eating some green vegetation.

(COMMON) WOODPIGEON ▲

SCIENTIFIC NAME:	*Columba palumbus*
FAMILY:	Columbidae
LENGTH:	41 cm (16in)
HABITAT:	Woodland, farmland, urban parks and backyards
DISTRIBUTION:	Occurs throughout most of Europe, east into central Asia, south to North Africa
IDENTIFICATION:	Large, robust pigeon. Blue-gray, with iridescent purple-green neck, purplish breast, and white neck and wing bars

Although the terms are somewhat interchangeable, the word "dove" is usually applied to the smaller members of this family of birds, and "pigeon" to the larger ones. The Woodpigeon is amongst the largest of its kind throughout much of its range, being the biggest in Europe, with a deep chest, rounded belly, and relatively long tail. As its name suggests, it is often found in woodland, but it is also increasingly common in urban parks and yards, where it may be heard producing deep cooing sounds. It usually forages in the open, feeding on seeds, grains, green crops, and some invertebrates, and it may congregate in large numbers in fields, sometimes damaging crops. In urban areas, however, it is a frequent visitor to bird tables. Having a relatively dry diet, the Woodpigeon drinks a great deal, and like other pigeons and doves, is unusual amongst birds in that it can drink without tipping back its head to swallow, using its bill rather like a straw to suck up water. Breeding may occur at almost any time of the year, with up to three clutches of two eggs being produced. It nests in trees, or occasionally on buildings, constructing a platform of sticks and twigs. Both parent birds incubate their eggs and care for the young following hatching.

COMMON/EUROPEAN TURTLE DOVE ▼

SCIENTIFIC NAME:	*Streptopelia turtur*
FAMILY:	Columbidae
LENGTH:	28cm (11in)
HABITAT:	Woodland, farmland, urban parks and backyards
DISTRIBUTION:	Occurs throughout most of Europe, east into central Asia, south to North Africa
IDENTIFICATION:	Fairly small, sandy or bronze above with dark mottling, gray head, pinkish breast, and white belly. Dark flight feathers, black and white patch on each side of neck

A small dove, the Turtle Dove was once far more common throughout its range, but its numbers have declined quite dramatically in recent years, and it is now considered to be severely threatened in the UK where it is a summer visitor. It is thought that its numbers may have fallen by as much as 80 percent since around 1970, partly because of changes in farming practices, which have led to a reduction in the weeds that it likes to eat, and by shooting in the Mediterranean during its migrations. It overwinters in Asia and North Africa, typically not reaching northern Europe until April, producing its clutch of one or two eggs in May or June. The arrival of this species is usually heralded by soft, purring calls from trees and hedgerows, and breeding begins with the males performing display flights, ascending quite steeply with claps of the wings, before making a gliding, circular descent. Following mating, the eggs are laid in a somewhat flimsy twig nest, usually placed in a low tree or on top of an overgrown hedge. These are incubated for around two weeks by both parent birds, with the chicks fledging around three weeks after hatching.

MOURNING DOVE

SCIENTIFIC NAME:	*Zenaida macroura*
FAMILY:	Columbidae
LENGTH:	30cm (12in)
HABITAT:	Open woodland, prairie, farmland, and urban parks and yards
DISTRIBUTION:	From Alaska and southern Canada, throughout the US, beyond into parts of Central and South America
IDENTIFICATION:	Streamlined, pinkish below, gray-brown above, with dark spots on wings and dark spot below eyes. Long, white-tipped tail feathers

Despite the fact that the Mourning Dove is amongst the most commonly hunted gamebirds in North America, it remains the most abundant and widespread dove throughout its range, inhabiting a variety of open and semi-open habitats. It is generally sedentary, but northernmost populations tend to migrate southward to avoid the harsh winters in Canada and Alaska. The Mourning Dove is a prolific breeder, frequently raising three or more broods in a season lasting from April to September. Both parent birds are involved in the care of their eggs and young, from nest construction, through incubation to brooding. They construct a flimsy platform nest of small twigs in a tree or large bush where two eggs are usually laid. Incubation lasts for about two weeks, and the nestlings fledge a further two weeks after hatching, although they continue to be cared for until they are around 30 days old. Like other pigeons and doves, the parents feed the young on a substance known as "pigeon milk," secreted from the lining of the crop. The adult birds meanwhile feed primarily on grain and the seeds of weeds, occasionally supplemented with invertebrates such as grasshoppers, spiders, and snails.

COLLARED DOVE ▲

SCIENTIFIC NAME:	*Streptopelia decaocto*
FAMILY:	Columbidae
LENGTH:	33cm (13in)
HABITAT:	Woodland, farmland, parks, and yards
DISTRIBUTION:	Throughout much of Europe, across central and southern Asia to parts of the Far East
IDENTIFICATION:	Pale gray overall, with dark flight feathers and black collar. Long tail with black and white underside

Fairly similar to the Turtle Dove in appearance, the Collared Dove may be distinguished by its slightly larger size and more uniform plumage, as it lacks the patterned wings of the aforementioned species. It is also far more common and more widely distributed. Perhaps somewhat surprisingly, the Collared Dove was until quite recently scarce in the colder north and west of Europe, inhabiting the warmer southeast and parts of Asia. However, beginning in the first half of the 20th century, it spread rapidly across Europe, to have colonized its present range by the 1960s, in one of the fastest and widest natural distribution expansions of any bird within living memory. It has also since been introduced to North America, where it is thriving and continuing to spread. Quite adaptable, it occurs in a range of habitats, typically establishing itself wherever trees are present, including in urban settings, where it seems quite unwary of man. However, it is more likely to be encountered in suburban parks and yards than in city centers. It requires trees in order to nest, constructing a flimsy twig platform where one or two eggs are laid. The Collared Dove feeds on seeds, berries, and other vegetation, and during the winter, large flocks are often formed close to farmland where grain may be available.

DIAMOND DOVE ▲

SCIENTIFIC NAME:	*Geopelia cuneata*
FAMILY:	Columbidae
LENGTH:	20cm (8in)
HABITAT:	Arid semidesert and desert regions, usually close to thickets or scrub vegetation
DISTRIBUTION:	Much of Australia, including the interior, absent from much of the south and east
IDENTIFICATION:	A small dove, gray-brown above with black-edged, white diamond-shaped markings on the wings. Head, neck, and breast blue-gray, pale below. The eyes are orange-red, surrounded by a red ring

The Diamond Dove is one of the smallest species of doves and the smallest in its native Australia, but it is quite striking in appearance on account of the diamond-shaped speckles on its wings, from which its name is derived. It occurs mainly in pairs or sometimes in small flocks, usually in quite open terrain, although it tends to be found close to bushes or small thickets of trees, often near to a source of water. Living in arid environments it needs to drink daily, and generally visits watering holes late in the afternoon or evening once it has fed. It forages on the ground, feeding on the seeds of grasses and other plants, and may be observed bobbing its relatively long tail as it does so. Diamond Doves may produce several clutches of eggs each year; prior to mating, the male displays by bowing and spreading his wing and tail feathers. As with most doves and pigeons, the female produces two eggs at a time that are laid on a platform nest of twigs, positioned in a tree, and these are incubated for about two weeks by both parent birds. The young are initially fed on "pigeon milk," progressing to regurgitated seeds within a matter of days. They develop quickly, fledging after a further two weeks. First domesticated in Europe around 1870, Diamond Doves are easily bred in captivity, and are now amongst the most common doves kept as aviary birds.

SPINIFEX PIGEON

SCIENTIFIC NAME:	*Geophaps plumifera*
FAMILY:	Columbidae
LENGTH:	21cm (8in)
HABITAT:	Arid desert and semidesert, typically where spinifex grass occurs
DISTRIBUTION:	Parts of northern Australia
IDENTIFICATION:	Small pigeon with reddish-brown plumage above, black and white throat and breast band, white belly, and black and gray barring on the neck and wings. Distinctive pointed crest on head and bare red skin around eyes

The Spinifex Pigeon is a highly distinctive species, which can be easily identified by its size, plumage, and slender crest. The Crested Pigeon, *Ocyphaps lophotes*, has a very similar arrangement of feathers on its head, but it is a much larger bird, with proportionately longer wings and tail. The Spinifex Pigeon has a noticeably short tail and wings, giving it a rather partridge-like appearance. It is amongst the most terrestrial of pigeons and rarely flies, preferring to seek cover amongst rocks or spinifex grass if threatened. However, it is also quite fearless of man and is often approachable. It is found in arid habitats, but as it tends not to fly it usually remains close to a source of water, and like other pigeons it is able to drink without tipping up its head. It feeds mainly on the seeds of grasses and other plants, also occasionally eating invertebrates, and is most commonly observed foraging in pairs or small flocks of up to around 12 birds. Breeding may occur at any time of year, but is usually prompted by rains in spring, and begins with a courtship display by the male which involves head-bobbing and the ruffling of his feathers. Nesting occurs on the ground in a shallow scrape, sometimes lined with grass stems. Two eggs are laid, which are incubated by both parent birds.

VICTORIA CROWNED PIGEON

SCIENTIFIC NAME:	*Goura victoria*
FAMILY:	Columbidae
LENGTH:	75cm (30in)
HABITAT:	Lowland tropical forests
DISTRIBUTION:	Northern parts of New Guinea and some surrounding islands
IDENTIFICATION:	An extremely large pigeon, blue-gray overall with a purplish breast and wing edge, light blue wing bar and tail tip. Fan-like crest, tipped with white

The Victoria Crowned Pigeon is the world's largest pigeon, growing to around the size of a large chicken, but it is rarely encountered, being found only on New Guinea and a few surrounding islands, in dense jungle habitats. It is also becoming increasingly rare due to hunting, habitat destruction, and illegal export, despite now being protected throughout much of its range. It spends much of its time on the ground, being a rather heavy flier, but it will retreat into trees if disturbed, and also roosts and nests off the ground. During courtship, the male performs bowing displays toward the female, lowering his head and displaying his tail and crest. This species constructs a fairly large nest of twigs and other vegetation, into which one egg is usually laid, and both parent birds are involved in incubation and in the care of their young. Incubation lasts around 28 days, with the downy young being quite helpless upon hatching. For the first few days they are fed on "pigeon milk," before this is supplemented with partially digested food. The young leave the nest at 35 to 40 days to begin foraging on the ground for fruit, seeds, and also invertebrates.

RAINBOW LORIKEET

SCIENTIFIC NAME:	*Trichoglossus haematodus*
FAMILY:	Psittacidae
LENGTH:	25cm (10in)
HABITAT:	Eucalypt forest, woodland, farmland, parks, and yards
DISTRIBUTION:	From Indonesia, through New Guinea and the Solomon Islands, and in Australia from parts of the north including Cape York, south along the east coast to the southeast
IDENTIFICATION:	Green above with a blue head and belly, variable breast, collar, and underwings, but often shades of yellow and red

A small parrot, the Rainbow Lorikeet is nevertheless a striking bird on account of its vivid plumage. It is bright green overall, but there is considerable variation in the color of the neck and breast, and over 20 subspecies have been identified. It is also a highly vocal bird, and flocks can be quite noisy, producing screeching and chattering sounds as they feed. The Rainbow Lorikeet eats fruit, seeds, flowers, and occasionally insects, but pollen and nectar are favored foods, and it is specially adapted to eat them. It has a rather unusual tongue, the tip of which is brush-like; covered in tiny projections, or papillae, to which the pollen adheres. Much of its time is spent feeding, but it is most active in the morning and evening, roosting in trees at night and during the hottest part of the day. It usually forages in flocks of around 20 to 30 individuals, but when roosting, flocks may contain hundreds or even thousands of birds. Breeding pairs are monogamous and tend to remain together for life. Nests are established in tree cavities, often high above the ground, where a clutch of two or three is laid. The female incubates the eggs for around 25 days, whilst the male brings food to her. Both parents feed the chicks.

GALAH (COCKATOO)/ROSEATE COCKATOO ▲

SCIENTIFIC NAME:	*Eolophus roseicapillus*
FAMILY:	Psittacidae
LENGTH:	35cm (14in)
HABITAT:	Grassland, cultivated fields, open woodland, and forest edges
DISTRIBUTION:	Most of Australia, including some offshore islands, but absent from much of the coast
IDENTIFICATION:	Rose-pink head, neck, and underparts, pale pink crown, gray back, wings, and tail

The Galah is amongst the most abundant and widespread of Australian cockatoos, occurring in large flocks across a variety of habitats. It requires trees for roosting and nesting, but tends to feed on the ground in more open country, usually close to water. It is also becoming increasingly common near human habitations. It spends much of its time sheltering amongst the foliage of trees and shrubs, avoiding the heat of the day, and feeding when it is cooler, on seeds, roots, buds, and insects. It is particularly fond of the seeds of cereal crops, which has led it to become something of an agricultural pest in some areas. It may breed at various times of the year, but the breeding season tends to occur earlier in the year in the north of its range than it does in the south, from February to July and July to December respectively. Galahs are monogamous and pair for life, although they will find a new partner if one of them dies. They nest in tree hollows lined with eucalyptus leaves, producing a clutch of two to four eggs. Both parent birds incubate the eggs and care for the young. Once the young have fledged, they tend to form flocks of juveniles, remaining together for the first few years of their lives. Cockatoos are sometimes placed in their own family Cacatuidae, with the Galah further assigned to the subfamily Cacatuinae.

SULFUR-CRESTED COCKATOO

SCIENTIFIC NAME:	*Cacatua galerita*
FAMILY:	Psittacidae
LENGTH:	45cm (18in)
HABITAT:	Forests, woodland, and open habitats such as heaths and farmland. Also in rural and urban areas
DISTRIBUTION:	From Indonesia and New Guinea, to northern, eastern, and south-eastern Australia. Also introduced in southwestern Australia and New Zealand
IDENTIFICATION:	Plumage white overall, with a narrow, yellow, curving crest. Some yellow on the underside of flight and tail feathers and pale yellow ear coverts. Feet and bill are gray-black

Instantly recognizable, the Sulfur-crested Cockatoo is a common and conspicuous species, being fairly large, noisy, and abundant in urban areas. It is also highly gregarious, often roosting in flocks of hundreds of individuals, and tends to be at its most vocal in the mornings and evenings when arriving and departing from its roosts, producing a raucous screeching. Whilst foraging during the day, these flocks tend to disperse into smaller groups however. It feeds mainly on the ground, foraging for seeds and insects, but also eats nuts, fruit, and flowers. Regarded as a pest for the damage it sometimes causes to agricultural crops, the Sulfur-crested Cockatoo is also known to strip timber from buildings, and in some areas licensed culling occurs. This practice is particularly common in Western Australia, where the species is considered to be non-native. Sulfur-crested Cockatoos usually nest high above the ground in the hollow limbs or trunks of trees such as eucalyptus, producing two or three eggs, which are incubated for up to 30 days by both parent birds. Following hatching, the young will remain in the nest until they are fledged at around 70 days old. Cockatoos are sometimes placed in their own family Cacatuidae, with the Sulfur-crested Cockatoo further assigned to the subfamily Cacatuinae.

COCKATIEL

SCIENTIFIC NAME:	*Nymphicus hollandicus*
FAMILY:	Psittacidae
LENGTH:	30cm (12in)
HABITAT:	Arid plains, open woodland, and thickets, usually close to water
DISTRIBUTION:	Throughout the interior of Australia. Absent from Tasmania and many coastal areas
IDENTIFICATION:	Gray overall, with paler underparts sometimes washed with brown. White wing bars, orange-red patch on ear coverts, yellow head and crest. Undertail black in males, yellow in females

Closely related to cockatoos, the Cockatiel is sometimes placed in the family Cacatuidae, and in its own subfamily, Nymphicinae. It differs physically in various ways, most notably in being small in comparison to other cockatoos, and it is also unusual in that it is the only cockatoo that may breed in its first year of life. The breeding season tends to vary according to weather conditions, and typically begins following the rainy season. Nests are usually located in the hollow of a eucalyptus tree, often close to, or even standing in, water. Clutches range from four to six eggs, with incubation lasting around 20 days. Both parent birds incubate the eggs and feed their chicks. This species tends to maintain close pair bonds, often mating for life, and pairs or small flocks commonly feed together. In agricultural areas where food is most plentiful, however, flocks may number several hundred birds and are frequently regarded as pests by farmers. Cockatiels feed on cereal grains, various seeds, buds, and berries. In the north of its range, this species is highly nomadic, wandering in search of food, but southern populations tend to have more fixed migratory patterns.

ECLECTUS PARROT

SCIENTIFIC NAME:	*Eclectus roratus*
FAMILY:	Psittacidae
LENGTH:	35cm (14in)
HABITAT:	Lowland rainforest and mangroves
DISTRIBUTION:	New Guinea and surrounding islands. A small population is also found in Australia on the Cape York peninsula
IDENTIFICATION:	Stocky, with a short, broad tail. Males are green with a red patch on the flanks and a yellow upper bill, the female is red with blue or purple underparts

The Eclectus Parrot displays amongst the most obvious sexual dimorphism within the avian world, for whereas many birds develop contrasting plumage when breeding, the genders of this species have a markedly different appearance throughout the year, with the males being mainly green, and the females red. At one time it was even thought that the sexes were different species. Breeding may occur at any time of the year, and if conditions are particularly favorable, a second clutch of eggs may be produced almost immediately after the first brood has fledged and left the nest. The female chooses the nest site, usually a hollow high in a tree on the edge of a forest, where two eggs are laid. These are incubated by the female, whilst the male provides her with regurgitated food. The chicks hatch after three or four weeks and are then fed by both parent birds. Eclectus Parrots tend to be highly sociable, roosting in large flocks before dispersing to feed amongst the trees in pairs or small groups. However, they may gather in large numbers where food is plentiful. They consume a variety of fruits, buds, seeds, and nuts.

EASTERN ROSELLA

SCIENTIFIC NAME:	*Platycercus eximius*
FAMILY:	Psittacidae
LENGTH:	32cm (13in)
HABITAT:	Open forests and woodlands, grasslands, cultivated fields, roadsides, parks, and yards
DISTRIBUTION:	Southeast Australia and Tasmania, also introduced in New Zealand
IDENTIFICATION:	Head and upper breast scarlet, cheeks white, yellow-green and black scalloping on back, yellow below with blue wings, Female slightly duller, with greenish patch on nape

A common species throughout much of its range, the Eastern Rosella is one of the most colorful parrots in Australia, and although it enjoys wooded habitats, it is also a familiar sight in towns and suburbs. It usually occurs in pairs or small family groups, tending to congregate in larger flocks in winter. It may feed on the ground or amongst bushes and trees, where it forages for seeds, nuts, flowers, nectar, and fruit, and it is sometimes considered as an agricultural pest for the damage it causes in orchards and cultivated fields. Its toes are arranged with two pointing forwards and two backwards, and as with other parrots, it is quite dextrous, able to use its feet to manipulate food. It nests in a hollow, usually fairly high off the ground in a tree, but occasionally in a stump or even a fence post. Following mating, the female produces a clutch of up to nine eggs; however, between four and seven is more common. The eggs are incubated solely by the female for around three weeks, although the male will often join her in the nest, and following hatching, the chicks are fed only by the female for the first couple of weeks. After this the male will join her in caring for the young, which are fledged a few weeks later. In the north of its range, the Eastern Rosella has been known to hybridize with the closely related Pale-headed Rosella (*Platycercus adscitus*).

BUDGERIGAR

SCIENTIFIC NAME:	*Melopsittacus undulatus*
FAMILY:	Psittacidae
LENGTH:	18cm (7in)
HABITAT:	Desert, semidesert, open forest, and grassland
DISTRIBUTION:	Most of Australia, but generally absent from coastal areas. Introduced elsewhere with little success
IDENTIFICATION:	Small and streamlined. Yellow forehead and throat, yellow and black barring on cheeks and crown, developing into scalloping across the back. Underparts and rump light green, tail blue-green. Cere, the skin at the base of the bill, is light brown in females and blue in males

Familiar as a domesticated species, the Budgerigar is probably the most well known pet bird in the world, and numerous attempts have been made to establish wild populations outside of its natural range,

notably in Britain and the US, generally without success. However, feral populations do exist in Europe, and in North America this species has become well established in Florida. It occurs in its wild state across most of Australia, living in large nomadic flocks. These move around almost constantly in search of food and water, although breeding colonies will be established in favorable conditions; especially after heavy rains, when water and their favored food of grass seeds are most abundant. Budgerigars nest in cavities in trees or posts, and are monogamous, but they do not incubate their eggs together. The female looks after the clutch of between four and eight eggs, whilst the male spends most of its time foraging for food. Several broods may be raised in succession where conditions allow. Budgerigars are diurnal, being active throughout the day, but they usually seek shade at midday and at other times when the weather is extremely hot, returning to their roosting sites just after sunset.

SCARLET MACAW/RED AND GOLD MACAW

SCIENTIFIC NAME:	*Ara macao*
FAMILY:	Psittacidae
LENGTH:	90cm (35in)
HABITAT:	Rainforest, forest edges, and savannah
DISTRIBUTION:	Southern Mexico, Central America, and South America, being most common throughout the Amazon Basin
IDENTIFICATION:	Scarlet head, shoulders, and tail, yellow back and mid-wing feathers, blue wingtips, white patches around eyes. Large bill is light above, dark below

The Scarlet Macaw is quite widely distributed in Central and South America, but its numbers have been seriously reduced by deforestation, illegal export, and hunting for its meat and feathers. However, attempts have been made to halt this population decline, including legal protection, which outlaws trade, and the provision of nest boxes where natural nesting sites have become scarce. Despite such provisions, the recovery of this species is made more difficult by its long breeding cycle. It often breeds only once every two years, with the young frequently remaining dependent upon their parents for this amount of time. Scarlet Macaws form monogamous pair bonds and remain together for life. Whilst they may be encountered in small flocks, sometimes in close association with other species of macaw, paired birds will spend almost all their time together apart from when breeding, with the female performing most of the incubation, whilst the male forages for food. Nests are established in hollow trees and a typical clutch contains two eggs. Scarlet Macaws feed mainly on fruit, nuts, and seeds, occasionally supplementing their diet with nectar and flowers. They have also been observed consuming clay found on cliffs and riverbanks, which is thought to aid in the digestion of toxins ingested when eating unripe fruit and other vegetation.

BLUE-HEADED PARROT/ BLUE-HEADED PIONUS

SCIENTIFIC NAME:	*Pionus menstruus*
FAMILY:	Psittacidae
LENGTH:	28cm (11in)
HABITAT:	Forest, farmland, and foothills
DISTRIBUTION:	Much of tropical Central and South America, from Costa Rica to southeast Brazil
IDENTIFICATION:	Green overall, with patch of pinkish red feathers on throat, and red undertail coverts. The head, neck, and upper breast are deep blue with a darker patch on the ear coverts

Widespread and abundant throughout most of its range, the Blue-headed Parrot, or Blue-headed Pionus as it is also known, is often encountered singly, or in pairs, although when it is not breeding, or where food is available in sufficient quantities, large flocks may gather. This is particularly evident on cultivated land, where this bird may feed in large numbers on fruit or maize crops, but it also congregates along with other parrots, to feed on mineral-rich soils, a behavior thought to neutralize toxins ingested from some of the vegetation that they consume. The Blue-headed Parrot forages mainly amongst the treetops, feeding on fruit, seeds, flowers, and nuts. When breeding, flocks disperse, and pairs establish nests in cavities in trees, usually quite far from the ground. A clutch consists of three or four eggs, which are incubated mainly by the female for around 28 days. Following hatching the young are cared for by both parent birds, and leave the nest after about eight weeks.

Hawk-headed Parrot/ Red-fan Parrot

Scientific name:	*Deroptyus accipitrinus*
Family:	Psittacidae
Length:	33cm (13in)
Habitat:	Lowland rainforest
Distribution:	Northern parts of South America, from Columbia, through Venezuela to French Guiana, south into Brazil
Identification:	Mainly green above, with dark primaries. Forehead and crown pale buff, face brown streaked with white. Nape, chest, and abdomen feathers dark red with blue edges. Very broad tail

The Hawk-headed Parrot, or Red-fan Parrot as it is also known, is a striking species, particularly when adopting its distinctive display posture, whereby it raises the feathers of its neck to form a large fan that frames its face. This is performed when the bird is alarmed, or otherwise excited, and is used in territorial displays during the breeding season, usually accompanied by loud vocalizations and swaying from side to side. These parrots are usually encountered in pairs or small groups, foraging amongst the treetops, where they feed on seeds, nuts, fruits, and leaves. They roost and nest in tree cavities, or abandoned woodpecker nests, usually high in the rainforest canopy, producing a clutch of two or three eggs. The chicks hatch after an incubation period of about 26 days, during which time the female rarely leaves the nest; the male, however, spends most of his time searching for food. Following hatching, both parents feed and rear the young. Although considered fairly common in some parts of its range, its numbers are declining overall, mainly as a result of widespread deforestation, and the sub-species *D. a. fuscifrons*, also known as the Brazilian Hawk-headed Parrot, is almost extinct in the wild.

Kea ▼

Scientific name:	*Nestor notabilis*
Family:	Psittacidae
Length:	48cm (19in)
Habitat:	Wooded valleys, grassland, and alpine scrub
Distribution:	Mountainous parts of South Island, New Zealand.
Identification:	Olive-brown overall, with a green back and wings, reddish-brown rump, and orange underwings. The upper mandible of the bill is enlarged and decurved

The Kea is a fairly large, stocky parrot that spends much of its time foraging for food on the ground. Its diet is highly varied and changes according to the season. It feeds on green vegetation, berries and other fruits, invertebrates, and carrion, eating flesh and bone marrow from carcasses. It also has a reputation for attacking sheep, which in the past led to large scale culling. However, it generally preys only on wounded or dying animals. The Kea is highly adaptable, inquisitive, and bold, and will scavenge around human settlements, sometimes being quite destructive. It is known to investigate, break, and steal belongings, damaging clothing and other objects, and stripping windshield wipers and wiring from cars. Keas may breed at almost any time of the year, except late fall, but the peak reproductive period typically lasts from July to January. They nest in burrows, amongst rocks and tree roots or in hollow logs, lining the cavity with moss and other plant material. An average clutch consists of two to four eggs, which are incubated for three or four weeks. The young fledge after about 13 weeks. Keas are quite gregarious, with a hierarchical social structure, and they live in family groups until sexually mature. This takes about three years for females, and four to five years for males, at which time the males usually disperse. Males will fight for dominance of a group, and during the breeding season, sometimes as few as ten percent of males within a group will be allowed to breed.

(COMMON) CUCKOO ▲

SCIENTIFIC NAME:	*Cuculus canorus*
FAMILY:	Cuculidae
LENGTH:	35cm (14in)
HABITAT:	Woodland edges, farmland, marshes, and grassland
DISTRIBUTION:	Throughout most of Europe and Asia, also North Africa, wintering to South Africa and the Philippines
IDENTIFICATION:	Gray overall with dark horizontal barring on white underparts. Wings are pointed and quite falcon-like, tail is long and broad. Rarely, females are red-brown

The distinctive call of the male Cuckoo, after which these birds are named, has long been regarded as heralding the start of spring in Europe, with this species returning from Africa in late March and early April and remaining for the duration of the summer. During this time the Cuckoo breeds, and it is probably for its reproductive behavior that the bird is best known. It is a brood parasite, laying its eggs in the nests of other birds, usually small songbirds such as Reed Warblers, Meadow Pipits and Dunnocks. The Cuckoo may produce around 20 eggs in a season, but it will lay only one egg in any single nest, usually specializing in a particular host species and laying eggs of similar size and color. Once hatched, the blind and naked Cuckoo then removes the host's eggs by pushing them out with its back. In the case of the host's eggs hatching first, the Cuckoo will also push chicks from the nest. The Cuckoo is tended by its foster parents, and grows rapidly, quickly outgrowing them to leave the nest in around three weeks. Cuckoos feed on invertebrates, particularly large caterpillars.

GREAT SPOTTED CUCKOO

SCIENTIFIC NAME:	*Clamator glandarius*
FAMILY:	Cuculidae
LENGTH:	40cm (16in)
HABITAT:	Forest edges, open grassland, and rocky hillsides with scattered trees
DISTRIBUTION:	Southern Europe and parts of Africa
IDENTIFICATION:	Silver-gray crest and crown, gray or olive-brown back and wings, spotted with white. Long dark gray tail, tipped with white, creamy-white underparts

Like the Common Cuckoo, the Great Spotted Cuckoo is parasitic in its reproductive habits, laying its eggs in the nests of other birds, particularly magpies and other members of the crow family. The female will usually remove at least one egg from the host's clutch, but unlike the Common Cuckoo, however, the young of this species will not remove any eggs upon hatching, but will be reared alongside the host's own chicks, remaining camouflaged by developing remarkably similar plumage and mimicking the calls of the other nestlings. The Great Spotted Cuckoo grows rapidly, leaving the nest after around 18 days to begin foraging for food. This species feeds mainly on the ground in lightly wooded areas, and is insectivorous, feeding especially on large, hairy caterpillars, which many other birds will not eat. Birds in the northern and southern extremes of this species' range typically undertake migrations, from Europe into Africa, and from South Africa farther north, and following the breeding season may form quite large flocks.

SMOOTH-BILLED ANI

SCIENTIFIC NAME:	*Crotophaga ani*
FAMILY:	Cuculidae
LENGTH:	35cm (14in)
HABITAT:	Open grassland, scrub, cultivated land, and lightly wooded areas
DISTRIBUTION:	From southern Florida, south through the Caribbean and Central America as far as northern Argentina
IDENTIFICATION:	Quite squat, with a large head and bill and long, rounded tail. Plumage is black

The Smooth-billed Ani is a member of the cuckoo family, but has a rather unusual appearance, with a heavy head and bill. It flies weakly, and spends much of its time on the ground, where it forages for large invertebrates such as grasshoppers, small vertebrates such as lizards, and some seeds and berries. It is also frequently encountered on ranches, where it will take ticks from cattle. Smooth-billed Anis are gregarious, usually feeding in small groups, sometimes in association with the highly similar Groove-billed Ani (*Crotophaga sulcirostris*). They also nest collectively and do not parasitize other birds' nests, as many Old World cuckoos do, but construct large cup-shaped nests in thorny bushes or trees, into which several females may lay their eggs. A female usually produces three to five eggs, but up to 30 may be found in the same nest, and groups of nesting pairs will share in incubation and rearing of the young.

GREATER ROADRUNNER ▲

SCIENTIFIC NAME:	*Geococcyx californianus*
FAMILY:	Cuculidae
LENGTH:	58cm (23in)
HABITAT:	Open grassland, scrub, and desert
DISTRIBUTION:	Southwestern US and Mexico
IDENTIFICATION:	Plumage buff with white streaks above, white below, long tail and legs, blue stripe behind eye and spiky crest

A large, ground dwelling cuckoo, the Greater Roadrunner rarely flies, but runs well on its long legs, reaching speeds of around 25km/h (15m.p.h.) whilst foraging in open, arid habitats for small rodents, reptiles such as lizards and small snakes, and large invertebrates including scorpions. Roadrunners have black skin which rapidly absorbs heat, and in cool conditions, such as early in the morning, may be observed basking to warm themselves with their feathers outstretched. Roadrunners pair for life and occupy a permanent territory, nesting amongst cacti or in thorny scrub, constructing a cup-shaped nest of twigs. Following mating, the female produces a clutch of three to six eggs, which are incubated by both parent birds for around three weeks. The eggs hatch at intervals, and if food is scarce the younger, smaller hatchlings often starve, or are sometimes eaten by their parents or siblings.

GREAT BLUE TURACO

SCIENTIFIC NAME:	*Corythaeola cristata*
FAMILY:	Musophagidae
LENGTH:	75cm (30in)
HABITAT:	Tropical forest
DISTRIBUTION:	Parts of West and Central Africa
IDENTIFICATION:	Large and long-tailed bird with a permanently erect crest, blue above, red and yellow below

Sometimes also known as the Giant Turaco, the Great Blue Turaco is the largest turaco, a group of African birds closely related to cuckoos. It inhabits forests and spends much of its time moving amongst the trees, but it is something of a weak flier, with quite short, rounded wings, and tends to glide or to climb from branch to branch. It feeds mainly on various fruits, but also consumes some invertebrates. During the breeding season it constructs a flimsy platform nest of twigs and leaves in the fork of a tree or large bush, usually quite far from the ground. Normally two eggs are laid, which are incubated solely by the female for around 18 days, during which time the male will bring her food. The young possess rudimentary claws on their wings which aid in climbing. This species is not often easy to spot on account of its dense habitat, but it may flock in small groups, and be heard producing a variety of whining and short barking calls.

HOATZIN

SCIENTIFIC NAME:	*Opisthocomus hoazin*
FAMILY:	Opisthocomidae
LENGTH:	64cm (25in)
HABITAT:	Forest edges or thickets close to swamps, lakes, or rivers
DISTRIBUTION:	Northern parts of South America, including Venezuela, Brazil, and Bolivia
IDENTIFICATION:	Large, heavy body, broad tail, long neck and long, spiky crest. Plumage is olive-brown above, with buff streaking, buff throat and breast, and brown underparts

The Hoatzin is a rather unusual bird, both in its appearance, and because it is thought to be a surviving link to reptilian ancestors for, like turacos, the juveniles of this species possess rudimentary claws on their wings, which enable them to clamber amongst the trees before they are able to fly, after which time the claws are shed. The Hoatzin tends to nest above water, and the young may drop into it whilst climbing, either accidentally or to escape a threat, but they are able to swim well, and will normally return to the nest. During the breeding season, this species lives in small groups of up to about ten birds, with the entire group incubating eggs and caring for young, but they may also be found in much larger flocks. The Hoatzin feeds primarily on the leaves and shoots of marsh and swamp plants, requiring a large crop to aid digestion. Large amounts of food may be stored in this crop, sometimes hampering flight.

BARN OWL

SCIENTIFIC NAME:	*Tyto alba*
FAMILY:	Tytonidae
LENGTH:	38cm (15in)
HABITAT:	Open woodland, grassland, and cultivated land, often close to human habitation
DISTRIBUTION:	Worldwide; found in Europe, most of Africa, southern and south-east Asia, Australia and most of the Americas
IDENTIFICATION:	White, heart-shaped face, whitish underparts. Light orange-brown above, with dark spots on the head and shoulders. Long legs

The Barn Owl, and its close relatives, the Masked, Grass, and Bay Owls, belong to the family Tytonidae, one of two families of owls, the other being Strigidae, or the typical owls. The two groups differ somewhat in the arrangement of their bone structures and the Tytonid owls have heart-shaped facial disks. The two groups share many characteristics, however, being mainly nocturnal, with large, forward-facing eyes and soft, dense plumage that enables almost silent flight. Although predatory, owls are more closely related to nightjars than the diurnal raptors. The Barn Owl is a distinctive and widely distributed species, and as its name suggests it often nests and roosts in barns, although it may also utilize other buildings or cavities in trees and cliffs. It hunts at night, or at dawn and dusk, preying on small rodents, bats, and birds, reptiles, amphibians, and large invertebrates and, unlike many owls, which carry their prey in their talons, the Barn Owl tends to use its bill. During the breeding season, a clutch of four to seven eggs are laid, which are incubated by the female for about a month, whilst the male provides her with food. Both parent birds care for their chicks once hatched.

BUFFY/MALAY FISH-OWL

SCIENTIFIC NAME:	*Ketupa ketupa/Bubo ketupa*
FAMILY:	Strigidae
LENGTH:	45cm (18in)
HABITAT:	Dense forest close to water
DISTRIBUTION:	Southeast Asia, from Thailand, through Malaysia and Indonesia to Burma
IDENTIFICATION:	Dark brown above, orange-brown below with dark streaking. Large yellow eyes, ear tufts and large feet with huge, curved claws

The Buffy or Malay Fish-Owl is a fairly large species, which looks much like an eagle owl, and although it may feed on a variety of small creatures, including rodents, amphibians, reptiles, and invertebrates, it specializes in hunting fish, using its elongated talons and scaly feet to secure its favored prey. It hunts at night, watching for fish or amphibians from a waterside perch, before swooping down and plunging its outstretched feet into the water to grasp its prey in much the same way as an Osprey. The Buffy Fish-Owl lacks the downy wing feathers that provide most owls with near-silent flight, and this is thought to be due to its mainly aquatic feeding habits, whereby it relies on its vision rather than hearing, also being unlikely to disturb its underwater prey whilst in flight. During the day, this species is usually to be found roosting amongst dense vegetation, often in pairs. It makes its nest in a natural cavity in a tree, or in the abandoned nest of another bird, producing a clutch of two or three eggs.

SNOWY OWL

SCIENTIFIC NAME:	*Nyctea scandiaca*
FAMILY:	Strigidae
LENGTH:	65cm (26in)
HABITAT:	Woodland, tundra, and coastal marshes
DISTRIBUTION:	Circumpolar, high in the Northern Hemisphere
IDENTIFICATION:	A large owl, with dense white plumage and yellow eyes. Males may be pure white, whilst females are typically barred and spotted with gray

With its dense, white plumage, the Snowy Owl is both insulated and camouflaged in its harsh arctic habitats. It lives year-round on the tundra, where it feeds on rodents, rabbits, and birds, hunting either by day or night, usually watching for its prey from a low vantage point, such as a stump or rocky outcrop, before swooping in to make a kill. Lemmings are a particularly important prey item, and in years when their numbers are low, the Snowy Owl may produce smaller clutches, or even forfeit breeding at all. At such times it may also be forced far south of its normal range in search of other food. Nesting on the ground in a shallow scrape, the Snowy Owl will defend its nest aggressively against any intruders, including large predators such as wolves. A clutch usually consists of five to eight eggs, but in years when food is abundant up to 14 may be produced. They are incubated solely by the female for about 32 days. Following hatching, the downy young are cared for by both parent birds. They may leave the nest after around three weeks, but will normally not be able to fly for at least another month.

GREAT GRAY OWL

SCIENTIFIC NAME:	*Strix nebulosa*
FAMILY:	Strigidae
LENGTH:	68cm (27in)
HABITAT:	Coniferous and deciduous woodland, wooded bogs and adjacent open habitats
DISTRIBUTION:	Northern parts of Europe, Asia, and North America
IDENTIFICATION:	A large owl, gray overall, mottled with brown. Has a prominent facial disk, marked with concentric circles, white above the throat. Tail is relatively long, yellow eyes and bill

The Great Gray Owl is a very tall species, and amongst the largest of the owls, but it is relatively slender, lacking the power of species such as the Great Horned Owl, which probably represents the only major predator to regularly attack and kill this bird. It tends to inhabit northerly forests and may be nocturnal, crepuscular, or even active by day, particularly in the far north of its range. It feeds mainly on small rodents and shrews, and its facial disk contributes to its excellent hearing; at times it will even locate prey beneath deep snow. It usually hunts over quite open ground, perching at the edge of woodland before swooping down silently to make a kill. The breeding season begins in late winter, with a pair establishing a nest in a hollow tree or an abandoned raptor's nest, with two to five eggs being laid from spring to early summer. The clutch is incubated by the female for around four weeks, and following hatching both parent birds will provide food for their young.

Tawny Owl

Scientific name:	*Strix aluco*
Family:	Strigidae
Length:	40cm (16in)
Habitat:	Mature woodland, but also farmland, parks, and yards with tall trees
Distribution:	Throughout most of Europe, east across Asia to China. Also in parts of North Africa
Identification:	A medium sized owl, quite plump, with mottled brown plumage and a round facial disk

The Tawny Owl is the most numerous and widely distributed owl in Europe, and is the most common owl in its range that is regularly found in suburban and urban environments. It is primarily nocturnal, roosting by day, high amongst the branches of a tree or in a hollow trunk, and occasionally in a crevice in a rocky outcrop or the wall of a building. It will also nest in such sites, utilizing woodpecker holes or the abandoned nests of crows and birds of prey. More rarely, it has been known to nest in burrows. It produces a clutch of two to five eggs, which are incubated for around four weeks by the female, whilst the male provides her with food. Following hatching, both parent birds will care for their brood, and may be highly aggressive, even toward people. The Tawny Owl feeds predominantly on rodents and small birds, but as is common with many owls, if it is discovered by other birds whilst roosting during the day, they will frequently mob it and attempt to drive it away. The "tu-whit tu-whoo," commonly used to represent the sound of an owl, is a combination of the abrupt call of the female and the softer hooting of the male of this species.

BURROWING OWL ▼

SCIENTIFIC NAME:	*Speotyto cunicularia/Athene cunicularia*
FAMILY:	Strigidae
LENGTH:	25cm (10in)
HABITAT:	Open grassland and lightly wooded areas
DISTRIBUTION:	From western Canada, south through the western US and Central America to southern South America. Also populations in Florida and the Caribbean
IDENTIFICATION:	Small, long legged, short tailed owl. Plumage is mainly brown with white spots and streaks, becoming more buff toward the belly and undertail

The Burrowing Owl is a fairly unusual species, spending most of its time either on or below the ground, living throughout the year in a burrow. It also frequently lives in small colonies. These owls may take over the burrows of mammals such as prairie dogs and gophers, or they may dig their own. At times they may even share their burrows with larger rodents, or reptiles such as the gopher tortoise. The Burrowing Owl is predominantly diurnal, foraging above ground by day for insects, amphibians, reptiles, and small rodents. Nesting takes place in the burrow, at which time the nest chamber is lined with grass and other vegetation. Following mating, the female produces a clutch of five to seven eggs, which she incubates alone for a period of around four weeks; the chicks are cared for by both parent birds upon hatching. Whilst in the nest, the young may deter predators by producing hissing sounds that sound much like snakes.

(EURASIAN) PYGMY OWL ▲

SCIENTIFIC NAME:	*Glaucidium passerinum*
FAMILY:	Strigidae
LENGTH:	18cm (7in)
HABITAT:	Mainly coniferous woodland, often in mountainous regions
DISTRIBUTION:	Northern and Central Europe, east to Siberia
IDENTIFICATION:	A very small owl, dark brown above with white spots and barring, buff below, with dark streaks. Prominent white eyebrows

The Eurasian Pygmy Owl is amongst the smallest of the world's owls, and is the smallest found in Europe. It is typically crepuscular, being most active at dawn and dusk, but it may also hunt during the day. It hunts for small rodents, reptiles, and terrestrial insects by swooping to the ground from a perch, but also catches small birds on the wing, and has a rapid, if somewhat undulating, flight. It will usually prey on tits and small finches, but is capable of killing birds approaching its own size. When breeding, this species often nests in woodpecker holes, usually in conifer trees, but it will also use nest boxes. The female produces a clutch of between three and eight eggs, which she incubates alone, whilst the male provides her with food. Incubation lasts for approximately four weeks, after which time both birds will attend to their brood. The young leave the nest after around 30 days, but will continue to be fed for about six or seven weeks, initially by both parents, until the female leaves to undergo a molt.

LITTLE OWL

SCIENTIFIC NAME:	*Athene noctua*
FAMILY:	Strigidae
LENGTH:	25cm (10in)
HABITAT:	Fairly open habitats; lightly wooded areas, rocky terrain, and cultivated fields, sometimes also in urban areas
DISTRIBUTION:	From Britain, across Europe and Asia to China. Also in North Africa
IDENTIFICATION:	Small and squat, plumage brown above, spotted with white, pale below with dark streaking. Small facial disk is mainly whitish

Despite its diminutive size, the Little Owl is often quite conspicuous. It is frequently active during the day, and may be found close to human habitations, particularly in rural areas, where it may be observed perching on fence posts, telegraph poles, or in trees, as it keeps watch for a potential meal. It feeds on insects and other invertebrates such as worms, but it is quite capable of tackling larger prey, including rodents and small birds. It nests in a variety of locations, using holes in trees, buildings, and rocky outcrops, but will also make use of nest boxes and even rabbit burrows. This species breeds in spring, producing a clutch of three to five eggs, which are incubated for around four weeks by the female alone. The male will bring food to the female whilst she is at the nest, and will care for the young once they are hatched. If food is abundant, two clutches may be produced in a year.

LONG-EARED OWL

SCIENTIFIC NAME:	*Asio otus*
FAMILY:	Strigidae
LENGTH:	38cm (15in)
HABITAT:	Deciduous woodland, coniferous forests, heaths, and thickets
DISTRIBUTION:	Across the Northern Hemisphere, from North America, to Eurasia, as far east as Japan
IDENTIFICATION:	Buff-brown plumage streaked with darker feathers, paler belly. Has long ear-tufts, and deep orange eyes surrounded by a golden-orange facial disk

The Long-eared Owl is so called due to its earlike tufts, although these are not actually its ears, which are to be found lower down on the sides of its head. Like some other owls, it has asymmetrical ear openings, with the left ear positioned higher than the right, providing acute directional hearing that enables it to catch its prey, such as small birds, mice, and voles, in complete darkness. Being largely nocturnal and secretive, it may be difficult to observe, but during migration it may be more diurnal. It hunts almost exclusively at night, using its sense of hearing to locate prey whilst flying low over open ground, and kills its prey with a bite to the back of the head. Following this, it generally swallows its meals whole. During the breeding season, the Long-eared Owl does not construct its own nest, but uses nests built by other birds, such as crows, or may nest in a squirrel drey. Occasionally it may also nest in a cavity in a tree, cliff, or on the ground. An average clutch consists of between three and five eggs, which are incubated by the female for a period of up to four weeks. Following hatching, the young are fed solely by the female bird, although the male will provide her with food, close to or at the nest. When food is scarce, the largest nestling, typically the first to have hatched, will be fed, whilst the others may be left to starve, often to be eaten by their surviving sibling.

SHORT-EARED OWL ▲

SCIENTIFIC NAME:	*Asio flammeus*
FAMILY:	Strigidae
LENGTH:	40cm (16in)
HABITAT:	Open grassland, moorland, dunes, and marshes
DISTRIBUTION:	Much of North and South America, northern Africa, and Eurasia
IDENTIFICATION:	Mottled brown overall, with four bold tail stripes, short ear-tufts, and yellow eyes surrounded by black patches

The Short-eared Owl is so named because of the short, sometimes inconspicuous, ear-tufts on its head. It is similar in appearance to the Long-eared Owl, but is generally somewhat larger, and has longer, thinner wings. Unlike the Long-eared Owl, the Short-eared Owl is frequently diurnal and can be seen hunting during the daytime, flying low over moors and marshland, searching for small mammals, such as mice, voles, and lemmings, as well as birds and amphibians. It may be seen flying low over vegetation, or hovering to spot its prey. Occasionally Short-eared Owls also hunt from perches. During the breeding season it nests on the ground in a shallow hollow lined with grass, usually in the shelter of vegetation such as heather, grass, or reeds. An average clutch consists of between four and six eggs, which are incubated solely by the female for a period of around four weeks, whilst the male will provide her with food. Following hatching, the nestlings leave the nest after about two weeks, but may remain flightless for a further 14 days.

SOUTHERN BOOBOOK

SCIENTIFIC NAME:	*Ninox novaeseelandiae*
FAMILY:	Strigidae
LENGTH:	33cm (13iin)
HABITAT:	Found in a variety of habitats, from tropical forest to open woodland, desert scrub, and also towns and suburbs
DISTRIBUTION:	Throughout Australia, Tasmania, and some coastal islands, also in southern New Guinea
IDENTIFICATION:	Dark brown above, reddish-brown below, streaked and spotted with white. The eyes are large and yellow

The Southern Boobook is the smallest and most common of Australian owls, and frequently inhabits suburban areas, but being primarily nocturnal it is more often heard than seen, with its name being derived from its low-pitched "boo-book" call, which is quite similar to that of a cuckoo. Although it is most active at night, or at dawn and dusk, on overcast days this species may also be seen in daylight hours. It feeds on insects such as beetles and moths, which are usually caught in flight, as well as small rodents and lizards that it catches on the ground. The Southern Boobook normally breeds from September to February, nesting in a hole in a tree, which may be left bare, or contain a small amount of vegetation. The clutch of two to four eggs is incubated solely by the female, whilst the male provides her with food. Following hatching, both parent birds care for their young, which leave the nest at between five and six weeks of age.

OILBIRD

SCIENTIFIC NAME:	*Steatornis caripensis*
FAMILY:	Steatornithidae
LENGTH:	48cm (19in)
HABITAT:	Caves and cliffs in forested areas and on coastlines
DISTRIBUTION:	Parts of northern South America and the Caribbean
IDENTIFICATION:	Owl-like with a rounded face, large eyes, and a hooked bill. Reddish-brown overall with black-edged white spots and a long, barred tail

The Oilbird is closely related to the nightjars and frogmouths, but unlike these birds, which feed at night on invertebrates and small vertebrates, the Oilbird is a nocturnal fruit eater, the only bird in the world to display such behavior. By day it rests in huge colonies in caves, before emerging at night in search of fruit, which is plucked from the trees in flight and carried back to the roost to be eaten. It is this species' preference for oil-rich fruits, such as those from palms, which gives the bird a thick layer of fat and its name, and it is sometimes hunted for this fat, which is used as a fuel for cooking and is also burned for light. Oilbirds are extremely vocal, producing a range of screeches and snarls, but they also emit sharp, high pitched calls and clicks which operate as a form of echo-location, in much the same way as bats. The Oilbird nests in caves, constructing a nest of droppings and regurgitated fruit and seeds, where it will generally lay two to four eggs.

COMMON POTOO ▶

SCIENTIFIC NAME:	*Nyctibius jamaicensis*
FAMILY:	Nyctibiidae
LENGTH:	40cm (16in)
HABITAT:	Tropical forest
DISTRIBUTION:	From southern Mexico and the Caribbean, through Central America, south to northern Argentina
IDENTIFICATION:	Quite large and squat with mottled gray-brown plumage. The bill is short, but reveals a large gape when open

Potoos are closely related to the nightjars and share a similar appearance, with cryptic plumage that camouflages them during the day when they are inactive; however, they tend to be somewhat stockier. The Common Potoo spends the daylight hours resting motionless in the trees, frequently with its head pointing vertically, its eyes closed, and its feathers somewhat ruffled, giving it the appearance of part of a branch. It also incubates in this position, having laid a single egg in a bare depression on a branch or stump. It becomes active at night, swooping from its perch to catch large flying insects on the wing. Potoos take their name from the sound made by the Giant Potoo (*Nyctibius griseus*) but they are capable of producing a wide variety of whistles, shrieks, and booming sounds.

LARGE FROGMOUTH

SCIENTIFIC NAME:	*Batrachostomus auritus*
FAMILY:	Podargidae
LENGTH:	40 cm (16in)
HABITAT:	Tropical forest
DISTRIBUTION:	Malaysia, Sumatra, and Borneo
IDENTIFICATION:	Large and squat with reddish-brown upperparts marked with white spots and buff barring, a white collar and buff belly. The mouth is large and surrounded by bristles

Perhaps not surprisingly, the frogmouths take their name from their huge frog-like gape, which enables them to feed on large invertebrates such as scorpions, centipedes, and snails, as well as reptiles, amphibians, small birds and rodents. Like their close relatives the nightjars, frogmouths are nocturnal, resting by day amongst the trees, becoming active at night to begin hunting. The Large Frogmouth is almost twice the size of many of its group, but it is not a strong flier; however, it may fly quickly and silently, swooping from a perch to seize its prey on the ground. When breeding, this species constructs a loose nest of leaves and down in the fork of a tree, where up to three eggs may be laid. These are incubated by the male during the day and by the female at night. The Large Frogmouth is not particularly common, being quite scattered throughout its range. It is at some risk from habitat destruction, but seems to show a preference for secondary-growth forest, which may make it less vulnerable than some other species.

(Eurasian/European) Nightjar ▲

Scientific name:	*Caprimulgus europaeus*
Family:	Caprimulgidae
Length:	28cm (11in)
Habitat:	Moorland, heaths, open woodland, and forest clearings
Distribution:	Much of Europe, Asia and Africa
Identification:	Long wings and tail, mottled gray-brown plumage with bristles around the bill and white stripe below the eyes. Males also have white areas on the wings

The nightjar is a nocturnal bird and is rarely seen, being well camouflaged by its cryptic plumage, but its churring mating call may be a familiar sound during the summer months in parts of Europe, when these birds arrive from Asia and Africa. Once far more common, the Nightjar has suffered badly from the destruction of heathland across much of its breeding range, but there have been some increases of late, particularly in the United Kingdom. It typically spends the day resting on the ground, usually amongst leaf litter or other vegetation, although it will sometimes roost on a branch. At night it becomes active, hunting for moths, beetles, and other flying insects, which it catches on the wing. Nightjars nest on the ground, laying a clutch of two eggs, which are incubated for around 18 days by both parent birds. In addition to being protected by its plumage, the Nightjar is capable of emitting loud hissing sounds if disturbed, which will often deter a potential predator.

Standard-winged Nightjar

Scientific name:	*Macrodipteryx longipennis*
Family:	Caprimulgidae
Length:	23cm (9in)
Habitat:	Arid, rocky country, savannah, and scrub
Distribution:	In a band across Central Africa from Senegal to Ethiopia
Identification:	A small nightjar with mottled brown plumage. When breeding, the male develops a long streamer-like feather on each wing

The male Standard-winged Nightjar is one of several African species which develops extremely long, streamer-like feathers during the breeding season. These usually extend from the tail or trailing edge of the wing, but in the case of the Standard-winged Nightjar, the feathers protrude from the center of each wing. These plumes may grow up to 47cm (18in) in length and are held erect whilst the bird performs its display flight, acting as an advertisement to female birds. Following the breeding season, the feathers are shed. This species nests on bare ground, usually producing two eggs. It is a nocturnal bird, resting on the ground by day in a sheltered spot, to begin hunting at dusk for moths, beetles, and other flying insects. It may also be observed catching insects which are forced into flight by forest fires.

COMMON POORWILL

SCIENTIFIC NAME:	*Phalaenoptilus nuttallii*
FAMILY:	Caprimulgidae
LENGTH:	20cm (8in)
HABITAT:	Arid scrub, desert, and open woodland
DISTRIBUTION:	The western US, wintering south to Mexico
IDENTIFICATION:	A small nightjar, mottled gray-brown plumage with small white spots on the wings, white collar, and long bristles around the bill

The Common Poorwill is the smallest member of the nightjar family to be found in North America, and is highly unusual amongst birds for its ability to hibernate. When food is scarce in winter, it finds a sheltered spot such as a crevice amongst rocks, where it will enter a state of torpor, slowing its breathing and heart rate and lowering its body temperature from around 40ºC (104ºF) to less than 20ºC (68ºF). It may remain in such a state for several days or even weeks until conditions are more favorable. During the warmer months, this species spends much of its time on the ground, resting by day, and making short flights at night to catch flying insects such as moths and beetles. It also nests on the ground, usually around June, laying two eggs on the bare earth.

COMMON SWIFT

SCIENTIFIC NAME:	*Apus apus*
FAMILY:	Apodidae
LENGTH:	16cm (6in)
HABITAT:	Airborne except when nesting. Found particularly in urban areas or at cliffs and over grassland, often close to water
DISTRIBUTION:	Most of Europe, across Asia to northern India and China, wintering in Africa
IDENTIFICATION:	Slender, with long, pointed wings and a short, forked tail. Plumage sooty overall, with small pale throat patch

The Common Swift is amongst the most aerial of birds, spending almost its entire life in flight; feeding, sleeping and even sometimes mating on the wing, landing only when nesting. Its feet are not designed for perching, although it can cling vertically to trees, cliffs, or buildings, where it makes its cup-shaped nest in a crevice or roof space. This species tends to reuse nest sites and in cases where a pair has taken over another's nest, vicious fights may ensue. Mating normally occurs in the nest, following which a clutch of two to three eggs is produced. Both parent birds take turns to incubate their eggs and to care for their young. Swifts may be seen soaring at great heights or gliding low over rooftops or water in large numbers, taking flying insects on the wing, and even drinking in flight, skimming the water's surface with their bills. A summer visitor to Europe, the Common Swift undertakes extensive migrations from Africa in order to breed.

ALPINE SWIFT

SCIENTIFIC NAME:	*Tachymarptis melba*
FAMILY:	Apodidae
LENGTH:	23cm (9in)
HABITAT:	Mainly airborne, nests in hilly or mountainous regions, on coasts and in urban areas
DISTRIBUTION:	Southern Europe, the Middle East, and North Africa, wintering throughout Africa and into India
IDENTIFICATION:	A large swift with very long swept-back wings. Brown above with a black collar, white throat, breast, and belly

Despite its name, the Alpine Swift occurs over a wide range of habitats, although hilly and mountainous regions provide suitable nesting sites, in the form of rocky crags and cliff faces. In addition, this bird nests at cliffs along coastlines, and utilizes tall buildings in urban areas. Like other swifts, it is a highly aerial bird, spending much of its time on the wing, typically gliding at high altitude and feeding on flying insects. Unlike the Common Swift, however, this species roosts nightly, retreating to crevices and within roof spaces at dusk, or clinging to the vertical surfaces of cave or building walls. The Alpine Swift normally breeds in colonies, returning to the same sites year after year, where cup-shaped nests are made and maintained. The nests are constructed from feathers and plant material, cemented with saliva. Two to three eggs are laid, which are incubated by both parent birds.

CHIMNEY SWIFT

SCIENTIFIC NAME:	*Chaetura pelagica*
FAMILY:	Apodidae
LENGTH:	13cm (5in)
HABITAT:	Nests in urban areas, usually feeds over more open habitats
DISTRIBUTION:	From eastern parts of North America, migrating south to parts of the Amazon Basin
IDENTIFICATION:	Small swift, gray-brown, darker above than below. Long, slender wings, short square tail

Before widespread urban development in North America, the Chimney Swift is likely to have roosted and nested in hollow trees and caves, but as its name suggests, it is now more often to be found in chimneys. It is a gregarious species, and large numbers of these birds may roost together, but when breeding only one pair will nest in a single chimney, although a pair may allow other swifts to roost with them. The nest is constructed from small twigs, or other vegetation such as straw, cemented together and held in place by saliva. The Chimney Swift produces a clutch of between one and five eggs, which are incubated by both parent birds for around three weeks. Like other swifts, this species is highly aerial, and when not roosting or incubating, it spends all of its time in flight, feeding on flying insects.

HUMMINGBIRDS

Hummingbirds belong to the family Trochilidae and have traditionally been placed in the order Apodiformes, along with the swifts. However, in some more recent taxonomies, they have been classed as belonging to a new and distinct order, Trochiliformes, which contains only the hummingbirds. There are around 340 species of hummingbirds, all of which are found only in the Americas. Most inhabit South and Central America, but there are about 30 species that are found in North America either as residents or when breeding. The name hummingbird is derived from the characteristic humming sound produced by the rapid wingbeats of these birds, which may reach speeds of between 80 and 200 beats per second. Such fast wing movements provide hummingbirds with incredible agility, enabling them to hover, to fly left, right, up, down, backwards, and even upside down. In contrast, hummingbirds can barely move on their tiny feet, which are used almost exclusively for perching. They are small birds, and in fact the family includes the smallest bird in the world, the **Cuban Bee Hummingbird** (*Mellisuga helenae*), which often grows to only 6 centimeters (just over 2 inches). However, due to the energy required in order to sustain their hovering flight, which itself is necessary to their feeding habits, hummingbirds must feed almost constantly, sometimes consuming two thirds of their body weight in a single day. Sugary nectar and sap constitute the majority of a hummingbird's diet, but pollen and insects are also important foods.

Most species have long, sometimes downcurved bills, and correspondingly long tongues, which are used to probe deep into tubular flowers in search of food, and in so doing, hummingbirds tend to collect pollen as they feed and transfer it from flower to flower, helping many plants to reproduce. Some flowers, such as penstemons, even seem to be designed to accommodate hummingbirds and may rely on them heavily for pollination to take place. The males of most species are brightly colored, with iridescent plumage, which serves to attract mates, whilst the females, which incubate their eggs alone, are generally somewhat duller, in order to provide them with camouflage whilst they are nesting.

The nests of most species take the form of neat, open cups, constructed from lichen, moss, and cobwebs, placed in the fork of a branch, although some hummingbirds suspend their nests below leaves, amongst roots, or in caves. A clutch typically contains one or two eggs, which are incubated for between 14 and 19 days. Both males and females generally establish and maintain feeding territories and

White-tipped Sicklebill

Rufous Hummingbird

will usually mate in neutral areas, often fighting with each other to defend a good food supply. At times, these frequently bold birds will also even attack other birds, including potential predators such as hawks and crows. The longest-billed species tend not to be territorial, however, since the flowers from which they obtain their food are largely inaccessible to other birds and many insects. **The Sword-billed Hummingbird** (*Ensifera ensifera*) is one such species, with an overall length of around 20 centimeters (8 inches), about half of which may be accounted for by its bill, and in fact, its bill may even exceed its body length. It feeds from trumpet-like passion flowers, in the mountainous forests of the Andes, from Venezuela to Bolivia. The **White-tipped Sicklebill** (*Eutoxeres aquila*) which also occurs in north-western parts of South America has a comparatively shorter bill, but one which is remarkable for its highly downcurved shape, enabling it to feed from flowers less accessible to other species. However, its bill shape also often makes feeding on the wing difficult, and unlike most hummingbirds it will tend to settle on a plant in order to probe its flowers.

The largest of the hummingbirds, the **Giant Hummingbird** (*Patagonia gigas*), which may attain a length of about 23 centimeters

(9 inches), will hover in order to feed, but it has characteristically slow wingbeats. It is also recognizable by its metallic green upperparts and reddish underparts. It is found throughout the Andes from Ecuador to Chile, and also in the lowland scrub of western Argentina, often migrating seasonally from higher altitudes in winter. Many hummingbirds undertake long migrations considering their size, and the **Rufous Hummingbird** (*Selasphorus rufus*) breeds along the west coast of North America as far north as Alaska, wintering in California and around the Gulf of Mexico. It grows to around 10 centimeters (4 inches), and the male is reddish overall, with a white breast, dark wings, and a bright red throat. The female is similar, but greenish above, with a patchy throat. The most familiar hummingbird in North America, and a frequent garden visitor, is the **Ruby-throated Hummingbird** (*Archilochus colubris*) which is also the only member of the family regularly found in the east for much of the year, although it tends to overwinter in Central America. It grows to around 9 centimeters (3 1/2 inches), and the male of this species has an iridescent red throat, whilst both sexes are green above and white below.

Broad-tailed Hummingbird

BLUE-NAPED MOUSEBIRD ▲

SCIENTIFIC NAME:	*Urocolius macrourus*
FAMILY:	Colidae
LENGTH:	34cm (13in)
HABITAT:	Thorny scrub
DISTRIBUTION:	In a band across sub-Saharan Africa, from Senegal to Somalia, south to Tanzania
IDENTIFICATION:	Slender, gray-brown, with long, narrow central tail feathers, a spiky crest and blue nape

With its small body, gray hair-like body feathers and long, slender tail, the Blue-naped Mousebird has a very mouse-like appearance, added to by the way it scurries amongst the scrub bushes in which it lives. It has a unique toe arrangement, whereby the two outer toes of each foot may be rotated to point either forward or backward, providing a grip that affords the bird a high degree of agility. At times it may even roost whilst hanging upside down and it also runs well on the ground. Mousebirds are highly sociable, living in groups of 20 to 30 birds, roosting, dust-bathing, and foraging together. They also indulge in mutual preening. The Blue-naped Mousebird feeds on fruit, flowers, shoots, buds, and leaves, occasionally supplemented with insects. When breeding, a neat, bowl-shaped nest is constructed in a dense bush, where three eggs are usually laid, to be incubated for around two weeks.

BLUE-CROWNED TROGON

SCIENTIFIC NAME:	*Trogon curucui*
FAMILY:	Trogonidae
LENGTH:	25cm (10in)
HABITAT:	Tropical rainforest, often close to water
DISTRIBUTION:	Northeastern parts of South America
IDENTIFICATION:	Male has iridescent green upperparts with bluish sheen on crown, neck, and tail, red underside, orange eye-ring. Female is blue-gray above with white upper breast. Both sexes have black and white barred tail feathers

Although brightly colored, the Blue-crowned Trogon is rarely encountered, being fairly uncommon and often inhabiting quite dense rainforest, typically close to rivers and streams or in swampy habitats. It is also quite sluggish, spending much of its time resting motionless amongst the branches of trees, darting from its perch to seize insects in flight, briefly hovering as it does so. It also feeds on other invertebrates such as snails, and vegetation such as fruit. It is usually solitary, pairing to breed, at which time it nests in a cavity. It sometimes uses an abandoned woodpecker nest, but it is capable of excavating its own hollow in soft material, like rotten wood or in a termite nest in a tree, with both birds in a breeding pair taking turns to dig the hole. The female produces two to five eggs, which are incubated for around three weeks.

NARINA TROGON

SCIENTIFIC NAME:	*Apaloderma narina*
FAMILY:	Trogonidae
LENGTH:	33cm (13in)
HABITAT:	Lowland forests and forest edges
DISTRIBUTION:	Much of sub-Saharan Africa
IDENTIFICATION:	Metallic green upperparts, crimson below. Wings gray with fine black and white barring on flight feathers. Female has cinnamon throat and breast

Like other trogons, the Narina Trogon is brightly colored, but it is unobtrusive, spending much of its time perching motionless in an upright position amongst high branches, and when disturbed, it may turn around to conceal its crimson belly. It is also generally solitary or found in pairs, but it may sometimes associate with mixed-species flocks. It feeds mainly on insects, particularly caterpillars, usually plucking its prey from a branch before returning to its perch to eat, but it will occasionally take invertebrates from the ground. In addition to caterpillars, the Narina Trogon will consume spiders, moths, beetles, and even small vertebrates such as arboreal lizards. When breeding, it nests within an unlined cavity in a tree or stump, producing two to four eggs, which are incubated for just over two weeks. Both parent birds incubate the eggs and care for their young.

BELTED KINGFISHER ▼

SCIENTIFIC NAME:	*Ceryle alcyon*
FAMILY:	Alcedinidae
LENGTH:	33cm (13in)
HABITAT:	Rivers, ponds, streams, and estuaries
DISTRIBUTION:	Throughout most of North America, wintering as far south as northern South America
IDENTIFICATION:	Slate-blue head, wings, and breast band, white collar and underparts. Female has rust-red band across belly. Both have shaggy crest

The only kingfisher found throughout most of North America, the Belted Kingfisher is a common and conspicuous species in suitable habitats through much of its range. It feeds mainly on fish, but will also consume aquatic invertebrates and even terrestrial vertebrates, including small mammals and reptiles. The Belted Kingfisher normally rests on a perch watching for prey, before plunge-diving to retrieve a fish or other meal. At times the bird will also dive from a hovering position above the water. During the breeding season, this bird excavates a tunnel in a riverbank in which to nest, usually in sandy soil. A pair take turns to dig their burrow, which may be over two meters (6 1/2 ft) long, and ends in a nesting chamber, where six or seven eggs are laid. Both parents incubate the eggs for up to 24 days. The chicks are naked and blind upon hatching, but the young are ready to leave the nest and begin to learn to fish within about four weeks. After the breeding season, the birds become solitary, defending their own territories.

WHITE-COLLARED KINGFISHER/ COLLARED KINGFISHER

SCIENTIFIC NAME:	*Todirhamphus chloris*
FAMILY:	Alcedinidae
LENGTH:	28cm (11in)
HABITAT:	Inland at woodland edges, rainforest, and mangrove swamps, as well as at ponds, streams, and coastal areas
DISTRIBUTION:	Scattered from East Africa across to western India, and through southeast Asia to northern and eastern Australia
IDENTIFICATION:	Variable, but typically greenish-blue above, including crown, white underparts, face, and collar, with a black eye-stripe and upper mandible

There are several subspecies of the White-collared Kingfisher occurring across a wide geographical range and in a wide variety of habitats. It hunts from a perch, either above water or open ground, diving down to seize its prey of fish, crustaceans, or small vertebrates such as reptiles and amphibians. Fish are usually swallowed whole and head first, whilst prey such as crabs may be dismembered prior to consumption. Collared Kingfishers are territorial and may be highly aggressive, both to their own kind and other bird species, particularly during the breeding season. At this time, courtship flights are performed and the male may also offer food to the female. Both parents construct the nest, digging a tunnel in a riverbank, or hollowing out a tree or termite nest. They may also use an abandoned woodpecker hole. A typical clutch consists of two to four eggs, and two broods may be raised in a season. Both parent birds are responsible for incubation and caring for their young.

(COMMON) KINGFISHER

SCIENTIFIC NAME:	*Alcedo atthis*
FAMILY:	Alcedinidae
LENGTH:	18cm (7in)
HABITAT:	Lakes, canals, and riverbanks with overhanging vegetation. Sometimes also at the coast, particularly in winter
DISTRIBUTION:	Much of Europe and parts of North Africa, across to southeast Asia
IDENTIFICATION:	Iridescent blue above, bright orange below, with orange markings around the eyes, white-ear tufts and white throat, and long pointed bill

The only kingfisher found in western Europe, the Common Kingfisher is also one of the region's most brightly colored birds, yet it may be difficult to spot as it rests on a secluded riverside perch, keeping a watchful eye for prey in the water below. It feeds mainly on fish and some aquatic insects and crustaceans, making spectacular plunge-dives in order to catch its prey. Once it has seized a fish, it will return to its perch, strike the fish against the branch and rotate it so that it can be swallowed head first, avoiding damage from its scales. The Kingfisher may also catch insects in flight. During the breeding season this bird makes display flights, flying low over the water and high above surrounding trees, making trilling calls in order to attract a mate. Pairs will then nest in long burrows in the riverbank, which are excavated with the bill and feet. A clutch normally consists of six or seven eggs, which are incubated by both parent birds for about three weeks. The young hatch blind and naked, but are fully fledged within a month, and fed by their parents until they can fish for themselves.

LAUGHING KOOKABURRA ▲

SCIENTIFIC NAME:	*Dacelo novaeguineae*
FAMILY:	Alcedinidae
LENGTH:	45cm (18in)
HABITAT:	Woodland and scrub
DISTRIBUTION:	Parts of southern and eastern Australia, introduced to Tasmania
IDENTIFICATION:	Stocky, with a large head and dagger-like bill. Gray-brown above, grayish-white head and underparts. Dark eye-stripe and barred tail

The Laughing Kookaburra is the largest member of the kingfisher family, and is regarded as a forest or tree kingfisher, inhabiting woodland quite far from water. It is probably best known for its loud call, which sounds like raucous human laughter, and which is usually heard in the mornings and evenings, earning this bird the nickname "the bushman's clock." It is territorial, living in small family groups comprising an adult breeding pair and their offspring. When breeding, the Laughing Kookaburra nests high in a hollow tree, where it lays two to four eggs in an unlined cavity, which are incubated for around 25 days. The Kookaburra feeds on invertebrates, such as insects, worms, and snails, also taking larger prey including amphibians, small birds, rodents, lizards, and snakes. Larger prey is dispatched by being bashed against a branch, or sometimes dropped from a height.

SPANGLED KOOKABURRA

SCIENTIFIC NAME:	*Dacelo tyro*
FAMILY:	Alcedinidae
LENGTH:	32cm (13in)
HABITAT:	Tropical forest, mangrove swamps, and open grassland
DISTRIBUTION:	Southern New Guinea and the Aru Islands
IDENTIFICATION:	Stocky, with a large head and heavy bill. Wings and tail are iridescent blue, head is spangled black and white and underside is white

Also known as the Aru Giant Kingfisher, the Spangled Kookaburra is similar in appearance to the better known Laughing Kookaburra, but has stunning blue flight and tail feathers. It may be found in swampy habitats, but it is essentially a forest or tree kingfisher, dwelling amongst the low branches of trees and shrubs, and foraging mainly on the ground for its prey. It feeds mostly on insects, including ants and beetles, and during the breeding season makes its home in a termite nest, usually quite high in a tree. This species produces a variety of sounds, including a laughter-like call.

RUFOUS MOTMOT

SCIENTIFIC NAME:	*Baryphthengus martii*
FAMILY:	Momotidae
LENGTH:	45cm (18 in)
HABITAT:	Tropical forest
DISTRIBUTION:	From Central America into north-western parts of South America
IDENTIFICATION:	Fairly squat, with a long tail, large head and bill. Head and underparts are orange-red, wings and tail green with blue edges. Black eye-stripe

The Rufous Motmot is the largest of the motmots, a small family of brightly colored birds found in the tropical forests of Central and South America, closely related to the kingfishers. It is relatively inactive, spending much of its time perching high amongst the branches of a tree in wait for a passing meal, darting out to catch flying insects, or to pick them from a nearby branch or leaf. It also feeds on small vertebrates such as rodents and reptiles, sometimes taking prey on the forest floor. It also will consume fruit, plucking it from the trees whilst in flight. Larger prey is often beaten against a branch before consumption, and may be dismembered. Additionally, the Rufous Motmot may follow columns of army ants, preying on small animals disturbed as they traverse the forest floor. This species is typically solitary or found in pairs and, during the breeding season, pairs will nest in long burrows in soft soil, usually in a bank, or between tree roots. These birds may also use such burrows for roosting outside of the breeding season.

Bee-eaters

The Bee-eaters belong to the family Meropidae, a highly distinctive group of birds, characterized by their vivid plumage, slender wings and bodies, and narrow tails, which often have elongated central feathers. They also possess long, slightly downcurved bills. They are found mainly in tropical and subtropical parts of the Old World, with slightly over half of all species occurring in Africa. Most inhabit open country, such as dry scrub and more moist savannah habitats, with some species moving between the two seasonally, whilst still others, such as the **Red-bearded Bee-eater** (*Nyctyornis amictus*), are found in more dense forest habitats. This species is found in the rainforests of southeast Asia, and is fairly large, growing to around 30 centimeters (12 inches) in length, but it is rather more squat than most species, with a large head, and shorter, more rounded wings, typical of birds which live in forests, enabling them to fly between trees and branches more easily. Additionally it lacks the tail extensions common to many species. It is green overall, and as its name might suggest, it has a red face and throat; however, this characteristic is lacking in juveniles. It

tends to occur singly or in pairs, another trait that sets it apart from most Bee-eaters, which are generally highly sociable; breeding, roosting, and feeding in colonies.

As is implicit in the common name of this family, Bee-eaters eat bees, with honey bees comprising the majority of the diet of most species. However, other flying insects are also routinely eaten, including wasps, locusts, grasshoppers, and winged termites. Almost all prey is taken on the wing, usually after flying from a perch such as a dead branch, although many African species will also perch on grazing animals and even large grassland birds such as bustards or storks, dashing off to catch insects disturbed from the grass below. Bee-eaters will often take advantage of bush fires, too, flocking to feed on insects flushed out by the flames. In fact, in parts of its range, the Carmine Bee-eater is known as "the cousin to the fire" for this reason. There are two distinct populations, usually regarded as separate species, and known as the **Northern** and **Southern Carmine Bee-eaters** (*Merops nubicus* and *M. nubicoides* respectively). Northern

Carmine Bee-eater

populations are found in a band just south of the Sahara, whilst the southern birds inhabit parts of the southern African interior. Both species are a vivid red overall, with a dark face and crown, but the Northern Carmine may be distinguished by its turquoise throat.

Bee-eaters have a certain level of immunity to the stings of bees and wasps, but they are nevertheless careful with their prey. Once captured, an insect will be taken back to a perch, where it will be knocked against the branch to immobilize it, and in the case of a stinging insect, it will be dragged back and forth in order to dislodge the sting before consumption. Bee-eaters are sometimes regarded as pests by bee keepers, but they may also be beneficial as they prey on many insects such as hornets which also feed on bees. The **White-throated Bee-eater** (*Merops albicollis*) is unusual in that in addition to insects, it also feeds on some plant material, eating strips of palm nut skin, which is discarded by squirrels and other animals feeding in the forest canopy. It is found in a band across sub-Saharan Africa, dwelling in scrub and open country when breeding, before migrating farther south to forest clearings and moist grassland in winter. It grows to about 23 centimeters (nine inches), including an elongated tail, and is distinctively colored, with yellow-green upperparts and a black and white head and throat.

The **European Bee-eater** (*Merops apiaster*) is also highly distinctive, growing to around 28 centimeters (11 inches) long, with brown and yellow upperparts, green wings, a yellow throat, dark eye and throat stripes, and bluish underparts. It breeds in southern Europe, parts of North Africa and western Asia, and is a strongly migratory bird, wintering throughout tropical Africa and in north-western India. At times it is also found slightly farther north of its natural breeding range, and has been known to reproduce in Britain. Like most Bee-eaters, this species is gregarious, nesting in large colonies, and like all members of the family, it nests in burrows, which both parent birds excavate in sandy banks with their feet and bills. Clutches vary between two and ten eggs, depending upon the species, and are incubated by both adult birds for about three weeks.

(European) Bee-eater

HOOPOE

SCIENTIFIC NAME:	*Upupa epops*
FAMILY:	Upupidae
LENGTH:	28cm (11in)
HABITAT:	Open woodland and scrub
DISTRIBUTION:	Much of Europe, Asia, and Africa, with northern birds wintering in the south of this range
IDENTIFICATION:	Pinkish-brown or orange, with black and white barred wings and tail, a black-tipped crest, and a long, downcurved bill

Unmistakable, with its boldly patterned wings and fan-like crest, the Hoopoe is amongst the most striking of birds occurring in Europe, occasionally straying to Britain in spring when birds from Africa migrate northward. Its crest is normally held flat, to be raised during courtship, or when this bird is otherwise excited, but it also frequently raises its crest upon alighting from flight. It feeds mainly on the ground, using its long downcurved bill to probe in the soil for worms and other invertebrates, but it will also catch larger prey, such as small lizards. During the breeding season, the Hoopoe makes its nest in a hole in a tree, or sometimes in the wall of a building, lined with feathers and vegetation, where the female lays between four and seven eggs. These are incubated solely by the female for just over two weeks, whilst the male brings food to her. The Hoopoe's nest is well known for being foul smelling, as this bird produces a pungent fluid as a defense, particularly whilst nesting. The Hoopoe is named after its call, which is a soft repetitious "hoop."

EUROPEAN ROLLER ▲

SCIENTIFIC NAME:	*Coracias garrulus*
FAMILY:	Coraciidae
LENGTH:	30 cm (12in)
HABITAT:	Savannah, open woodland, cultivated land, and rocky areas, often close to water
DISTRIBUTION:	Southern and eastern Europe into Asia and North Africa, wintering to South Africa
IDENTIFICATION:	Thickset, with a large head and stout bill. Plumage blue overall, with chestnut back and wings, with a vivid blue wing-patch and black primaries

Somewhat crow-like, with a stocky appearance, the European Roller is a striking and highly visible bird, being particularly conspicuous in its brighter breeding plumage when it is found in parts of Europe. It also tends to perch in prominent positions such as on telephone wires or posts close to open ground, where it watches for its prey of large insects, which are either taken on the ground or caught in flight. The European Roller will also consume small vertebrates, such as amphibians, reptiles, and young birds, usually returning to its perch to feed. The rollers take their name from the acrobatic, rolling display flights that are performed by the male birds during courtship. Following mating, around four eggs are usually produced, with nesting taking place in a woodpecker hole, or in a hole in a bank, cliff, or building.

COMMON SCIMITARBILL

SCIENTIFIC NAME:	*Rhinopomastus cyanomelas*
FAMILY:	Phoeniculidae
LENGTH:	28cm (11in)
HABITAT:	Woodland and lightly wooded savannah
DISTRIBUTION:	From southern Africa to Angola and Kenya
IDENTIFICATION:	Slender, long tailed bird with iridescent deep blue plumage and a long, highly downcurved bill

The Common Scimitarbill belongs to a group of birds called the wood-hoopoes, and it is sometimes also known as the Scimitar-billed Wood-Hoopoe. It is usually found alone or in pairs, but may occur in small flocks of around five birds, sometimes also associating with the closely related Green Wood-Hoopoe (*Phoeniculus purpureus*). It is a highly agile bird, and is often be seen clinging upside down to the bark of a tree as it forages for food. It feeds on insects, their eggs and larvae, probing crevices with its specialized bill, also occasionally feeding on nectar. During the breeding season, pairs nest in abandoned woodpecker holes or natural cavities in trees, where two to four eggs are laid. These are incubated for around two weeks by the female, which is brought food by the male. The young hatch blind and naked, but fledge after about two weeks. Like other hoopoes, both the young and adults are capable of producing a foul smelling secretion, which is used to deter potential predators.

GREAT HORNBILL/GREAT INDIAN HORNBILL

SCIENTIFIC NAME:	*Buceros bicornis*
FAMILY:	Bucerotidae
LENGTH:	125cm (49in)
HABITAT:	Tropical forest
DISTRIBUTION:	Parts of India and Thailand, through Malaysia to Sumatra
IDENTIFICATION:	Large, with a huge downcurved bill topped with a bony casque. Head, neck, upper breast, tail, and lower underparts are creamy white, whilst the body and wings are mainly black, with white wing bands and tips. Black band across the face and tail

The Great Hornbill is amongst the largest of this group of birds, and looks almost vulture-like in flight with its broad wings and tail. It flies powerfully and steadily over the forest canopy, usually in pairs or small groups, and hops high amongst the branches as it forages for food. It feeds on a variety of foods, primarily fruit and seeds, but also consumes large insects, amphibians, reptiles, and small mammals. Other than its large bill, perhaps the Great Hornbill's most noticeable feature is the large bony casque over the forehead and bill. It is thought that this may be used to amplify the bird's call, act as an indication of its age, and also be used as a weapon in territorial or courtship disputes. The Great Hornbill's breeding behavior, like that of most hornbills, is highly unusual. The female nests in a large hollow in the trunk of a tree where she incubates two eggs. The entrance to the nest is sealed with a cement of regurgitated food, droppings, and mud, leaving only a small hole, through which she is fed by the male. The female may remain holed-up in this way for around 100 days, leaving the nest around a week or two before the young, which are resealed in the nest to be fed by both parent birds.

RHINOCEROS HORNBILL ▶

SCIENTIFIC NAME:	*Buceros rhinoceros*
FAMILY:	Bucerotidae
LENGTH:	110cm (43in)
HABITAT:	Tropical forest
DISTRIBUTION:	Southeast Asia from the Malay Peninsula to Java and Borneo
IDENTIFICATION:	Large, with a huge downcurved bill topped with a large up-curved, orange casque. Plumage is mainly black, rump is white, tail is white with a broad black band

This species takes its name from the large upcurved casque on its bill, reminiscent of a rhinoceros' horn. It is amongst the largest of the hornbills, but despite its size, it is reasonably agile and flies strongly, with powerful and loud wingbeats. It is also highly vocal, producing loud resonant calls, thought to be amplified by the hollow casque. It is usually found in pairs, but small groups may congregate where food is plentiful, such as at large trees which are bearing fruit. Additionally, this species feeds on insects and small vertebrates such as amphibians and reptiles. As with other arboreal hornbills, the Rhinoceros Hornbill nests in a large hollow in a tree, in which the female is sealed, being fed through a small hole by the male. It is thought that this is a defensive measure, protecting the female, her eggs and young from predators such as snakes. A clutch consists of two eggs; however, usually only one chick in a brood will reach maturity. Whilst the female is incubating, and therefore unable to fly, she undergoes a molt, leaving the nest a week or so before her young, to join the male in foraging for food.

SOUTHERN GROUND-HORNBILL

SCIENTIFIC NAME:	*Bucorvus cafer*
FAMILY:	Bucorvidae
LENGTH:	105cm (43in)
HABITAT:	Open grassland and lightly wooded areas
DISTRIBUTION:	Parts of sub-Saharan Africa
IDENTIFICATION:	Large hornbill, black overall with white wing bar visible in flight, bare red skin around the eye, and a throat wattle that is red in males, blue in females. Large downcurved bill, relatively small bony casque

The Southern Ground-Hornbill is one of two species of ground-hornbills, both of which are found in Africa. As its name would suggest, it spends most of its time on the ground, but tends to roost in trees. It lives in small groups of up to about ten birds, and forages in grassland, scrub, or open woodland for large insects, amphibians, reptiles, and small mammals. Like other hornbills, this species nests in hollow trees, and although the female will incubate her eggs whilst the male brings food to her, ground-hornbills do not wall up their nesting chambers. The clutch usually consists of two eggs which are incubated for about a month, but frequently only one chick from each clutch is raised, the second chick to hatch dying due to competition with the first. The remaining chick may stay in the nest for up to three months, being cared for by the parents for an additional nine months, and remaining with the family group until it reaches sexual maturity at about four years. With numbers of these birds in decline, programmes have been established to rescue, rear, and release hornbill chicks.

PARADISE JACAMAR ◀

SCIENTIFIC NAME:	*Galbula dea*
FAMILY:	Galbulidae
LENGTH:	30cm (12in)
HABITAT:	Rainforest
DISTRIBUTION:	Northern parts of South America
IDENTIFICATION:	A small, long tailed bird with a long pointed bill, dark green plumage, iridescent wings, white throat, and brown crown

With its pointed bill and iridescent green wings, the Paradise Jacamar looks somewhat like a very large hummingbird. However, it does not feed on nectar, but almost exclusively on flying insects. It catches its prey in flight, spending its time waiting on a perch for a passing meal, usually quite high in the canopy. At other times it may be found flying over water, or in forest clearings, frequently with mixed-species flocks. It consumes flies, beetles, and moths, but butterflies are a favored prey. During the breeding season, the Paradise Jacamar nests in a burrow that is excavated by both birds in a pair. This is usually positioned in a soft earthen bank, alongside water, between tree roots, or sometimes in a termite nest in a tree. These burrows may be as much as 50cm (20in) long. The female produces a clutch of two to four eggs, which are typically incubated by both birds during the day, and the female alone at night, with incubation lasting around three weeks.

GREATER HONEYGUIDE

SCIENTIFIC NAME:	*Indicator indicator*
FAMILY:	Indicatoridae
LENGTH:	20cm (8in)
HABITAT:	Open woodland and scrub
DISTRIBUTION:	Much of sub-Saharan Africa
IDENTIFICATION:	Slender, male slate-gray above with white-edged wing coverts and ear patch, pale gray below with a black throat. Female brown above, yellowish below

The Greater Honeyguide is a rather plain bird, but it is highly unusual in its behavior. Honeyguides are in fact unique in the bird world for their ability to consume and digest beeswax. They feed mainly on insects, but also eat the honeycombs, wax, and larvae from bees' nests, although they do not often eat honey, adult bees, or their pupae. Protected from stings by their thick skin, honeyguides are, however, unable to break open the nests themselves, and instead lead humans, or the ratel, also known as the honey badger, to nests. Another interesting aspect of the greater honeyguide's behavior is that, like some cuckoos, it is a brood parasite, laying a single egg in the nest of another bird. It favors the nests of birds such as bee-eaters and barbets that utilize burrows or hollows, and upon hatching, the young bird then kills its host's brood with a sharp egg-tooth on its bill.

TOUCAN BARBET

SCIENTIFIC NAME:	*Semnornis ramphastinus*
FAMILY:	Capitonidae
LENGTH:	20cm (8in)
HABITAT:	Mountainous rainforest
DISTRIBUTION:	Western Colombia and Ecuador
IDENTIFICATION:	Thickset, with a large head and powerful bill. Olive-brown above, orange-red below, black crown, gray head with white tufts behind the eyes

A colorful bird, the Toucan Barbet is so named as its plumage is similar to that of certain mountain toucans, which are also found in the local area. Barbets are closely related to the woodpeckers, and have a similar toe arrangement, enabling them to move around in a similar way, clinging to tree trunks supported by their tails, or hopping amongst the branches as they forage. They feed on fruit, buds, and insects, sometimes also taking small vertebrates such as lizards. This species may be found singly, in pairs, or small groups, sometimes with birds of other species, although, when breeding, they tend to become territorial. Nesting occurs in hollow trees, and the Toucan Barbet usually excavates its own hole, using its sturdy bill. The female normally produces two eggs, which are incubated by both parent birds. The young hatch naked and blind, to be cared for in the nest by their parents for around five weeks, initially being fed on insects, which are more easily digested than fruit or other vegetation.

TOCO TOUCAN

SCIENTIFIC NAME:	*Ramphastos toco*
FAMILY:	Ramphastidae
LENGTH:	60cm (24in)
HABITAT:	Rainforest, also savannah and around human habitations
DISTRIBUTION:	Venezuela and Brazil, south to northern Argentina
IDENTIFICATION:	Black overall, with large white bib, red undertail coverts bare, yellow skin around eye, and massive orange-yellow bill, black at base and tip

Probably the most familiar of the toucans, the Toco Toucan is also the largest, and as with all members of the toucan family, it possesses a huge bill. This may appear somewhat impractical, but the bill is in fact light, and toucans are able to use them with some skill in order to grasp fruit or other food that might otherwise be out of reach. In addition to fruit, the Toco Toucan also consumes birds' eggs, insects, and other small animals, including reptiles and nestlings, and it seems that other birds are wary of the toucan's bill, making predation from their nests much easier. The Toco Toucan nests in a natural cavity in a hollow tree, or sometimes in an abandoned woodpecker hole, where a clutch of two eggs is laid. These are incubated alternately by both parent birds for around 16 days. The chicks hatch naked and blind, and may take over two weeks to open their eyes, and over a month to begin developing feathers, usually leaving the nest two to three weeks later.

PLATE-BILLED MOUNTAIN-TOUCAN

SCIENTIFIC NAME:	*Andigena laminirostris*
FAMILY:	Ramphastidae
LENGTH:	50cm (20in)
HABITAT:	Mountainous rainforest
DISTRIBUTION:	Western Colombia and Ecuador
IDENTIFICATION:	Blue-gray below, black crown, olive-brown wings, and yellow patches on flanks. Large bill is black and red with bony yellow plates on each side

Although the bill of this species, and that of other mountain-toucans, tends to be smaller than that of those birds belonging to the Ramphastos genus, it is highly distinctive, bearing plates on each side, which provide the common name. It is unclear what purpose these serve. As its name also suggests, this bird is often found at quite high altitudes, living in mountainous forests, where it forages for fruit, insects, and small vertebrates amongst the trees. Like other toucans, its wings are relatively small and rounded, and it is not a vigorous flier, but it has a strong grip that affords it a certain amount of agility whilst moving along the branches in search of food. The Plate-billed Mountain-Toucan usually occurs in pairs or small flocks, sometimes associating with other rainforest birds when foraging. It nests in a woodpecker hole or natural cavity, usually producing two or three eggs, which are incubated by both parent birds.

RED-BILLED TOUCAN

SCIENTIFIC NAME:	*Ramphastos tucanus*
FAMILY:	Ramphastidae
LENGTH:	55cm (22in)
HABITAT:	Rainforest, often close to water
DISTRIBUTION:	Parts of Colombia and Venezuela to northern Brazil
IDENTIFICATION:	Fairly large toucan, black overall with a white bib, yellow rump, and bare blue skin around the eye. The massive bill is predominantly red along the sides, with black, yellow, and blue markings

The Red-billed Toucan is a fairly large species, and like other toucans it has a somewhat undulating flight, usually gliding, interspersed with brief wingbeats in order to gain height. Amongst the branches of the rainforest canopy, however, it tends to appear more agile, hopping around whilst it forages for food. It feeds mainly on fruit, but also eats insects, birds' eggs, nestlings, and other small vertebrates such as lizards. It usually feeds by taking food in the tip of its bill and tossing it back into the mouth with its head thrown back. Perhaps somewhat surprisingly, toucans have very long, slender tongues, which may reach almost the full length of the bill, and which are often notched. It is generally thought that this might aid the toucan in manipulating its food. Larger items of food are often held in one foot and broken into smaller pieces with the bill. The Red-billed Toucan nests in a natural hollow in a tree, or in a woodpecker hole, producing a clutch of two to four eggs, which are incubated by both parent birds.

GREAT SPOTTED WOODPECKER ▼

SCIENTIFIC NAME:	*Dendrocopos major*
FAMILY:	Picidae
LENGTH:	23cm (9in)
HABITAT:	Woodland, parks, and backyards
DISTRIBUTION:	Throughout Europe and northern Asia, also parts of northwest Africa
IDENTIFICATION:	Black and white plumage, with white shoulders, cheeks, neck, breast and spotted wings. Lower belly and rump is red, and male has red patch on nape

The Great Spotted Woodpecker is the commonest and most widely distributed of the black and white woodpeckers, and certainly the commonest in Britain, although it is absent from northern Scotland and also Ireland. It forages in a variety of wooded habitats, working its way up the vertical surfaces of trees, tapping and probing at the bark to locate insects and their larvae, which are extracted with its long, sticky tongue. When insect prey is scarce, it will also feed on acorns, berries, and nuts. As with most woodpeckers, during the breeding season this species announces its presence with loud drumming, created by repeatedly tapping its bill against a tree, also making display flights to attract a mate. Following mating, a cavity is excavated in a dead or decaying tree, and a nesting chamber hollowed out. The Great Spotted Woodpecker usually makes a new hole each year, although it will often use the same tree more than once. A clutch of four to seven eggs will be laid, to be incubated by both parent birds. The chicks hatch after about two weeks, and fledge around three weeks later.

EURASIAN WRYNECK ▲

SCIENTIFIC NAME:	*Jynx torquilla*
FAMILY:	Picidae
LENGTH:	17cm (7in)
HABITAT:	Open woodland, heaths, and orchards
DISTRIBUTION:	Europe, Asia and North Africa
IDENTIFICATION:	Gray-brown overall, with dark brown and buff mottling and barring

The Eurasian Wryneck belongs to a small subfamily of woodpeckers, Jynginae, or wrynecks, which take their common name from the snake-like manner in which they are able to move their necks, a characteristic used in defensive posturing toward potential predators. These displays are also combined with hissing and the raising of feathers on the crown. Like woodpeckers, the Eurasian Wryneck has a large head, long tongue, and feet characterized by two toes facing forwards and two backwards, but its bill is shorter and it lacks the stiff tail which enables woodpeckers to brace themselves against tree trunks. For this reason, wrynecks do not climb vertical trunks or branches, are more often seen perching, and will also feed on the ground. The Eurasian Wryneck feeds almost exclusively on ants. During the breeding season, this bird does not make its own holes for nesting, but will make use of abandoned woodpecker holes, or natural cavities in trees and walls. An average clutch consists of seven to ten eggs, which are incubated for about two weeks, with the young fledging up to three weeks later.

(European) Green Woodpecker

Scientific name:	*Picus viridis*
Family:	Picidae
Length:	33cm (13in)
Habitat:	Open woodland, orchards, parks, and farmland
Distribution:	From Britain, throughout much of Europe to southwest Asia
Identification:	Dark green above, yellow-green below, with crimson crown and nape, black around eyes and black mustache, center of which is red in male. Primaries barred black and white

The Green Woodpecker is a fairly large species. It is found in a variety of mainly open habitats, and may be inconspicuous on account of its green plumage, although its red markings can betray its whereabouts on an exposed tree. However, its presence is most likely to be betrayed by its loud, somewhat laughing call, or seen in characteristic undulating flight as it crosses an open area. It climbs tree trunks whilst foraging, in much the same way as other woodpeckers, but it also spends a great deal of time feeding on the ground, often some distance from trees, where it will break open ant nests, ants being a particularly favored food. Whilst this species will drum upon wood with its bill during the breeding season in late April or early May, it does not use this call as frequently as many woodpeckers. Following mating, it makes a large nest hole in a hollow tree, sometimes quite close to the ground. Here the female produces a clutch of five to seven eggs, which are laid upon the bare wood chips, to be incubated for around 18 days. Following hatching, the young fledge at around three weeks of age, but will usually not stray great distances from the nest site.

Yellow-bellied Sapsucker

Scientific name:	*Sphyrapicus varius*
Family:	Picidae
Length:	21cm (8in)
Habitat:	Deciduous and coniferous forests and woodland
Distribution:	Much of North America, but largely absent from western US. Winters south to Central America and the Caribbean
Identification:	Black back and wings with white bars, black head with white stripes, red forehead and crown, yellowish upper belly and breast with black patch, white lower belly and rump, and a black tail with a white central stripe. Throat red in male, white in female

As its name suggests, the Yellow-bellied Sapsucker specializes in feeding on tree sap, which it extracts by means of making a series of holes in a suitable tree with its bill, and waiting for the sap to emerge. However it also feeds on insects which are attracted to the sap, and will supplement its diet with fruit. This species is the only North American woodpecker that is entirely migratory, probably due to a dependence on sap, which can be found in most of its range only during the breeding season in spring and summer. As with most woodpeckers, it performs rapid bill-drumming against hollow trees to advertise its presence at this time, but will also drum against man-made structures such as road signs. When nesting it also produces a rather cat-like call. It nests in cavities in trees, which it excavates itself, where a clutch of up to seven eggs will be incubated for around two weeks. Following the breeding season, it migrates south, being found from the southeastern US as far as the Caribbean and Panama, with females tending to migrate farther than males.

Hairy Woodpecker ▲

SCIENTIFIC NAME:	*Picoides villosus*
FAMILY:	Picidae
LENGTH:	23cm (9in)
HABITAT:	Dense forest, open woodland, farmland, parks, and yards
DISTRIBUTION:	Most of North America, south to parts of Central America
IDENTIFICATION:	Black above, but with a white back, wing spots, and bar above and below eyes. White below. Male has red patch on back of head

The Hairy Woodpecker is North America's most widespread woodpecker, being found across Canada and the US in a variety of habitats, being absent from only the harshest, cold, arid, and treeless areas. It is probably also the most familiar, for whilst it is perhaps less bold than some species, it will readily feed at bird tables and feeders when other food is more scarce. It will usually forage on trees, gleaning insects from bark and foliage, or extracting them from cavities with its long bill and tongue. Additionally it will consume fruit, nuts, berries, and also sap from trees. During the breeding season, particularly, this species produces a loud and fast drumming on tree trunks to proclaim its territory, also emitting sharp call notes and rattling cries. It nests in unlined tree cavities, which are excavated by both birds in a pair, where a clutch of up to seven eggs will be incubated for around two weeks. The Hairy Woodpecker is generally a resident species, although individuals in the far north may move southwards in winter, and birds at high elevations may move to lower-lying woodland. There is considerable variation in Hairy Woodpeckers across their range, with around 18 subspecies having been currently identified.

Northern Flicker ▼

SCIENTIFIC NAME:	*Colaptes auratus*
FAMILY:	Picidae
LENGTH:	30cm (12in)
HABITAT:	Forest edges, open woodlands, and suburbs
DISTRIBUTION:	Throughout North America, south to Central America
IDENTIFICATION:	Brown above, with black bars on the back and wings, underside buff with black spots, white rump, and black crescent at base of throat. Male also has black mustache. Underwings red in western birds, yellow in eastern

A common woodpecker throughout North America, the Northern Flicker occurs in two color forms, a yellow-shafted form, which is common across the eastern and northern parts of North America, and a red-shafted form, found in the west. These were formerly considered to be separate species, but it is now widely accepted that they are one and the same, and they hybridize where their ranges overlap. Like other woodpeckers this species may be seen climbing vertically up tree trunks, excavating and gleaning insects and their larvae, but it has a somewhat more upright posture, and tends to perch more often. It also spends a great deal of time on the ground, foraging for seeds, fruit, and insects, with ants being a favorite food. During the breeding season, it excavates a hole in a tree, where up to 12 eggs are incubated for around two weeks. Following nesting, many individuals migrate southward, particularly those found farthest north.

PASSERINES

LONG-TAILED BROADBILL

SCIENTIFIC NAME:	*Psarisomus dalhousiae*
FAMILY:	Eurylaimidae
LENGTH:	25cm (10in)
HABITAT:	Tropical and subtropical forests
DISTRIBUTION:	Eastern Himalayas through southeast Asia to Borneo and Sumatra
IDENTIFICATION:	Quite small and squat, with a long tail, large head, and short, wide bill. Plumage is green overall, with a black crown, yellowish face and throat, and white collar

The Long-tailed Broadbill is the most widely distributed of the broadbills, but its populations are rather scattered across its range. Unlike most members of its family, which are solitary, this species is a highly sociable bird, particularly outside of the breeding season, when it may be observed moving around its forest habitats in small flocks. Interestingly, broadbills have very primitive vocal organs, but they are nevertheless noisy birds, and the Long-tailed Broadbill may be identified by its particularly shrill call. As their name would suggest, these birds have a wide bill, which when opened reveals a huge gape, much like that of a frogmouth, enabling them to consume large insects, which may be either taken on the wing, or foraged for high amongst the branches of trees. During the breeding season, the Long-tailed Broadbill constructs a large, pear-shaped nest from twigs and grasses, which it suspends from a branch or vine. Both parents participate in building the nest, and subsequently in incubating their clutch of two to three eggs and in feeding the young.

(LESSER) GREEN BROADBILL

SCIENTIFIC NAME:	*Calyptomena viridis*
FAMILY:	Eurylaimidae
LENGTH:	20cm (8in)
HABITAT:	Tropical and subtropical forests
DISTRIBUTION:	Found across southeast Asia, from Thailand to Papua New Guinea
IDENTIFICATION:	Green overall, with black wing bars, wingtips and small cheek patch. Wide bill is largely concealed by crest at the front of head. Tail is short

Like most members of the broadbill family, the Green Broadbill has quite vivid plumage, but it tends to remain camouflaged in the half light of the dense rainforests it inhabits, as it forages for food in the lower branches. This species occasionally eats insects, but feeds primarily on soft fruits such as figs, and other vegetation, playing an important role in the ecosystem of the forest by disseminating seeds in its droppings. Although there are some fears for the future of this bird due to habitat destruction, it is also found in secondary woodland, where trees have regrown following forest clearance, implying that it may not be immediately threatened. During the breeding season, the Green Broadbill produces a clutch of one to three eggs, which are incubated by both parent birds. The nest is an elaborate, pear-shaped construction made of vegetation, which is suspended from a slender branch.

RED-BILLED SCYTHEBILL

SCIENTIFIC NAME:	*Campylorhamphus trochilirostris*
FAMILY:	Dendrocolaptidae
LENGTH:	28cm (11in)
HABITAT:	Tropical forests and swamps
DISTRIBUTION:	Much of South America, except Chile, Uruguay, and southern Argentina
IDENTIFICATION:	Slender, with a very long, downward-curving bill. Plumage is reddish-brown overall; head, neck, and underside speckled lighter brown

The Red-billed Scythebill is the most widespread and common of the scythebills, and is a member of the woodcreeper family, a group of birds with strong grasping feet and stiff tails, which climb well on tree trunks, in much the same way as woodpeckers. This species is aptly named due to its elongated, curving bill, which may account for up to a fourth of its length. It uses this to probe amongst loose bark, flowers and other vegetation as it forages for its insect prey. It is relatively sociable, and is frequently observed feeding in mixed-species flocks, no doubt benefiting from being able to reach food that other birds cannot. During the breeding season it nests in broken stumps or other tree cavities, where it makes a cup-shaped nest, lined with moss, leaves, and other soft plant material. The female generally produces a clutch of two eggs, which are incubated for about two weeks.

OCELLATED ANTBIRD

SCIENTIFIC NAME:	*Phaenostictus mcleannani*
FAMILY:	Thamnophilidae/Formicariidae
LENGTH:	20cm (8in)
HABITAT:	Rainforest
DISTRIBUTION:	Found in southern parts of Central America, Colombia, and Ecuador
IDENTIFICATION:	A fairly large antbird, reddish-brown back and wings with dark eye-spots, olive-brown crown, darker tail feathers and a patch of bare, blue skin around the eye. Black throat and collar, nape and underside orange-red

With its ocellated plumage, this species is quite a striking bird, but it may be easily overlooked amongst the dense undergrowth of its preferred habitats. It is also a fairly large antbird, and as such, it tends to dominate smaller species by securing the best feeding positions when following columns of army ants, typically being found at the front of the swarm, or amongst the lowest branches where it can most easily prey on the small animals that the ants disturb. It feeds on various insects and other invertebrates, but also preys on small vertebrates such as reptiles and amphibians.

GREAT ANTSHRIKE ▲

SCIENTIFIC NAME:	*Taraba major*
FAMILY:	Thamnophilidae/Formicariidae
LENGTH:	20cm (8in)
HABITAT:	Rainforest, particularly secondary growth
DISTRIBUTION:	From Mexico to southern Argentina
IDENTIFICATION:	Stout, with a large head, heavy, hooked bill, and red eyes. Male black above, with a black crest, white markings on the tail and wings, and a white underside. The female is brown above, buff below, and lacks crest

Like most antshrikes, this species is usually found close to the rainforest floor, foraging through thickets and amongst dense undergrowth for its prey. It feeds on both terrestrial and flying insects, and a number of other invertebrates, but will also consume much larger animals, including vertebrates such as frogs and small lizards, seizing and killing them with its heavy, hooked bill. Despite its name, it does not normally forage for ants; instead, as with many species of antbird, it will follow columns of army ants to prey upon the creatures that flee their path. During the breeding season, both members of a pair construct a cup-shaped nest of vegetation, which is usually attached to a branch by its rim. An average clutch consists of two eggs, which are incubated by both parent birds for around two weeks. During the day, a pair will incubate the eggs in turn for short periods, with the female incubating them alone at night.

FASCIATED ANTSHRIKE

SCIENTIFIC NAME:	*Cymbilaimus lineatus*
FAMILY:	Thamnophilidae/Formicariidae
LENGTH:	17cm (7in)
HABITAT:	Rainforest
DISTRIBUTION:	Central America, and northern parts of South America
IDENTIFICATION:	Stout, with a large head, heavy, hooked bill, and red eyes. Male is black above with fine white barring, finely barred black and white below. Female is similarly barred with brown and buff

The Fasciated Antshrike does not habitually feed upon ants, but like other antbirds, it may follow columns of army ants as they move along the rainforest floor, preying on insects and other small creatures that attempt to escape from the advancing swarm. At other times, however, this bird feeds much higher amongst the trees, and it is usually found at forest edges, in clearings or along watercourses, preying on flying insects, such as moths and beetles, which are caught on the wing. The Fasciated Antshrike is thought to pair for life, and during the breeding season the male often initiates courtship and simultaneously reaffirms the pair bond by offering items of food to his mate. The breeding pair will then construct a nest together, making a cup-shaped structure in the fork of a tree or bush. A typical clutch consists of two eggs, which are incubated by both parent birds.

VERMILION FLYCATCHER ▼

SCIENTIFIC NAME:	*Pyrocephalus rubinus*
FAMILY:	Tyrannidae
LENGTH:	15cm (6in)
HABITAT:	Open woodland in arid areas, but often close to ponds or streams
DISTRIBUTION:	Southern US, Central and South America, rarely farther north as far as easternmost Canada
IDENTIFICATION:	Male has vermilion head, chest, and underparts, with a brown-black mask, wings, tail, and back. Female is gray-brown above, with whitish brow and forehead, white breast lightly colored with brown, black tail, and a pale pink belly

The Vermilion Flycatcher is probably the most distinctive of the tyrant flycatchers on account of its vivid plumage, and it tends to remain perched on an exposed branch for long periods, making short flights in order to catch passing insect prey. During the breeding season, the male will spend almost all his time perching, but will make noisy display flights over the treetops in order to gain the female's attention, and bring gifts of food to the female prior to mating. Following mating, the female will produce a clutch of two to four eggs in a loose, cup-shaped nest of twigs and grasses, lined with animal hair and feathers, placed in the fork of a tree. The eggs are incubated solely by the female for about two weeks, during which time the male will defend the nest aggressively. Once the eggs have hatched, both parent birds will care for their young. There are some twelve recognized subspecies of Vermilion Flycatcher, some birds in South America having almost entirely dark plumage, with only a few red feathers around the head or under the tail.

ROYAL FLYCATCHER

SCIENTIFIC NAME:	*Onychorhynchus coronatus*
FAMILY:	Tyrannidae
LENGTH:	16cm (6in)
HABITAT:	Rainforest and subtropical open woodland
DISTRIBUTION:	From Mexico south to northern parts of South America
IDENTIFICATION:	Orange-brown to cinnamon overall, with erectable fan-like crest, which is yellow in females, red in males, with blue edge and black spots. Bill tip is hooked

The Royal Flycatcher is a small, seemingly rather nondescript bird, which tends to remain inconspicuous for much of the time, spending long periods remaining motionless amongst foliage in the middle to lower levels of tropical and subtropical forests in wait for passing insects, before darting from its perch to catch them on the wing. However, both males and females possess a spectacular fan-like crest which is normally folded flat on the head, but may be erected when the bird is excited. It also has long bristles on either side of its bill which may help it to catch insects, but possibly also serve as protection for its eyes while hunting. The Royal Flycatcher tends not to be very sociable, usually staying alone or in pairs. During the breeding season, this species nests in an elongated, sac-like nest which it suspends from a branch, often overhanging water.

FORK-TAILED FLYCATCHER

SCIENTIFIC NAME:	*Tyrannus savana*
FAMILY:	Tyrannidae
LENGTH:	23cm (9in)
HABITAT:	Open grassland and scrub
DISTRIBUTION:	South and Central America, straying to the US and central and eastern Canada
IDENTIFICATION:	Black head with yellow stripe on crown, gray back, and white underparts. Tail is extremely long and forked, sometimes longer in males

Although typically a bird of tropical and subtropical South America, the Fork-tailed Flycatcher is regularly also found in eastern North America, probably straying when migrating northward in South America following the breeding season, when it may often be encountered perching on fences and telephone wires. During the winter it often associates in huge flocks, particularly when roosting and foraging. It feeds mainly on flying insects, darting from perches to catch them on the wing, although it also consumes berries and other fruit. During the breeding season, the Fork-tailed Flycatcher constructs a cup-shaped nest of twigs and grasses, in which two to five eggs are normally laid. These are incubated by the female for around two weeks, with both parent birds caring for the young following hatching.

WESTERN WOOD-PEWEE

SCIENTIFIC NAME:	*Contopus sordidulus*
FAMILY:	Tyrannidae
LENGTH:	16cm (6in)
HABITAT:	Open woodland, parks, orchards, and mountain forests
DISTRIBUTION:	Western Canada and North America, Central America, wintering south to western parts of South America
IDENTIFICATION:	A medium sized flycatcher, olive-brown above with whitish wing bars, pale gray below, with darker wash on breast and flanks.

An inconspicuous species in terms of appearance, this bird characteristically advertises its location with a harsh and persistent call of "pee-eer." It generally perches in an upright position, watching for passing insects, which it catches on the wing or plucks from foliage, before returning to its vantage point to eat its meal. Favored prey includes moths, flies, and mosquitoes, but this species has also been known to feed on berries, particularly in colder months when insects may be scarce. During the breeding season, the Western Wood-Pewee constructs a fairly shallow cup- or saucer-shaped nest of grass, moss, and lichens on a horizontal branch, where the female produces a clutch of three to four eggs, which are incubated solely by the female for around two weeks. This species and the Eastern Wood-Pewee (*Contopus virens*) are almost identical in appearance and were once thought to be the same species. However, it has subsequently been proved otherwise, and there is no evidence that they interbreed where their ranges overlap.

BLACK PHOEBE ▲

SCIENTIFIC NAME:	*Sayornis nigricans*
FAMILY:	Tyrannidae
LENGTH:	16cm (6in)
HABITAT:	Open areas near water, agricultural areas, streams, lakes, and along cliffs. Often found near buildings.
DISTRIBUTION:	Southwestern North America through Central America to Bolivia and northwestern Argentina
IDENTIFICATION:	Small songbird, black above and below, with a white belly and undertail. White on belly extends onto chest in an inverted V-shape

Like the Eastern Phoebe, the Black Phoebe can often be found near water, wagging its tail whilst hunting for insects. However, this species also occasionally catches very small fish in the shallows of ponds and streams and may even feed fish to its young. The nest is almost always positioned near water, and consists of an open cup formed with mud and dry vegetation, often cemented to the wall of a building or bridge with mud, although it is sometimes placed amongst roots at the top of a bank. The male will direct the female to potential nesting sites, but she will take the sole responsibility for nest construction. The clutch consists of around two to six eggs, which are incubated for between two and three weeks. A second brood will force the nestlings into independence about three weeks later. Outside of the breeding season, the Black Phoebe is solitary and territorial, often remaining in its established area throughout the year, although nonbreeding juveniles may wander farther afield.

EASTERN KINGBIRD ▼

SCIENTIFIC NAME:	*Tyrannus tyrannus*
FAMILY:	Tyrannidae
LENGTH:	21cm (8in)
HABITAT:	Forest edges, woodland clearings, and farmland, often close to water
DISTRIBUTION:	Found across much of North America, wintering south as far as Argentina
IDENTIFICATION:	Large flycatcher, with a black head, gray back and wings, and pale gray chest band. Also has reddish crown feathers, usually concealed by short dark crest

A large and conspicuous flycatcher, the Eastern Kingbird is amongst the most familiar of its family, also being particularly widespread. It is found throughout much of North America during the breeding season, at which time it is highly aggressive and territorial. In addition to attacking members of its own species, it will drive much larger birds from its nest sites, including crows, herons, and large birds of prey, relentlessly pecking at them in flight. It builds a large, bulky nest of twigs, grass, and straw, lined with plant material and animal hair, which it places in the fork of a branch, on a horizontal tree limb or sometimes on a fence post. The female lays between two and five eggs, which are then incubated for two to three weeks. Following hatching, the young will be fed by their parents for about seven weeks. The Eastern Kingbird typically hunts for flying insects from a perch, but it will also eat seeds and berries, particularly as winter approaches. At this time of year, it becomes more sociable, gathering in large flocks to migrate.

GREAT KISKADEE

SCIENTIFIC NAME:	*Pitangus sulphuratus*
FAMILY:	Tyrannidae
LENGTH:	23cm (9in)
HABITAT:	Fairly open country, often near water
DISTRIBUTION:	From the southern US, through Central America, south to northern Argentina
IDENTIFICATION:	Large flycatcher, brown above, with a black and white striped head, inconspicuous yellow crown patch, white throat, and yellow underside

The Great Kiskadee is amongst the largest and most common of the tyrant flycatchers throughout much of its range, and it is a conspicuous bird, with its bright yellow underside and loud "kis-ka-dee" call. Like other flycatchers it feeds on flying insects such as beetles, flies, and wasps, but being large, with a powerful bill, it also preys on vertebrates, including lizards, frogs, small rodents, and nestlings. Additionally, at times the Great Kiskadee hunts for fish, diving from a waterside perch, and when other food is scarce, it will consume seeds and fruit. This species is usually found in pairs, and is often highly aggressive to other birds, particularly during the breeding season, which usually begins in March. At this time, the Great Kiskadee constructs a bulky, domed nest of plant stems and moss high in a tree, where the female will lay two to five eggs.

STRIPED MANAKIN ▲

SCIENTIFIC NAME:	*Machaeropterus regulus*
FAMILY:	Pipridae
LENGTH:	10cm (4in)
HABITAT:	Rainforest and secondary woodland
DISTRIBUTION:	Found in the northern parts of South America
IDENTIFICATION:	Very small, with olive-brown upperparts and red and white striped underside. Male has scarlet crown

A small bird, this species is somewhat less conspicuous than many of its close relatives. This is partly on account of its size, but also due to the fact that it is rather less brightly colored than other manakins. However, during the breeding season, large groups of males congregate in clearings in order to perform courtship dances to attract a mate. Little is known about the nesting habits of this species, but it is thought that following mating, the female constructs the nest, incubates her eggs, and rears the chicks alone. The nest itself takes the form of a small cup or hammock-like construction of woven vegetation, positioned in the fork of a tree or bush, or suspended between two branches. A typical clutch consists of one or two eggs, which are likely to be incubated for two to three weeks, with the young leaving the nest around two weeks after hatching. The Striped Manakin usually inhabits the lower levels of tropical forests, where it forages for small insects, seeds and berries.

SWALLOW-TAILED MANAKIN

SCIENTIFIC NAME:	*Chiroxiphia caudata*
FAMILY:	Pipridae
LENGTH:	15cm (6in)
HABITAT:	Rainforest and secondary woodland
DISTRIBUTION:	Eastern parts of South America
IDENTIFICATION:	Male is blue overall, with mainly black wings, a black head, bright red crown, and long blue tail feathers. Female is dull green, darker on wing edges and paler on belly, with an olive throat and breast

The Swallow-tailed Manakin gets its name from its forked central tail feathers, and is a fairly common species, found in the tropical and subtropical forests of Brazil, Paraguay, and Argentina. During the breeding season, up to 50 males may gather at a communal display site, or lek, in order to perform their courtship dances and attempt to attract a mate. Each bird will select a small area in a clearing where it will take up position amongst the lower branches of surrounding trees or bushes to await its turn to display to a female. During the display the males will leap from the ground, calling and making whirring sounds with their wings. The female will select a male, and following mating will take sole responsibility for constructing the nest, incubating her eggs, and rearing the chicks. The nest takes the form of a finely woven cup, usually positioned in branches overhanging water, where two eggs are laid. The Swallow-tailed Manakin feeds on insects, berries, and other small fruits.

WIRE-TAILED MANAKIN

SCIENTIFIC NAME:	*Pipra filicauda*
FAMILY:	Pipridae
LENGTH:	13cm (5in)
HABITAT:	Rainforest and secondary woodland, often near water
DISTRIBUTION:	Peru, Ecuador, Colombia, Venezuela, and Brazil
IDENTIFICATION:	Male has black upper plumage, red crown, yellow face and underparts, long, wiry black tail feathers. Iris is white. Female is green, darker on the wings and tail tip, with a yellow belly

Although the adult male of this species is quite striking in appearance, with the brightly colored plumage of its head and underside and its long, wiry tail feathers, it is a rather uncommon bird, and may be hard to spot amongst the dense vegetation of its preferred habitat. The

Wire-tailed Manakin may be found in reasonably open forest and forest edges, but usually inhabits the thick undergrowth close to the forest floor. At times it also occurs high in the rainforest canopy, particularly when trees are bearing fruit. It feeds on a variety of fruit, but like other manakins it is omnivorous, also consuming insects. This bird is at its most conspicuous during the breeding season, when large groups of males may congregate at leks, or communal display sites, in order to attract a mate by performing courtship dances. Individuals are typically quite widely spaced, with each male selecting a number of display perches in the lower branches of a tree or bush. The display itself consists of jumps, short flights, the ruffling of feathers, and raising of the tail filaments.

Bare-throated Bellbird

Scientific name:	*Procnias nudicollis*
Family:	Cotingidae
Length:	26cm (10in)
Habitat:	Mountainous tropical forests
Distribution:	Eastern parts of South America
Identification:	Male has entirely white plumage, with bare blue skin on face and throat. Female is dull green above, with a darker head, and underparts streaked yellow

The Bare-throated Bellbird occurs from eastern Brazil into adjacent parts of Paraguay and northern Argentina, where it inhabits montane rainforest during the breeding season, moving to lower altitudes for the winter. It is rarely observed, being rather sedentary, and usually living high in the forest canopy. However, as its name might suggest, it emits a highly distinctive, metallic, bell-like call, which is in fact amongst the loudest produced by any bird. The females are usually silent, whilst the males are most vocal during the breeding season, calling to attract a mate. This is usually performed from an exposed position, with the head thrown back and the bill wide open. Once a female is in the vicinity of a male, he will often continue his display by hopping from perch to perch, with tail feathers spread. Following mating, the females nest alone in a cup-shaped nest placed in the fork of a tree, where a single egg is incubated.

ANDEAN/SCARLET COCK-OF-THE ROCK ▼

SCIENTIFIC NAME:	*Rupicola peruviana*
FAMILY:	Cotingidae
LENGTH:	30cm (12in)
HABITAT:	Forest and wooded gorges, often by streams
DISTRIBUTION:	Colombia, Ecuador, Venezuela, Bolivia, and Peru
IDENTIFICATION:	Male is bright red overall, with black wings and tail, enlarged pale gray wing coverts, and an arcing crest from the back of the head to the bill. Female is duller, reddish-brown with smaller crest

The Andean or Scarlet Cock-of-the-Rock is found in the mountainous subtropical forests of eastern South America, often close to rocky outcrops and upland streams, where it forages for fruit, insects, and, at times, small vertebrates. The females are quite dull, and may be more easily overlooked, but the male of this species has stunning scarlet plumage, and may be highly visible, particularly during the breeding season, when males gather at leks, or communal courtship sites, in numbers of up to 50 individuals. Here they display on exposed branches or rocks, calling loudly and fanning their crests to attract females. Following mating, the female constructs a nest of mud, which is secured to a cliff face or cave, where she will incubate two eggs alone. However, females may sometimes nest quite closely together at suitable sites. The major threat to this species comes from encroachment upon its habitat, but on account of their plumage, the males are particularly vulnerable to predation from birds of prey and snakes.

PURPLE-THROATED FRUITCROW

SCIENTIFIC NAME:	*Querula purpurata*
FAMILY:	Cotingidae
LENGTH:	28cm (11in)
HABITAT:	Rainforest
DISTRIBUTION:	Costa Rica, Panama, and northern parts of South America
IDENTIFICATION:	Black overall, with long, rounded wings, and a broad bill. Adult male has purple throat ruff

Despite its name, the Purple-throated Fruitcrow is not closely related to true crows, but is a member of the cotinga family, a fairly primitive group of perching birds, in which many of the males bear ornate or brightly colored plumage. In the case of this species, both males and females are almost completely black, but the male has a red or purplish ruff on its throat which may be raised for the purposes of courtship display. These birds are found in tropical and subtropical forests, where they typically dwell amongst the upper levels, high in the branches, which may make them difficult to observe. Of the cotingas, the Purple-throated Fruitcrow is probably the most sociable, living in small family groups, and sometimes also associating with mixed-species flocks, particularly when foraging for food. As its name suggests, this bird is mainly frugivorous, that is, a fruit eater, but it also consumes insects. During the breeding season, the female produces one egg, which is laid in a cup-shaped nest high in a tree. Although the female is the sole incubator, the rest of the group will help to raise the young.

INDIAN PITTA

SCIENTIFIC NAME:	*Pitta brachyura*
FAMILY:	Pittidae
LENGTH:	20cm (8in)
HABITAT:	Tropical and subtropical forests, and scrub
DISTRIBUTION:	Indian subcontinent, with some birds wintering in Sri Lanka
IDENTIFICATION:	Squat, with a large head, eyes, and bill. Plumage is green above, with blue wing patches, black and white head, and orange-yellow underparts

As with other Pittas, the Indian Pitta is a ground dwelling bird, which runs and hops quickly amongst the undergrowth of its wooded or scrubland habitat, and although it prefers to move along the ground, it both roosts in and calls from the branches of trees. It also flies well, and some northern populations will migrate as far south as southern India and Sri Lanka. It forages amongst leaf-litter, where it searches for fruit, seeds, insects, other invertebrates, and small vertebrates, using its strong bill to overturn debris or to dig in the ground. It will also hold snails in its bill, smashing them against logs or stones in order to extract them from their shells. During the breeding season, the Indian Pitta constructs a large, ball-shaped nest from twigs and other vegetation, which it lines with moss. The nest is usually located in a bush close to the ground, but may be positioned in a similarly sheltered spot, such as amongst logs, tree roots, or rocks. An average clutch consists of around three eggs.

GIANT PITTA ▼

SCIENTIFIC NAME:	*Pitta caerulea*
FAMILY:	Pittidae
LENGTH:	30cm (12in)
HABITAT:	Rainforests and secondary woodland
DISTRIBUTION:	Malay Peninsula, Sumatra, and Borneo
IDENTIFICATION:	A large pitta, stocky, with a large head and short tail. Mail is blue above and on tail, buff below, with a dark stripe along the crown and through the eyes. Female has brown back and wings

As its name might suggest, the Giant Pitta is the world's largest pitta, but like its close relatives, it is a somewhat shy and elusive bird, which may be more often heard than seen. It produces a trilling whistle, often from a perch, most commonly at dusk or on moonlit nights. This bird is usually found alone or in pairs, and is territorial, with calls often being answered by birds in adjacent territories. It normally inhabits lowland forests with quite dense vegetation, where it spends most of its time on the ground amongst the undergrowth. It forages in leaf-litter, searching for invertebrates such as worms, snails, insects, and spiders, also consuming small lizards and snakes. During the breeding season, the Giant Pitta constructs a round nest of twigs and roots, lined with moss, where the female generally produces a clutch of two eggs. The nest may be placed in a bush, amongst logs, tree roots, or rocks.

BANDED PITTA ▲

SCIENTIFIC NAME:	*Pitta guajana*
FAMILY:	Pittidae
LENGTH:	23cm (9in)
HABITAT:	Rainforests and secondary woodland
DISTRIBUTION:	Found in southeast Asia, from Thailand to Papua New Guinea
IDENTIFICATION:	Plump, brown above with white wing bar, yellow and black barred underside, short blue tail, white throat, yellow head with black crown and broad eye-stripes. Female duller than male

Usually occurring alone or in pairs, the Banded Pitta is quite a shy bird, and may be more commonly heard, emitting its whistling call, than seen. However, it is sometimes observed dashing across a path or clearing as it forages for food. It is a ground dwelling species, and will often run from danger rather than take flight. It favors shady forests where it moves along the ground or over dead logs, overturning leaves and other debris, sometimes also probing the soil with its bill in order to find its prey. It consumes insects, other invertebrates including spiders and snails, and some small vertebrates such as lizards. It is sometimes also found in the lower branches of bushes and trees, and tends to roost above the ground. During the breeding season, the Banded Pitta creates a globular nest of small sticks, which it places in a bush or amongst tree roots, where two eggs are usually laid.

SUNBIRD-ASITY

SCIENTIFIC NAME:	*Neodrepanis coruscans*
FAMILY:	Philepittidae
LENGTH:	10cm (4in)
HABITAT:	Dense rainforest
DISTRIBUTION:	Eastern Madagascar
IDENTIFICATION:	Very small bird with decurved bill. Breeding male has yellow underparts, iridescent blue upperparts and a blue-green wattle around the eye. Female is olive-green with mottled white and green or yellowish underparts

This tiny bird is also sometimes known as the Wattled False Sunbird, on account of the eye-wattles of the male, which are most prominent during the breeding season. The male also undergoes two molts each year, developing iridescent blue upper plumage when breeding, being much duller and more similar to the female for much of the year. Sunbird Asities construct untidy globular or pear-shaped nests, which are suspended from the tips of branches, and it is thought that only the female constructs the nest, building a hollow sphere before making an entrance hole in the side. Here she produces a clutch of three somewhat elongated eggs. This species forages for food at all levels of the forest, feeding on nectar, using its long decurved bill to probe within flowers, and also consuming insects such as termites.

◀RIFLEMAN

SCIENTIFIC NAME:	*Acanthisitta chloris*
FAMILY:	Acanthisittidae
LENGTH:	8cm (3in)
HABITAT:	Forest
DISTRIBUTION:	New Zealand
IDENTIFICATION:	Very small, golden-brown upper plumage, with black patches on its short, rounded wings. It has a broad head, white eyebrow, and white underparts

The Rifleman, or Titipounamu as it is also known, is a member of the New Zealand wren family, of which there is thought to be just one other surviving member, the Rock Wren (*Xenicus gilviventris*). It is a tiny bird, in fact New Zealand's smallest, and it feeds on small insects, probing for them amongst lichen, moss, and bark. The Rifleman forages by spiraling up a tree in short hops before dropping to the base of another with open wings to repeat the process. It is usually found in pairs, which maintain contact with short, high pitched calls. When breeding, this species nests in a cavity in a tree where it makes a small, domed structure of vegetation, often held together with spiders' webs and lined with moss and feathers. The female produces a clutch of around four eggs, and whilst laying the male will provide her with food. The male also performs much of the nest-building and incubation, and following hatching, both parent birds will provide food for their nestlings. Occasionally the chicks from a first brood may also help to feed a second brood.

SUPERB LYREBIRD

SCIENTIFIC NAME:	*Menura novaehollandiae*
FAMILY:	Menuridae
LENGTH:	80–90cm (32–35in) Male larger than female
HABITAT:	Eucalyptus forests
DISTRIBUTION:	Southeast Australia, including parts of Tasmania
IDENTIFICATION:	Brown upperparts with rufous wings and grayish underparts. Adult male has an ornate tail, with prominent curved feathers that resemble a lyre when raised. Females also have long tails, but lack the specialized feathers

Although not closely related, the Superb Lyrebird somewhat resembles a pheasant, with its long legs and tail, slender body and small head. It is a ground dwelling species, which inhabits damp eucalyptus forests, and it tends to be solitary, although females and their young may forage together. It searches for food by scratching in leaf-litter and soil with its feet, feeding on insects, spiders, worms, and other invertebrates, sometimes also consuming seeds. The Superb Lyrebird breeds from April to October, during which time the male secures a territory in which he constructs a mound of debris covered in soil, from where he displays to attract a mate. The display involves a great deal of singing and dancing, with the tail thrown forward over the body and shaken. A male may mate with several females, which will go on to nest alone in large, domed structures, placed amongst vegetation. The female produces one egg that is incubated for around seven weeks. The Superb Lyrebird is well known for its vocalizations, most of which consist of the mimicry of both natural and mechanical sounds. It also emits a series of whistles, cackling notes, and loud shrieks.

(COMMON) SKYLARK

SCIENTIFIC NAME:	*Alauda arvensis*
FAMILY:	Alaudidae
LENGTH:	18cm (7in)
HABITAT:	Open grassland, particularly pasture
DISTRIBUTION:	From western Europe, across Eurasia and also in North Africa
IDENTIFICATION:	Streaked brown and white plumage on head, throat, back, wings, and tail, underparts lighter. Male has small brown crest

Although once far more numerous, the Skylark remains a fairly common and widespread species. It occurs across a variety of open habitats, including farmland, marshes, and moors, favoring areas of relatively short grass or immature crops. It spends much of its time on the ground, but remains well camouflaged on account of its plumage, and its presence is most likely to be announced by its warbling song. This bird may call from the ground, but it is perhaps best known for its aerial vocalizations, usually given at great height, and most frequently at the beginning of the breeding season, which lasts from around April to August. The nest takes the form of a small cup placed in a fairly deep scrape on the ground, usually well concealed by vegetation. The female produces a clutch of three to five eggs that she incubates alone for around 11 days. Both parents feed their young, which leave the nest after about ten days, remaining dependent on their parents for a further week or two, before the adult birds go on to raise further broods. Successful pairs may raise up to four broods in a season. In winter, Skylarks gather in large flocks, particularly on lowland stubble fields. This species feeds on insects, seeds, and other vegetation.

CRESTED LARK

SCIENTIFIC NAME:	*Galerida cristata*
FAMILY:	Alaudidae
LENGTH:	20cm (8in)
HABITAT:	Open woodland, grassland, and agricultural areas
DISTRIBUTION:	North Africa, Europe, and the Middle East to northern India, China, and Korea
IDENTIFICATION:	Quite a stout lark, with streaked brown plumage, orange-buff underwings, and a conspicuous, pointed crest, noticeable even when depressed

The Crested Lark looks much like the skylark, and has similar habits, but it is slightly larger, and may be distinguished by its more pointed crest, which it raises in display. It is a common bird that breeds across most of temperate Eurasia and parts of Africa; however, it is nonmigratory, and its sedentary nature is evidenced by the fact that it is only very rarely found in Britain, although it may breed as close as northern France. The Crested Lark favors dry, open country with low vegetation, but may also be found close to sparsely wooded areas, and although it spends much of its time on the ground, it will sometimes perch in the lower branches of a tree or in a bush. Like other larks, during the breeding season it nests on the ground, laying two to three eggs in a deep cup-shaped nest, located in a hollow. This species forages for food on the ground, and although it eats mainly seeds, it also eats invertebrates such as beetles, particularly during the breeding season. The Crested Lark produces a loud, musical song.

SHORE LARK/HORNED LARK

SCIENTIFIC NAME:	*Eremophila alpestris*
FAMILY:	Alaudidae
LENGTH:	18cm (7in)
HABITAT:	Cultivated land, open grassland, coastal and mountainous regions
DISTRIBUTION:	Breeds in the Arctic, Eurasia, and most of North America, wintering in the south of this range. Also an isolated sedentary population in the Andes
IDENTIFICATION:	Upperparts lightly streaked sandy-colored or gray, white underparts, white or yellow face with thick black eyestripe and throat. Black horn-like tufts present on head when breeding

The Horned Lark is a widely distributed species, and is the only true lark native to North America, the Skylark having been introduced to some areas. It is a common bird of open country, occurring in a range of habitats, despite its name. However, in winter, it is often found in coastal regions in small flocks. It also tends to prefer somewhat more barren, stony ground than the short-grass areas favored by its close relatives. Like other larks, the Horned Lark forages for its food on the ground, feeding primarily on weed and grass seeds, but it also consumes insects, particularly during the breeding season, and will feed them to its young. It nests on the ground, laying two to five eggs in a cup woven of fine grasses, placed in a cavity. The song of this species consists of a series of high pitched, musical notes.

Swallow/Barn Swallow

SCIENTIFIC NAME:	*Hirundo rustica*
FAMILY:	Hirundinidae
LENGTH:	20cm (8in)
HABITAT:	Open country near water
DISTRIBUTION:	Found throughout much of the Northern Hemisphere, moving south in winter
IDENTIFICATION:	Glossy dark blue back, pale underparts, and a red throat. The elongated forked tail feathers have white subterminal markings. Female is duller, with shorter tail feathers and paler underparts

Along with martins, the swallows are quite unlike most birds in appearance and behavior, with the exception of swifts, which, whilst not closely related, have evolved in a similar way. The Swallow, or Barn Swallow as it is known in America, spends much of its time on the wing, and its extraordinary powers of flight, forked tail, and manner of hawking for insects makes it quite distinctive. Its flight, whilst graceful, is marked by seemingly random changes in direction and height. Unlike swifts, which are unable to perch, the Swallow is often seen at rest on telephone wires, and although it is seldom found on the ground, it will land in order to collect nesting material. Both sexes contribute to the building of the nest, using mud, straw, and feathers to create a bowl-shaped structure, which is usually secured to the wall of a building or cave. A typical clutch consists of four to six eggs and incubation is undertaken solely by the female for around 14 or 15 days. Following hatching, the young are cared for by both parents. The chicks are able to fly after about three weeks, and their feeding will largely take place in the air from that day forth. They are highly gregarious birds, often roosting in their hundreds, and are usually found in groups at other times, although less commonly during the breeding season.

TREE SWALLOW

SCIENTIFIC NAME:	*Tachycineta bicolor*
FAMILY:	Hirundinidae
LENGTH:	15cm (6in)
HABITAT:	Grassland and open woodland, usually near water
DISTRIBUTION:	North America, moving south as far as Colombia in the winter
IDENTIFICATION:	Metallic-blue upperparts, white beneath, with a shallow forked tail and broad wings

Like other swallows, the Tree Swallow is mainly an aerial feeder, catching small flying insects on the wing. However, it also feeds on some berries and, interestingly, it is one of the few species of bird that can digest the berries of the wax myrtle plant, another being the Myrtle Warbler, a subspecies of the Yellow-rumped Warbler (*Dendroica coronata*). Generally highly sociable, the Tree Swallow may be found in vast flocks of thousands of individuals, particularly when migrating, but during the breeding season it may become aggressively territorial. This species constructs a cup-shaped nest of vegetation in a hole such as a tree cavity or abandoned woodpecker nest, but it will also make use of nesting boxes. Both males and females construct the nest, where a clutch of four to six eggs is laid, with incubation being performed solely by the female for around 14 or 15 days. Following hatching, the nestlings fledge between 16 and 30 days, after which most will become totally independent of their parents.

HOUSE MARTIN

SCIENTIFIC NAME:	*Delichon urbica*
FAMILY:	Hirundinidae
LENGTH:	12cm (5in)
HABITAT:	Grassland near waterways, parks, and woodland edges, nesting on suburban buildings
DISTRIBUTION:	Much of Eurasia, wintering in Africa, India, and southeast Asia
IDENTIFICATION:	Iridescent blue-black upperparts, white below. Wings are brownish-black and pointed, tail is forked

The House Martin is a strong and agile flier which spends much of its time on the wing, catching its insect prey, over grassland, farmland, and at woodland edges, often close to water. It is a summer visitor to most of its range, including Britain, where it comes to reproduce, typically wintering in Africa, northern India, and some parts of southeast Asia. It is generally a colonial nester, and although some birds continue to nest at cliffs, it has almost entirely adapted to the manmade environment, and now nests under the eaves of suburban houses, building a cup-shaped nest of mud, which it collects at the banks of ponds or lakes. The same nesting sites, and indeed nests, tend to be reused for many years, either by returning adults or their offspring, and an average clutch consists of three to five eggs, which are incubated in turn by both parent birds for around two weeks. Both adults also feed their young, which fledge at about three or four weeks of age. Being such fast and acrobatic fliers, and nesting in sheltered locations, House Martins do not suffer from a great deal of predation; however, they are frequently driven from their nests by House Sparrows, which may have contributed to a decline in their numbers in recent years.

SAND MARTIN

SCIENTIFIC NAME:	*Riparia riparia*
FAMILY:	Hirundinidae
LENGTH:	12cm (5in)
HABITAT:	Grassland, sandy riverbanks, lakeshores, and quarries
DISTRIBUTION:	Across North America, the Middle East, and Eurasia, wintering in Central and South America, parts of India and southeast Asia
IDENTIFICATION:	Small martin, dark gray-brown above, paler below with dark breast bar

The Sand Martins are the smallest members of the martin and swallow family, but are amongst the most widespread, and being powerful and agile fliers, they frequently undertake vast migrations between their wintering and breeding grounds. As its name might suggest, the Sand Martin nests in sandy earth or riverbanks, excavating a burrow with its feet and bill. It tends to be gregarious throughout the year, but particularly during the breeding season, when it nests colonially, often with several hundred pairs utilizing a suitable nesting site. These sites are frequently used year after year, particularly where broods have been raised successfully in the past, but females nesting for the first time will not always return to the site where they were hatched. A clutch may contain up to five eggs, which will be incubated for about two weeks by both parent birds. Sand Martins return quite early to their breeding grounds, usually in April or May, and it is not uncommon for them to produce two broods in a season. Sometimes a female will leave her mate to raise the young alone, going on to mate with another male. This is particularly likely if some nestlings from the first brood have not survived. The Sand Martin may be observed catching its insect prey on the wing, often over water, or be seen at rest, perched on telephone wires.

PURPLE MARTIN ▼

SCIENTIFIC NAME:	*Progne subis*
FAMILY:	Hirundinidae
LENGTH:	20cm (8in)
HABITAT:	Urban, agricultural, and desert areas, also open woodland and rainforests
DISTRIBUTION:	Southern Canada, south to Mexico. Overwinters in eastern South America
IDENTIFICATION:	Large martin. Male is glossy blue-black overall, female is blue-black above with gray collar and underparts

The Purple Martin is the largest member of the martin and swallow family found in North America, and is common in a range of habitats, including urban and suburban areas. In fact, in the east of its range, it now nests almost exclusively in nest boxes, whilst elsewhere it may use natural cavities in trees, large cacti, cliffs, or frequently take over abandoned woodpecker nests. It often nests in colonies, with numbers tending to be greatest where large numbers of nest boxes have been provided, rather than at natural sites. The Purple Martin is monogamous, and paired birds will cooperate in lining a chosen site with mud and vegetation, although the female will undertake the incubation of up to seven eggs alone, for a period of approximately two weeks. Both parent birds will then feed the young for around four weeks until fledging, and continue to feed them for one or two weeks after that. Like its relatives, the Purple Martin is an aerial insectivore, taking all of its prey on the wing. It will also drink in flight, skimming over the surface of a pond or stream to collect water in its bill.

Gray Wagtail

Scientific name:	*Motacilla cinerea*
Family:	Motacillidae
Length:	18cm (7in)
Habitat:	Rocky streams, woodland brooks, marshes, rivers, and ponds
Distribution:	Europe, northern and eastern parts of Africa, and Asia
Identification:	Slate-gray upperparts, sulfur-yellow breast, white outer-tail feathers, and a greenish-yellow rump. Male has a black throat, becoming white in winter, whilst the female is a paler gray above and lacks the black throat

The wagtails are aptly named for their habit of constantly moving their tails up and down, and despite the name of this species, it is actually quite a colorful bird, with yellow underparts. It is almost always found near water, often alongside fast flowing upland waters during the breeding season, but tends to spend the winter months in lowland areas, including marshes, and increasingly along canals, and in parks and yards in urban and suburban locations. Whilst this species is relatively common, in harsh winters its populations can be badly affected. It feeds mainly on small invertebrates, flying from a perch to seize flying insects above the surface of a stream or pond, or probing amongst bankside stones and vegetation. It will also sometimes forage in the shallows, taking small aquatic snails and even tadpoles. During the breeding season, the Gray Wagtail nests in a crevice in a wall, bridge, or bank, constructing a shallow cup-shaped nest, where the female lays four to six eggs. The clutch is incubated solely by the female for up to two weeks, but following hatching, both parent birds care for their young.

MEADOW PIPIT

SCIENTIFIC NAME:	*Anthus pratensis*
FAMILY:	Motacillidae
LENGTH:	15cm (6in)
HABITAT:	Open country, tundra, moorland, farmland, and coastal marshes
DISTRIBUTION:	Present from Greenland through Europe to North Africa and central Asia
IDENTIFICATION:	Small brown bird, with a buff chest streaked with brown, and dark markings on the back and wings

The Meadow Pipit looks much like a small thrush or lark, with its streaked plumage, but it belongs to the same family as the wagtails, and is in fact the smallest pipit species. It prefers quite moist, open habitats, breeding on upland heaths, moors, and also coastal marshes, being more common on farmland and urban fields in winter. During the breeding season, the male makes a distinctive display flight, launching itself almost vertically from a perch, before gliding back down, all the while producing a loud, rising song, which ends in a trill. This species nests on the ground in a cup-shaped nest of grass, usually well concealed amongst vegetation, where the female lays and incubates three to five eggs for around two weeks. Following hatching, both adult birds feed their young on insects, worms, and spiders. The adult birds will also consume seeds. The Meadow Pipit is one of the species whose broods are regularly parasitized by the Common Cuckoo.

PIED WAGTAIL   ▲

SCIENTIFIC NAME:	*Motacilla alba yarrellii*
FAMILY:	Motacillidae
LENGTH:	18cm (7in)
HABITAT:	Riverbanks, lake edges, farmland, coasts, parks, and gardens
DISTRIBUTION:	Most of Eurasia. Moves south to North Africa, India and south-east Asia in winter
IDENTIFICATION:	Male has black crown, throat, breast, and upperparts. Forehead, cheeks and belly white. Female has a gray back and less black on breast and crown

The Pied Wagtail is a common and widespread bird, which is found from Iceland, throughout Europe and Asia, and into North Africa. It occurs in a variety of open habitats, including farmland, meadows, and parks, but displays a distinct preference for areas close to water, where it forages for insects and other invertebrates, wagging its long tail almost incessantly as it darts around on the ground, or whilst perching. It usually breeds from April to August, nesting in holes in buildings, amongst vegetation or rocks, sometimes also using the abandoned nests of other birds, including those of Swallows. Its own nest is usually constructed from twigs, leaves, and grass, lined with feathers and hair. The female produces three to five eggs, which she incubates alone for a period of 11 to 15 days. Following hatching, both parent birds care for their young for some weeks, even after they have fledged at around two weeks old. During the winter months, large flocks of Pied Wagtails may gather to roost communally in trees or on rooftops.

BLACK-FACED CUCKOO-SHRIKE ▲

SCIENTIFIC NAME:	*Coracina novaehollandiae*
FAMILY:	Campephagidae
LENGTH:	33cm (13in)
HABITAT:	Forest and open woodland
DISTRIBUTION:	Most of Australia, with some birds migrating to New Guinea
IDENTIFICATION:	Black face, gray upperparts, slightly paler below. Wingtips are darker gray, and tail is tipped with white

Despite its name, this species is not closely related to either cuckoos or shrikes, but is so-called due to its appearance; possessing a rather cuckoo-like shape, and a powerful, slightly hooked bill, reminiscent of that of a shrike. This bird and others in its family are also sometimes known as "shufflewings," due to their habit of shuffling their wings upon landing. The Black-faced Cuckoo-Shrike is both common and widespread, occurring in most kinds of wooded habitat, although it is normally absent from rainforest areas. It may also be familiar in suburban areas where it is often observed perching on telephone wires or rooftop aerials. Outside of the breeding season, this bird tends to be found in quite large numbers, with some flocks migrating, whilst others are often more nomadic. The Black-faced Cuckoo-Shrike breeds mainly from August to February, at which time a pair will construct a small, saucer-shaped nest of sticks and bark, bound with cobwebs. An average clutch consists of three eggs, and upon hatching, both parents will care for their young birds until they are fledged at around three weeks old. Successful Black-faced Cuckoo-Shrikes may pair with the same partner each year, also repeatedly using the same territories. They feed on insects and other invertebrates, which may be caught on the wing, plucked from foliage or taken on the ground. Additionally, some fruits and seeds are also consumed.

STRAW-HEADED BULBUL ▼

SCIENTIFIC NAME:	*Pycnonotus zeylanicus*
FAMILY:	Pycnonotidae
LENGTH:	28cm (11in)
HABITAT:	Woodland and forest edges
DISTRIBUTION:	Borneo, Sumatra, Java, and the Malay Peninsula
IDENTIFICATION:	Large, pale-headed bulbul with conspicuous black mustache. Crown and ear coverts orange, back, wings, and tail olive-brown, chin and throat white, underparts gray

The Straw-headed Bulbul is the largest of its family, and is quite a common species in much of its range. However, it is a popular cage-bird on account of its melodious, warbling song, and it constantly faces pressure from illegal trapping. It occurs in secondary woodland and rainforest edges, where it feeds on a variety of fruit and invertebrates, foraging on the ground, often alongside streams, or catching insects on the wing, flying low over the surface of rivers. Favored food includes beetles, snails, dragonflies, and grasshoppers. This species tends to live in small groups of up to around eight birds, which breed throughout the year, and it is thought that family groups are cooperative, with nonbreeding birds helping to feed the nestlings of other pairs. They nest in the lower branches of trees or in bushes, laying a clutch of two or three eggs in a cup-shaped nest of roots, leaves, and twigs. Both adults in a breeding pair incubate their eggs for about 16 days.

RED-WHISKERED BULBUL

SCIENTIFIC NAME:	*Pycnonotus jocosus*
FAMILY:	Pycnonotidae
LENGTH:	20cm (8in)
HABITAT:	Open forest, thickets, and yards
DISTRIBUTION:	China, Assam, Nepal, India, also introduced to North America and Australia
IDENTIFICATION:	A crested bird with a black head, red and white cheek patches, white throat and breast, and buff belly. Its back and long tail are brown

The Red-whiskered Bulbul is an active and often quite conspicuous bird, occurring in small but noisy flocks, producing short, loud notes and warbling songs. It tends to spend much of its time amongst vegetation, but is found in large suburban backyards and may perch in the open on telephone wires or posts. This species is omnivorous, feeding on a variety of fruits, flowers, buds, and invertebrates, particularly favoring the berries of various shrubs. The young, however, are fed mainly on large, plump insects such as caterpillars, consuming more vegetation as they approach adulthood. The breeding season typically lasts from January to August, and up to three broods may be raised in a year. A clutch consists of two or three eggs, although occasionally as many as five may be produced. The nest takes the form of a shallow cup of vegetation, usually bound with spiders' webs, located in a bush or tree. The nestlings hatch blind and naked, and are fed by both parent birds for around two weeks until they fledge, also returning for food for a few days after leaving the nest, before becoming completely independent.

ASIAN FAIRY BLUEBIRD

SCIENTIFIC NAME:	*Irena puella*
FAMILY:	Irenidae
LENGTH:	27cm (11in)
HABITAT:	Dense tropical forests
DISTRIBUTION:	Southern India, and from Nepal to southeast Asia
IDENTIFICATION:	Male is glossy black overall, with blue on the back extending onto the wings and tail. Female is similarly marked, but duller. Both have red eyes

The fairy bluebirds are thought to be closely related to the ioras and leafbirds, but their exact taxonomic relationships remain somewhat uncertain, and some studies suggest closer links to the bush shrikes.

There are only two species: the wide-ranging Asian Fairy Bluebird, which occurs on the Indian subcontinent, and from the Himalayas to the Philippines, and the Philippine Fairy Bluebird (*Irena cyanogaster*), which is endemic to the major Philippine islands. The Asian Fairy Bluebird is a medium sized, arboreal inhabitant of rainforests, where it forages mostly high in the canopy for fruit, particularly figs, insects, spiders, and nectar. It usually occurs in pairs or small flocks, but may gather in large numbers where fruit or flowers are abundant. During the breeding season, this species builds a rough cup-shaped nest of twigs, lined with a layer of moss and rootlets, usually placed quite low in the fork of a tree. The female builds the nest and incubates the clutch of two to four eggs alone, but both parent birds are involved in feeding their young.

COMMON IORA ▲

SCIENTIFIC NAME:	*Aegithina tiphia*
FAMILY:	Irenidae
LENGTH:	14cm (6in)
HABITAT:	Forest, open woodland, and cultivated land
DISTRIBUTION:	India and Sri Lanka, through southeast Asia to Java and Borneo
IDENTIFICATION:	Olive or yellowish-green above, with black wings and tail, and white wing bars, yellow below. Breeding male has yellow head and neck

The Common Iora occurs mainly in rainforest habitats, but is also found in woodlands and yards in much of its range. It is a fairly small bird, which tends to remain high in the rainforest canopy, or in the uppermost branches of tall garden trees, and therefore it may be difficult to observe. It is most likely to be encountered during the breeding season, at which time it builds its nest at much lower levels. The nest takes the form of a small but deep cup of grass and animal hair often attached to the fork of a branch with spiders' webs. Two eggs are usually laid, although a clutch may contain as many as four, and both parent birds will share responsibility for their brood. Prior to nesting, the male Common Iora performs an acrobatic display flight, darting into the air from a perch before spiraling back down with its feathers puffed out, fanning its tail upon landing. Throughout this performance the bird emits a long, high pitched whistle or constant chirruping sound. The Common Iora forages high in the trees for insects and spiders, usually moving around in pairs, but also associating with mixed-species flocks.

ORANGE-BELLIED LEAFBIRD

SCIENTIFIC NAME:	*Chloropsis hardwickii*
FAMILY:	Irenidae
LENGTH:	20cm (8in)
HABITAT:	Mountainous forest regions
DISTRIBUTION:	Eastern Himalayas and southern China to the Malay Peninsula
IDENTIFICATION:	Quite slender, green above with blue flight feathers, a dark face and throat, and a yellow or orange belly. Male has a blue tail

Closely related to the ioras, the leafbirds are also birds of the high rainforest canopy, and despite their colorful plumage, they may be hard to spot from the ground. The Orange-bellied Leafbird is an active species, which usually moves quickly amongst the treetops in pairs, or in mixed-species flocks, as it forages for food. It hunts for insects and spiders, picking them from foliage, but will also consume various fruits, and use its brush-like tongue to take nectar from flowers, a behavioral trait that aids in the pollination of many plant species. During the breeding season, the Orange-bellied Leafbird constructs a cup-shaped nest quite high in the fork of a tree, weaving together grasses, animal hair, and cobwebs. The nest is built largely by the female bird, who also takes most of the responsibility for incubating her clutch of two or three eggs, and for caring for the nestlings once they are hatched.

SHRIKES

The shrikes are sometimes referred to as the "butcherbirds", due to their habit of impaling their prey on thorns or barbed wire; however, they are not closely related to the butcherbirds of Australia, which share some similar traits, and there are also some shrikes that do not indulge in this practice. The taxonomy of shrikes is a much debated subject, with the group often being divided into three or more separate families; the true shrikes, of the family Laniidae, the helmet-shrikes of the family Prionopidae, and the bush shrikes and their allies of the family Malaconotidae, which often includes puffback shrikes, tchagras, boubous, gonoleks, vangas, and the batises and wattle-eyes. Some of these later groups are sometimes given the status of families in their own right. The true shrikes are widespread in Europe, Asia, and Africa, but there are only a few species found in North America. They are medium sized predatory birds with hooked bills, which feed on large invertebrates, and small vertebrates such as mice, small lizards, and nestlings. Most have black, white, and gray plumage, with black eye-masks, but some also bear reddish-brown wings and heads. They occur mainly in quite open country, typically grasslands, open woodland, and scrub, and they are sit-and-wait predators; their usual foraging behavior involves swooping to the ground from a perch such as a bush, or chasing flying insects. Many species impale their prey for later consumption.

The **Loggerhead Shrike** (*Lanius ludovicainus*) is a North American species, occurring from southern Canada, south to Mexico. Its name is derived from its relatively large head, and it is dark gray above, white below, with a black face, tail, and primaries. It grows to a length of around 22 centimeters (9 inches). During the breeding season, it nests in a dense bush or tree, where a clutch of up to six eggs will be incubated for a little over two weeks.

Another well known species is the **Red-backed shrike** (*Lanius collurio*). However, it has declined in numbers throughout much of its range, which includes most of western Europe. In winter it is found in Africa and northern India. The male has a gray head with a black eye-mask, white throat, a gray-brown underside, and reddish back and wings. The female has a white face with a brown eye-mask and crown, and a pale, speckled underside. This species grows to around 18 centimeters (7 inches) in length. During the breeding season, it constructs a nest of twigs and other vegetation, usually positioned in a dense bush or tree. An average clutch consists of five or six eggs, which are incubated for between 15 and 17 days. Following hatching, the young remain in the nest for up to 20 days, and may continue to be fed by their parents for several weeks after fledging.

Although classed as a typical or true shrike, the **Magpie-shrike** (*Corvinella melanoleuca*) is monotypic, being the only member of its

Crimson-breasted Shrike

genus, and it is sometimes regarded as representing a link between the true shrikes and the bush shrikes, helmet-shrikes, and their allies. Unusually for a true shrike, it is a sociable species, occurring in small but noisy flocks of ten or more individuals. It is found in parts of eastern and southern Africa, inhabiting open woodland and scrub, where it forages for small reptiles and invertebrates, usually hawking insects in flight, gleaning them from foliage, or descending from a perch to take its prey on the ground. It is black overall, with a somewhat ruffled appearance, with white patches on its back and wings and a gray rump. Including its elongated tail, it grows to a length of around 46 centimeters (18 inches). During the breeding season, it constructs an untidy cup-shaped nest of twigs, grasses, and other vegetation, where a clutch of up to six eggs is laid, to be incubated by the female for a little over two weeks. The young will generally leave the nest around two weeks after hatching, but may be unable to fly for several more days. Both adult birds care for their young, with the help of other members of the flock, and often birds from a first brood will cooperate to feed a second. The helmet-shrikes are also sociable, living in similarly sized groups, which usually feed, breed, and roost communally.

The **White Helmet-Shrike** (*Prionops plumatus*), or **White-crested Helmet-Shrike**, as it is also known, is found in open grassland, scrub, and woodland in much of sub-Saharan Africa. As its name suggests, it has a white forehead, which extends into a small crest over its bill. It also has a small yellow wattle around each eye, white wingtips, and a gray crown, whilst the rest of its plumage is black. It grows to around 20 centimeters (8 inches) in length. Like other shrikes, it forages amongst foliage, on the ground, or takes prey in the air, feeding on a variety of invertebrates, including termites and spiders, but it will also occasionally eat small lizards. During the breeding season, a nest of twigs, bark, and other vegetation is constructed on a horizontal branch or tree fork, where a clutch of up to nine eggs is laid. These are frequently incubated cooperatively by all members of a group, who will also go on to care for the nestlings.

The **Crimson-breasted Shrike** (*Laniarius atrococcineus*) or **Crimson-breasted Gonolek**, as it is also known, is fairly typical of the bush shrikes. It inhabits open woodland and scrub in parts of southern Africa, and possesses a hooked bill, sharing similar feeding habits to many shrikes. It may seize its prey by dropping from a perch, hawk insects in flight, or forage on the ground. It too feeds mainly on invertebrates, but may also take small reptiles. Like many bush shrikes it is vividly colored, with an intensely crimson underside and starkly contrasting black upper plumage. It also has noticeable white wing bars. An adult generally attains a length of 23 centimeters (9 inches).

Red-backed Shrike

◀ BOHEMIAN WAXWING

SCIENTIFIC NAME:	*Bombycilla garrulus*
FAMILY:	Bombycillidae
LENGTH:	18cm (7in)
HABITAT:	Coniferous forests, often wintering in gardens and parkland
DISTRIBUTION:	Found across northern Eurasia and much of North America, often wintering in the south of this range
IDENTIFICATION:	Medium sized, crested songbird, gray-brown overall, with white and yellow wing edges, waxy, red-tipped secondaries, yellow tail tip, and reddish rump. Black throat and mask

The Bohemian Waxwing is a highly sociable bird that is almost always seen in small colonies, even during the breeding season. It has developed a range of vocalizations and display behaviors in order to communicate with others of its kind, particularly during courtship. These include dancing, and the passing back and forth of food or other small objects such as stones. After pairing, the Bohemian Waxwing builds its cup-shaped nest high in a conifer, usually quite close to the trunk, where the female produces a clutch of four to six eggs. These are incubated for a period of around two weeks, mainly by the female bird. Waxwings feed largely on berries, and are the only birds in the Northern Hemisphere which mainly consume fruit, although they will also eat insects. The Bohemian Waxwing does not maintain regular territories, and in addition to migrating south in winter, it generally wanders in search of food throughout the year. It is from its nomadic movements that its name arises.

CEDAR WAXWING

SCIENTIFIC NAME:	*Bombycilla cedrorum*
FAMILY:	Bombycillidae
LENGTH:	15cm (6in)
HABITAT:	Open woodland, farms, suburban parks and yards
DISTRIBUTION:	Throughout most of North America, and to northern South America in winter
IDENTIFICATION:	Medium-sized songbird, gray-brown overall, with yellow belly and tail tip. It has a crested head, white-edged black mask, and a black chin patch

The Cedar Waxwing, like most of its close relatives, is a highly sociable bird, occurring in large flocks for most of the year, except during the breeding season when it is more likely to be seen in pairs. Its favored nesting sites include open woodland, fields containing trees and shrubs, and suburban backyards, where it constructs a loose, cup-shaped nest of twigs, grass, and moss, on a horizontal branch. The female normally produces a clutch of three to six eggs which will be incubated for 12 to 14 days. Following hatching, the young birds are usually ready to fend for themselves between 17 and 19 days later. The Cedar Waxwing moves around nomadically in winter in search of food, feeding mainly on berries, and it is one of the few birds dwelling in temperate regions that can survive on fruit alone for several months. However this bird is known to be vulnerable to alcohol intoxication, and may die after eating fermented fruit. It will also feed on insects, particularly in the warmer months, usually catching them on the wing.

PHAINOPEPLA

SCIENTIFIC NAME:	*Phainopepla nitens*
FAMILY:	Bombycillidae
LENGTH:	20cm (8in)
HABITAT:	Desert, scrubland, and open woodland
DISTRIBUTION:	Southwestern US and Mexico
IDENTIFICATION:	Male is glossy black, female is gray with pale-edged wing feathers. Both sexes have a white underwing patch, pointed crest, and red eyes

The Phainopepla is regarded as a silky flycatcher, a small group of birds closely related to the waxwings, which are usually considered to be within the same family, Bombycillidae; however they are sometimes placed in their own family, Ptilogonatidae. As with waxwings, these birds are heavily reliant upon berries and other fruit, and the Phainopepla feeds mainly on the berries of mistletoe. The berries pass through the birds' digestive systems undamaged, and in this way Phainopeplas help to disseminate the seeds of the plant. Additionally, this species feeds on insects, often catching them on the wing. The Phainopepla is gregarious, living in small nomadic flocks, but where berries are abundant it may congregate in its hundreds. The breeding season typically begins in early spring, at which time this species nests in mesquite scrub, placing its cup-shaped nest in a tree or bush. The female produces a clutch of two or three eggs, which are incubated by both parent birds for around two weeks. Following hatching, the young are taken care of for up to about 20 days before leaving the nest. As the weather becomes warmer, the adults may then move to a more moist habitat in order to raise a second brood.

(Common) Dipper

Scientific name:	*Cinclus cinclus*
Family:	Cinclidae
Length:	18cm (7in)
Habitat:	Mountainous regions with fast flowing streams
Distribution:	Europe, northwest Africa and central Asia
Identification:	Coffee-brown head and nape, white bib, bordered with brown, and darker, gray-black plumage on the rest of the body

Dippers are the only passerine birds that are truly aquatic, being found along the banks of streams and rivers in hilly or mountainous country, where they feed on insect larvae and other aquatic invertebrates such as snails, also consuming tadpoles and small fish. It hunts either amongst vegetation on the bank, or in the water itself, diving from a rock and walking along on the stream bed, or swimming underwater by flapping its wings. The Dipper has a number of adaptations for its lifestyle, including thick downy plumage for insulation, and enlarged preen glands, which produce secretions that keep it from becoming waterlogged. It also has opaque, moveable "third eyelids," known as nictitating membranes, to protect its eyes whilst diving. When out of the water, it blinks these frequently, also making the regular bobbing movements from which this species gets its name. The breeding season begins in late winter or early spring, with pairs building spherical nests in holes or on ledges in the riverbank, where the female lays and incubates three to six eggs. These hatch after about two weeks, and the young remain in the nest for a further three weeks, usually emerging to take to the water a few days before being fully fledged.

(Northern) Wren/Winter Wren

Scientific name:	*Troglodytes troglodytes*
Family:	Troglodytidae
Length:	10cm (4in)
Habitat:	Open forests, stream edges, meadows, and backyards
Distribution:	Much of Europe, into North Africa and temperate parts of Asia, also North America
Identification:	Tiny bird with a large head and short tail. Reddish-brown plumage above with dark barring, lighter underside and eyebrows

The Northern Wren is known in North America as the Winter Wren, but as it is the only wren found outside North America, it is often known simply as the Wren in other parts of its range. It is a very small bird, in fact it is amongst the smallest of birds found in Europe, but it is relatively stocky. Although it spends much of its time amongst dense vegetation, the Wren is a highly active bird, and may be seen darting about when in the open, typically flicking its erect tail repeatedly. It forages on the ground amongst leaf-litter, or probes crevices in the bark of trees with its long, thin bill for the small insects and spiders that constitute most of its diet. During the breeding season, the Wren may use nest boxes, but usually the male bird will construct several ball-shaped nests from leaves, grass, and moss, positioned in crevices in walls, banks, or trees. The female will then choose a nest, which she will line with feathers, before producing a clutch of up to ten eggs. Incubation is performed only by the female, during which time the male may mate with a second female; however, he will usually help to feed the nestlings of any broods which he is responsible for. Despite its small size, the Wren is known for its very loud voice, and its warbling and trilling will often announce its presence when it might otherwise remain unnoticed.

BLACK-CAPPED DONACOBIUS

SCIENTIFIC NAME:	*Donacobius atricapillus*
FAMILY:	Troglodytidae
LENGTH:	23cm (9in)
HABITAT:	Swampland, marshes, and damp meadows
DISTRIBUTION:	Eastern Panama to Bolivia, and northern Argentina
IDENTIFICATION:	Fairly large songbird, black crown, dark brown upperparts and tail. Underparts orange-yellow, orange eye

The Black-capped Donacobius is usually considered to be the largest member of the wren family, but it looks much like a member of the mockingbird family with its long legs, tail, and bill. In fact, it was assigned to the family Mimidae for many years, and known as the Black-capped Mockingthrush, until behavioral studies saw it transferred in the 1980s. More recently, however, DNA evidence has suggested a potential relationship with the Old World prinias, or wren-warblers, but it is possibly monotypic, being the only example of its kind. The Black-capped Donacobius is quite common, and tends to live in pairs, which maintain year-round territories, and which are often quite conspicuous, perching close together on exposed branches to sing noisily whilst bobbing their heads and fanning and wagging their tails. Such displays are used in order to confront intruders, also forming part of courtship during the breeding season. This species nests in a large, open cup amongst reeds or grass,

DUNNOCK ▲

SCIENTIFIC NAME:	*Prunella modularis*
FAMILY:	Prunellidae
LENGTH:	15cm (6in)
HABITAT:	Woodland, hedgerows, scrubland, parks, and gardens
DISTRIBUTION:	Throughout Europe, and parts of the Middle East
IDENTIFICATION:	Overall plumage of brown, streaked with black, with gray head, throat, and breast. It has a brown patch beneath its eyes, and on its crown

Although this bird is sometimes also known as the hedge sparrow due to its appearance, it is not closely related to the sparrow family. Rather, it is regarded as an accentor, a group of small, ground dwelling birds found mainly in upland regions, which also includes the Alpine Accentor (*Prunella collaris*). The Dunnock, however, favors hedgerows, yards, and woodland edges, largely in lowland areas. This bird forages on the ground, or hops around the lower branches of bushes in search of invertebrates, feeding mainly on caterpillars, beetles, worms, and spiders. In the winter, when insect prey is less plentiful, the Dunnock will supplement its diet with seeds and berries. During the breeding season, the female will usually build a cup-shaped nest in a bush or hedge, although it may also occasionally use the disused nest of another bird. An average clutch consists of four to six eggs which are incubated by the female alone for around two weeks, following which the hatchlings will be fed by both parents until they are fledged at about 12 days old.

GRAY CATBIRD

SCIENTIFIC NAME:	*Dumetella carolinensis*
FAMILY:	Mimidae
LENGTH:	23cm (9in)
HABITAT:	Woodland, farmland, scrub, and residential areas
DISTRIBUTION:	Southern Canada, North America, migrating to parts of the Caribbean and Central America
IDENTIFICATION:	Slate-gray plumage overall, with a black crown and chestnut beneath its long tail

Like the mockingbirds, to which this species is closely related, the songs of the Gray Catbird contain mimicry of other bird songs and sounds. However, the characteristic "mew" that gives this bird its name is not an imitation. The Gray Catbird is often heard, rather than seen, frequently inhabiting dense thickets on farmland, by roads or streams, or in forest areas, where it forages on the ground for insects, although it also consumes seeds and berries. It nests low down in a tree or shrub, using twigs and bark to build a bulky cup lined with rootlets and animal hair. The female lays around two to five eggs, which she incubates for around two weeks. The Brown-headed Cowbird will often lay eggs in the nests of Gray Catbirds, but the catbird will usually remove them, recognizing its own clutch. However, if the cowbird replaces the first ejected egg quickly enough, the catbird is liable to become confused into mistaking the cowbird's egg as its own, and may then even remove the remainder of its own clutch. This is a fairly unusual situation, however, and few catbirds actually end up incubating cowbird eggs.

BROWN THRASHER ▼

SCIENTIFIC NAME:	*Toxostoma rufum*
FAMILY:	Mimidae
LENGTH:	28cm (11in)
HABITAT:	Woodland, scrubland, hedgerows, and backyards
DISTRIBUTION:	Southern Canada and central and eastern North America
IDENTIFICATION:	Reddish-brown above, with two white wing bars, white outer tail feathers, and yellow eyes. Buff below with dark streaks

A fairly large songbird, the Brown Thrasher is nevertheless a relatively shy member of the mockingbird family, and although it may be found close to human habitations, it usually prefers more remote areas, typically dwelling in dense hedgerows and thickets. It searches for its food on the ground, foraging for insects such as beetles, nuts, seeds, and fruit, by moving its bill from side to side along the ground amongst leaf-litter, sweeping or thrashing away soil and leaves. It also often nests on the ground, or in low undergrowth, building a well hidden, bulky cup of twigs, lined with leaves and rootlets, in which between two and six eggs are laid. Both parent birds undertake incubation, which may last for up to two weeks, and the young may leave the nest as early as nine days after hatching. However at times they will remain for up to two weeks. As with most of its close relatives, this bird is known to be an aggressive defender of its nest, and reports of attacks on humans and dogs are not uncommon, sometimes with enough force to draw blood.

NORTHERN MOCKINGBIRD ▲

SCIENTIFIC NAME:	*Mimus polyglottos*
FAMILY:	Mimidae
LENGTH:	25cm (10in)
HABITAT:	Open grassland, semidesert, woodland, farmland, and urban areas
DISTRIBUTION:	Southern Canada, through the US to Mexico and the Caribbean
IDENTIFICATION:	Gray plumage above, with darker wings, white below, white wing bars, and long black tail with white outer feathers

Although found in much of North America, and in a variety of habitats, the Northern Mockingbird prefers the warmer climate of the southern states of America, and the "Northern" of its name distinguishes it from mockingbirds found in the Southern Hemisphere, whilst the group as a whole are known and named for their long and complex songs which invariably include imitations of other birds, animals, and other ambient sounds. This species may be heard throughout the day, and often into the night, with males without a mate usually singing most loudly. The calls of the Northern Mockingbird are also related to territory, and its repertoire will increase throughout its life as it learns from other birds it encounters. It often nests in fairly open areas containing shrubby vegetation, such as cultivated fields and parkland, where it will build a cup-like nest of twigs, fairly low down in trees or bushes. The two to six eggs are incubated solely by the female for a period of about 12 to 13 days, and the young will be ready to fly between 9 and 12 days after hatching. The Northern Mockingbird can often be seen flashing its wings to reveal large white patches on the underside while foraging for food on the ground, and whilst the precise reason for this behavior is unknown, it has been suggested that it is an attempt to flush out insects and spiders. In addition to invertebrates, it will also feed on seeds, berries, and other fruit.

(COMMON) NIGHTINGALE ▼

SCIENTIFIC NAME:	*Luscinia megarhynchos*
FAMILY:	Turdidae
LENGTH:	17cm (7in)
HABITAT:	Woodland and dense thickets
DISTRIBUTION:	Europe, North Africa, central Asia, and the Middle East, wintering in Africa
IDENTIFICATION:	Slender, with smooth brown plumage, paler underparts, and a chestnut colored tail

Once far more common throughout its range, Nightingale populations have declined throughout much of Europe, and particularly in Britain, although they remain fairly common in southern Europe. This decline can be mainly attributed to habitat destruction, with this species favoring secluded and densely overgrown woodland for nesting and feeding. The Nightingale forages mainly on the ground for small invertebrates, probing the soil for worms with its slender bill, but it may supplement its diet with seeds and berries. It also nests close to the ground, building a cup-shaped structure in low vegetation. The female typically produces a clutch of four to five eggs, which she incubates for around two weeks. The Nightingale is crepuscular, being mainly active at dawn and dusk which, along with its dense habitat and drab plumage, may make it difficult to observe, and it is more likely to be heard than seen. In fact it is famed for its loud, melodious, and distinctive song, which may continue into the night.

(EURASIAN) ROBIN ▲

SCIENTIFIC NAME:	*Erithacus rubecula*
FAMILY:	Turdidae
LENGTH:	15cm (6in)
HABITAT:	Forest, open woodland, gardens, and parks
DISTRIBUTION:	Europe and northern Africa, to western Siberia and the Middle East
IDENTIFICATION:	Brown above, white beneath, with an orange-red face and breast

The Robin is a familiar and distinctive species on account of its red breast, and it is sometimes also known as the "Robin Redbreast," yet it is not merely conspicuous due to its plumage, but is a bold and often highly vocal species, and one of the few birds that may be heard singing melodiously throughout the winter months. However, its numbers can be badly affected in years when there is heavy snow, as it takes most of its food from the ground. It feeds mainly on insects, worms, and spiders, but also consumes seeds and berries, foraging amongst vegetation or in more open areas. Robins are territorial throughout the year and often maintain a territory for life; however, during the breeding season, the male will allow a female into his territory prior to mating, and she will construct a cup-shaped nest of leaves and moss, in a sheltered spot, such as among ivy, in a crevice on a wall, or sometimes in a more unusual spot, like a flowerpot or on a shelf in a garden shed. The female produces a clutch of between four and six eggs, which she will incubate for up to 15 days.

BLUETHROAT

SCIENTIFIC NAME:	*Luscinia svecica*
FAMILY:	Turdidae
LENGTH:	15cm (6in)
HABITAT:	Forests, wooded tundra, scrubland, and thickets
DISTRIBUTION:	Eurasia, North Africa, and Alaska
IDENTIFICATION:	Gray-brown above, with a white belly and eyebrow. The male has a blue bib, underlined with black, which usually has a central patch of red or white

Although a rather secretive bird, the male Bluethroat may be conspicuous due to its striking throat coloring and reddish tail that can be clearly seen in flight or while this bird is singing in the open. It will often flash its tail, especially when alighting, briefly fanning its feathers to reveal the rufous patches. While all male Bluethroats have striking blue bibs, there are two distinct subspecies; *L.s. svecica*, the more northern of the two, has a red center to its blue throat feathers, whilst *L.s. cyanecula*, which inhabits more southerly regions, usually has a white spot, although sometimes it may lack this mark, resulting in an entirely blue throat. The Bluethroat feeds mainly on insects but it will supplement its diet with seeds and fruits in winter, when invertebrates are more scarce. It nests in a cup of woven twigs, grasses, sedges, and rootlets, lined with animal hair, often in a thicket on the ground or in a dense clump of grass. The female produces a clutch of between five and seven eggs, which are then incubated for about two weeks, with the young birds ready to leave the nest a further two weeks after hatching.

(COMMON) REDSTART

SCIENTIFIC NAME:	*Phoenicurus phoenicurus*
FAMILY:	Turdidae
LENGTH:	15cm (6in)
HABITAT:	Forests, yards, orchards, and heaths
DISTRIBUTION:	Europe and parts of the Middle East
IDENTIFICATION:	Male has gray upperparts, a white forehead, black face, rusty-red tail, and orange breast and flanks. The female is light grayish-brown above, pale orange below

The Redstart is a small, slender member of the thrush family that looks somewhat like a robin, but it may be distinguished by its black face and rusty-red tail. It also tends to spend its time higher up in trees or hedgerows, and although it is found in backyards, it is usually less bold, being more inclined to inhabit mature woodland. Many Redstarts overwinter in Africa, before returning to Europe in order to breed, and it is usually the males which will return first and begin to establish territories. The male will select a territory, and then begin singing to attract a female, and following mating, he will lead her to several possible nest sites, usually holes in trees, or cavities in walls. At each possible nest site, the male Redstart will perform a display, repeatedly flying in and out of the hole, whilst singing and flashing his rump and tail. Once the female has selected a site, she will construct a nest of twigs, leaves, moss, and grass, where she alone will incubate a clutch of six or seven eggs for around two weeks. During this time, and for around two weeks after the eggs have hatched, the male will bring food to the nest, including spiders, ants, moths, and beetles. In winter the Redstart will also feed on berries.

EASTERN BLUEBIRD ▼

SCIENTIFIC NAME:	*Sialia sialis*
FAMILY:	Turdidae
LENGTH:	18cm (7in)
HABITAT:	Farmland, open woodland, forest edges, and parks
DISTRIBUTION:	Eastern parts of North and Central America
IDENTIFICATION:	Deep blue above, chestnut throat, neck, breast, and flanks, white belly and under-tail coverts. Female is similar but grayer, with more white on the belly

Once in decline, mainly due to competition with other birds for suitable nesting sites, the popularity of the Eastern Bluebird has helped to reverse this negative population trend, and seen the erection of specifically designed nest boxes. This has increased their nesting options, but they will otherwise find a natural cavity or woodpecker hole in which to place their loose, cup-shaped nests woven of grasses, pine needles, and other vegetation, lined with feathers, animal hair, or fine grass. However, before nest-building begins, the male Eastern Bluebird will perform a kind of nest demonstration display, involving him going in and out of the proposed cavity with nest material, and waving his wings while perched above it. The female will then take the role of nest builder, as well as incubating the eggs. Although clutch size varies with location, it will usually consist of between three and seven eggs. Eastern Bluebirds often have more than one successful brood annually, with young from later broods often remaining with their parents over the winter. They feed on insects, spiders, and berries, but are also frequent, and welcome, visitors to bird-feeders.

MOUNTAIN BLUEBIRD ▲

SCIENTIFIC NAME:	*Sialia currucoides*
FAMILY:	Turdidae
LENGTH:	18cm (7in)
HABITAT:	High meadows and mountainous regions
DISTRIBUTION:	Western North America, migrating as far south as Mexico
IDENTIFICATION:	Male is a sky-blue color, with a lighter blue breast, and white belly. The female is gray, with a blue wash on her wings, tail, and rump, and a white belly

Preferring more open habitat than other bluebirds, the Mountain Bluebird has become a rather common sight, particularly on the ranchland of the American West, and the male is often easily spotted due to its striking sky-blue feathers. Being a popular bird, many nest boxes have been erected with it in mind, but it will also use a natural cavity such as a woodpecker hole. This species will compete for territory with the Western Bluebird (*Sialia mexicana*), and where their ranges overlap, the Eastern Bluebird, usually dominating both. The nest, which is constructed of woven grasses lined with fine grass, feathers, animal hair, and soft bark, is built entirely by the female, but the male may bring some nesting material to the site. More commonly, however, gathered material is dropped on the way back to the nest, or the male may simply go back and forth, as if helping, but often collecting no material at all. The female will produce between four and eight eggs, which are incubated for about two weeks. Feeding on insects and small fruits, the Mountain Bluebird will often drop to the ground from a perch or hovering position, but will also catch flies and other flying insects on the wing.

(Eurasian) Blackbird

Scientific name:	*Turdus merula*
Family:	Turdidae
Length:	25cm (10in)
Habitat:	Gardens, hedgerows, and woodland
Distribution:	Most of Europe, parts of Asia and North Africa, also introduced to southern Australia and New Zealand
Identification:	Male is entirely black, with an orange-yellow bill and eye-ring. Female is dark brown above, with streaked lighter brown underparts, and a pale chin

The male Blackbird is rather striking and conspicuous, on account of the contrast of its plumage with its bright bill and eye-ring, and this species is also very common, with a pleasing, mellow song. In much of its range, the Blackbird is sedentary; however, those of more northerly regions, such as Scandinavia, will move south in winter, often migrating to Britain. It may be found on open lawns or in more dense thickets and hedgerows, where it forages for fruit and berries, insects, worms, slugs, and snails. However, it is usually no expert at breaking the shells of mollusks, and will sometimes attempt to rob Song Thrushes of snails once they have broken them open. The Blackbird usually nests a few feet up in a bush or hedge, but it may also find a site in a building, on the ground, or even at a considerable height in a tree. It is normally the female that builds the nest, using grass, twigs, mud, and moss, in which she will lay between three and five eggs, and incubate them on her own for about two weeks. Following hatching, both parent birds will feed the young, which will begin to fly around two weeks later.

FIELDFARE ▲

SCIENTIFIC NAME:	*Turdus pilaris*
FAMILY:	Turdidae
LENGTH:	25cm (10in)
HABITAT:	Woodland, orchards, and open grassland
DISTRIBUTION:	Europe and northern Asia, winters in southwest Asia
IDENTIFICATION:	Gray head, nape, and rump, reddish-brown back, golden-brown breast and white underside, with arrow-shaped markings

The Fieldfare is a fairly large thrush found across much of Europe, but it is relatively uncommon in Britain, and in fact, its numbers vary considerably from year to year across its range, as it tends to move around in nomadic flocks. In the fall and winter these groups may be quite large, and are usually found in open habitats, foraging for food on the ground, taking invertebrates from the soil or feeding on fallen fruit. The Fieldfare also often roosts on the ground, sheltering amongst vegetation or in the furrows of a plowed field. During the breeding season, small colonies are more likely to be encountered in woodland, where they will defend their territory aggressively and noisily. The Fieldfare constructs a fairly large, cup-shaped nest of mud and grass lined with moss, where the female will incubate a clutch of five or six eggs, for ten to twelve days. Following hatching, the nestlings are fed by both parent birds for around two weeks until they are fledged.

HERMIT THRUSH

SCIENTIFIC NAME:	*Catharus guttatus*
FAMILY:	Turdidae
LENGTH:	18cm (7in)
HABITAT:	Coniferous or mixed woodland and thickets, often in mountainous regions
DISTRIBUTION:	Present throughout much of North America, wintering south to Central America
IDENTIFICATION:	A stocky thrush, olive-brown upperparts and flanks, buff below, with dark speckles on the breast, a reddish tail, and a white eye-ring

Hermit thrushes are widely distributed throughout the forests of North America during the breeding season, expanding their range into Central America during the winter. They forage both on the ground and amongst vegetation, and are omnivorous, feeding on small invertebrates such as beetles, wasps, and flies, as well as fruits, particularly berries, typically consuming more vegetation in the winter, when insects are more scarce. During the breeding season, the males will establish and defend breeding territories, into which they will accept a female in order to mate. The female constructs a cup-shaped nest of grass, leaves, and moss, either on the ground amongst vegetation, or in a bush, hedge, or tree. Here she will produce a clutch of three to six eggs, which she will incubate alone. During incubation, however, the male will bring food to the nest, and he will continue to do so once the eggs have hatched at around 12 days. The nestlings usually fledge after about two weeks, following which a further brood is often reared. This species often suffers from brood parasitism by the Brown-headed Cowbird, which will lay a single egg in its nest, to be raised by the unsuspecting hosts.

SONG THRUSH

SCIENTIFIC NAME:	*Turdus philomelos*
FAMILY:	Turdidae
LENGTH:	23cm (9in)
HABITAT:	Backyards, hedgerows, thickets, and woodland
DISTRIBUTION:	Europe to central Asia and North Africa, also introduced to Australia and New Zealand
IDENTIFICATION:	Rich brown upperparts, buff speckled breast and flanks. It has a slender bill, and fairly long, slender legs

The Song Thrush is a familiar garden bird in much of Western Europe, well known for its musical voice, although its numbers have declined dramatically, particularly on farmland where hedgerows have been cleared. In other parts of its range, however, it continues to thrive in woodland habitats. Although the Song Thrush may spend much of its time in the cover of bushes, it feeds mainly on the ground, and may be seen hopping tentatively into open areas in search of food, with snails being a favored item. It breaks these open against suitable stones, which have come to be known as "snail anvils." The Song Thrush is also often conspicuous when delivering its melodious song, perching high in a tree on an exposed branch, particularly on evenings during the breeding season. This species lays its clutch of three to five eggs in a cup-shaped nest in a bush or tree, incubating them for around two weeks. The young fledge after a further two weeks, and once the breeding season is over, many Song Thrushes will migrate for the winter, with northernmost populations typically moving farthest south.

MISTLE THRUSH ▼

SCIENTIFIC NAME:	*Turdus viscivorus*
FAMILY:	Turdidae
LENGTH:	28cm (11in)
HABITAT:	Woodland, open grassland, hedgerows, and gardens
DISTRIBUTION:	Europe to central Asia, and parts of northwest Africa
IDENTIFICATION:	Large thrush, gray-brown above with a gray breast and buff underparts spotted with dark brown or black

The Mistle Thrush is amongst the largest of the thrushes, and it is often quite conspicuous, either when foraging in the open or singing its flute-like song from a prominent perch, high in a tree. It is sometimes also encountered in small groups, but it can be an aggressive and territorial bird, particularly during the breeding season, when males are also likely to be at their most vocal; singing to attract a mate, or emitting a harsh, rattling call to warn off intruders. Once a pair has formed, the female will construct a fairly large, cup-shaped nest of mud, grass, roots, moss, and leaves, often quite high in a tree, where she will incubate her clutch of three to five eggs for around two weeks. Following hatching, the young are fed by both parent birds and fledge at around two weeks of age. The Mistle Thrush feeds on small invertebrates, such as insects and worms, relying more heavily on berries in winter, and during the colder months a bush laden with berries may be vigorously defended. The Mistle Thrush often sings in bad weather, earning it the alternative name of "Stormcock."

AMERICAN ROBIN ▲

SCIENTIFIC NAME:	*Turdus migratorius*
FAMILY:	Turdidae
LENGTH:	25cm (10in)
HABITAT:	Woodland, gardens, parks and swamps
DISTRIBUTION:	Throughout North America, wintering in Mexico and Guatemala
IDENTIFICATION:	Gray-brown above, a reddish-orange breast, white throat, brown-black head and tail, and a yellow bill

Although somewhat similar to the Eurasian Robin on account of its orange-red breast, the American Robin is a much larger species, and is regarded as a true thrush. It is also the most widespread American thrush, and probably one of the best known birds throughout its range, having developed a tolerance for human-modified habitats. It is common in both suburban and urban areas, where it is a frequent visitor to parks and backyards, but this bird is also found in meadows, woodland, and orchards, requiring trees and shrubs for nesting and roosting, and more open ground in order to forage. It feeds on a variety of wild and cultivated fruits, berries, worms, insects, and other invertebrates. American Robins are migratory, with the entire population moving south in the fall, to return in spring, and during migrations they may be found in huge flocks, often roosting together in swamps. The breeding season begins soon after these robins return to their northerly habitats, at which time the female will construct a cup-shaped nest on the ground, in a bush or high in a tree. Sometimes it will also be positioned in a hole in a wall. Three to five eggs are usually laid, to be incubated by the female for a period of about two weeks.

Chestnut-crowned Babbler

Scientific name:	*Pomatostomus ruficeps*
Family:	Pomatostomidae
Length:	23cm (9in)
Habitat:	Open woods, scrub, and semi-desert
Distribution:	Found in the southeast Australian interior
Identification:	Slender, with a long broad tail, and narrow downcurved bill. Plumage is mottled gray-brown above, with a darker crown, white-tipped tail, white throat, breast, eyebrows, and wing bars

Once classified with the Old World babblers of the family Timaliidae, the Australo-Papuan babblers are now generally recognized as a family in their own right; Pomatostomidae. They are small or medium sized birds endemic to Australia and New Guinea, named for their incessant chattering. Like other babblers, the Chestnut-crowned Babbler is an active and highly sociable bird, living in flocks of around 20 individuals, which forage together in scrub vegetation or on the ground. It is an omnivorous species, consuming both vegetation and small invertebrates, with insects comprising the majority of its diet. During the breeding season, it constructs a large, roughly spherical nest of twigs, lined with softer material such as grass or animal hair, usually positioned in a tree. Despite being a lively and noisy bird, the Chestnut-crowned Babbler is rather nervous of people, and flocks may be difficult to approach.

SILVER-EARED MESIA

SCIENTIFIC NAME:	*Leiothrix argentauris*
FAMILY:	Timaliidae
LENGTH:	13cm (5in)
HABITAT:	Scrubland and mountainous forest
DISTRIBUTION:	From eastern Nepal through Indo-China to Sumatra
IDENTIFICATION:	Olive-green above, with red wing bar and rump, black crown and silver-gray ear coverts. Red throat blends to orange-yellow underparts

The Silver-eared Mesia is a small and attractive babbler that may usually be found in family groups of about six to ten individuals, sometimes also gathering in larger flocks of up to 30, particularly where there is an abundant supply of food. It feeds mainly on insects, but will also consume soft fruit and nectar, foraging through low, dense vegetation and feeding on or close to the ground. During the breeding season, which lasts from March to June in much of its range, the Silver-eared Mesia constructs a small but deep cup-shaped nest in the fork of a tree, often quite close to the ground. An average clutch consists of three to four eggs, which may be incubated by both parent birds for about two weeks. The chicks leave the nest after around 12 days, but may spend the first few days climbing amongst low branches before they are able to fly, and can remain dependent on their parents for around six weeks. Occurring in montane habitats, these birds are fairly hardy and able to tolerate quite low temperatures, but they are likely to be found at lower altitudes in winter.

BEARDED TIT　▲

SCIENTIFIC NAME:	*Panurus biarmicus*
FAMILY:	Panuridae/Paradoxornithidae
LENGTH:	17cm (7in)
HABITAT:	Reed-beds in marshland
DISTRIBUTION:	Found in parts of Europe and across Asia to the Pacific
IDENTIFICATION:	Plumage is tawny-brown overall, with white, brown, and black bands on the wing, and black under-tail coverts. Male has a pale gray crown, white head, and black mustache. Female has a brown crown, and lacks the mustache

The Bearded Tit is not a true tit, but belongs to the parrotbill family, Panuridae (or Paradoxornithidae), and it is also known frequently as the Bearded Reedling or Bearded Parrotbill. Unlike most parrotbills, and the closely related Old World babblers which are confined to warm climates, the Bearded Tit occurs in Europe and temperate parts of Asia, and is found almost exclusively in wetland habitats, living in quite large colonies amongst reeds in marshlands. It is sociable throughout the year, and also noisy, producing a distinctive "ping" and a "tink-tink" sound, akin to stones being knocked together. During the breeding season, it constructs a loose cup-shaped nest above water, or close to the ground, in reeds and sedges, which it lines with fine grass, and where a clutch of five to seven eggs is laid, usually between April and August. During the summer months, the Bearded Tit feeds mainly on insects, reverting to a diet of seeds in winter; however, this bird is particularly vulnerable to harsh winters, and in recent years its numbers have moderately declined.

REED PARROTBILL

SCIENTIFIC NAME:	*Paradoxornis heudei*
FAMILY:	Panuridae/Paradoxornithidae
LENGTH:	18cm (7in)
HABITAT:	Marshland
DISTRIBUTION:	Parts of eastern Asia
IDENTIFICATION:	Plumage is tawny-brown overall, with black and white markings on the wings and tail, and a silvery-gray head with a dark crown. The bill is short and stout

The parrotbills are a small family of birds which are closely related to the Old World babblers, although they are much like tits in their general appearance and behavior. Unlike tits, however, their bills are normally short, stout and laterally compressed much like those of parrots, hence the common name for the family. Most species are found in tropical southeast Asia, where they inhabit quite open terrain, although they are also found in bamboo groves, forests, and marshland. As its name suggests, the Reed Parrotbill occurs in marshland, where it feeds on seeds and small invertebrates, using its heavy bill to break open the stems of reeds in search of insects and their larvae. During the breeding season, it constructs a small but deep cup-shaped nest of leaves and stems, which it secures between the stalks of reeds, usually just above the surface of the water, and where the female will lay a clutch of up to about five eggs.

BLUE-GRAY GNATCATCHER

SCIENTIFIC NAME:	*Polioptila caerulea*
FAMILY:	Polioptilidae
LENGTH:	12cm (5in)
HABITAT:	Deciduous woodland, thickets, and scrub
DISTRIBUTION:	Throughout much of North America from southern Canada, south to Mexico and Cuba
IDENTIFICATION:	Blue-gray above, white below, with white eye-ring, and long black tail with white outer-feathers. Male has black eyebrow in summer, and is generally paler than the female

The Blue-gray Gnatcatcher is fairly common throughout North America for much of the year, being found primarily in deciduous woodland in the east, and juniper scrub in the west. It is also generally quite conspicuous, being an active and noisy bird. It produces a melodic warbling song, and also a distinctive whining call. It forages amongst foliage for insects, gathering them from the leaves and branches of trees or bushes, constantly flicking its long tail as it does so. The breeding season tends to last from April to early June, during which time the Blue-gray Gnatcatcher constructs a small cup-shaped nest on a horizontal limb, using grass, lichen, and spiders' webs. A clutch consists of four or five eggs, which are incubated by both adult birds for around two weeks. Following hatching, the young will be tended by both their parents for around a further 12 days. The nests of this species are also known to be parasitized by the Brown-headed Cowbird. At the end of the breeding season, northern populations undertake migrations to the southern US and into Central America.

CETTI'S WARBLER ▲

SCIENTIFIC NAME:	Cettia cetti
FAMILY:	Sylviidae
LENGTH:	15cm (6in)
HABITAT:	Reedbeds, marshes, and thickets
DISTRIBUTION:	From Britain and France, through Mediterranean Europe, North Africa, the Middle East, and central Asia
IDENTIFICATION:	Chestnut-brown, with a buff underside, and a broad, rounded tail

Cetti's Warbler favors habitats with dense vegetation, usually close to water, and tends to inhabit the tangled undergrowth adjacent to reedbeds. It is also a "skulking" bird that creeps around close to the ground as it forages for insects. For this reason it can be very difficult to observe, but the male of this species is highly vocal, and produces an incredibly loud call for a bird of its size, often revealing its presence. Its song is not especially melodious, but rather an abrupt and explosive succession of notes, which sounds much as though the bird is repeating its name; "cetti-cetti-cetti." This call may be heard throughout both the day and night, particularly during the breeding season in spring and summer. Cetti's Warbler nests in bushes or other low vegetation close to water, building a substantial cup of grass and other plant material. Here the female produces a clutch of four or five eggs, which are incubated for a little over two weeks.

GRASSHOPPER WARBLER

SCIENTIFIC NAME:	Locustella naevia
FAMILY:	Sylviidae
LENGTH:	13cm (5in)
HABITAT:	Marshes, moist heaths, and thickets
DISTRIBUTION:	From Britain, across Europe to China, wintering in North Africa and India
IDENTIFICATION:	Olive-brown above, streaked with darker brown, buff underparts. The breast often has a tinted band and faint streaks of brown

Although it is insectivorous, the Grasshopper Warbler's name is not derived from its diet, but from its high pitched, whirring song that is reminiscent of the chirping of a grasshopper or cricket. It is a secretive bird, and more often than not, its call will be the only indication of its presence. It can be heard singing mostly at dawn and dusk, but it will often continue to sing through the night. It spends much of its time foraging for insects, creeping mouse-like in low scrub and dense vegetation, usually in marshy habitats, and particularly in coastal areas when returning from migration. It generally breeds between May and July, with the female producing a clutch of around four to six eggs, which are laid in a grassy, cup-shaped nest, frequently positioned in a tuft of long grass or in a small bush. These are incubated for between 12 and 15 days, and the nestlings fledge around 12 days after hatching.

SEDGE WARBLER

SCIENTIFIC NAME:	*Acrocephalus schoenobaenus*
FAMILY:	Sylviidae
LENGTH:	13cm (5in)
HABITAT:	Reedbeds, lakes, and marshes
DISTRIBUTION:	Europe and central Asia, wintering in sub-Saharan Africa
IDENTIFICATION:	Rich brown upper plumage, streaked with both lighter and darker browns, light brown underside and a light eyebrow

The Sedge Warbler is amongst the most common and widespread of the marsh-dwelling warblers, with a breeding range that extends from central Asia throughout most of Europe, reaching as far as northern Scandinavia. It is found across a range of wetland habitats, from the edges of lakes and rivers to reedbeds in marshes and flooded gravel pits. However, it is also sometimes found in drier, adjacent scrub areas such as hawthorn and bramble thickets. It usually inhabits dense undergrowth, and may be difficult to observe, but it is a highly vocal species, advertising its presence with a variety of chattering and warbling calls. At times it will also call from a more exposed perch and display by launching itself almost vertically from a branch, before making a spiraling descent with its wings and tail outspread. During the breeding season the Sedge Warbler constructs a cup of grass, leaves, and moss in low vegetation, where a clutch of five or six eggs is incubated for around two weeks. This species feeds mainly on insects, also consuming seeds and berries in the fall. As winter approaches, the entire breeding population undertakes a migration to Africa.

(Eurasian) Chiffchaff

Scientific name:	*Phylloscopus collybita*
Family:	Sylviidae
Length:	11cm (4in)
Habitat:	Open woodland and thickets
Distribution:	Europe, central Asia, Siberia, and North Africa, moving to sub-Saharan Africa and India in the winter
Identification:	Overall olive-green plumage, with a paler underside, and faint eye-stripe. Slight color variations occur geographically

The Chiffchaff is a common and widespread warbler, which spends the breeding season in much of Europe and in temperate parts of Asia, dwelling in open woodland, with some dense undergrowth to provide cover when nesting. It is a migratory species, and is amongst the first birds to return to its breeding range from southern Asia, Africa, and the Mediterranean, and it is also often one of the last species to leave at the end of the fall. The nest is usually placed on or just above the ground in a bush or other low vegetation, and takes the form of a domed structure composed of leaves, moss, and grasses. A typical clutch will consist of between four and seven eggs, which are incubated for up to 15 days, and following hatching, the young fledge at around two weeks of age. The Chiffchaff is very similar to the Willow Warbler (*Phylloscopus trochilus*) in appearance, but may be distinguished by its somewhat duller plumage and the distinctive, monotonous "chiffchaff" call, from which its name is derived. Like other warblers, it is insectivorous, and typically forages amongst foliage for its food.

BLACKCAP (WARBLER) ▼

SCIENTIFIC NAME:	*Sylvia atricapilla*
FAMILY:	Sylviidae
LENGTH:	14cm (6in)
HABITAT:	Forests, open woodland, parks, and yards
DISTRIBUTION:	Much of Europe, North Africa, the Middle East, and parts of central Asia
IDENTIFICATION:	Olive-green back, wings, and tail, white underside, gray face, and a black cap. The female's plumage is gray-brown, and her cap is a rusty-brown color

The Blackcap is a common and distinctive, if somewhat drab, warbler, but its song is highly melodious, and it is sometimes referred to as the "northern nightingale" for this reason. It is found throughout most of Europe, and although a large proportion of individuals migrate to the warmer parts of its range in winter, it is quite a hardy bird, and may be found in Britain and other parts of western Europe throughout the year. It is usually found in both mixed and deciduous woodland, mainly where dense undergrowth is present, but it also occurs in parks and backyards, particularly during the colder months. It breeds in spring and summer, building a cup-shaped nest of grass, rootlets, and animal hair, often amongst brambles or similar cover, where a clutch of four or five eggs will be incubated for around 12 days. It feeds mainly on insects during the breeding season, relying more heavily on seeds and berries at other times of the year.

GOLDCREST ▲

SCIENTIFIC NAME:	*Regulus regulus*
FAMILY:	Sylviidae
LENGTH:	9cm (4in)
HABITAT:	Coniferous and mixed woodland
DISTRIBUTION:	Europe, parts of North Africa, and central Asia to Japan
IDENTIFICATION:	Olive-green plumage, darker above than below, with black and white banded wings. Both sexes have a bright, black-bordered crest; yellow in females and fiery orange in males

Along with the Northern Wren and the Firecrest (*Regulus ignicapillus*), the Goldcrest, often also known as the Golden-crested Wren, is amongst the smallest of Europe's birds. It is found throughout much of Europe, across southern Siberia and the Himalayas to Japan and China, and although it tends to inhabit quite cold northern forests, in years of severe weather its numbers may be seriously affected. It is closely associated with conifers, and although it may be found in deciduous woodland, parks, and yards, it will only visit them if there are conifers nearby. The breeding season begins in late April, at which time it will construct a hammock-like nest, where it will typically incubate a clutch of around ten eggs for a period of about 16 days. Present all year round in parts of its range, the Goldcrest may form mixed-species flocks in winter, associating with other small birds such as tits. However, some individuals undertake extensive southward migrations, particularly for a bird of this size. It feeds on small insects and spiders, usually foraging amongst the foliage in trees, but will also feed on the ground at times, and take berries when invertebrates are scarce.

SPOTTED FLYCATCHER

SCIENTIFIC NAME:	*Muscicapa striata*
FAMILY:	Muscicapidae
LENGTH:	14cm (6in)
HABITAT:	Woodland, parks, and backyardss
DISTRIBUTION:	Europe, Africa, the Middle East, and central Asia
IDENTIFICATION:	Gray-brown upperparts, with off-white underparts, a streaked crown and breast, and large eyes

The Spotted Flycatcher is a fairly quiet bird, and would be inconspicuous but for its habit of darting from its perch in order to catch its prey. It adopts an alert, watchful posture on a branch in wait for a passing meal, before flying out to catch an insect on the wing, rapidly twisting and turning in flight as it does so. As its name suggests, it feeds on flies and other flying insects such as beetles and wasps. It is encountered in mature deciduous woodland with clearings, but will also inhabit parks, yards and hedgerows where tall trees are present. The Spotted Flycatcher is a long distance migrant, overwintering in South Africa and northern India, reaching more northerly parts of its range in early summer in order to breed. It constructs a small, cup-shaped nest from twigs, grass, and moss in a sheltered spot such as a crevice in a wall or tree trunk, where the female will incubate a clutch of four or five eggs. The male may mate with two females, but will usually provide food for both broods when this is the case. Females may also go on to raise a second, normally smaller, brood, sometimes being assisted by the young from the first.

PIED FLYCATCHER

SCIENTIFIC NAME:	*Ficedula hypoleuca*
FAMILY:	Muscicapidae
LENGTH:	13cm (5in)
HABITAT:	Deciduous woodland, yards, and orchards
DISTRIBUTION:	Europe, North Africa, and western Siberia
IDENTIFICATION:	Male in summer is black with large white wing bars, forehead spot, tail edges, and underside. The female and winter male are brown and white with smaller wing bars

The Pied Flycatcher is a summer visitor to much of Europe and parts of Siberia, spending the winter months in the warmer climate of southern Europe and North Africa. It generally arrives in April to begin establishing nests in open, deciduous, or mixed woodland, usually in upland areas. It tends to nest in holes in trees, although it will also use nest boxes where they are provided. A clutch may consist of up to eight eggs, which are incubated by both parent birds for around two weeks. Following hatching, the young are fed by both adult birds for a further two weeks. Spending much of its time high in trees, this bird may be difficult to observe, and it is likely to be heard before it is seen, producing either a musical warbling song, or a distinctive metallic call. Like other flycatchers, this species feeds mainly on flying insects, catching them on the wing, or gleaning caterpillars from foliage. The Pied Flycatcher may be hard to distinguish from the Collared Flycatcher (*Ficedula albicollis*), and where the ranges of the species overlap, hybrids sometimes occur.

FAIRY-WRENS

The fairy-wrens belong to the family Maluridae, a small group of birds which are found in Australia and parts of southeast Asia. They are not closely related to the true wrens in the family Troglodytidae, being more closely linked to the Old World warblers, Sylviidae, but all are quite small, similar in shape, and share the characteristically cocked tail, although the tails are much longer in fairy-wrens. The fairy-wrens are also sometimes known as blue wrens, with the adult males of many species bearing at least some vivid blue plumage, particularly during the breeding season. However, on account of the social structure of these birds, groups will frequently contain only one brightly colored male, whilst the others may be quite drab, often closely resembling the females. Usually, there is a dominant male which will bear bright breeding plumage, his mate, and several subordinate, nonbreeding males. In other cases there may be two breeding males and a varying number of siblings and females, but generally females disperse from their family groups in order to pair with a male. In some species, pairs may also be found alone.

Fairy-wrens occur in a variety of habitats; in Australia they are found mainly in open grassland with dense shrubs or undergrowth, but they also inhabit more arid scrub areas in the interior, as well as forest edges and swampland. In southeast Asia many species are to be found in tropical rainforests and subtropical woodland. The **Orange-crowned Fairy-Wren** (*Clytomyias insignis*), for example, dwells in the mountain rainforests of New Guinea. It grows to around 15 centimeters (6 inches) in length, and unusually, both males and females share the same plumage. The back and wings are a warm, reddish brown and the head is orange, whilst the throat and breast are golden or buff. It is neither widespread nor common, and also tends to inhabit the dense rainforest undergrowth, therefore it may be difficult to observe; however, it lives in family groups of up to about ten birds, which may be quite noisy, with members constantly calling to each other whilst foraging. It feeds on small insects, spiders, and

Splendid Fairy-Wren

236

other invertebrates, which may be gleaned from foliage, or taken on the ground. Little is known of the breeding habits of this species, but like other fairy-wrens it probably constructs an ovoid or ball-shaped nest of leaves and grasses, placed in a bush or other low vegetation, where a clutch of two to four eggs will be laid, to be incubated by the female alone, or both parent birds. Following hatching, nonbreeding members of a flock tend to cooperate to help feed the young.

The **White-winged Fairy-Wren** (*Malurus leucopterus*) is amongst the most widespread of the family, occurring across much of Australia in scrub, grassland, and the arid interior. However it is absent from large parts of the north and east. The breeding male is distinctive, being blue overall with white wings and brown primary feathers, whilst the females are buff above and white below. The males of some subspecies found on islands off Western Australia are black with a blue tail. This is a tiny species, growing to only around 12 centimeters (5 inches) long. Like other fairy-wrens, it dwells in bushes, thickets, and undergrowth close to the ground, feeding on

small insects. It constructs a spherical nest of grasses, where a clutch of three to four eggs will be laid. In some species juveniles and females in a flock will help to feed the young once hatched, but it has been observed amongst White-winged Fairy-Wrens that the helpers are usually adult males.

The breeding male **Red-backed Fairy-Wren** (*Malurus melanocephalus*) is another very small, yet highly distinctive species, being mainly black, with orange or crimson shoulders, back, and rump. Females and nonbreeding birds are sandy-colored overall, although males may exhibit traces of red plumage. The Red-backed Fairy-Wren is found in northern and eastern parts of Australia, in tropical and subtropical grasslands, open woodland, and swampy habitats, and is often quite common. It feeds on small insects and larvae, foraging at low levels amongst the undergrowth. During the breeding season the male will display to the female by fluffing up his red plumage, and following mating a clutch of around three eggs will be laid in a domed grass nest.

Red-backed Fairy-Wren

WEEBILL

SCIENTIFIC NAME:	*Smicrornis brevirostris*
FAMILY:	Acanthizidae
LENGTH:	8cm (3in)
HABITAT:	Dry forests and open woodland
DISTRIBUTION:	Most of Australia
IDENTIFICATION:	Mostly yellow, with a pale face and eyebrow, and an olive-colored back

The Weebill is arguably Australia's smallest bird, for although the Mallee Emu-wren (*Stipiturus mallee*) has a smaller body, its long tail alone is around the same size as the Weebill. This species occurs throughout mainland Australia, and is found in a wide range of timbered habitats; however, it is largely absent from the most humid rainforest areas, and favors open eucalypt woodlands. It spends much of its time high in trees, usually in pairs or small groups, where it forages for small insects amongst the foliage, picking them from leaves with its short, stubby bill. Weebills are sedentary, tending to maintain the same territory throughout the year, although they will roam about a small range in search of food. During the breeding season, this species constructs a neatly-woven, domed nest of grass and other vegetation, with a spout-like entrance hole. Here the female incubates a clutch of two to three eggs alone, which hatch after about 12 days. Both parent birds then care for their young, which will remain in the nest for about 10 days after hatching.

SOUTHERN WHITEFACE

SCIENTIFIC NAME:	*Aphelocephala leucopsis*
FAMILY:	Acanthizidae
LENGTH:	10cm (4in)
HABITAT:	Open arid country
DISTRIBUTION:	Southern Australia
IDENTIFICATION:	Gray-brown above, off-white below with buff flanks, a white face, black line on forehead, and a brown, white-tipped tail

The Southern Whiteface is a sociable bird, usually found in flocks of between 15 and 20 birds; however, flocks may reach numbers of up to 50 strong, and if disturbed they will take to the air suddenly and simultaneously. Largely a ground dwelling bird, it forages for seeds and invertebrates in open, dry land, particularly around dead trees or low scrub vegetation, but it also feeds on nectar and soft fruit. Hollow trees are often the favored nesting sites for the Southern Whiteface, but a low bush or shrub may also be used. The nest itself consists of a large, roughly-constructed sphere of grass and other vegetation, with a side entrance.

CRIMSON CHAT

SCIENTIFIC NAME:	*Epthianura tricolor*
FAMILY:	Acanthizidae
LENGTH:	12cm (5in)
HABITAT:	Inland plains, rocky hills, and desert areas
DISTRIBUTION:	Australia, in arid regions
IDENTIFICATION:	Male has crimson crown, forehead, breast, flanks, and rump, white throat and under-tail coverts, dark nape, eye-stripe and tail, and a dark brown back. Female light brown above, with a white belly and throat, and pale red and buff patches on breast, rump, and flanks

The Crimson Chat is nomadic in nature, traveling widely in search of food, and the arid nature of its habitat regularly forces it to search out areas where there has been sufficient rainfall to produce fresh plant growth. Although primarily an insectivore, it will consume nectar from desert flowers to supplement its diet, and invertebrates are also more likely to be encountered where vegetation is present. Like all chats, it most commonly forages for food on the ground, and its long legs are ideal for walking from plant to plant. Importantly, as it does so, this species helps to pollinate a variety of flowering desert vegetation. During the breeding season it nests close to the ground, constructing a deep cup of grass and twigs, usually positioned under the cover of vegetation. A sociable species, the Crimson Chat is usually encountered in flocks, which will sometimes associate with other chats to form mixed groups.

ASIAN PARADISE FLYCATCHER

SCIENTIFIC NAME:	*Terpsiphone paradisi*
FAMILY:	Monarchidae
LENGTH:	Male: 50cm (20in), female: 20cm (8in)
HABITAT:	Forest and scrubland
DISTRIBUTION:	Much of Asia and Oceania
IDENTIFICATION:	Male has black head and nape, pale body, blue bill and eye-ring, and a long, white tail, terminating in two streamers. Female has brown upper plumage and wings, a pale underside, and a dark head. Regional variations occur in the male's plumage

The male Asian Paradise Flycatcher is an impressive looking bird, with striking white plumage that contrasts with its dark head, and long tail streamers. However it generally resembles the somewhat more drab female for at least the first four years of its life. Some plumage differences also occur geographically, with individuals in Sri Lanka, for example, never developing white plumage. During the breeding season, the male uses his tail streamers to attract a mate, flicking them repeatedly whilst perching on an exposed branch. This species constructs an inverted cone-shaped nest high in a tree, using grass plastered with spiders' webs, and lined with soft down. As its name suggests it is insectivorous, and its prey is usually caught on the wing, snatched from the air during short chases.

Tomtit ▶

Scientific name:	*Petroica macrocephala*
Family:	Eopsaltriidae
Length:	13cm (5in)
Habitat:	Forests and open woodland
Distribution:	New Zealand
Identification:	Small and plump, the male has a dark head and upper plumage, with a white wing bar, yellow throat band, and a white underside. Female has brown upper plumage and pale underside

The Tomtit is a rather bold bird, showing little fear of people, and generally displaying an aggressive and inquisitive nature. It feeds mainly on invertebrates, foraging for them on trees or on the ground, and often employs a patient "watch and wait" method, whereby it will scan an area from a perch before flying to catch its prey. It will, however, also consume small fruits in fall and winter. Pairs of Tomtits will generally remain together year after year, and maintain the same territory. During the breeding season, the female alone constructs a bulky cup of twigs, bark, feathers, and moss, placed either in a tree cavity, at the end of a broken branch, or amongst a tangle of thick vines.

Willie Wagtail

Scientific name:	*Rhipidura leucophrys*
Family:	Monarchidae
Length:	20cm (8in)
Habitat:	Almost any habitat, apart from very dense forests
Distribution:	Throughout much of Australia, the Solomon Islands and New Guinea
Identification:	Glossy black overall, with white underparts and eyebrow

The Willie Wagtail is the largest and probably best-known species of Australian fantail, being common across a range of habitats, including parks, gardens, farmland, and forests, where it forages on the ground amongst leaf-litter, for small invertebrates. It is usually seen on its own or in pairs, although flocks may form in winter, often associating with other species. During the breeding season, the Willie Wagtail builds a neat, cup-shaped nest of grass and spiders' webs, lined with hair, which may sometimes be plucked directly from an animal. Nests are usually positioned on a horizontal tree branch, or alternatively on a post or rooftop. A typical clutch consists of three eggs, which are incubated by both parent birds for around two weeks, with the young leaving the nest after a further 14 days. Up to four broods may be raised in a single season, and the young from previous clutches will often remain with their parents until the next clutch begins to hatch, at which time they will be driven away from the nest.

TITS

The tits of the family Paridae, which also contains the chickadees and titmice of the Americas, are small, somewhat stocky, yet agile birds, mainly occurring in woodland, parks and yards in Britain, Eurasia and North Africa. They feed mostly on insects and other small invertebrates such as spiders, supplementing their diets with seeds, nuts and berries, and often also frequenting bird tables and feeders provided in gardens, particularly during the winter months, when other food may be scarce. Perhaps the most distinctive, well known, and amongst the most colorful, is the **Blue Tit** (*Parus caeruleus*). It grows to around 11 centimeters (4 inches) and has a greenish back, yellow underside, blue wings with a white bar, a blue tail and crown, and a white face with a black eye-stripe. It also has a dark, narrow stripe down its belly. It is common in deciduous or mixed woodland, parks, and hedgerows, also frequenting gardens with nest boxes in summer or which provide food in winter, when it may also be seen in association with other tit species in small mixed feeding flocks. It feeds on insects and their larvae, including caterpillars, but also seeds, nuts, and berries. Being highly inquisitive and resourceful, the Blue Tit has also been known to puncture or tear open the foil tops of milk-

bottles in order to drink milk, particularly in winter. During the breeding season, this species nests in a hole in a tree, wall, or post, or in a nest box, making a cup-shaped nest lined with grass, moss, feathers, and animal hair. It produces large clutches for a small bird, often laying seven or eight eggs, but clutches containing over 15 eggs have been recorded. These are incubated by the female for around two weeks, whilst the male brings food to her at the nest, but following hatching, both parent birds will feed their young, which fledge at about three weeks of age.

Somewhat similar in appearance is the **Great Tit** (*Parus major)*, with its yellow underside, greenish back, and blue-gray wings. However it has more black on the wings, tail, and head, and a broad black stripe down its breast, and some Asian birds lack the yellow plumage. It is also larger than the Blue Tit, reaching a length of about 15 centimeters (6 inches). It is found in mixed woodland, parks, and backyards, where it may be observed gleaning insects from foliage, or hanging from narrow branches or stems to reach seeds and berries. Being larger than most other tits, it tends to feed more readily on the ground. The Great Tit is a common bird, and its numbers appear to

Coal Tit

Crested Tit

be increasing, probably as a result of the provision of nest boxes and bird-feeders, and although it will form mixed flocks when foraging in winter, it can be aggressive, outcompeting smaller tits for food. When nesting, it will line a nest box or natural cavity in a tree or wall with soft material such as grass and moss, before laying a clutch of up to eleven eggs, which will be incubated by the female for around two weeks. Both adult birds will feed their young once hatched, until they fledge at around three weeks old.

Another common tit, although perhaps a little less common in gardens, the **Coal Tit** (*Parus ater*) is also rather less colorful than some of its relatives. It is small, around 11 centimeters (4 inches), with a gray back and wings, gray-brown underside, and black head, with large white cheek patches and a white nape. It feeds primarily on insects, but having a more slender bill than most other tits, it is also well adapted to feeding on conifer seeds, and is often more likely to be encountered in coniferous, rather than deciduous, woodland. During the breeding season, it nests in a hole in a tree or bank, and will even use abandoned mouse burrows, lining its chosen site with soft material. It produces a clutch of up to 12 eggs, which are incubated

solely by the female for about two weeks. As with other tits, however, both adult birds will care for their young.

The **Crested Tit** (*Parus cristatus*) is almost exclusively found in coniferous woodland, and in Britain it tends only to be seen in the highlands of Scotland, although here it will visit gardens with large or plentiful conifers. It tends to forage quite low in such trees, or on the ground, feeding on insects, spiders, berries, and seeds. It is a distinctive tit, with a large, grayish head, a black crescent behind the eye, a black throat and collar, and black and white pointed crest. Its upperparts are grayish-brown, and it is buff below. It grows to around 12 centimeters (5 inches) in length. It tends to nest in rotting stumps or branches, excavating a cavity itself, in which it will construct a small, cup-shaped nest of vegetation. Here it will produce a clutch of up to eight eggs, which will be incubated by the female for about two weeks. Both adult birds will care for their young, which fledge around three weeks after hatching.

Blue Tit

243

TUFTED TITMOUSE

SCIENTIFIC NAME:	*Parus bicolor*
FAMILY:	Paridae
LENGTH:	15cm (6in)
HABITAT:	Parks, deciduous forests, orchards, suburban areas
DISTRIBUTION:	Southeast Canada, the eastern US, and northeast Mexico
IDENTIFICATION:	Small gray songbird with a white underside, orange flanks and gray crest. Black eyes and forehead marking prominent on pale gray face

The Tufted Titmouse is the largest of the American tits, and is often quite conspicuous, mainly on account of its loud and varied vocalizations. It is widespread in the eastern US, and has extended its range northward, able to find food by visiting bird-feeders in gardens during the winter months. Its natural diet, however, consists of insects, fruit and seeds. It is an active and sociable bird, usually seen in pairs or small groups, but during the colder months it may join other small birds to form larger, mixed-species flocks. During the breeding season, it makes a cup-shaped nest in a tree hole or nest-box, using grass, leaves, animal hair, and wool, where up to eight eggs are laid. Once considered a distinct species, in Mexico and Texas, the Tufted Titmouse often possesses a black crest and white forehead, and is known as the Black-crested Titmouse. Where the two color variants overlap, hybridization is common, resulting in offspring with dark crests and orange or brown foreheads.

VERDIN

SCIENTIFIC NAME:	*Auriparus flaviceps*
FAMILY:	Remizidae
LENGTH:	10cm (4in)
HABITAT:	Desert and mesquite scrub
DISTRIBUTION:	Southern US to central Mexico
IDENTIFICATION:	Small songbird with a gray body, yellow face, and reddish shoulder patches

The Verdin is a fairly inconspicuous, though active, bird of desert and scrub areas, occurring particularly in the southwestern US, where it forages amongst mesquite and other vegetation in search of food. It feeds on insects, seeds, and berries, but will also take nectar from flowers. During the breeding season the Verdin constructs domed nests of thorny twigs, placed low in a tree or in a bush. The male will usually begin constructing one or more nests, to be aided by the female once successful pairing has taken place. The female will then produce a clutch of around three to six eggs, which she alone incubates for between two and three weeks. However, the male will remain in attendance, and should the female go on to produce a second clutch, he will take responsibility for feeding the first brood. Outside of the breeding season, the Verdin is usually solitary, but continues to construct similar, but usually smaller, roosting nests all year round. Winter roosting nests have thicker insulation than those built throughout the rest of the year, and those built in summer tend to open toward the prevailing winds.

BLACK-CAPPED CHICKADEE

SCIENTIFIC NAME:	*Parus atricapillus*
FAMILY:	Paridae
LENGTH:	13cm (5in)
HABITAT:	Woodland, parks, gardens, fields, and forest edges
DISTRIBUTION:	Southern Canada and the northern US
IDENTIFICATION:	Small songbird with a large head. Gray above, buff below, with white-edged wing and tail feathers, white face, black crown and throat patch

A familiar and fairly common bird throughout its range, the Black-capped Chickadee is mainly confined to southern Canada and the northern US, although in the southeast its range overlaps slightly with that of the very similar Carolina Chickadee (*Poecile carolinensis*), with which it may hybridize. Nesting normally takes place in May and June, at which time the Black-capped Chickadee produces a clutch of around eight eggs in a hole in a tree, lined with moss or other soft plant material. Outside of the breeding season, pairs and solitary birds form flocks, which often combine with small flocks of other bird species. It remains highly active throughout even the harshest of winters, during which time it is a frequent visitor to bird-feeders in backyards, where it may even be bold enough to alight on a human hand. This species naturally forages in thickets for insects, seeds and berries, and habitually stores items of food during the winter months. The chickadees are named after their "chick-a-dee" calls, and that of the Black-capped Chickadee is quite low and slow.

WHITE-BREASTED NUTHATCH ▼

SCIENTIFIC NAME:	*Sitta carolinensis*
FAMILY:	Sittidae
LENGTH:	15cm (6in)
HABITAT:	Mature deciduous and mixed forests, suburban parks and gardens with large trees
DISTRIBUTION:	Much of North America, from southern parts of Canada, south to Mexico
IDENTIFICATION:	A fairly large nuthatch with blue-gray upperparts, bright white face and underparts, and black outer tail feathers. Tail is short, bill is long and slightly upturned. Male has black crown, the female's is grayer

Inquisitive and acrobatic, the White-breasted Nuthatch can often be seen hopping headfirst down tree-trunks as it forages for food. Originally known as "nut-hacks," these birds break open seeds and nuts by jamming them into crevices in tree bark and hammering them with their bills, although they also consume fruit, insects, and other small invertebrates such as spiders. Territorial throughout the year, pairs of White-breasted Nuthatches will, however, often remain together after the breeding season, sometimes joining foraging flocks of titmice or chickadees in winter, possibly for protection. During the breeding season, the White-breasted Nuthatch nests in tree holes or nest-boxes, which it lines with bark chips, leaves, grass, and animal hair, where the female will incubate a clutch of up to nine eggs for around two weeks.

(EURASIAN) NUTHATCH ▲

SCIENTIFIC NAME:	*Sitta europaea*
FAMILY:	Sittidae
LENGTH:	14cm (5in)
HABITAT:	Woods, parks, and yards
DISTRIBUTION:	Much of Europe and across Asia to the Pacific
IDENTIFICATION:	Small, plump bird with a short tail. Plumage is blue-gray above, buff below, with reddish flanks and rump, and black eye-stripes

The Nuthatch is a lively, alert bird that is often seen clinging upside down as it traverses tree trunks and branches in search of spiders and insects; indeed, these are the only birds that can climb down tree trunks as easily as they climb up them, gripping with their relatively large feet and long claws. As its name suggests, in addition to invertebrates, this species also eats nuts, which it may first wedge into a crevice before breaking the shell with its bill. It nests in tree holes, which it lines with bark and other vegetation such as leaves, also using mud to plaster over large cracks or crevices inside the nest, and to reduce the size of the entrance hole. The female alone will incubate up to nine eggs for around two weeks but the male will remain near by, providing food for her, and, following hatching, for the young. Although the Nuthatch can be hard to spot, it is made conspicuous in woodland by its loud "chit-chit" calls, and it may also visit garden feeders.

COMMON TREECREEPER ▶

SCIENTIFIC NAME:	*Certhia familiaris*
FAMILY:	Certhiidae
LENGTH:	13cm (5in)
HABITAT:	Mature woods, parks, and backyards
DISTRIBUTION:	Much of Europe, through central Asia to Japan
IDENTIFICATION:	Speckled gray-brown upperparts, silvery white underparts, with a white eye-stripe, and long, slender, curved bill

Although quite common in woods, parks, and backyards throughout much of its range, the Treecreeper manages to remain fairly inconspicuous due to the camouflage afforded by its mottled upper plumage, and its somewhat mouse-like method of creeping up tree trunks and moving along branches in short spurts. However, it cannot climb down the trunks, so it instead flies from the upper trunk of one tree to the base of the next, continuing up the trunk in a spiraling manner. It uses its narrow bill to probe crevices for spiders and insects as it does so, while using its stiff tail to press against the trunk for balance, in much the same way as a woodpecker. During the breeding season, the Treecreeper nests amongst ivy, behind loose bark, or in the cavity of a tree, using vegetation, animal hair, and feathers to make a sort of pocket. Both the male and the female build the nest; however, the female will incubate the clutch of three to nine eggs by herself. These hatch after around two weeks, with both parent birds then feeding the young for around a further 15 days.

BROWN CREEPER

SCIENTIFIC NAME:	*Certhia americana*
FAMILY:	Certhiidae
LENGTH:	13cm (5in)
HABITAT:	Coniferous and mixed forests, often in mountainous regions
DISTRIBUTION:	Much of North America, south to parts of Central America
IDENTIFICATION:	Mottled brown and white upperparts, whitish underparts, long, thin, curved bill, and stiff tail

Like the closely related Eurasian Common Treecreeper, the Brown Creeper climbs up tree trunks, using its tail as a brace to aid its spiraling ascent, as it forages for invertebrates such as insects and spiders. It then flies to the base of the next tree, being unable to climb down the trunks. It was once thought to be the same species as the Eurasian Treecreeper, but studies have shown that they do not respond to each other's songs, supporting the idea that they are a separate species. During the breeding season, it nests amongst ivy, loose bark, or in a split in a tree, making a pocket from bark, moss, and other plant material, where a clutch of five or six eggs is usually laid, to be incubated solely by the female for around two weeks. Outside of the breeding season, the Brown Creeper is generally a solitary bird, but it may sometimes join flocks of other small birds in winter.

◄ MISTLETOEBIRD

SCIENTIFIC NAME:	*Dicaeum hirundinaceum*
FAMILY:	Dicaeidae
LENGTH:	10cm (4in)
HABITAT:	Rainforest, open woodland, hedgerows, and thickets, wherever mistletoe grows
DISTRIBUTION:	Throughout Australia, and in parts of Indonesia
IDENTIFICATION:	Male has glossy blue-black upperparts, scarlet throat, breast and under-tail coverts, with grayish-white underparts. Female is gray-brown above, grayish-white below, with pale scarlet under-tail coverts

The Mistletoebird belongs to the family of flowerpeckers and berrypeckers, a group of fairly small, typically plump birds, which forage for insects, nectar, and fruit in bushes and trees in the forested habitats of Australasia and Asia. As its name suggests, the Mistletoebird specializes in feeding on mistletoe berries. Due to the short gut of this bird, the mistletoe fruit passes through relatively quickly, and the sticky seeds of the plant are deposited on branches undamaged, where they grow, insuring a future supply of its food. In this way the bird forms a symbiotic relationship with the mistletoe plant. It will also feed on insects, flower petals, and nectar. Unlike most members of the flowerpecker family, which are sedentary, the Mistletoebird is nomadic, living in small flocks that may range over long distances in search of food. During the breeding season, which occurs from October to March, this species constructs a huge, domed nest of plant material and spiders' webs, woven around the branches of a tree, where a clutch of three or four eggs is laid.

WHITE-BROWED TREECREEPER

SCIENTIFIC NAME:	*Climacteris affinis*
FAMILY:	Climacteridae
LENGTH:	15cm (6in)
HABITAT:	Open woodland and scrubland
DISTRIBUTION:	Interior of Australia
IDENTIFICATION:	Bold black and white striped belly, with gray-brown upperparts, white eyebrow, and yellow wing bars

Once far more common and widespread in Australia, the White-browed Treecreeper is currently classified as near threatened, having suffered badly from habitat destruction. It occurs in acacia and spinifex scrubland, particularly where cypress pines are present. Although a treecreeper by name, the White-browed Treecreeper spends much of its time feeding on the ground, foraging largely for ants, and although it does also glean insects from the trunks and branches of trees, it tends not to use its tail as a brace, and is more likely to be seen perching or hopping around between branches than clinging to the trunk. During the breeding season, this species produces a clutch of one to three eggs, which are laid in a hollow lined with grass and animal hair, usually in a cypress pine tree or stump, quite close to the ground.

STRIATED PARDALOTE

SCIENTIFIC NAME:	*Pardalotus striatus*
FAMILY:	Dicaeidae
LENGTH:	10cm (4in)
HABITAT:	Eucalyptus forests and woodland
DISTRIBUTION:	Throughout most of Australia
IDENTIFICATION:	Variable, but generally dark above, with white edged flight feathers, yellow and gray underparts, and orange or yellow throat, facial markings, and wing spot

The Striated Pardalote occurs in a variety of habitats where trees or shrubs are present, but favors eucalyptus forests and woodlands, ranging over most of Australia, being absent from only the most arid areas. It usually forages high in the foliage of trees, occasionally feeding in shrubs closer to the ground. It consumes a variety of invertebrates, including spiders, insects, and their larvae, which are usually picked from leaves. Often found in small flocks, the Striated Pardalote occurs in pairs or groups of up to around six birds during the breeding season, which takes place between June and January. The nest takes the form of a ball-shaped structure of twigs, bark and grasses, usually constructed in a tree hollow or at the end of a burrow in an earthen bank. The Striated Pardalote produces a clutch of three to five eggs, which are incubated by both adult birds. Following hatching, both parents also care for their young, and other members of a group may cooperate to help with their feeding.

SUNBIRDS & SPIDERHUNTERS

The sunbirds and spiderhunters are a group of fairly small Old World birds belonging to the family Nectariniidae. They are found in Africa, India, southeast Asia and Australia, where they occur primarily in tropical and subtropical woodland, grassland and scrub habitats. They are characterized by their long, downcurved bills, which are used mainly for obtaining nectar from flowers, and the males of almost all species of sunbird are vividly colored with iridescent plumage, particularly when breeding, whilst the females are more drab. Spiderhunters usually also possess duller plumage.

Although they are not closely related, they are often described as being the Old World equivalent to the hummingbirds of the Americas, their similar traits being ascribed to convergent evolution; that is, they have independently acquired common characteristics as a response to similar environmental conditions. Like hummingbirds, they also have long, brush tipped tongues, and may hover whilst feeding at flowers. However, they are somewhat less agile, are unable to fly backwards and more commonly perch to feed. Their breeding habits are also different, for whilst most hummingbirds are polygamous, with males mating with several females, which tend their

young alone, sunbirds and spiderhunters are monogamous, and both parent birds in a pair cooperate to raise their nestlings. Their nests are usually pear-shaped, spherical or ovoid, constructed from grass and other vegetation, usually bound with spiders' webs, and suspended from the end of a narrow branch. An average clutch will normally consist of two or three eggs which will be incubated by the female for around two weeks. In addition to nectar, sunbirds will eat small fruits and insects which may be gleaned from foliage or taken in flight. As their name suggests, the spiderhunters feed largely on spiders and other small invertebrates, although fruit and nectar also make up a proportion of their diet.

Most sunbirds are found in Africa, and the **Malachite Sunbird** (*Nectarinia famosa*) is found in mountainous regions in much of East and South Africa. The male is notable for its extended tail feathers, which account for it being up to 10 centimeters (4 inches) longer than the female, with an average overall length of about 25 centimeters (10 inches). The male is iridescent green, and as with most species, the female is olive-green or brown above, with a pale underside. Like other sunbirds, the Malachite Sunbird is generally solitary, territorial,

Bronze Sunbird

and may be aggressive to other birds, especially when breeding. The male uses his long tail and shimmering plumage to attract a mate, and following mating, two eggs are laid in an ovoid nest, placed low in a shrub.

The **Bronze Sunbird** (*Nectarinia kilimensis*) is another species found in East Africa, in the same kinds of habitats, often also in mountainous regions. Like the Malachite Sunbird, males of this species possess long tails. On account of this, the male is around 23 centimeters (9 inches) long, whilst the female is about 15 centimeters (6 inches). The male tends to look almost black from a distance, but a bronze iridescence is noticeable on the head and back at close range. The female is olive-green above with a white throat, and a buff, slightly speckled underside. This species is often seen in pairs, and is thought to mate for life.

The **Purple Sunbird** (*Nectarinia asiatica*) is one of the most common and widespread of the Asian species, being found from Iran, throughout India, with the exception of the extreme north and west, to China and southeast Asia, where it occurs in deciduous woodland and scrub, and also in parks and gardens. It is quite small, growing to around 10 centimeters (4 inches), and the male is dark purple-blue, whilst the female is olive above and yellowish below. This species constructs a pear-shaped nest, suspended in a bush or low tree.

The **Purple-rumped Sunbird** (*Nectarinia zeylonica*) is another fairly common species, found throughout much of India, east to parts of southeast Asia. The male is vividly colored, with a maroon breast-band, which extends to the sides of its head, green crown, bright purple throat, and yellow underparts bordered with white. The female is duller, with an olive-green back, brown wings and yellowish breast. It too is often found close to human habitation, in backyards, and on cultivated land, as well as in scrub habitats.

The **Gray-breasted Spiderhunter** (*Arachnothera affinis*) is found in much of southeastAsia, where it inhabits forests, gardens and also plantations. It grows to around 18 centimeters (7 inches), and can be identified by its olive-green upperparts and gray underparts, with streaking on the breast and throat. When breeding, it constructs an elongated, cup-shaped nest of grasses, which it suspends beneath a large leaf, such as a banana leaf. It often decorates its nest with flowers.

Greater Double-collared Sunbird

ORIENTAL WHITE-EYE ▲

SCIENTIFIC NAME:	*Zosterops palpebrosus*
FAMILY:	Zosteropidae
LENGTH:	12cm (5in)
HABITAT:	Lowland forest edges and scrubland
DISTRIBUTION:	Most of India, southern China, and parts of southeast Asia
IDENTIFICATION:	Greenish upper plumage, a yellow head and throat, with a white underbelly and eye-ring

A highly active and sociable bird, the Oriental White-eye occurs in fairly large flocks, usually numbering around 30 individuals. However, it will also associate with loose, mixed-species flocks, and outside of the breeding season may even be found in its hundreds. In such numbers, these birds can cause substantial damage to fruit crops, but are also useful in controlling insect pests. Additionally, the Oriental White-eye consumes nectar, collecting it from flowers with its long, brush-tipped tongue. During the breeding season, flocks tend to disperse, and pairs of this species construct a deep, cup-shaped nest of grasses, woven amongst the branches of a small tree or bush, or attached to bamboo stems. The female produces a clutch of two eggs, which are usually incubated for a little under two weeks, with the young fledging around 12 days after hatching.

BROAD-RINGED WHITE-EYE

SCIENTIFIC NAME:	*Zosterops poliogaster*
FAMILY:	Zosteropidae
LENGTH:	12cm (5in)
HABITAT:	Mountainous forest
DISTRIBUTION:	Northeast Africa
IDENTIFICATION:	Olive-green plumage, yellow eyebrow, and large white eye-ring

Like other members of its family, The Broad-ringed White-eye possesses a distinctive ring of feathers surrounding the eye, which, as its name suggests, is particularly conspicuous in this species. It is often found in large flocks, moving around its rainforest habitat noisily as it searches for insects, berries, and other fruits. It usually forages high in the trees, and its strong legs and feet enable the Broad-ringed White-eye to move around the branches with a great deal of agility. Occasionally however, it may also feed on or near to the ground. During the breeding season, pairs construct a deep, cup-shaped nest from grasses, lichens, and moss, lined with finer fibers, which they attach to the branches of a small tree or bush. The female produces a clutch of two to four eggs, which are incubated for the relatively short period of 11 to 12 days.

NEW HOLLAND HONEYEATER ▼

SCIENTIFIC NAME:	*Phylidonyris novaehollandiae*
FAMILY:	Meliphagidae
LENGTH:	18cm (7in)
HABITAT:	Heaths, scrub, woodland, parks, and yards
DISTRIBUTION:	Southern Australia, including Tasmania
IDENTIFICATION:	Black and white, with a large yellow wing and tail patches, small white ear patch, white whiskers at base of the bill, and a white eye

The New Holland Honeyeater is nomadic, and common across a range of habitats, including heaths, woodland, parks, and backyards, and it is an active and inquisitive bird, bold enough to approach humans. However, should it sense danger it will tend to emit a loud alarm call, often joined by others of its kind. It may forage alone at times, but will typically be found in quite large groups, sometimes also in association with other species of honeyeaters. New Holland Honeyeaters forage mainly in the lower branches of trees and bushes, where they feed mostly on the nectar of flowers, however; they will also consume fruit, spiders and other small invertebrates, which are usually plucked from foliage. The New Holland Honeyeater may breed at almost any time of the year, but most nesting occurs in summer and winter. It constructs a cup-shaped nest of bark and grass, secured with spiders' webs, and lined with soft vegetation, which is placed in a bush or tree. The female produces a clutch of two to three eggs, which are incubated for about 18 days, and following hatching, both parent birds feed the young, which leave the nest after around a further 16 days. Due to the relatively long breeding season, two or three broods may be raised in a year.

BLUE-FACED HONEYEATER ▲

SCIENTIFIC NAME:	*Entomyzon cyanotis*
FAMILY:	Meliphagidae
LENGTH:	30cm (12in)
HABITAT:	Open woodland and scrub
DISTRIBUTION:	Northern and eastern Australia, also southern New Guinea
IDENTIFICATION:	A large honeyeater, olive-green above, with a black crown and breast stripe, white underparts, white patch at the back of the head, and large areas of bare blue skin around the eyes

The Blue-faced Honeyeater of northern Australia and New Guinea is a large and conspicuous species, particularly notable for the large patches of bright blue skin around its eyes, from which its common name is derived. It inhabits quite open woodlands and scrub, where it forages amongst thickets for fruit and nectar. Like all honeyeaters, it has a long, specially adapted tongue which terminates in brush-like projections or papillae, which enable it to collect nectar from deep inside flowers. It is frequently an aggressive species, particularly during the breeding season, and it will use the nests of Australo-Papuan babblers and miners as its own, sometimes forcibly evicting the original occupants. At other times it may construct its own nest, building a large, cup-shaped structure of twigs and other vegetation, and in many cases this will be aggressively defended against perceived intruders, including humans that venture too close.

NOISY FRIARBIRD ▼

SCIENTIFIC NAME:	*Philemon corniculatus*
FAMILY:	Meliphagidae
LENGTH:	35cm (14in)
HABITAT:	Eucalypt forest and open woodland
DISTRIBUTION:	Eastern Australia, but absent from much of the Cape York Peninsula
IDENTIFICATION:	Large gray bird, with bare black head, white plumes on throat, long, white-tipped tail, and red eyes. Large curved bill with an upright knob

Also known as the "Leatherhead," this large, stocky species of honeyeater is rather vulturine in appearance, with its bald head, heavy bill, and ruff-like neck feathers. Despite its large size and distinctive look, however, the Noisy Friarbird spends much of its time high in the forest canopy, and were it not for its raucous, cackling voice, it might be more difficult to locate. Like other honeyeaters, it feeds on nectar from flowers, but it will also consume berries, fruit, insects, and the eggs of other birds. Some large honeyeaters are also known to occasionally feed on nestlings, small amphibians, and reptiles. This species is often found in small, rowdy flocks for much of the year, but during the breeding season, which lasts from August to February, pairs tend to become more retiring. The Noisy Friarbird constructs a deep cup-shaped nest of bark, grasses, leaves, spiders' webs, and other available materials, positioned in dense foliage in the outer branches of a tree, sometimes above water. Here the female produces a clutch of two to three eggs.

YELLOW-THROATED MINER

SCIENTIFIC NAME:	*Manorina flavigula*
FAMILY:	Meliphagidae
LENGTH:	28cm (11in)
HABITAT:	Open woodland and agricultural areas
DISTRIBUTION:	Throughout most of Australia, except for the southeast and parts of the northeast
IDENTIFICATION:	Buff-white underparts, gray wings washed with yellow, black around eyes with a yellow eye spot, throat patch, bill and feet

The Yellow-throated Miner is a large honeyeater that feeds on some nectar, fruit, and seeds, but forages mainly for insects, both on the ground and in trees, prying under bark and amongst foliage for ants, beetles, wasps, and caterpillars. It is a highly sociable bird, living in nomadic colonies of between 12 and 50 birds, which usually form smaller groups when feeding. During the breeding season, which takes place from July to December, nesting also occurs in colonies, and this species demonstrates cooperative breeding, with several birds helping to feed and protect nestlings. The young also band together after leaving the nest and continue to be fed by adults. The nest itself takes the form of a large saucer-shaped structure composed of twigs, leaves, and grass, and an average clutch consists of two to three eggs. The Yellow-throated Miner is a noisy and aggressive bird, particularly when breeding, and groups will attack other species that encroach upon their feeding, roosting, and nesting sites.

YELLOW WATTLEBIRD

Scientific name:	*Anthochaera paradoxa*
Family:	Meliphagidae
Length:	48cm (19in)
Habitat:	Eucalypt forest, woodland, heaths, and backyards
Distribution:	Tasmania
Identification:	Very large honeyeater. Plumage is gray-brown streaked with white overall, with a yellow belly. A yellow wattle hangs from each cheek

The Yellow Wattlebird is the largest honeyeater, and a species which is endemic to, or found only in, Tasmania. In addition to its large size, it is also highly distinctive on account of the pendulous, yellow cheek wattles from which its name is derived, and its guttural call. It does feed on nectar and fruit (as with other members of its family it plays an important role in the pollination of many flowering plants) but as with most of the larger honeyeaters, its diet consists predominantly of insects. It forages in Eucalyptus forests amongst trees and bushes, searching for food at all levels, but it is also present on coastal heaths and regularly visits backyards to eat at bird tables and feeders. It is a fairly common species throughout its range, but its numbers have declined somewhat due to habitat loss. During the breeding season it constructs a large, loose, cup-shaped nest of twigs, bark and other vegetation, lined with feathers and soft plant material, where a clutch of two or three eggs is laid.

CAPE SUGARBIRD ▲

Scientific name:	*Promerops cafer*
Family:	Meliphagidae
Length:	22–45cm (9–18in) Female is smaller than male
Habitat:	Scrub and heathland
Distribution:	South Africa
Identification:	Slender honeyeater with long, slightly curved bill and long tail, which is much longer in the male. Plumage brown above, white below, speckled with brown. Rump is yellow

The sugarbirds are the only members of the honeyeater family that occur in Africa, with all others being found in Australasia and parts of southeast Asia, and the Cape Sugarbird is also amongst the largest of the honeyeaters. However, it is not a stocky bird, and much of its length can be attributed to its long tail. This is particularly true in the case of the male, whose tail may account for around two thirds of its total length. Its diet contains some invertebrates which may be caught in the air or taken from foliage, but it is essentially a nectar-feeding species, using its long bill and long, brush-tipped tongue to probe amongst flowers. Of particular importance is the protea plant, which provides food in the form of nectar, and during the breeding season is used extensively by the male as a vantage point when defending territory. It is also used for nesting materials. The Cape Sugarbird usually nests quite low in a bush, constructing a cup-shaped nest of twigs and other vegetation, which it lines with plant down, positioned quite close to the ground amongst the branches of a bush. The breeding season is during the winter months, from March to August, and is heralded by display flights by males, in which they fly with the tail held high, whilst clapping their wings together.

YELLOWHAMMER

SCIENTIFIC NAME:	*Emberiza citrinella*
FAMILY:	Fringillidae
LENGTH:	16cm (6in)
HABITAT:	Open country, hedgerows, and coniferous woodland
DISTRIBUTION:	Much of Europe and central Asia, also parts of northwest Africa
IDENTIFICATION:	Male has yellow head and underparts, streaked brown back, and white outer tail feathers. Female is less boldly colored and more heavily streaked

The Yellowhammer is widespread in areas of grassland and hedged fields, although its numbers have declined in parts of its range, particularly in Britain, where breeding numbers have fallen by as much as 50 percent in recent years. When seen, however, it is easily identified by its coloration, particularly the male, with its brightly colored head. It feeds mainly on seeds and small insects, foraging on the ground in open country such as cultivated fields and heaths, or in hedgerows and bushes. In the winter and spring, it may also visit backyards in search of food. During the winter this species is often encountered in small flocks with finches and buntings. The breeding season begins with a rather boisterous courtship, in which the male pursues the female in a twisting flight that often ends with both birds tumbling through the branches of trees or bushes. The nest, which is built by the female, consists of a tidy cup of grass and moss, lined with animal hair, which may be placed low in a bush or hedge, or on the ground amongst vegetation. A clutch of three to five eggs is incubated for up to two weeks, with both parent birds caring for their young.

SNOW BUNTING

SCIENTIFIC NAME:	*Plectrophenax nivalis*
FAMILY:	Emberizidae
LENGTH:	17cm (7in)
HABITAT:	Tundra, barren fields, and rocky shores
DISTRIBUTION:	Circumpolar, high in the Northern Hemisphere, farther south in winter
IDENTIFICATION:	White overall with black wingtips, central tail feathers, and shoulder patch. Breeding male has black back, winter male has buff crown and mottled back. Female is white with a rust-colored crown, collar, and back

Snow Buntings are highly sociable birds, and migrate in large flocks between their arctic breeding grounds and more southerly winter habitats. In winter, these flocks are usually composed only of Snow Buntings. However, in other seasons Snow Buntings may associate with pipits and other small birds. The breeding season begins around late May, with older male birds arriving at the breeding grounds first, to begin to establish territories. Once the females arrive, the males attract them with a finch-like warbling, before a chase ensues, which will usually end with mating. The female builds a cup-shaped nest of grass and moss lined with feathers, placed amongst rocks for shelter and to minimize predation. Four to six eggs are laid, and incubated solely by the female for four to ten days, during which time the male brings her food. In a habitat where it can become extremely cold, the eggs require constant warmth. The chicks fledge around two weeks after hatching, to join the larger flocks. Snow Buntings forage on the ground, feeding primarily on seeds, buds, insects, and other invertebrates.

REED BUNTING ▲

SCIENTIFIC NAME:	*Emberiza schoeniclus*
FAMILY:	Fringillidae
LENGTH:	15cm (6in)
HABITAT:	Reedbeds, river margins, farmland, and forest edges
DISTRIBUTION:	Most of Eurasia, from western Europe to the Far East. Also in North Africa
IDENTIFICATION:	Streaked brown plumage above, pale with dark speckles below. Male has a black head and bib, white collar and mustache. Female has lighter head, with heavy brown mustache

As its name suggests, the Reed Bunting is traditionally a wetland bird but the loss of some reedbed habitats has also had two distinct results. There has been a marked decline in this species' number and at the same time the Reed Bunting has extended its range into drier areas such as farmland and forests, and has also been known to visit backyards on occasion. Waterside habitats remain preferred during the breeding season, however, with the adult female constructing a cup-shaped nest of grass and moss, placed amongst reeds or other dense vegetation, on or near to the ground. Here the female incubates a clutch of between four and seven eggs for a period of up to two weeks, and following hatching, both parent birds will care for their young, which fledge at around 12 days. The Reed Bunting feeds largely on the ground, its diet consisting of seeds and insects, and although it is generally a well-camouflaged bird, it has white outer tail feathers which may be flicked conspicuously as it flies into cover.

FOX SPARROW

SCIENTIFIC NAME:	*Passerella iliaca*
FAMILY:	Emberizidae
LENGTH:	18cm (7in)
HABITAT:	Scrub, thickets, and mixed woodland
DISTRIBUTION:	Most of Canada and the US
IDENTIFICATION:	Stocky bunting. Plumage variable, upperparts often dark brown or gray in the west, more rufous in the east. Underparts pale with heavy streaks, meeting in a large spot on breast

Amongst the largest of the New World sparrows, the Fox Sparrow is quite common, but it tends to inhabit areas of dense undergrowth, and therefore may be difficult to observe. It may be detected by its melodious song or noisy scratching as it searches for food. It is essentially a ground dwelling bird, foraging amongst soil or leaf-litter for insects, spiders and other invertebrates, although it will also feed on vegetation such as buds. However, as with many songbirds, its nestlings are fed exclusively on invertebrates. During the breeding season, it builds a cup-shaped nest of twigs and grasses, which it places on or close to the ground, in a bush or, rarely, low in a tree. Here a clutch of between two and five eggs will be laid. The eggs are incubated solely by the female for around two weeks, although following hatching, both parent birds will care for their young. As with some other species that nest on the ground, the adult Fox Sparrow has been known to feign a broken wing in order to lure potential predators away from the nest, before rapidly taking flight.

SONG SPARROW

SCIENTIFIC NAME:	*Melospiza melodia*
FAMILY:	Emberizidae
LENGTH:	17cm (7in)
HABITAT:	Scrub, thickets, woodland, suburbs, overgrown grassland, often close to water, also swamps and coastal marshes
DISTRIBUTION:	Much of North America, south to Mexico
IDENTIFICATION:	Variable plumage, but has striped head, darkly streaked back and rump, brown wings, pale breast and flanks, usually streaked or spotted, merging to a large breast patch. Rounded tail, short rounded wings

The Song Sparrow is common throughout much of North America in a wide range of habitats, and in a variety of forms; in fact some 31 distinct subspecies are recognized, the most of any species, with considerable variation in plumage. Alaskan individuals also tend to be somewhat stockier. As its name would suggest, the Song Sparrow is a prolific singer, particularly throughout the breeding season in spring and summer, when the male will sing both to attract a mate and to declare his territory. Following mating, nest construction and incubation is undertaken by the female, which builds a cup-shaped nest of small twigs and grasses, placed on the ground or in a low bush or thicket. The female produces a clutch of around three to five eggs, which she incubates alone for around two weeks. Following hatching, both parent birds initially care for the nestlings, until the young are almost fledged around a further two weeks later. The male will then assume care of the young birds, whilst the female will typically go on to lay and incubate another clutch. Three clutches a season is not uncommon. The young are fed on insects, the major constituent of their parents' diet, but the adult birds will also consume seeds, berries, and other vegetation.

WHITE-THROATED SPARROW ▲

SCIENTIFIC NAME:	*Zonotrichia albicollis*
FAMILY:	Emberizidae
LENGTH:	16cm (6in)
HABITAT:	Scrub, hedgerows, and dense thickets, also parks and backyards
DISTRIBUTION:	Much of North America, south to Mexico, but absent from parts of the west
IDENTIFICATION:	Upperparts streaked brown, underparts gray, with white throat patch. Crown may be striped black and white or black and tan

This species commonly breeds across Canada, but rarely much farther south; however, during the winter months its range extends to northern Mexico. It is found in a variety of habitats, and of all the New World sparrows, it is probably the most common to be found in urban environments. The White-throated Sparrow occurs in two color forms or morphs, white-crowned and tan-crowned. Interestingly, during the breeding season, individual birds nearly always mate with a bird of the opposite morph, and this species has also been known to hybridize with the Dark-eyed Junco. The White-throated Sparrow constructs a cup-shaped nest on the ground or low in a bush, where a clutch of four to six eggs will be laid, to be incubated solely by the female for around two weeks. The male will then help to feed the chicks on insects and other small invertebrates. The adult birds are more omnivorous, also feeding on seeds, and other vegetation.

SAFFRON FINCH

SCIENTIFIC NAME:	*Sicalis flaveola*
FAMILY:	Emberizidae
LENGTH:	15cm (6in)
HABITAT:	Open grassland and scrubland
DISTRIBUTION:	Various parts of South America, also introduced to parts of Central America and the Caribbean
IDENTIFICATION:	Male has bright yellow plumage, with dark wing feathers and tail tip and an orange-yellow forehead. Female is usually gray-brown above, whitish below, with a yellow collar

The Saffron Finch is a fairly common bird which occurs mainly in open and semi-open lowland areas in much of South America, but it is absent from the Amazon Basin, and there are three distinct populations in the surrounding areas, with the species occupying northern Colombia and Venezuela, Ecuador, and Peru, and being found from northeastern Brazil to central Argentina. The male is quite striking, being bright yellow in color, and it may be distinguished from other yellow finches which occur within its range by its orange crown patch. The female may be more difficult to identify as it can vary in appearance somewhat, usually being gray-brown above and pale below with a yellow collar, although sometimes its plumage is very much like the male, but duller. The Saffron Finch is sociable, and may be observed in small flocks, foraging on the ground for seeds. During the breeding season, this species often makes its nest in a hole in a tree or a roof cavity, but it will also frequently use the abandoned nest of another species. A clutch consists of three to four eggs, which are incubated for about two weeks. This bird has a melodious, repetitious song which, in addition to its plumage, has led to it being widely kept as a cage bird.

DARK-EYED JUNCO ▼

SCIENTIFIC NAME:	*Junco hyemalis*
FAMILY:	Emberizidae
LENGTH:	15cm (6in)
HABITAT:	Mixed and coniferous woodland, thickets, parks, and backyards
DISTRIBUTION:	Throughout most of North America, south to northern Mexico
IDENTIFICATION:	Fairly small sparrow with variable plumage. Typically gray or brown above with a darker hood and pale belly

This small and common New World sparrow is confined to Canada, and the far northern and mountainous parts of the western US for much of the year, extending its range widely across the US in winter, when it is a frequent visitor to bird-feeders in backyards. In spring it returns north to woodland or thickets in order to breed. It is mainly a ground dwelling bird, and tends to nest on the ground, amongst vegetation or in cavities amongst rocks or tree roots, commonly on a sloping or near vertical bank. Both birds in a pair cooperate to construct a small, cup-shaped nest of small twigs, grasses, roots, leaves, moss, and other vegetation. The female Dark-eyed Junco incubates the clutch of around three to five eggs alone, for a period of around two weeks. Following hatching, the young are cared for by both parent birds, and will leave the nest at about two weeks of age. The Dark-eyed Junco forages mainly on the ground, sometimes in flocks, where it searches amongst undergrowth and leaf-litter for insects, spiders, and other invertebrates, seeds, buds, and berries.

EASTERN TOWHEE ▲

SCIENTIFIC NAME:	*Pipilo erythrophthalmus*
FAMILY:	Emberizidae
LENGTH:	23cm (9in)
HABITAT:	Open fields, thickets, scrubland, and forest edges
DISTRIBUTION:	From southern Canada, throughout the US to Mexico
IDENTIFICATION:	Male is black overall, with rusty-red flanks and a white belly. Female is brown where the male is black

Formerly considered to be races of the same species, known as the Rufous-sided Towhee, the Eastern Towhee and the Spotted Towhee (*Pipilo maculatus*) are now generally recognized as being separate species, although where their ranges overlap, the two forms may hybridize. It is one of the largest of the New World sparrows or buntings, and may also be conspicuous due to its red flanks. It spends much of its time on the ground, where it forages for insects, spiders, seeds, and fruits, often scratching at the ground or leaf-litter with a two-footed technique. During the breeding season, the Eastern Towhee also tends to nest on the ground, typically amongst a clump of tall grass or other vegetation, although it may also place its cup-shaped nest of twigs and grasses in the lower branches of a bush. The female takes responsibility for constructing the nest, and will incubate a clutch of between two and six eggs alone, for a period of around two weeks. Following hatching, both parent birds will tend to their offspring, which fledge about a further two weeks later. The family will then usually remain together until the end of summer.

DICKCISSEL ▲

SCIENTIFIC NAME:	*Spiza americana*
FAMILY:	Cardinalidae
LENGTH:	15cm (6in)
HABITAT:	Open meadows, cultivated land, and prairies
DISTRIBUTION:	Southeast Canada and the eastern US. Overwinters as far south as northern South America
IDENTIFICATION:	Small, stocky bird with gray-brown back and head, buff underside, yellowish breast, and yellow eyebrows. Breeding male has bright yellow breast, black bib, and white throat.

Although formerly classified in the family Emberizidae, the Dickcissel is now more commonly placed in the family Cardinalidae. It is a small, sparrow-like bird which occurs in open, grassy habitats in eastern parts of North America. Like sparrows and other closely related species such as finches, it is a seed eating bird, and it forages for its food mainly on the ground. However, when singing, it is more likely to be observed perching on a post or telephone wire. It is highly sociable, usually occurring in small flocks, but it will gather in much larger groups during migration and where there is a particularly abundant food supply. During the breeding season, the female takes responsibility for nest-building, incubation, and the care of the young. The nest takes the form of a loose cup-shaped structure of leaves and grasses lined with fine vegetation, which is placed low in a bush or amongst dense vegetation on the ground. An average clutch consists of four eggs, which are incubated for just under two weeks. Following hatching, the young fledge at around ten days old.

RED-CRESTED CARDINAL

SCIENTIFIC NAME:	*Paroaria coronata*
FAMILY:	Emberizidae/Cardinalinae
LENGTH:	20cm (8in)
HABITAT:	Grassland with scattered trees and scrubland, often near water
DISTRIBUTION:	Southeast Brazil, northern Argentina, and southeast Bolivia. Introduced in Hawaii
IDENTIFICATION:	Gray back, wings, and tail, white underside and collar, with a red crest, face, and throat patch

This species is sometimes also known as the Brazilian Cardinal, however this name can be somewhat misleading, as it is often also used to refer to several different, although closely related, species, which can be found in Brazil and the surrounding areas. As its more common name suggests, one of the most distinctive characteristics of this bird is its raised red crest. It is a fairly active and sociable bird, often encountered in small family groups or in pairs, which tend to forage on the ground for seeds, although when perching it will usually be found high in a tree or large shrub. During the breeding season, mating is preceded by a courtship dance, which is performed by the male. He hops around with his tail feathers outspread, often with an item of food or nesting materials held in his bill. The nest takes the form of a compact, neatly woven cup, commonly placed fairly low down in a bush or tree. The female produces a clutch of three or four eggs, which are incubated by both parent birds for around two weeks. The young leave the nest about two weeks after hatching, but may be fed by their parents for a further week. Due to its attractive appearance, the Red-crested Cardinal is often kept as a cage bird.

COMMON/NORTHERN CARDINAL

SCIENTIFIC NAME:	*Cardinalis cardinalis*
FAMILY:	Cardinalidae
LENGTH:	23cm (9in)
HABITAT:	Forests, thickets, hedgerows, suburban parks, and backyards
DISTRIBUTION:	Southeastern Canada, and the central, eastern and southern US, south to Mexico and Belize
IDENTIFICATION:	Medium sized bird with a large crest, heavy triangular bill, and black face mask. Male's plumage is brilliant red, whilst the female is gray-tan, with red in wings, crest, and tail

Sometimes classified in the family Emberizidae, the Common Cardinal is now often placed in the family Cardinalidae. The male of this species is a highly distinctive bird, with its bright red plumage and pointed crest, and it is a familiar sight in a variety of habitats across its range. It is a common visitor to parks and gardens, particularly during the winter months, although it prefers areas with plenty of cover in the form of shrubs and bushes. It forages on or close to the ground, feeding mainly on seeds, buds,and berries, although it will supplement its diet with insects. This species is thought to pair for life, and will usually return to the same nesting sites each year. The male will defend this territory aggressively, whilst the female incubates a clutch of three or four eggs alone, in a loosely woven, cup-shaped nest of twigs and grasses, which it places amongst the densely tangled branches of a bush or small tree. Following hatching, both parent birds will initially care for their young and the male will often care for them alone for a short time once they have fledged, allowing the female to produce a second brood.

PAINTED BUNTING

SCIENTIFIC NAME:	*Passerina ciris*
FAMILY:	Cardinalidae
LENGTH:	13cm (5in)
HABITAT:	Thickets, hedges, and woodland edges
DISTRIBUTION:	South-eastern US and Mexico, wintering in Cuba, the Bahamas, Jamaica, and Central America
IDENTIFICATION:	Male is red below, with indigo-blue head, red eye-rings and bright green back, with darker green wings and tail. Female has lime-green back, crown, and nape, with a yellow-green throat, belly, and chest, occasionally with blue feathers on the head

The Painted Bunting is probably North America's most colorful bird, but perhaps somewhat surprisingly it may be difficult to spot, as it has a tendency to remain hidden amongst dense vegetation, sometimes even when it is singing. Its diet consists of seeds, insects, insect larvae, and spiders, and it may forage amongst low branches or on the ground, and will take insects from spiders' webs. During the breeding season males become highly territorial and aggressive to others of their species, and fights, which are common, may sometimes result in death. The nest takes the form of a neatly woven cup of twigs and grasses, lined with fine vegetation or animal hair, which is normally placed quite low in a small tree or bush. Following mating, the female incubates a clutch of around three or four eggs alone, for a period of about two weeks. The male Painted Bunting was once widely kept as a cage bird on account of its beautiful plumage, and although it is now protected, it continues to be illegally trapped, which has had an adverse affect on population numbers in recent years. Formerly classified in the family Emberizidae, the Painted Bunting is now often placed in the cardinal family Cardinalidae.

INDIGO BUNTING ▲

SCIENTIFIC NAME:	*Passerina cyanea*
FAMILY:	Cardinalidae
LENGTH:	15cm (6in)
HABITAT:	Open woodland and hedgerows
DISTRIBUTION:	Southeastern Canada and the eastern US, moving south as far as the Caribbean and Central America in winter
IDENTIFICATION:	Male breeding plumage is blue overall, deepest on head, with black in front of eyes, and dark tail and wing feathers, edged in blue. Usual plumage is brown with blue-edged feathers and whitish lower belly and undertail. Female is brown, often with faint streaks on chest, and faint buff wing bars

Common in summer in a range of open and lightly wooded habitats in much of North America, the male Indigo Bunting is most notable for his brilliant blue breeding plumage and his song, which is normally delivered from an exposed perch high in a tree or on a telephone wire. During the breeding season, males establish small territories, and it is interesting to note that birds in adjoining territories will share very similar or even identical songs, whilst those of individuals slightly farther apart may vary enormously. After a mate has been attracted and mating has occurred, the female will produce and incubate a clutch of three to four eggs in an open cup-shaped nest of leaves, twigs, and grasses, lined with fine vegetation, feathers, and animal fur, held together with spiders' webs. The nest is usually placed quite close to the ground, in the lower branches of a small tree or in a shrub. After the breeding season, this species tends to congregate in small flocks to forage together before migrating south in winter. It feeds on seeds, buds, berries, insects, and spiders. Although formerly classified in the family Emberizidae, the Indigo Bunting tends now to be placed in the family Cardinalidae.

BLUE GROSBEAK

SCIENTIFIC NAME:	*Guiraca caerulea*
FAMILY:	Cardinalidae
LENGTH:	17cm (7in)
HABITAT:	Woodland edges, hedgerows and thickets
DISTRIBUTION:	Much of North America south to the Caribbean
IDENTIFICATION:	Male is dark blue with chestnut wing bars, a black face, and a sturdy, conical bill. Female is dark brown above with two buff wing bars, and paler underneath

The Blue Grosbeak breeds in temperate North America during the summer before migrating south to spend most of the year in Mexico, Central and South America, and the Caribbean, where there are also resident populations. During the breeding season, the males typically sing from high perches, such as treetops or telephone wires, producing a long, warbling song that serves both to attract a mate, and to declare territory to other males. It is thought that the female constructs the nest alone, using a variety of vegetation to build a cup-shaped nest in a shrub or low in a small tree. Incubation of the clutch of three to four eggs and feeding of the young is also undertaken almost exclusively by the female, although once the young have fledged, the male may continue to care for them whilst the female sets about constructing a new nest in which to raise a second brood. The nests of this species are frequently parasitized by the Brown-headed Cowbird; however, Blue Grosbeaks have been documented constructing a new story on top of a parasitized nest, and they sometimes also successfully raise both cowbirds and their own young. Following the breeding season, Blue Grosbeaks form flocks that feed together prior to migration. This species feeds on a variety of insects, particularly beetles and grasshoppers, also consuming various seeds. Although formerly classified in the family Emberizidae, the Blue Grosbeak is now more commonly placed in the family Cardinalidae.

TANAGERS

The tanagers are a large group of small, colorful birds that belong to the family Thraupidae, which includes the typical tanagers, the honeycreepers, the euphonias, chlorophonias, and flowerpiercers. They are found mainly in tropical and subtropical regions in South and Central America, with just four species breeding in North America. These represent some of the most vividly colored birds occurring north of Mexico. The **Scarlet Tanager** (*Piranga olivacea*) overwinters in Central and South America, but breeds throughout much of the eastern US, north to southern Canada. This species reaches a length of 18 centimeters (7 inches), and the breeding male is highly distinctive, being bright red overall, with black wings and tail. The female and winter males are olive-green above and yellow below, with a dark tail and wings. They prefer mature deciduous or mixed woodland, but are also found in parks and backyards. Tanagers occur in a variety of arboreal and open shrub habitats, particularly in damp forests and around woodland edges, usually avoiding the darker, densest rainforest interiors in South America, although they may be found in clearings, or in the canopy where conditions are generally lighter and more open. These birds are also often seen close

to human habitation or on plantations. Owing to their bright plumage and habit of foraging in the open in small flocks, tanagers are often highly visible, and most species are common and numerous. They are generally marked with patches of yellows, reds, greens, and blues, and are quite stocky birds, mainly with short tails and stout bills. The honeycreepers and flowerpiercers have elongated, usually slightly downcurving bills.

The **Purple Honeycreeper** (*Cyanerpes caeruleus*) is found in a variety of habitats, including woodland, forest edges, and gardens in northern South America. The male is violet-blue overall, with a bright blue head, black wings and eye-stripe. The female is olive-green above, with pale, streaked underparts and brown markings around its eyes. Both possess a long, curved bill, and grow to around 10 centimeters (4 inches) long. Tanagers vary in length from around 10 to 28 centimeters (4 to 11 inches). Most associate in mixed-species flocks, comprising various tanager species and other birds, which move around together whilst foraging. They feed predominantly on small fruits and berries, and may be found feeding at all levels of the forest. Many will also feed on insects, gleaned from foliage, caught in

Green-and-gold Tanager

flight, or taken on the ground, whilst some species specialize in ground-feeding. The flowerpiercers and honeycreepers feed predominantly on nectar taken from flowers. These birds help to pollinate many plants. Being mainly fruit eaters, tanagers commonly ingest seeds, and as a result, disperse them in their droppings, aiding the spread of plants and trees. Euphonias, for example, play a highly important role in the life of the mistletoe plant, consuming its berries and depositing the seeds on branches, where they germinate and grow.

The **Golden-rumped Euphonia** (*Euphonia cyanocephala*) is found in forests and open woodland in much of South America, particularly in the Andes, parts of Brazil, Paraguay, and Argentina. The male is black above, with a blue crown and golden underside. The female is paler overall, with olive upper plumage. This species grows to around 10 centimeters (4 inches) long. When breeding, it builds a domed nest of moss with an entrance in the side, placed amongst a mound of moss or in the fork of a tree. Most tanagers are monogamous, and pairs frequently remain together throughout the year, with breeding often prompted by heavy rains, which bring about

an abundance of food. Males tend to display to females prior to mating, showing off their plumage and sometimes also offering food. Nest designs and locations vary, from cup-shaped nests placed in trees or bushes, to domed nests positioned in a crevice on a cliff or bank. The pair may construct the nest together, but often this is undertaken solely by the female. An average clutch consists of two eggs, which are incubated for up to 18 days by the female alone. Following hatching, the nestlings are cared for by both adult birds for a similar period.

The **Blue-naped Chlorophonia** (*Chlorophonia cyanea*) is a cliff-nesting species, often being found around cliffs in parts of South America, including areas of Venezuela and northern Argentina. The male has a blue back, green head with a blue eye-ring, green wings, and a yellow underside. The female is duller, with olive-green upper plumage and a blue nape. It is usually seen in pairs or small flocks in the forest canopy, and like the euphonias, its diet consists largely of mistletoe berries, although it will also feed on other small fruits and insects.

Western Tanager

YELLOW-RUMPED WARBLER ▼

SCIENTIFIC NAME:	*Dendroica coronata*
FAMILY:	Parulidae
LENGTH:	15cm (6in)
HABITAT:	Coniferous and mixed forest
DISTRIBUTION:	North and Central America
IDENTIFICATION:	Breeding male dark blue-gray above, streaked with black, dark breast and flanks. Rump, crown, and parts of breast yellow. Western male has yellow throat, white wing patch. Eastern male has white throat and wing bars. Females and nonbreeding males are streaked gray-brown

Once thought to be two separate birds, the eastern Myrtle Warbler and the western Audubon's Warbler are now considered to be one species, the Yellow-rumped Warbler. It is a common and widespread species, found throughout most of North America, south through Mexico to Guatemala. The ranges of the two forms are quite distinct, with only a relatively narrow overlap, although in such areas the Myrtle Warbler and Audubon's Warbler will interbreed. In addition to plumage differences, which are particularly noticeable in breeding males, there is a distinct difference in call notes between the eastern and western varieties, with Audubon's Warbler producing somewhat softer tones. The Yellow-rumped Warbler feeds on insects, spiders, seeds, and berries, and is the only warbler that can digest the waxes present in wax myrtles and bayberries, enabling this species to spend the winter farther north than other warblers. During the breeding season, it builds a cup-shaped nest of twigs and stems, usually high in a conifer tree, where a clutch of four or five eggs is laid.

YELLOW WARBLER ▲

SCIENTIFIC NAME:	*Dendroica petechia*
FAMILY:	Parulidae
LENGTH:	13cm (5in)
HABITAT:	Woodland, often near water
DISTRIBUTION:	From Canada, south to northern parts of South America
IDENTIFICATION:	Yellow overall, with darker wings and tail, and a dark eye. Males have light brown streaks on the breast and flanks, whilst females are duller with fainter stripes

The Yellow Warbler is a fairly common and widespread species, usually found in damp open woodland, often alongside streams. In Central and South America, mangrove swamps are a favored habitat. This species typically forages in the mid-level foliage of trees, where it hunts for insects and spiders, which may be caught in flight or gleaned from vegetation. During the breeding season, it builds a cup-shaped nest from grasses and other plant materials in the fork of a shrub or small tree, usually near water. In North America, the nests of Yellow Warblers are frequently parasitized by the Brown-headed Cowbird; however, the warbler will often recognize the foreign egg, and will then build an additional floor above it and begin constructing another nest in which to lay a new clutch. Occasionally, where the Brown-headed Cowbird has gone on to deposit further eggs, a nest may end up with several tiers. The Yellow Warbler usually lays a clutch of four or five eggs, but may produce as many as seven. These are incubated solely by the female for around 12 days; following hatching both parent birds care for their young.

BLACK-AND-WHITE WARBLER

SCIENTIFIC NAME:	*Mniotilta varia*
FAMILY:	Parulidae
LENGTH:	13cm (5in)
HABITAT:	Mixed woodland
DISTRIBUTION:	Much of North and Central America, traveling as far south as Peru in the winter
IDENTIFICATION:	Black and white striped plumage overall. Male has white chin in winter, black throat and cheeks when breeding. Female has buff, gray-streaked flanks, and whitish throat and cheeks

The Black-and-white Warbler is a highly unusual wood warbler, which behaves much like a nuthatch or treecreeper, and may commonly be seen creeping around on the trunks and large branches of trees, foraging for insects, conspicuous due to its barred plumage. It has an unusually long hind toe and claw on each foot, an adaptation that allows it to securely grip the tree bark as it probes any crevices with its long bill, hunting for prey such as beetles, ants, and caterpillars. During the breeding season, this species builds its nest in a sheltered spot on the ground, such as under a log or amongst tree roots, using plant material to make a thick woven cup. An average clutch consists of between four and six eggs, which are incubated by the female for up to two weeks. The Black-and-white Warbler can be rather aggressive for a warbler, and will sometimes attack other small birds, including nuthatches, chickadees, and other warbler species.

American Redstart

Scientific name:	*Setophaga ruticilla*
Family:	Parulidae
Length:	13cm (5in)
Habitat:	Open, deciduous woodland
Distribution:	Mainly eastern parts of North America, wintering in Central America and northern South America
Identification:	Male is black above, with orange wing patches, tail base, and sides of breast, with a white belly. Female has gray-green back, light gray head and white underside, with yellow wing patch, outer tail feathers, and side of breast

The American Redstart is a vividly patterned warbler, made more conspicuous by its habit of flashing its wings and tail in order to flush out insect prey from amongst foliage. Most of its food is taken on the wing, but this species will also glean insects from leaves or bark, and occasionally supplement its diet with berries. During the breeding season, the female constructs a neat, cup-shaped nest of plant material, animal hair, and spiders' webs, in a tree or bush, where she will incubate a clutch of three to five eggs alone. Occasionally male American Redstarts are polygamous, and will go on to mate with a second female once the first has begun to incubate her eggs. The females will incubate alone, but the male will help to feed the young once they have hatched. Unlike most polygamous birds, the male will establish and defend two separate territories which may be some distance apart.

COMMON YELLOWTHROAT

SCIENTIFIC NAME:	*Geothlypis trichas*
FAMILY:	Parulidae
LENGTH:	13cm (5in)
HABITAT:	Forests, thickets, moist grasslands, and marshes
DISTRIBUTION:	From southern Canada, through most of the US to Mexico. Winters as far south as Colombia and Venezuela
IDENTIFICATION:	Male is olive-green above with a black mask edged with white, yellow below, with a buff belly. Female is olive-brown above, buff below, with a yellow throat

The Common Yellowthroat is a rather skulking warbler, which often inhabits dense thickets and reedbeds, and as such, it may be more frequently heard than seen, producing a fast and rather cheerful sounding song. However, it is in fact one of the most abundant warblers, and occurs in several forms across its range, with more than 12 subspecies having been identified. Generally, the lower plumage of western birds tends to be brighter than that of those found in the east. Although associated with wetland habitats, the Common Yellowthroat is also found in drier areas with abundant, dense undergrowth, where it can forage for insects and spiders, which are gleaned from foliage or taken from the ground. During the breeding season, the male displays by ascending into the air whilst singing, before dropping back to the ground. The female constructs the cup-shaped nest, usually on or close to the ground amongst vegetation, or occasionally amongst reeds over water. A clutch consists of around four eggs, which are incubated by the female for about 12 days. Both parents care for their young for up to four weeks, although they may leave the nest after just over a week. The nests of Common Yellowthroats are often parasitized by the Brown-headed Cowbird; however, if the egg is discovered, a second nest may be constructed above the parasite's egg, where a new clutch will be laid.

YELLOW-BREASTED CHAT

SCIENTIFIC NAME:	*Icteria virens*
FAMILY:	Parulidae
LENGTH:	20cm (8in)
HABITAT:	Thickets in open woodland and scrubland
DISTRIBUTION:	Southern Canada and the US. Winters south to Panama
IDENTIFICATION:	Olive-green above, bright yellow throat and breast, white belly, gray head with a white eye-ring

The Yellow-breasted Chat is unusually large for a wood warbler, and is in fact the largest species in North America. However, it is rather shy and may be difficult to observe amongst the dense thickets in which it forages for insects and fruit. Due to its large size, this species somewhat resembles a thrasher or mockingbird, and it is sometimes known as the Yellow Mockingbird. Additionally, it also mimics the calls of other birds, and often sings during the night. They will sometimes nest in loose colonies even though the males tend to be somewhat territorial. During courtship, the male makes display flights, ascending from a perch whilst singing, before making a fluttering descent. The female constructs the large, cup-shaped nest of bark, twigs, and grasses, placed amongst the dense vegetation of a large bush. A clutch consists of four or five eggs, which the female incubates alone for around 12 days. Following hatching, the young are cared for by both parents, and leave the nest after about ten days. As with many wood warblers, the nests of this species are often parasitized by the Brown-headed Cowbird.

WARBLING VIREO

SCIENTIFIC NAME:	*Vireo gilvus*
FAMILY:	Vireonidae
LENGTH:	15cm (6in)
HABITAT:	Forests and open woodland
DISTRIBUTION:	From southern Canada, south to Mexico. Winters south to Nicaragua
IDENTIFICATION:	Gray above, buff below, white eyebrow, and pale yellow flanks

The Warbling Vireo is a rather drab and secretive bird which may be difficult to observe amongst the higher branches of trees, where it tends to forage for caterpillars and spiders, which are gleaned from the bark and foliage. It will also supplement its diet with berries. During courtship the male displays to the female by strutting around with his wings and tail outspread whilst singing and, if receptive, the female will vibrate her wings in response. Following mating, a clutch of around three or four eggs will be laid in a basket-like nest, suspended in the fork of a branch, usually quite high in a tree. Most of the nest construction is undertaken by the female, although the male will help, and the eggs are also incubated by both parent birds, for a period of around 12 days. Following hatching, the young fledge at around 16 days old. As with many small woodland birds, the nest of the Warbling Vireo is often parasitized by the Brown-headed Cowbird.

YELLOW-THROATED VIREO

SCIENTIFIC NAME:	*Vireo flavifrons*
FAMILY:	Vireonidae
LENGTH:	15cm (6in)
HABITAT:	Thickets and forest edges
DISTRIBUTION:	Southeastern Canada and the eastern US, south to northern parts of South America in winter
IDENTIFICATION:	Olive upper plumage, yellow breast and throat, and white belly. Bright yellow eye-rings and white wing bars

Despite its abundance and bright plumage, the Yellow-throated Vireo may be hard to spot, as it often remains high in the dense foliage of the forest canopy, where it forages for insects. However, it is a relatively bold species and may tolerate the close proximity of observers. Commonly a solitary bird, the Yellow-throated Warbler pairs during the breeding season just long enough to raise its brood, although at other times of the year, it may form loose associations with mixed-species flocks whilst foraging. During the breeding season, the female constructs a tightly woven, cup-shaped nest of grass, roots, leaves, and animal hair, which is held together with spiders' webs. As is typical with vireos, the nest is suspended, basket-like, from a branch. An average clutch contains between three and five eggs, which are incubated for around 12 days. Following the breeding season, this species will undertake a southward migration to spend the winter in warmer climes, including northern South America and the Caribbean.

RED-EYED VIREO

SCIENTIFIC NAME:	*Vireo olivaceus*
FAMILY:	Vireonidae
LENGTH:	15cm (6in)
HABITAT:	Forest and open woodland
DISTRIBUTION:	Most of Canada and the US, moving as far south as Uruguay in winter
IDENTIFICATION:	Light gray back, gray crown, white eyebrows, white underside, and red eyes

The Red-eyed Vireo is a very abundant bird, particularly in the east of its range; however, it tends to spend much of its time high in the forest canopy, and may be more easily heard than seen, producing a broken song from morning until night. Although the Red-eyed Vireo may live entirely on fruit, such as berries, throughout the winter, like most small woodland birds, it feeds largely on insects for much of the year. When hunting for insects it will usually fly from a perch and glean its prey from bark or foliage with a brief, hovering flight, or hop around on the branches of trees and shrubs, searching particularly for caterpillars on the underside of leaves. During the breeding season, the Red-eyed Vireo nests in an intricately woven, cup-shaped nest composed of plant material and spiders' webs, which is lined with animal hair and grasses and hung from a branch. A clutch of one to five eggs is usually produced. As with many vireos and warblers, the Brown-headed Cowbird often parasitizes the nest of the Red-eyed Vireo, laying a single egg which the vireo will subsequently incubate, almost certainly to the detriment of its own brood.

RED-WINGED BLACKBIRD

SCIENTIFIC NAME:	*Agelaius phoeniceus*
FAMILY:	Icteridae
LENGTH:	23cm (9in)
HABITAT:	Grassy wetland, marshes, and reedbeds
DISTRIBUTION:	Throughout most of North America, south to the Caribbean
IDENTIFICATION:	Male is black overall, with bright red patch on shoulder, bordered below with yellow. Female is brown, with heavily streaked buff underside and buff eye-stripe

The Red-winged Blackbird is common and widespread, but favors moist habitats throughout its range. It is a highly sociable bird, and may form huge flocks, particularly outside of the breeding season when it may roost in flocks of millions of birds, often with other similar species, before dispersing to forage at dawn. It feeds on seeds, and can be something of a pest in agricultural areas; however, it also eats many insects which are capable of causing extensive damage to crops. During the breeding season, the male becomes extremely territorial, and is also highly polygamous, sometimes having over ten females nesting in his territory, whose nests he will aggressively defend from birds, large animals, and even people. However, many of these females are likely to produce offspring from mating with other males. The nest takes the form of a sturdy cup, usually placed low in a bush, close to the ground amongst reeds and tall grasses, or positioned in vegetation over water. The female produces a clutch of three to four eggs, which are incubated for a period of around 12 days, with the young becoming independent around two weeks after hatching.

◄ BOBOLINK

SCIENTIFIC NAME:	*Dolichonyx oryzivorus*
FAMILY:	Icteridae
LENGTH:	18cm (7in)
HABITAT:	Moist open grassland and cultivated fields
DISTRIBUTION:	Southern Canada and parts of the northern US. Winters in South America to Argentina
IDENTIFICATION:	Breeding male is mainly black, with buff nape, white shoulders and rump. Winter male and female buff overall, with dark streaks, and a buff and black striped crown

The Bobolink is fairly common in damp meadows and in hayfields in summer, when it is found in the northern US and southern Canada, but it is a long-distance migrant, departing in the fall to travel to South America for the winter, before returning in spring; a round-trip of perhaps some 20,000 kilometers (12,430 miles). At both the breeding and wintering sites, the Bobolink undergoes a complete molt, and is one of the few songbirds that will molt twice in a year. It forages for seeds and insects, and is considered something of an agricultural pest, particularly on its wintering grounds, where it may feed extensively on grain and rice. As a result it is frequently hunted in these areas, and its numbers have experienced declines in recent years. The problem is also compounded by the loss of suitable nesting sites in its breeding range, where hay is often cut early. During the breeding season it nests on the ground, constructing a rather loose, cup-shaped nest of grass and other plant materials, usually placed amongst a dense clump of grass or similar vegetation. A clutch consists of between four and seven eggs, which are incubated for a little under two weeks.

OLIVE OROPENDOLA

SCIENTIFIC NAME:	*Psarocolius bifasciatus*
FAMILY:	Icteridae
LENGTH:	Male 40–50cm (16–20in) Male larger than female
HABITAT:	Rainforest
DISTRIBUTION:	Northern parts of South America, from Colombia to Bolivia and western Brazil
IDENTIFICATION:	Large and stocky, with a long, heavy black bill tipped with red. Back and wings brown, head, neck, and underparts olive-green. Long tail is yellow below, bright pink, bare cheek patch

A highly distinctive and somewhat unusual member of the New World blackbird family, the Olive Oropendola is amongst the largest of the group. Its bill is also much larger than that of its close relatives, and is used for picking fruits, which are usually swallowed whole. This bird will also supplement its diet with insects from time to time. It is most commonly found high in the rainforest canopy, living in fairly small but noisy colonies, and it will also tend to nest in groups. During the breeding season, the males make display flights, whilst producing a loud babbling song, and will also make a bowing display toward females. The nests, of which there may be several positioned in a single tree, take the form of elongated basket shaped constructions, which are woven from grass and other vegetation, and suspended from the ends of branches.

WESTERN MEADOWLARK

SCIENTIFIC NAME:	*Sturnella neglecta*
FAMILY:	Icteridae
LENGTH:	25cm (10in)
HABITAT:	Open grassland, farmland, and roadsides
DISTRIBUTION:	From southern Canada, south through much of the US, but absent from large parts of the east. Winters south to Mexico
IDENTIFICATION:	Gray-brown overall, heavily streaked above, with a dark eye-stripe. Underparts are yellow, edged with white, with a black V shape on its breast

A familiar and common bird throughout its range, the Western Meadowlark is abundant in open, grassy habitats, where it may be seen foraging on the ground for invertebrates and seeds, or perching on posts whilst singing melodiously. This species is almost identical to the Eastern Meadowlark (*Sturnella magna*) in appearance, which usually has a more whistling call. However, the species often learn each other's calls where their ranges overlap, and the two species will occasionally interbreed. During the breeding season, the Western Meadowlark constructs a cup-shaped nest on the ground, amongst vegetation, usually with a domed roof. Here the female will incubate the clutch of three to seven eggs alone for around two weeks, whilst the male will defend the territory. Following hatching, males may offer some help in feeding their young, but this is mostly performed by the female. It is also common for males to have two mates simultaneously.

COMMON GRACKLE

SCIENTIFIC NAME:	*Quiscalus quiscula*
FAMILY:	Icteridae
LENGTH:	33cm (13in)
HABITAT:	Woodland, open grassland, cultivated land, marshes, parks, and backyards
DISTRIBUTION:	From Canada south through US, mainly east of the Rockies, but range is expanding westwards
IDENTIFICATION:	Male black overall, with a bronze sheen, a blue sheen on the breast and head, and a purple gloss on the tail. Female is smaller and duller. Both sexes have long, keel-shaped tails and yellow eyes

A familiar sight on garden lawns as well as in woodland and more open habitats, the Common Grackle is a distinctive bird on account of its iridescent plumage and long tail, the outer feathers of which curve upward to form a keel shape. It is also highly gregarious, and may be encountered in large, noisy flocks, often with other blackbird species. It forages on the ground, and is something of an opportunist, feeding on acorns, grain, invertebrates, birds' eggs, and even small vertebrates, including mice, amphibians, small fish, and small birds. Once quite rare in the west of North America, this species is expanding its range where land has been cleared for agricultural use, benefiting in winter particularly where grain may be easily available. During the breeding season, it constructs a large, rather bulky, cup-shaped nest of twigs and grasses, usually placed quite high in a conifer. Here, the female produces a clutch of between four and seven eggs, which are incubated for around two weeks. Following hatching, the young leave the nest at around three weeks of age.

Brewer's Blackbird

SCIENTIFIC NAME:	*Euphagus cyanocephalus*
FAMILY:	Icteridae
LENGTH:	23cm (9in)
HABITAT:	Open grassland, farmland, and urban areas
DISTRIBUTION:	From southern Canada through the US to Mexico
IDENTIFICATION:	Breeding male is black overall, with a glossy violet-green sheen, iridescent purple head, and yellow eyes. When not breeding, the male is less glossy. Female has gray-brown plumage and brown eyes

A common blackbird, often seen in backyards, Brewer's Blackbird is somewhat more numerous in the east of its range, where it is often found in flocks with similar species. However, where its range overlaps with that of the larger Common Grackle, it is more likely to be encountered in open areas, with the Grackle being predominantly found in urban and suburban habitats. As with most of its close relatives, Brewer's Blackbird forages on the ground, feeding on a variety of seeds and invertebrates. During the breeding season, this species continues to be gregarious, and nests in loose colonies, numbering anywhere from a few to around a hundred pairs. The females construct their bulky, bowl-like nests in a bush or tree, and produce a clutch of between three and seven eggs. These are incubated for around two weeks, with the young leaving the nest about a further two weeks after hatching.

Brown-headed Cowbird

SCIENTIFIC NAME:	*Molothrus ater*
FAMILY:	Icteridae
LENGTH:	20cm (8in)
HABITAT:	Grassland, woodland edges, fields, pasture, orchards, and residential areas
DISTRIBUTION:	Most of North America, winters as far south as Mexico
IDENTIFICATION:	Medium-sized songbird with pointed wings. Male has shiny black and brown head and neck, and metallic green body. Female has light gray-brown plumage

The Brown-headed Cowbird gets its name from its frequent association with livestock or wild grazing animals, where it forages on the ground, consuming insects and other invertebrates disturbed by their feeding. Like the Common Cuckoo of Eurasia, this species is a brood parasite, the only bird to demonstrate such behavior that is common throughout North America. During the breeding season, it does not construct a nest of its own, but lays its eggs in the nests of other birds, particularly warblers, vireos, and other small birds of open woodland, which then incubate its egg and raise the hatchling. The female Brown-headed Cowbird will lay only one egg per nest, but may mate with several males and produce several eggs per season. Unlike the Common Cuckoo, it does not remove the host's eggs from the nest when laying, but its egg has a short incubation period, and will usually hatch first. The young cowbird will then out-compete the host's own chicks, which will commonly starve. In this way, the Brown-headed Cowbird can represent a serious threat to the breeding populations of some birds, particularly where those populations are already small.

CHAFFINCH

SCIENTIFIC NAME:	*Fringilla coelebs*
FAMILY:	Fringillidae
LENGTH:	15cm (6in)
HABITAT:	Woodland, open forest, and backyards
DISTRIBUTION:	Europe and North Africa, east to Siberia. Some birds winter in India
IDENTIFICATION:	Male is brown above, with olive rump, white shoulders and wing bars, a pinkish breast and crown and behind the eye slate-blue. Female is a dull olive-brown, darker above, with white wing bars

The Chaffinch is the commonest finch in much of its range, particularly in Britain where it is, in fact, the second commonest breeding bird species. It is found in a variety of habitats, including backyards, which it often visits in winter in small flocks. It forages mainly on the ground, feeding on seeds, but will also consume caterpillars, insects, and other small invertebrates, such as spiders. During the breeding season, males will establish and aggressively defend territories from others of their species, whilst the females will incubate a clutch of between two and eight eggs for a period of around two weeks. The nest itself takes the form of a cup-shaped structure, composed of spiders' webs, woven grasses, and other vegetation, lined with feathers, which is normally placed in the fork of a tree or bush. Following hatching, the young are fed primarily on insects and their larvae by both parent birds, and fledge at between 12 and 18 days.

(EUROPEAN) SERIN

SCIENTIFIC NAME:	*Serinus serinus*
FAMILY:	Fringillidae
LENGTH:	13cm (5in)
HABITAT:	Scrubland and open woodland
DISTRIBUTION:	Continental Europe, North Africa, and the Mediterranean
IDENTIFICATION:	Male is heavily streaked with green and yellow, with a yellow face patch, breast, and tail edge, and a whitish rump. Female is duller but heavily streaked, with a hint of yellow on the face, and whitish underside

Although reasonably widespread and common in much of western Europe and around the Mediterranean, the Serin is uncommon in Britain, although it may visit during migration, and has bred on England's south coast in small numbers each year since the late 1960s. During the breeding season, this species tends to nest together in small groups, often in suburban areas such as parks and gardens where there is sufficient cover in the form of thickets or dense bushes. It constructs a neat, cup-shaped nest of plant stems, grasses, and moss, which it lines with animal hair and feathers. A clutch consists of three to five eggs, which are usually incubated by the female bird alone, for a little under two weeks. Following hatching both parent birds will provide food for their young, which fledge at around two weeks of age. The Serin forages mainly on the ground, consuming small seeds from weeds, and trees such as birch, although it will supplement its diet with invertebrates, such as small insects and spiders.

Pine Siskin

Scientific name:	*Carduelis pinus*
Family:	Fringillidae
Length:	13cm (5in)
Habitat:	Coniferous forests, often in mountainous regions, also parks and grassland
Distribution:	North America, south to the mountains of Mexico, with northern populations migrating south in winter
Identification:	Heavily streaked brown plumage, paler underneath, with two buff wing bars, and yellow patches at the base of its wing feathers. Males tend to show more yellow

As with most finches, the Pine Siskin is a fairly gregarious species, which often forages in small groups. Outside of the breeding season, it may congregate in larger numbers, with flocks sometimes numbering hundreds of individuals. It may feed on the ground, searching for seeds, but will also feed in trees, and may be observed clinging upside down to pine cones and seedpods, demonstrating a high level of agility. Its diet consists mainly of seeds from birches, alders, and cedars, but it will sometimes feeds on buds and insects, and as with some other finches, it will also consume salt from roads, where it has been applied in order to melt the snow. During the breeding season, this species nests in small colonies, and will often remain in fairly cold climates, requiring the nest to be well insulated with thistledown, animal hair, and feathers. Additionally, the female will tend to incubate the clutch of three to four eggs almost constantly, with the male bringing food to her at the nest.

(EUROPEAN) GREENFINCH ▼

SCIENTIFIC NAME:	*Carduelis chloris*
FAMILY:	Fringillidae
LENGTH:	15cm (6in)
HABITAT:	Open woodland, farmland, and backyards
DISTRIBUTION:	Europe and northern Africa, east to western Asia
IDENTIFICATION:	Male olive-green overall, slightly paler beneath, with yellow markings on the tail and wing. Female duller, gray-brown above, paler below, with slightly duller yellow patches

A common visitor to parks and gardens, particularly in winter, the Greenfinch is a well known and easily recognized bird, and may be particularly conspicuous in flight, when its yellow outer-wing feathers are most visible. It is also frequently associated with farmland, where it may gather in large flocks, which sometimes contain hundreds or even thousands of birds. As with other finches, this species is primarily a seed eater, but it will also consume insects, especially during the breeding season, when it will also feed them to its young. It may nest in loose colonies, usually in hedgerows or dense bushes, where a simple, often somewhat untidy cup of twigs, plant stems, and moss is constructed in order to house a clutch of four to six eggs, which will be incubated for around two weeks. A further two weeks after hatching, the young will leave the nest, and the Greenfinch will then frequently go on to raise a second brood.

(EURASIAN/COMMON) LINNET ▲

SCIENTIFIC NAME:	*Carduelis cannabina*
FAMILY:	Fringillidae
LENGTH:	15cm (6in)
HABITAT:	Heaths, grassland, and thickets, also suburban parks and yards
DISTRIBUTION:	Most of Europe, northern Africa, east to central Asia
IDENTIFICATION:	Breeding male is largely brown, with a chestnut back, white-edged black tail, whitish rump and pale brown head, with a red patch on its crown and breast. Winter male and female duller, streaked brown above with paler underside

Once commonly kept as a cage bird on account of its musical song, the Linnet is now protected throughout most of its range due to a sharp decline in its numbers, but although it is less abundant, in winter it may still form fairly large flocks, sometimes associating with other small birds. It tends to forage in quite open country, feeding mainly on seeds, but it will also consume some insects. This finch has suffered a further decline in recent years due to habitat loss and the increased use of weedkiller and pesticides on farmland, which has badly affected its food supply. During the breeding season, the female Linnet constructs the nest alone, building a rather untidy cup-shaped nest of plant materials, lined with wool and fine grasses, which it places low in a tree or bush. A clutch consists of four to six eggs, which are incubated solely by the female for a period of up to two weeks. However, following hatching, the young are fed and cared for by both parent birds, and leave the nest around two weeks later. This bird's name is derived from lin, the old English word for flax, the seeds of which were once considered to be the favorite food of the Linnet.

EURASIAN/EUROPEAN GOLDFINCH ▼

SCIENTIFIC NAME:	*Carduelis carduelis*
FAMILY:	Fringillidae
LENGTH:	12cm (5in)
HABITAT:	Thickets and open grassland
DISTRIBUTION:	Europe and northern Africa, east to central Asia
IDENTIFICATION:	Brown back, white belly and rump, black wings with a broad yellow bar, black and white head, and a red face. Female duller, streaked brown, and lacking boldly marked head

The Eurasian Goldfinch is a popular bird due to its attractive plumage and melodious song, which has led to it becoming a heavily trapped cage bird. However, it remains abundant in a wild state throughout most of its range, and is a highly sociable species, often congregating in quite large flocks, particularly where food is abundant. It has a somewhat longer and more slender bill than most finches, which it uses to remove seeds from wild flowers such as dandelions and thistles, but it also feeds on the ground, and will supplement its diet with insects. During the breeding season, the female is the sole nest builder, and constructs a delicate cup using plant material, including thistledown, which it usually places on a horizontal branch of a small tree or bush. The nest is also sometimes decorated with flowers. A clutch consists of around three to seven eggs, which are incubated by the female for about two weeks. Following hatching, both adult birds will feed the young, initially on insects, before providing them with regurgitated seeds. The young fledge by 18 days, following which a second clutch may be produced.

AMERICAN GOLDFINCH

SCIENTIFIC NAME:	*Carduelis tristis*
FAMILY:	Fringillidae
LENGTH:	13cm (5in)
HABITAT:	Open grassland, backyards, and orchards
DISTRIBUTION:	Southern Canada and most of the US
IDENTIFICATION:	Breeding male has bright yellow plumage, black cap, white rump and under-tail coverts, black wings with white bars, and black tail with white-edged feathers. Winter male and female are olive above and yellow below

The American Greenfinch is a familiar and common bird throughout its range, and may be particularly conspicuous in summer, when the males are in their breeding plumage, although in winter this bird is likely to be found in larger numbers. Like its European counterpart, the American Goldfinch feeds mainly on the seeds of wildflowers and weeds, including thistles, and it will use thistledown to line its nest. It is a relatively late breeder, and usually does not begin nesting until late June or early July, when most other songbirds are finishing breeding. The nest takes the form of an open cup of plant materials, placed in the fork of a tree branch or a small shrub, and often bound to the limb with spiders' silk. A clutch consists of between two and seven eggs, which the female incubates alone. The American Goldfinch is mainly monogamous, but once a brood has been successfully hatched, the female may go on to produce a second clutch with a different male, leaving her original mate to look after the fledglings.

(COMMON) REDPOLL ▲

SCIENTIFIC NAME:	*Carduelis flammea*
FAMILY:	Fringillidae
LENGTH:	12cm (5in)
HABITAT:	Open woodland, forests, thickets, and scrubland
DISTRIBUTION:	Across much of the Northern Hemisphere, breeding in northern Canada and the US, Greenland, Iceland, and much of Eurasia
IDENTIFICATION:	Gray-brown above, streaked with brown above and below, red crown, dark wings and tail, and white wing bars. Male has pink chest, female has white or buff breast and is more heavily streaked

There are a number of subspecies of Redpoll, varying somewhat in size and coloration, but all are generally similar in appearance and habit. They are highly sociable birds, usually seen in large flocks, which forage for insects and small seeds, particularly from birch and conifer trees, in open northern forests. Like other finches, this species is highly agile, and may hang upside down to reach its food. Interestingly, the Redpoll possesses a throat pouch in which to store seeds. It may use this pouch especially when foraging in the open, returning to a more sheltered spot in order to eat its supply. During the breeding season, the female builds a cup-shaped nest of grasses and twigs, lined with animal hair and feathers, placed in a bush or small tree. The clutch of four or five eggs is incubated for around 12 days, with the nestlings fledging about two weeks after hatching.

JAPANESE GROSBEAK

SCIENTIFIC NAME:	*Eophona personata*
FAMILY:	Fringillidae
LENGTH:	23cm (9in)
HABITAT:	Open forest and woodland
DISTRIBUTION:	Southeastern Siberia, northern China and Japan, wintering in central China and southern Japan
IDENTIFICATION:	Buff to olive-brown overall, dark wing and tail feathers with blue patches, and a black face mask. Bill is extremely stout

Also sometimes known as the Masked Grosbeak, or Masked Hawfinch, the Japanese Grosbeak is a large finch which occurs in woodland in parts of Siberia, China, and Japan. The name grosbeak is derived from the large bills of these birds, and this species has a particularly powerful beak that it uses to break open pine nuts, which are a favored food. Its diet also consists of seeds, berries, and invertebrates, with insects being taken mainly during the breeding season, when they constitute an important part of the diet of both adult birds and their nestlings. Territorial during the breeding season, the Japanese Grosbeak may however be found foraging in flocks in winter, when southward migrations are also undertaken.

PINE GROSBEAK ▲

SCIENTIFIC NAME:	*Pinicola enucleator*
FAMILY:	Fringillidae
LENGTH:	23cm (9in)
HABITAT:	Woodland and forest edges
DISTRIBUTION:	Canada and parts of the northern US, northeastern Europe, and Siberia
IDENTIFICATION:	Male has pinkish-red head, breast, rump, and streaked back, with white under-tail coverts. Female has yellow head and rump, gray back and underparts. Both have dark wings and tail, with two white wing bars

The Pine Grosbeak is amongst the largest of the finches, but is a rather shy species, which breeds in the forests of northern Eurasia and North America, rarely venturing farther south, and hence, it is not commonly seen. However, in winter, when its normal food is more scarce, it may visit gardens in search of offerings at bird-feeders and tables. Its natural diet consists of buds, berries, seeds, and insects, and as its name might suggest, it has a large, sturdy bill, which it uses to break apart larger buds and seeds. During the winter months, the Pine Grosbeak can be encountered in seminomadic flocks, which may range in search of food until an adequate supply is found; however, when breeding, pairs become highly territorial. Interestingly, during the breeding season this species develops pouches in the floor of its mouth that enable it to transport large amounts of food to its young, usually insects and spiders, combined with some vegetation. The Pine Grosbeak generally constructs its nest high in a coniferous tree, building a cup-shaped structure of twigs, moss, and other vegetation. A typical clutch contains three or four eggs, which are incubated solely by the female for around 13-15 days, although the male will feed her whilst she is on the nest, and the young will be cared for by both parent birds.

EVENING GROSBEAK ▼

SCIENTIFIC NAME:	*Hesperiphona vespertina*
FAMILY:	Fringillidae
LENGTH:	20cm (8in)
HABITAT:	Open forest and woodland
DISTRIBUTION:	Southern Canada, and the western US, south to Mexico. May be found in eastern and central US in winter
IDENTIFICATION:	Male has brown head, neck, and breast, yellow underparts, back, forehead, and eyebrow, black wings and tail, and white wing patches. Female is grayish-brown above, paler below, with gray and white patches on black wings

The Evening Grosbeak is a large and vividly colored finch, which can often be found in sizeable, noisy flocks, particularly during the winter months, when it will wander nomadically in search of food. At such times it will stray from forested areas to backyards, and is a frequent visitor to bird-feeders, where it demonstrates a particular fondness for sunflower seeds. This species normally tends to forage high in the trees, and its natural diet consists of a wide variety of fruits and seeds, supplemented with insects, particularly when nesting. The large, strong bill of the Evening Grosbeak allows it to crack open very hard seeds, such as cherry stones, and during the breeding season the bill also changes from an ivory color to a more greenish-yellow. It builds a rather loose and flattened nest of roots and small twigs, lined with grasses and lichens, usually placed in a tree fork near the tip of a branch, amongst dense foliage. The female incubates a clutch of around three or four eggs for about two weeks, with the young fledging a further two weeks after hatching.

(RED/COMMON) CROSSBILL ▲

SCIENTIFIC NAME:	*Loxia curvirostra*
FAMILY:	Fringillidae
LENGTH:	16cm (6in)
HABITAT:	Coniferous forest
DISTRIBUTION:	From Alaska and southern Canada, south through the US to Central America. Also northern Eurasia and parts of North Africa
IDENTIFICATION:	Male has brick-red head and body, with dark wings and tail. Female is olive-gray, with a greenish breast and rump

The Crossbill is named after its rather peculiar, crossed mandibles that enable it to access the seeds in conifer cones, which constitute the majority of its diet. In fact, of all the finches, the Crossbills have the most specialized feeding habits. Even young Crossbills are fed on conifer seeds, allowing the Crossbill to reproduce at any time of the year, as long as there is a plentiful supply of food, although, as with many species of seed eating birds, the chicks are often initially fed on insects. During the breeding period, this species constructs a neat, cup-shaped nest of twigs and other vegetation, concealed high in a dense conifer tree, where the female alone will incubate a clutch of up to five eggs for around two weeks. However, both parent birds will care for their nestlings following hatching, with the young birds typically leaving the nest a little over two weeks later. Crossbills tend to be nomadic, and may wander great distances from year to year in order to find a good crop of pine cones.

(EURASIAN) BULLFINCH

SCIENTIFIC NAME:	*Pyrrhula pyrrhula*
FAMILY:	Fringillidae
LENGTH:	17cm (7in)
HABITAT:	Open woodland, orchards, and thickets
DISTRIBUTION:	Most of Europe, across central Asia to the Pacific
IDENTIFICATION:	Male has bright red breast and cheeks, black crown, tail and wingtips, gray upperparts, and white rump. Female is similar, but with a duller, pinkish breast

A rather attractively colored bird, at one time the Bullfinch was persecuted on a large scale due to the extensive damage that it caused to budding trees, particularly fruit trees, and it is thought that its slow recovery can be attributed to habitat loss. It remains rather uncommon in parts of its range. It has a voracious appetite, stripping buds at a rate of perhaps 30 or more per minute, but also feeds on insects, particularly during the breeding season. At this time, its young are also fed mainly on insects, and as with some other finch species, the parent birds develop specialized pouches within their mouths in order to maximize the amount of food carried to the young. Its clutch of four to six eggs is laid in a loose, shallow cup of twigs and moss, which is constructed by the female and placed low in a tree or hedgerow. The eggs are incubated for a period of around two weeks, with both parent birds feeding the nestlings upon hatching. The Bullfinch is usually seen in pairs, but may form small, nomadic flocks in the fall and winter. Unlike many other small seed-eating birds, it tends not to associate with mixed-species flocks.

HAWFINCH

SCIENTIFIC NAME:	*Coccothraustes coccothraustes*
FAMILY:	Fringillidae
LENGTH:	17cm (7in)
HABITAT:	Open woodland, forest edges, orchards, parks and gardens
DISTRIBUTION:	Europe, northwestern Africa, and parts of central and eastern Asia
IDENTIFICATION:	Stocky, with large head and heavy, conical bill, orange-brown head, chestnut upperparts and buff underparts, gray neck and black throat. Wings are dark, with blue-black and white wing patches. Bill is dark during the summer, yellowish in winter

The Hawfinch is a large and heavily built finch with a massive, powerful bill which, combined with strong jaw muscles enables this bird to crack open hard seeds such as cherry and olive stones. The inside of its bill contains special pads for gripping the stones, whilst the bird itself can exert a pressure equivalent to 45 kilograms, even though it usually weighs only 55 grams itself. Additionally, the Hawfinch consumes various buds, berries, and insects. During the breeding season, this species constructs a shallow cup-shaped nest of twigs, roots and other vegetation, which it places in a tree or bush. The female incubates a clutch of around two to six eggs for a period of about two weeks, with both parent birds taking responsibility for feeding their young following hatching. The Hawfinch is a rather shy bird, which spends much of its time high in the treetops, and it may therefore be difficult to observe, a factor that has made monitoring population numbers more difficult. However, it is thought to have declined in its traditional breeding areas across much of its range in recent years.

285

PURPLE GRENADIER

SCIENTIFIC NAME:	*Uraeginthus ianthinogaster*
FAMILY:	Estrildidae
LENGTH:	15cm (6in)
HABITAT:	Arid scrubland, grassland, and open forests
DISTRIBUTION:	Eastern Africa, from Ethiopia south to Tanzania
IDENTIFICATION:	Male is reddish-brown above, with a black tail, blue rump, purple underparts, red ring around eye, surrounded by blue. Female brown above, paler below, with buff-speckled breast and white patches around eyes. Both have red, conical bill

The Purple Grenadier is a brightly colored finch, which is often found in open or semi-open habitats. However, it tends to be quite secretive, preferring to feed in the vicinity of cover. It usually occurs in small flocks or family groups, feeding on the ground on grass seeds, and the seeds of various small herbaceous plants. It will also consume buds and insects, with termites being a favored food, particularly during the breeding season. The nest is constructed mainly by the male, and takes the form of a globular structure of grass stems and other vegetation, often densely lined with feathers and soft plant material, and usually positioned in a low bush or tree. Both parent birds incubate a clutch of between three and five eggs for a period of around two weeks, and care for their young following hatching, although most of the incubation is typically performed by the female bird. The nestlings are initially fed on soft bodied insects, progressing to soft seeds, with harder, ripe seeds being provided just prior to fledging at around three weeks of age.

COMMON/ST. HELENA WAXBILL

SCIENTIFIC NAME:	*Estrilda astrild*
FAMILY:	Estrildidae
LENGTH:	13cm (5in)
HABITAT:	Open grassland and scrub, often close to water
DISTRIBUTION:	Sub-Saharan Africa, also introduced widely elsewhere
IDENTIFICATION:	Small finch, grayish-brown overall with fine barring. Throat and belly paler than upperparts. Red eye-stripes and red, conical bill

The Common, or St. Helena, Waxbill, originates from Africa, but it has since been introduced to a number of areas outside of its natural range, including St. Helena, Mauritius, Reunion Island, the Seychelles, Tahiti, Portugal, Brazil, and Hawaii, where it has established small populations. It is also widely bred around the world as an aviary bird. In its natural state it inhabits open grassland, scrub, farmland, and marshes, often being found close to water in otherwise dry habitats. It tends to occur in large flocks, sometimes numbering thousands of birds, particularly at roosting sites. In fact, it is considered to be amongst the most numerous of all birds. It feeds almost exclusively on grass seeds, but supplements its diet with small insects at times. It shows a preference for areas of long grass, and may often be seen feeding by clinging to grass stems. During the breeding season it constructs a small globular nest of woven stems, usually placed close to the ground amongst the grass, or positioned in a shrub. The female produces a clutch of around four or five eggs, which are incubated for about two weeks, with the young fledging at about three weeks of age.

ZEBRA FINCH

SCIENTIFIC NAME:	*Taeniopygia guttata*
FAMILY:	Estrildidae
LENGTH:	13cm (5in)
HABITAT:	Open grassland, scrub and semidesert, usually close to water
DISTRIBUTION:	Throughout most of Australia, also eastern Indonesia
IDENTIFICATION:	Male has gray head and nape, olive-brown back and wings, black and white banded tail, barred throat and stripes below eyes, orange cheek patches, brown flanks spotted with white, and white underparts. Female is duller, and lacks orange cheeks

The Zebra Finch is amongst the most common and widespread of the Australian finches, and is also one of the most popular aviary birds. It is found throughout much of Australia in a range of habitats, including the arid interior, but in such areas, it will usually be found close to a source of water. It is a sociable bird, living in large flocks of 100 or more individuals, which forage on the ground for grass seeds. This species will also consume insects, particularly during the breeding season, when the nestlings are also more likely to be fed them. The breeding season typically occurs from October to April, but rainfall plays an important part in stimulating reproduction, as food is likely to be more plentiful following heavy rains. The Zebra Finch is thought to pair for life, with both adults in a pair caring for their eggs and young. The male tends to collect most of the nesting material, whilst the female will construct the dome-shaped nest of grasses in a shrub, or occasionally in a hollow in a tree or on the ground. An average clutch consists of between four and seven eggs, which will be incubated for around two weeks, with the young leaving the nest after about a further three.

GOULDIAN FINCH

SCIENTIFIC NAME:	*Chlobia gouldiae*
FAMILY:	Estrildidae
LENGTH:	13cm (5in)
Habitat:	Scrub, forest edges and open woodland, usually near water
DISTRIBUTION:	Northern Australia
IDENTIFICATION:	Bright green above, with a blue rump, purple breast, and yellow belly. Face is bordered with blue and may be black, red or orange. Female is similar, but duller

The Gouldian Finch is a strikingly colorful bird, which has led to it becoming one of the most widely kept aviary birds, a fact that will no doubt insure its survival in captivity. However, conversely, its numbers have dropped considerably in the wild, mainly due to trapping for the bird trade. This species also suffers high rates of predation, probably largely on account of its vivid plumage. It occurs in grassland, scrub, and open woodland in tropical northern Australia, usually close to water, where it forages in large flocks, which often number several hundred birds. They feed on grass seeds, tending to forage on the stems of grasses rather than on the ground, also consuming various small insects and spiders. Breeding typically occurs following or during the rainy season, when food is most plentiful. The nest takes the form of a loose structure of grasses, which may be placed in a hollow in a tree, termite mound or on the ground amongst long grass. An average clutch consists of between four and eight eggs, and successful pairs may produce two or three broods in succession. The eggs are incubated by both parent birds for around two weeks, with the hatchlings leaving the nest at about three weeks old.

JAVA SPARROW

SCIENTIFIC NAME:	*Padda oryzivora*
FAMILY:	Estrildidae
LENGTH:	16cm (6in)
HABITAT:	Tropical grassland, rice fields, scrubland, and thickets
DISTRIBUTION:	Java and Bali and Sumatra, also introduced in tropical regions throughout the world
IDENTIFICATION:	Gray above with black tail and crown, white cheeks, whitish below, with pink flanks. Bill of male is larger and darker red. Also dark red-eye ring, paler and pinker in females

The Java Sparrow is also sometimes known as the Java Rice Bird, and its scientific name relates both to the genus for domestic rice, and the method of its cultivation. This is on account of this species' fondness for eating rice, and where it occurs in large numbers, flocks of Java Sparrows can be devastating to rice crops. For this reason they are often killed by farmers seeking to protect their harvest. However, such culls seem not to affect overall population numbers too drastically, and this bird continues to thrive in its natural range. It has also been introduced with some success elsewhere, including Borneo, China, Japan, parts of Africa, and Hawaii. A small colony is also believed to be established in Florida, possibly from escapees, or otherwise released birds, for the Java Sparrow is a highly popular cage-bird. In addition to rice, the Java Sparrow feeds on grass seeds, also supplementing its diet with insects, particularly when nesting. During the breeding season, it constructs a domed nest of woven grasses, often positioned beneath the eaves of a building. Here a clutch of up to around seven or eight eggs will be incubated for a period of around two weeks.

SHAFT-TAILED WHYDAH ▲

SCIENTIFIC NAME:	*Vidua regia*
FAMILY:	Ploceidae
LENGTH:	13–30cm (5–12in) Male larger than female in breeding plumage
HABITAT:	Subtropical grassland
DISTRIBUTION:	Parts of southern Africa
IDENTIFICATION:	Breeding male is black above, including crown, with golden yellow nape, face, breast, and belly, with black lower flanks, thighs, and undertail. Tail is dark, with four highly elongated central feathers. Female and nonbreeding male buff above, with dark streaks, whitish or buff below

The name of the Shaft-tailed Whydah is derived from the breeding plumage of the male, which includes four very long, narrow, central tail feathers, which are shown off to females during courtship display flights. These are shed following nesting, when the male undergoes a molt, and his plumage then more closely resembles that of the female. This bird inhabits dry woodland and scrub, and is non-migratory, but following the breeding season it may become somewhat nomadic. It may be seen alone, but is usually found in flocks, which forage for seeds on the ground, with unusual two-footed hops, kicking away the dusty topsoil as they move in order to expose their food. This bird does not construct a nest during the breeding season, but is a brood parasite, parasitizing the nests of the Violet-eared Waxbill (*Uraeginthus granatina*). The female Shaft-tailed Whydah tends to produce around four or five eggs, which will usually be laid in separate nests, but sometimes two or more will be laid in the same nest, particularly, it seems, if the waxbill has a large clutch of its own. Although the whydah will sometimes remove or destroy the eggs of the host bird, it relies more heavily on mimicry, with its chicks developing similarly colored gapes and producing the same feeding calls, and even the adults will mimic the songs of the waxbills.

HOUSE SPARROW

SCIENTIFIC NAME:	*Passer domesticus*
FAMILY:	Ploceidae
LENGTH:	15cm (6in)
HABITAT:	Open grassland, scrub, farmland, suburban and urban areas
DISTRIBUTION:	Throughout Eurasia, parts of northern Africa and the Middle East, also introduced to Australasia and the Americas
IDENTIFICATION:	Male has gray crown, darkly streaked back, chestnut-brown nape, black eye-stripe and throat, pale cheeks, gray underparts and rump. Bill is yellowish-brown in winter, black in summer. Female is duller and lacks distinctive markings on head and neck

Although a widespread and familiar bird, the House Sparrow has suffered serious declines in parts of its range in recent years, particularly in Britain, where it is now considered as being severely threatened. Exact reasons for this decline are unclear, but the House Sparrow has come to live in close proximity to man, and has no doubt been affected by man's actions. Changes in agricultural practices are probably responsible for this species' spread into urban areas, and although it has adapted well in terms of foraging for scraps as well as insects, seeds, and other vegetation, those birds in urban areas tend to breed less successfully. During the breeding season, the House Sparrow constructs a loose, untidy nest, often under the eaves of a roof, in a nest box, or sometimes in a dense shrub. It is an aggressive bird when breeding, and may drive away swallows, martins, and tits in order to take over their nests. An average clutch consists of three to five eggs, which are incubated by both parent birds for up to two weeks. The young fledge around a further two weeks later. In winter the House Sparrow is a sociable bird, forming quite large foraging flocks.

Village Weaver

Scientific name:	*Ploceus cucullatus*
Family:	Ploceidae
Length:	18cm (7in)
Habitat:	Scrub and thickets, often close to human habitations
Distribution:	Much of sub-Saharan Africa apart from the most arid regions
Identification:	Breeding male is yellow overall, with a black face and black-streaked back and wings. Nonbreeding male has a yellow head and an olive crown. Female has olive crown, gray shoulders, white underparts and lacks black face

The weavers are so-called because of the large, elaborately woven nests that are constructed by most species. Many nest colonially, often constructing huge communal nests; however, the Village Weaver builds individual nests which are clustered together in trees. Made from grasses and twigs, they are generally oval or pear shaped, with a long, tubular entrance below, and are suspended near the tips of branches in thorny trees, deterring most predators, including snakes. However, its broods are frequently parasitized by various cuckoo species. Two to three eggs are usually laid, which are incubated for around two weeks. The Village Weaver is a very abundant bird, and Africa's most numerous weaver. It is found in a variety of habitats, often close to villages and even towns. It feeds mainly on seeds and grain, and at times can cause extensive damage to crops, although it will also take insects, particularly when feeding its young. The calls of the Village Weaver include harsh buzzing and chattering sounds.

Red Bishop/Orange Weaver

Scientific name:	*Euplectes orix*
Family:	Ploceidae
Length:	13cm (5in)
Habitat:	Reedbeds, moist open grassland, orchards, and agricultural land
Distribution:	Much of sub-Saharan Africa
Identification:	Breeding male has black forehead, face, throat, and belly, brilliant orange head, breast and rump, and brown or black wings. Female and nonbreeding male streaked buff and brown above, pale below with buff and brown streaks, tail and wings dark brown

The Red Bishop, or Orange Weaver, as it is also known, is a common weaver, found in moist habitats across much of the southern half of Africa. It is a highly sociable bird, found in large flocks for much of the year but these groups disperse during the breeding season, which usually occurs between December and March. The Red Bishop is polygamous, and when breeding, males may be found in association with several females. They display from perches, ruffling their feathers to attract mates, or make low display flights over reedbeds or tall grass. Males will often also pursue females and rival males. The females nest in a woven structure of grasses, which is constructed by the male, incubating a clutch of two to four eggs for around two weeks. The nest is usually placed amongst reeds or grasses above water, or sometimes amongst crops such as maize. The Red Bishop feeds on seeds, grain, and insects.

SUPERB STARLING

SCIENTIFIC NAME:	*Lamprotornis superbus*
FAMILY:	Sturnidae
LENGTH:	18cm (7in)
HABITAT:	Open grassland, scrub, and farmland, also suburban and urban areas
DISTRIBUTION:	Eastern Africa, from Sudan to Tanzania
IDENTIFICATION:	Glossy black upperparts with iridescent blue-green nape and shoulders, white breast band, undertail, and eyes, and rusty-red belly

The Superb Starling is very common throughout most of its range in a variety of habitats, including towns and cities, where it may be quite bold, sometimes begging for scraps from people. It is a gregarious species, occurring in flocks, often in association with the similar-looking Hildebrandt's Starling (*Lamprotornis hildebrandti*), and forages on the ground for a wide range of invertebrates, including insects, mollusks, crustaceans, and worms. It also feeds on various fruits and grains, and can be an agricultural pest in areas where it is particularly numerous. During the breeding season, both the male and female share responsibility for constructing the nest, incubation, and the feeding of the young. The nest takes the form of a spherical structure of grasses and twigs, placed low in a thorny bush, or hollow on a cliff face or tree. An average clutch consists of four eggs, which are incubated for around 12 days. The Superb Starling is a noisy bird and produces a number of whistling and warbling sounds, and also frequently mimics the calls of other species.

RED-WINGED STARLING ▼

SCIENTIFIC NAME:	*Onychognathus morio*
FAMILY:	Sturnidae
LENGTH:	28cm (11in)
HABITAT:	Rocky outcrops, and grassland, often at high altitudes. Also in urban areas
DISTRIBUTION:	Parts of sub-Saharan Africa, but largely absent from arid eastern regions
IDENTIFICATION:	Male glossy black overall, with reddish-brown primary feathers, tipped with black. Female similar, but has gray head, neck, and upper chest.

The Red-winged Starling is found in a variety of habitats, including towns, but it is particularly common in mountainous regions. It may be found singly, in pairs or in large flocks, sometimes in groups of several hundred, particularly in winter at communal roosts on cliffs, trees, and buildings. During the breeding season, this species becomes more territorial, but will breed in loose colonies. Both adult birds construct a bowl shaped nest of mud and vegetation on a rocky ledge, building, or in a tree, where a clutch of between two and five eggs is usually laid, to be incubated for about two weeks. The young fledge at around four weeks old, following which a second brood may be raised. The adults are highly aggressive when nesting, and may attack people that venture too close to the nest site. However, the nests of this species are often parasitized by the Great Spotted Cuckoo (*Clamator glandarius*). The Red-winged Starling feeds on the ground, in trees, or hawks for insects in the air, and is omnivorous, feeding on various invertebrates, including crabs, spiders, scorpions, millipedes, and termites. It has also been known to take small reptiles, nestlings, and carrion, in addition to various seeds, fruit, and nectar.

COMMON/EUROPEAN STARLING

SCIENTIFIC NAME:	*Sturnus vulgaris*
FAMILY:	Sturnidae
LENGTH:	23cm (9in)
HABITAT:	Urban areas, grassland, marshes, and open woodland
DISTRIBUTION:	From Europe and North Africa, across Asia to parts of India and China. Introduced to South Africa, Australia, and North America
IDENTIFICATION:	Black plumage, with iridescent purple and green feathers on nape, back, and breast. Feather tips are pale in winter

The Common or European Starling is a very common bird, and is also highly gregarious, occurring in flocks throughout the year, with a tendency to roost in vast numbers. This species also breeds in loose colonies, although males particularly may be somewhat aggressive to neighboring birds. They nest in cavities in trees, rocks, or buildings, constructing a cup-shaped nest of grass and other vegetation, where a clutch of between four and seven eggs is usually laid, to be incubated for around two weeks. Three clutches may be produced in a season, and although both parents normally care for their eggs and young, in later clutches the males may demonstrate little or no involvement. The young fledge after around three weeks, but may continue to be fed by their parents for a few more days. The Common Starling is omnivorous, feeding on a wide range of invertebrates, seeds, fruit, and nuts, and it will additionally feed on carrion. Despite the fact that it eats many insects that can damage crops, being so numerous it can itself cause serious damage on farmland at times, and also drive out other bird species. It is a highly vocal bird producing a wide range of clicks, warbles, and whistles, and it also mimics the sounds of other birds, animals, and even machinery.

ROTHSCHILD'S MYNA

SCIENTIFIC NAME:	*Leucopsar rothschildi*
FAMILY:	Sturnidae
LENGTH:	23cm (9in)
HABITAT:	Woodland and wooded grassland
DISTRIBUTION:	Bali in Indonesia
IDENTIFICATION:	Mainly white, with black-tipped wings and tail, bare blue skin around its eyes, and a long crest

Rothschild's Myna is the rarest member of the starling family, and also, in fact, one of the rarest birds in the world. It was discovered only comparatively recently, in 1912, by Walter Rothschild, from whom its name is derived. It is also sometimes known as Rothschild's Starling, and as the Bali Starling. It is endemic to Bali, where it inhabits woodland and savannah, in which it forages for invertebrates such as caterpillars, termites, and ants, as well as seeds and fruit. At one time, it could be found in quite large flocks, but its numbers are currently so small as to preclude this. It was also formerly more widespread, but now exists only in the Bali Barat National Park, where it is protected by armed guards. It has suffered mainly due to illegal trapping for trade, but habitat destruction and competition with other birds have also contributed to its rapid decline. Captive breeding and release programs have been established for around the last 20 years in an attempt to prevent the extinction of this species, and have yielded some success, but the future for Rothschild's Myna continues to be uncertain, particularly whilst trade in rare species persists. During the breeding season, this species nests in cavities in trees, producing a clutch of up to five eggs, which are incubated for about two weeks.

COMMON MYNA

SCIENTIFIC NAME:	*Acridotheres tristis*
FAMILY:	Sturnidae
LENGTH:	23cm (9in)
HABITAT:	Open grassland, scrub, farmland, and also suburban and urban areas
DISTRIBUTION:	From central to southeast Asia, also introduced to South Africa, the Middle East, Australasia, and various tropical islands
IDENTIFICATION:	Brown overall, with a darker, brown-black head and breast, white wing patch, and a whitish rump and under-tail. Small bare patch of yellow skin around eyes continuing into yellow bill

The Common Myna is something of an opportunist, and is highly adaptable; once a bird of open grassland, it now thrives in a range of habitats, including in and around human habitations, and it has also been successfully introduced to many areas outside of its natural range. It is omnivorous, consuming a wide range of vegetation, invertebrates, and even small vertebrates, and in some areas, including parts of Australia, it was deliberately introduced in order to control insect pests. However, this species' love of fruit has ironically sometimes seen it become a pest in turn, with large numbers decimating fruit crops. Outside of the breeding season, it may be found foraging in small groups or large flocks, but it tends to be found in its greatest numbers when roosting, with perhaps thousands of birds gathering to sleep in trees, bridges, buildings, and other suitable sites. These large flocks can be incredibly noisy, with the mynas producing a range of screeches, clicks, and growling sounds. During the breeding season, the Common Myna is less sociable, and is particularly aggressive to other bird species, often outcompeting them for food and nesting sites. The nest is usually placed in a cavity in a building or tree, and takes the form of an untidy bowl of twigs, leaves, grasses, feathers, and other, often manmade materials. An average clutch will contain between two and five eggs, to be incubated by both adult birds for around two weeks. The young fledge aged around four or five weeks, but may continue to beg for food from their parents for several more.

SPLENDID GLOSSY STARLING

SCIENTIFIC NAME:	*Lamprotornis splendidus*
FAMILY:	Sturnidae
LENGTH:	30cm (12in)
HABITAT:	Forest and open woodland, often close to water
DISTRIBUTION:	Western and central Africa
IDENTIFICATION:	Large starling with long wings and tail. Iridescent blue plumage above, with deep purple-blue underside, and bronze neck patches

Although a rather noisy bird, producing a variety of whistling, nasal, and more guttural calls, the Splendid Glossy Starling may be rather elusive, preferring to spend much of its time high in the treetops. However, it can also be observed on the ground from time to time, foraging in large flocks, often in association with closely related species. The Splendid Glossy Starling feeds on a variety of fruits and invertebrates, and seems to have a preference for figs and caterpillars. It is also fond of termites, and can be commonly found in large mixed-species flocks taking winged termites on the wing, particularly after heavy rains. It may be identified in flight by its rather stooped posture and loud, swooping wingbeats. The Splendid Glossy Starling is nomadic in nature, with flocks traveling together from place to place in order to find food, often traversing vast distances in order to do so. During the breeding season, this bird makes its nest in a cavity in a tree, which it lines with grass.

GOLDEN-BREASTED STARLING ▲

SCIENTIFIC NAME:	*Cosmopsarus regius*
FAMILY:	Sturnidae
LENGTH:	35cm (14in)
HABITAT:	Grassland, open woodland, and acacia scrub
DISTRIBUTION:	Eastern Africa, in Somalia, Ethiopia, eastern Kenya, and north-eastern Tanzania
IDENTIFICATION:	Large glossy starling, deep blue-green above, with a purple breast and golden-yellow underside

Also known as the Royal Starling, the Golden-breasted Starling is a highly distinctive bird on account of its vivid and unusual coloration, with few African birds sharing the intense golden-yellow of its lower plumage. It is a sociable bird, living in small family groups of around three to ten individuals, and during the breeding season, these groups nest in colonies, and breed cooperatively, sharing nest-building and feeding duties. They nest in natural cavities in trees, or abandoned woodpecker holes, which they line with dry grasses, roots, and leaves, where a clutch of between three and five eggs is usually laid. Following hatching, members of the group will bring food to the nest, which may be passed directly to the chicks, or often first to the female, which will beg for the food in a crouched position. Unlike most glossy starlings, which feed mainly on fruit, supplemented with invertebrates, the Golden-breasted Starling is unusual in that it feeds almost exclusively on insects, either taken in flight or on the ground. At times it may also eat other invertebrates such as snails, spiders and even crabs, and also small vertebrates such as lizards.

YELLOW-BILLED OXPECKER

SCIENTIFIC NAME:	*Buphagus africanus*
FAMILY:	Sturnidae
LENGTH:	23cm (9in)
HABITAT:	Open grasslands
DISTRIBUTION:	Sub-Saharan Africa
IDENTIFICATION:	Brown overall, with buff underparts, pale rump, yellow, red-tipped bill, and red eye. It has a short tail and strong claws

The oxpeckers are usually classified as belonging to the starling family Sturnidae, and sometimes placed in the subfamily Buphagidae, although some taxonomists elevate this status to that of a family in its own right, citing both physical and behavioral distinctions that set them apart from most starlings. These differences can be attributed to a large degree to the close association, if not co-dependency, of these birds with large mammals, particularly ungulates, that is, hoofed mammals, hence their common name. Oxpeckers spend most of their time traveling with herds, sitting on the backs of their hosts when roosting, preening, and even mating, and they feed almost exclusively on ticks and other parasites which they pluck from the hosts' fur or skin. The Yellow-billed Oxpecker is most commonly associated with thin-haired mammals such as buffalo or rhino, and although a variety of animals will tolerate their presence, elephants and some species of antelope will not. Whilst foraging, the Yellow-billed Oxpecker clings to its host with its strong claws, propping itself up with its tail. It is gregarious throughout the year, and will breed in small colonies, which demonstrate some degree of cooperation in feeding and caring for nestlings. They nest in holes in trees which they line with vegetation and animal hair, producing clutches of two or three eggs.

GREATER RACKET-TAILED DRONGO ▼

SCIENTIFIC NAME:	*Dicrurus paradiseus*
FAMILY:	Dicruridae
LENGTH:	63cm (25in)
HABITAT:	Rainforest, swamps, and bamboo jungle
DISTRIBUTION:	From India, east through the Himalayas to parts of southeast Asia, including Borneo, Java, and Bali
IDENTIFICATION:	Dark, iridescent blue-green plumage, long forked tail, with shafts of the two outermost feathers greatly extended, terminating in rackets. Shaggy crest is usually visible at back of head

The Greater Racket-tailed Drongo is generally easily distinguished from other Drongos on account of its pendant tail feathers; however, it may be confused with the Lesser Racket-tailed Drongo (*Dicrurus remifer*), although the latter is somewhat smaller and has a square, rather than forked, tail. There is also a Sri Lankan form, *D.p. ceylonicus*, which lacks the extended tail feathers. The Greater Racket-tailed Drongo occurs in a variety of forest habitats, but is most common in deciduous rainforest, where it forages amongst foliage for insects, or catches them on the wing. It may occur on its own, in pairs, or small groups, and will often associate with mixed-species flocks. As with other drongos, the Greater Racket-tailed Drongo is an aggressive and fearless bird, which will attack much larger species, particularly if its nest or young are threatened. During the breeding season, it constructs a cup-shaped nest of vegetation, usually bound together with spiders' webs, placed high in the fork of a tree. A typical clutch consists of three or four eggs.

CRESTED DRONGO

SCIENTIFIC NAME:	*Dicrurus forficatus*
FAMILY:	Dicruridae
LENGTH:	30cm (12in)
HABITAT:	Forests, cultivated land, savannah, and open scrubland
DISTRIBUTION:	Madagascar, and parts of the Comoro Islands
IDENTIFICATION:	Black overall, with a long, forked tail and a tuft of curving feathers on the head

Apart from its crest, the Crested Drongo is of rather plain appearance; however, its behavior is somewhat more interesting. It tends to occur singly or in pairs within mixed-species flocks, and is regarded as a "nucleus species," that is to say that it plays an important role in the dynamics of such groups. It has been discovered that this bird will even produce a particular call in order to attract flocks of other birds. Most large mixed flocks will be accompanied by one or two Crested Drongos, which act as sentries, fearlessly driving away birds of prey or other potential predators. Large feeding flocks tend to flush out greater numbers of insects, and the drongo probably also benefits by being afforded a greater degree of protection itself by associating with a group. It feeds mainly on insects, usually catching them in flight from a perch, and it will sometimes sit on the backs of large mammals, darting off to catch insects as they are disturbed by the animals' grazing. The Crested Drongo rarely flies any great distance, but it is capable of aerial acrobatics when hunting or fighting off other birds, using its long, forked tail to make sharp twists and turns. During the breeding season, this species constructs a cup-shaped nest between the forked branches of a tree, and other birds will often nest nearby for protection.

GOLDEN ORIOLE

SCIENTIFIC NAME:	*Oriolus oriolus*
FAMILY:	Oriolidae
LENGTH:	23cm (9in)
HABITAT:	Open deciduous woodland, scrub, orchards, and parks
DISTRIBUTION:	Much of Europe and Asia, as well as Africa in the winter
IDENTIFICATION:	Male has bright yellow plumage, black wings, black upper tail feathers with a yellow tip, and a black eye-stripe. Female is duller, olive-green above, with brown wings, speckled white underparts, and a yellow-tipped tail

Despite the brightly colored plumage of the male of this species, the Golden Oriole is a shy and generally solitary bird, which spends much of its time high up in the trees amongst foliage, and it may therefore be difficult to observe. Its presence is most likely to be noticed instead by its flute-like call. It has short, weak legs, which are poorly designed for walking, and so rarely descends to the ground; however, on occasion it may land briefly in order to feed on fallen fruit. Most foraging takes place in the forest canopy, with its diet of fruit being supplemented with insects. During the breeding season, the Golden Oriole constructs an intricately woven, hammock-like nest, which it suspends in a horizontal tree fork. The nest is built largely by the female, who incubates a clutch of three or four eggs for just over two weeks. Although somewhat scarce in Britain, the Golden Oriole is a visitor to the east coast of England during its migrations, also breeding in East Anglia in small numbers during the summer months.

GRAY BUTCHERBIRD

SCIENTIFIC NAME:	*Cracticus torquatus*
FAMILY:	Cracticidae
LENGTH:	27cm (11in)
HABITAT:	Forest, woodland, scrub, agricultural land, and suburbs
DISTRIBUTION:	Throughout much of Australia, but absent from desert areas
IDENTIFICATION:	Black head and tail, white collar, gray wings and back, white underparts, rump, and tail tip. Bill is long with a hooked tip

The Gray Butcherbird is found in a variety of wooded habitats but tends to favor dense forests where its food may be most abundant. It is an aggressive predator and hunts for a variety of small creatures, including insects, reptiles, rodents, and smaller birds. In addition, it will supplement its diet with fruit and seeds. This bird's name is derived from its habit of impaling its food on thorns, or in the fork of a branch in order to tear at it, and it will also store uneaten food in such places. It tends to hunt by watching from an exposed perch, before pouncing on its prey on the ground, although flying insects and small birds may also be taken on the wing. During the breeding season, this species constructs a bowl-shaped nest of twigs and leaves, usually lined with grasses and other fine material, and placed in the fork of a tree. Here the female will incubate a clutch of three to five eggs for around 25 days. Following hatching, both parent birds feed their young, which fledge at around four weeks of age. The young will often remain close to their parents for around a year or so, and will help to raise subsequent broods.

MAGPIE-LARK ▼

SCIENTIFIC NAME:	*Grallina cyanoleuca*
FAMILY:	Grallinidae
LENGTH:	27cm (11in)
HABITAT:	Open areas, usually near water; cultivated land, lake shores, and swamps
DISTRIBUTION:	Australia, and a small part of southern New Guinea
IDENTIFICATION:	Black above, white below, with white, black-tipped tail, white eye and bill. Male has a black throat and white eyebrow, whilst the female has a white face and throat

The Magpie-Lark, also known as the Mudlark and Peewee in various parts of its range, is a very common and widespread species, occurring throughout Australia, with the exception of Tasmania and some parts of the desert in the far northwest of the Australian mainland. As with many Australian birds, it was named for its apparent similarity to birds known to European settlers; however, it is in fact not particularly closely related to either the European Magpie or Lark, and whilst it is sometimes placed in the same family as the drongos, Dicruridae, Magpie-Larks are often classified in their own family, Grallinidae. This species is found in a variety of habitats; wherever there is open ground for foraging and trees in which to nest. It is often found close to water, and may appear much like a wader as it probes in the shallows on its long legs, searching for insects and aquatic invertebrates. The Magpie-Lark usually pairs for life, and will defend a territory throughout the year. When breeding, a bowl-shaped nest of mud and vegetation is constructed on a flat branch near water, where both parent birds will incubate a clutch of three to five eggs.

BLACK-FACED WOODSWALLOW ▲

SCIENTIFIC NAME:	*Artamus cinereus*
FAMILY:	Artamidae
LENGTH:	18cm (7in)
HABITAT:	Open forests and scrub
DISTRIBUTION:	Throughout Australia, Timor, and southern New Guinea
IDENTIFICATION:	Smoky-gray above, with paler underparts, a white tail tip, black face and rump

Although somewhat stockier, the Black-faced Woodswallow is similar to the true swallows in habit, and spends much of its time in the air, flying effortlessly to take insects on the wing in its gaping mouth. It rarely descends to the ground, being quite awkward on its short legs, but may be seen perching in groups on high branches or similar vantage points. This species tends to live in small flocks that consist of a breeding pair and their offspring, and they frequently roost together, huddled in cavities or forks in trees, often with several other groups to form quite large colonies. During the breeding season, woodswallows also often nest colonially. Breeding pairs will construct a shallow bowl-like nest of twigs, grass, and roots on a stump or branch, where a clutch of three or four eggs is usually incubated for around two weeks. Following hatching, the offspring from the previous year's brood will commonly cooperate with their parents to feed the new nestlings.

AUSTRALASIAN MAGPIE   ▲

SCIENTIFIC NAME:	*Gymnorhina tibicen*
FAMILY:	Cracticidae
LENGTH:	40cm (16in)
HABITAT:	Open forest, woodland, agricultural land, and suburban areas
DISTRIBUTION:	Throughout Australia, and in parts of southern New Guinea, also introduced to New Zealand and Fiji
IDENTIFICATION:	Variable black and white plumage. Nape, upper tail, and shoulders, white in males, gray in females. In much of Australia, remainder of body is black. In the southeast and parts of the southwest, interio,r and Tasmania, the back and rump are white

The Australasian Magpie is a common and conspicuous bird, which is found in a variety of habitats where there are both trees and adjacent open areas, and tends to be absent only from the driest desert regions and very dense forest. It is a sociable bird, living in flocks of 20 or so individuals, which maintain territories throughout the year, defending them most aggressively during the breeding season. A group is led by a dominant male, who will mate with all the females in the group, following which they will go on to nest separately, constructing a platform of twigs in a tree, on which a bowl-shaped nest is placed. A clutch consists of two to five eggs, which are incubated by the female for around three weeks. Following hatching, the dominant male will then help to feed his chicks. Although other males in a group may mate with females opportunistically, they will take no part in caring for nestlings. The flock will drive away other birds that encroach upon their territory, and may even attack humans if they approach a nest site. However, for much of the year, this species is often quite tame, and may beg for food from people. The Australasian Magpie feeds on a variety of invertebrates, which are dug from the ground with its powerful bill, but will supplement its diet with seeds and other vegetation.

PIED CURRAWONG

SCIENTIFIC NAME:	*Strepera graculina*
FAMILY:	Cracticidae
LENGTH:	50cm (20in)
HABITAT:	Open forests, woodland, scrub, agricultural land, and suburbs
DISTRIBUTION:	Much of eastern Australia, but absent from Tasmania
IDENTIFICATION:	Black overall, with a large white crescent on the wing, white base and tip of tail, and bright yellow eye. Bill is large and hooked

The name of the Pied Currawong is derived from its black and white coloration, and its main call, which is a loud "currawong." Other vocalizations include croaking and whistling sounds. It is a common and familiar bird, found in a variety of habitats, but it prefers forests and woodlands, particularly during the breeding season. In the north of its range it tends to be sedentary, whilst farther south it will often move between upland and lowland areas according to seasonal variations in temperature. This species tends to breed from July to January, when the female will construct a bowl-shaped nest of sticks, lined with finer material, placed high in the fork of a tree. The female incubates a clutch of around three eggs for about three weeks, whilst the male will bring food to the nest. He will continue to do so for a further week after the young have hatched. The female will continue to care for her young until they fledge at around 30 days. After the breeding season, Pied Currawongs may form large feeding flocks. They consume a variety of foods, including carrion, small vertebrates, birds' eggs, insects, and berries. As with the butcherbirds of the same family, uneaten food may be stored on thorns or placed in a crevice or fork in a tree.

GOLDEN BOWERBIRD

SCIENTIFIC NAME:	*Prionodura newtoniana*
FAMILY:	Ptilonorhynchidae
LENGTH:	23cm (9in)
HABITAT:	Rainforest, usually in mountainous regions
DISTRIBUTION:	Parts of the northeastern coast of Australia and New Guinea
IDENTIFICATION:	Male has yellow underparts, central crown, and nape, with golden-brown upperparts and central tail feathers. Female is olive-brown, with ash-gray underparts

The courtship behavior of male bowerbirds is amongst the most complex of all species. They construct highly elaborate structures, or bowers, of twigs and other vegetation, often decorated with flowers, or other brightly colored objects. These bowers serve to display a male's skill, and are also used as mating sites. Although the Golden Bowerbird is the smallest bowerbird, it builds the largest bowers, constructing a tower around the trunk of a sapling, which may reach over two meters (6½ feet) in height. Often a second tower is built nearby, and may be joined to the first with a slender branch. Bower sites tend to be reused year after year, and may be used by several successive generations. The male displays with calling and dancing at the bower to attract females, and will mate with several in a season. The females will go on to nest alone, building a cup-shaped nest in a tree, where they will incubate one or two eggs. The Golden Bowerbird feeds mainly on fruit, but will also eat insects such as beetles and cicadas.

BIRDS OF PARADISE

The birds of paradise belong to the fairly small family Paradisaeidae, which contains just over 40 species. They are found in northeastern Australia and New Guinea, inhabiting woodland, forests, and coastal bush, and are perhaps best known for the striking plumage possessed by the males of most species, which are used in courtship displays in order to attract females. Many species also have highly elongated and elaborate feathers extending from the tail, wings, or head. The most strikingly colored and decorated birds tend to be polygamous, attracting and mating with several females, whilst those species in which the males have duller plumage often share monogamous pair bonds, and the males help with nest-building, incubation, and care of their young. Females are also usually quite drab, in order to remain camouflaged whilst incubating their eggs. Male birds of paradise take up to five years to become sexually mature and gain their ostentatious plumage; females, however, tend to breed at around two years of age. In the polygamous species, most males display alone, but some visit a communal site, known as a lek, where several males will gather, swaying, showing off their plumage, and singing loudly. Females then come to the lek and select a mate. Following mating, the females will nest alone.

There are various nest types, including large cup-shaped nests and domed structures, and sites may vary from tree forks to amongst dense foliage or rocks. Some species suspend their nests beneath branches. Most produce a clutch of one, two or occasionally three eggs, which are incubated for around 18 days. Following hatching, the young commonly fledge at around three weeks of age. Amongst the polygamous birds of paradise, there is a great deal of interbreeding between different species, and more than 20 hybrids have been recorded in the wild.

Some birds of paradise include nectar in their diets, whilst others eat amphibians and reptiles; most feed predominantly on invertebrates, supplemented with berries and other small fruits. Foraging usually occurs quite high in the forest canopy, and birds of paradise are frequently encountered in mixed-species flocks, often in association with such birds as drongos and babblers.

The **King Bird of Paradise** (*Cicinnurus regius*) is the smallest of its kind, growing to between 17 and 28 centimeters (7–11 inches), with the male being longer on account of its extended tail feathers, but it is amongst the most vividly colored of the birds of paradise, and during courtship displays will ruffle its back and breast feathers to form an impressive fan. It is bright glossy red above, white below, with yellow-green, gray and emerald upper breast feathers and bright blue

King Bird of Paradise

legs and feet. Two elongated shafts extend from the tail, terminating in emerald disks. The female is much duller, being brown, with a barred underside allowing her to remain camouflaged whilst incubating her eggs. Despite the male's plumage, it too may be difficult to observe, as these birds spend much of their time hidden in dense foliage as they forage for food. The King Bird of Paradise is found in lowland rainforest in New Guinea, and it is omnivorous, its diet consisting largely of fruit, insects, snails, and other invertebrates. Once a male has successfully attracted a mate and mating has taken place, the female will go on to nest alone, building a cup-shaped nest of vegetation, particularly from palms, which somewhat unusually for birds of paradise will be constructed deep inside a cavity in a tree, rather than placed amongst its branches. As with many birds of paradise, the feathers of this species were often used in ritual headdresses by local tribes. Demand for the plumage of the male, particularly for use in the millinery trade in the West, once severely threatened the survival of some species until such practices were outlawed.

The **Blue Bird of Paradise** (*Paradisaea rudolphi*) is another species found in New Guinea, specifically in eastern parts, where it inhabits rainforest in the foothills of mountainous areas. Both males and females possess a bright blue back, wings, and tail, black upper body and head with white eye-rings. The male has dark underparts, whilst the female is chestnut-brown below. The male also has two elongated tail feathers which provide an overall length of up to 63 centimeters (25 inches), whilst the female is around 29 centimeters (12 inches) long. The Blue Bird of Paradise inhabits dense, humid, tropical and subtropical forests, and is found mainly in the forest canopy, where it forages for food. Fruit comprises the majority of its diet, but insects and other invertebrates are also gleaned from foliage. Females and juvenile males may be found in small groups, whilst the adult males are typically solitary. During the breeding season, males also tend to display alone, although lekking behavior has been noted in this species. The displays of the Blue Bird of Paradise are particularly flamboyant, involving the male bird first calling from a branch in order to attract potential mates, before swinging backwards to hang upside down, whilst fanning the iridescent feathers of his wings and flanks and producing a humming call. Following mating, the female constructs a shallow, cup-shaped nest in a tree. Habitat loss, due to the clearance of forested areas for agriculture, remains a serious threat to the Blue Bird of Paradise, whilst it was once threatened by hunting for its plumes.

Magnificent Bird of Paradise

(Eurasian) Jay ▲

Scientific name:	*Garrulus glandarius*
Family:	Corvidae
Length:	35cm (14in)
Habitat:	Open woods, hedgerows, orchards, parks,and backyards
Distribution:	Europe, north-west Africa, central, eastern and southeast Asia
Identification:	Pinkish-brown overall, with black and white speckled crown, black wings with blue and white barring, white rump, and black tail

A highly distinctive and colorful bird, the Jay is, however, also quite shy and secretive, and whilst it may be glimpsed fleetingly as it crosses a woodland clearing or other open ground with its bouncing flight, it is more likely to be heard, producing its screaming alarm call. It is particularly defensive, and will attack owls, crows, and birds of prey, also mimicking their calls in order to deter such species from entering its territory. It is quietest during the breeding season in spring, when a clutch of around five eggs will be incubated by both parent birds for a period of just under three weeks. The nest takes the form of a large, bowl-like structure of twigs, lined with grass and animal hair, usually placed quite high in a tree. Although the Jay may be found in coniferous and mixed forests, deciduous woodland where oaks are present is favored, as acorns are generally its preferred food. In autumn this species will bury hundreds or even thousands of acorns, which will serve as a cache during the winter months. Additionally, the Jay feeds on seeds and various invertebrates, and when nesting will take birds' eggs and even nestlings.

Crested Jay

Scientific name:	*Platylophus galericulatus*
Family:	Corvidae
Length:	33cm (13in)
Habitat:	Tropical lowland and sub-montane forest
Distribution:	Southeast Asia, from Thailand to Java and Borneo
Identification:	Dark or reddish-brown to black overall, with a short, broad tail and white neck patches. Crest is extremely long, with broad, forward facing feathers

Sometimes also known as the Shrike Jay, or Crested Shrike Jay, this species was once thought to belong to the true shrike family Laniidae, but is now recognized as a corvid, or member of the crow family. It is highly distinctive on account of its long crest, which it tends to flick repeatedly whilst producing its rattling calls. Uncommon, and tending to be found in quite isolated areas, this species has not been extensively studied; however, it is typically a very bold bird, and is not shy of human contact. In fact, pairs or small groups may even mob people on occasion, particularly during the breeding season, when defending nesting sites. The nest takes the form of a shallow cup, placed on a sturdy platform of twigs between the branches of a tree, and a clutch will usually consist of just one or two eggs. The Crested Jay forages mainly amongst the foliage of trees in the mid to lower levels of the forest, feeding on large insects and other invertebrates.

Blue Jay

Scientific name:	*Cyanocitta cristata*
Family:	Corvidae
Length:	28cm (11in)
Habitat:	Woodland, and suburban parks, and backyards
Distribution:	Central and eastern parts of North America
Identification:	Blue above, with a small blue crest, black neck ring, black and white barred wings, and black-barred tail. Underparts are light gray or whitish

A fairly common and familiar woodland bird, the Blue Jay has adapted well to suburban habitats, and may be found in parks and yards, particularly during the winter months, when it will take advantage of food provided at bird tables and feeders. It is far more numerous in eastern North America, from southern Canada, south to the Gulf of Mexico, although whilst there has been a slight decline in its numbers in this part of its range, the population is gradually expanding westward. Generally sedentary, some birds also undertake short migrations from more northerly parts in winter, at which time this species may be encountered in quite large flocks. However, pairs or small family groups are more common. During the breeding season, the Blue Jay constructs a bulky, cup-shaped nest in a tree, where a clutch of between three and six eggs is normally laid, to be incubated by the female for around 17 days. This species feeds mainly on fruit, seeds, nuts, and insects, and may bury nuts to insure a food supply in winter. In spring, it may also take the eggs and nestlings of other birds, but the extent to which it does so is generally exaggerated. It is a highly vocal bird, and may mimic the calls of other species, particularly birds of prey, which may serve as a warning to others of its kind, or deter other birds from its territory.

Steller's Jay

Scientific name:	*Cyanocitta stelleri*
Family:	Corvidae
Length:	30cm (12in)
Habitat:	Coniferous forests, pine-oak woodland, and suburbs
Distribution:	North American west coast, from Alaska to California, and beyond into parts of Central America
Identification:	Dark-crested jay, with a black head, throat, chest, and upper back, and deep blue belly, rump, tail, and wings, blue and white forehead streaks. Some individuals have white eyebrows

Steller's Jay is the largest jay found in North America, and is a common bird in hilly and mountainous woodland in the west, although it also tends to occur in lowlands in winter. Additionally, from time to time, large numbers of mainly young birds may be found far from their normal range, and where the ranges of this species and the Blue Jay (*Cyanocitta cristata*) overlap, they will also occasionally interbreed to produce hybrids. During the breeding season, Steller's Jay constructs a bowl-shaped nest of twigs, leaves, moss, and mud, placed on a horizontal branch, usually close to the trunk of a tree. An average clutch consists of between two and six eggs, which will be incubated mainly by the female for a little over two weeks, with the young becoming fledged at around three weeks of age. This species forages on the ground and amongst trees, feeding on a variety of invertebrates, nuts, seeds, and fruit, and even small vertebrates. Acorns are a favored food, and may be buried to provide a cache in winter. As with other members of the crow family, it will often hold and manipulate food items with its feet.

COMMON MAGPIE ▼

SCIENTIFIC NAME:	*Pica pica*
FAMILY:	Corvidae
LENGTH:	48cm (19in)
HABITAT:	Grassland, thickets, forest edges, farmland, parks, and backyards
DISTRIBUTION:	Much of Eurasia, northwest Africa, and northwest North America
IDENTIFICATION:	Black head, back, and breast, white shoulders and belly, with blue-green patches on wings and tail. Stout black bill, long tail, and shows white wing patches in flight

The Common Magpie has been frequently maligned for a number of reasons, probably mainly for its habit of eating the eggs and nestlings of other birds, although it has a wide diet, consisting of small mammals, reptiles, amphibians, various invertebrates, including insect pests, and vegetable material. It is also known as something of a thief, with a habit of collecting shiny or brightly colored objects, and has been associated with bad luck in folklore. It is found in a variety of habitats, and is a sociable bird for much of the year, gathering in noisy flocks and often roosting communally. During the breeding season, however, the Common Magpie becomes aggressively territorial, and fights may occur. Both males and females construct a large, untidy, domed nest of twigs, with the male collecting most of the nest material, which is then put in place by the female. An average clutch consists of around six eggs, which are incubated for about 18 days. Following hatching, the young remain in the nest for up to four weeks, and may rely on their parent birds for food for several more weeks once fledged. They will then typically remain as a group until the following spring.

CLARK'S NUTCRACKER ▲

SCIENTIFIC NAME:	*Nucifraga columbiana*
FAMILY:	Corvidae
LENGTH:	30cm (12in)
HABITAT:	Mountainous coniferous forests
DISTRIBUTION:	Parts of the western US, Canada, and northern Mexico, more rarely in central US
IDENTIFICATION:	Light gray overall, with long black wings, short black tail with white outer feathers, and white face and belly

Occurring mainly in the high coniferous forests of western North America, south to Mexico, Clark's Nutcracker specializes in feeding on pine seeds, which it extracts from cones with its sturdy but narrow bill. However, it will also consume carrion, small vertebrates, and, in summer particularly, a wide range of invertebrates. During the winter months, when this species may also be found at lower elevations, it will feed on caches of seeds collected earlier in the year, and has a pouch within its mouth that enables it to carry seeds over long distances. Storing food also allows Clark's Nutcracker to breed early in the year, even in late winter, as it will feed its nestlings on these pine seeds. During the breeding season, it constructs a cup-shaped nest of twigs, high in a conifer, where a clutch of two or three eggs will be incubated for up to 18 days. Unlike most members of the crow family, where incubation is performed solely by the female, both parent birds take turns to incubate their eggs. Following hatching, the young fledge at around three weeks of age.

CHOUGH

SCIENTIFIC NAME:	*Pyrrhocorax pyrrhocorax*
FAMILY:	Corvidae
LENGTH:	38cm (15in)
HABITAT:	Coastal cliffs, farmland, mountains, and steppes
DISTRIBUTION:	Parts of Europe, North Africa, the Middle East, Russia, and Asia
IDENTIFICATION:	Glossy black plumage, scarlet legs, and a long, curved, scarlet bill

The Chough has a rather patchy distribution throughout its range, and its numbers have suffered severe declines over many years. In Britain, this bird is almost exclusively found in South Wales, Northern Ireland, and some Scottish islands, although it has begun to breed again in parts of southwest England, where it was once far more common. In fact, it was so numerous in Cornwall that at one time it was also known as the Cornish Chough. The fall in its numbers is believed to have been brought about by a combination of hunting for sport and changes in agricultural practices. Today, however, it is protected. It feeds mainly on insects and their larvae, foraging under stones and probing the ground with its bill, and will also pick parasites from livestock. During the breeding season, this species usually nests in small colonies, constructing an untidy nest of twigs, heather, and other materials, usually located on a rocky ledge, in a cave, mine, or disused building. The female incubates a clutch of between two to six eggs alone, for a period of up to 18 days, whilst the male will bring food to her at the nest. The male will also do much of the feeding of the young once hatched. They fledge at up to six weeks, remaining dependent on their parents for perhaps a further five weeks.

(EURASIAN) JACKDAW

SCIENTIFIC NAME:	*Corvus monedula*
FAMILY:	Corvidae
LENGTH:	33cm (13in)
HABITAT:	Woodland, farmland, coastal and inland cliffs, also suburban and urban areas
DISTRIBUTION:	Much of Eurasia, and the tip of northwest Africa
IDENTIFICATION:	A small crow, black or dark gray overall, with a lighter gray nape

Very common throughout much of its range, including Britain, with the notable exception of far northwest Scotland, this sociable member of the crow family is commonly seen in flocks of several dozen or even hundreds, particularly on farmland, where it is often found in association with birds such as starlings and rooks. As with those species, it is primarily a ground feeder, foraging for invertebrates by probing the soil. Additionally it will also feed on carrion, fruit, seeds, and small vertebrates, including the nestlings of other birds. During the breeding season, the Jackdaw nests in colonies, and a large, untidy nest of twigs is constructed in a hole in a tree, building, or on a cliff. Alternatively, the nest of a larger bird, such as a rook, may be used. The female incubates a clutch of up to nine eggs for a period of about 17 or 18 days, whilst the male will share the feeding duties once the young have hatched. The young will typically begin to take flight after roughly 30 days. As with some other members of the crow family, the Jackdaw has a propensity for caching food at times, as well as other objects, particularly those made from shiny materials.

AMERICAN CROW ▲

SCIENTIFIC NAME:	*Corvus brachyrhynchos*
FAMILY:	Corvidae
LENGTH:	45cm (18in)
HABITAT:	Grassland, open woodland, farmland, and suburban and urban areas
DISTRIBUTION:	Most of North America
IDENTIFICATION:	A large crow, entirely black, with a short, rounded tail, broad wings, and large bill

The adult American Crow is a large bird, and is in part a voracious predator, feeding on large invertebrates, rodents, and nestlings. However, it is omnivorous, and will also consume grain and fruit. Additionally, carrion forms quite a large part of its diet, but its bill is not particularly strong, and it must often wait for another animal to break the skin before it may feast on a carcass. Highly sociable, in towns and cities this bird will often be found in huge flocks at refuse heaps, and roosting sites may contain millions of birds. As with other members of the crow family, the American Crow is notoriously intelligent and resourceful, with a well developed social structure and advanced communication system, enabling it to describe the location of food or to warn of approaching danger. During the breeding season, the female produces a clutch of between three and six eggs, which are incubated for a period of about 17 days in a large, cup-shaped nest in a tree or large bush. The young leave the nest around five weeks after hatching, but will often remain in the family group and help their parents to raise subsequent broods.

CARRION CROW

SCIENTIFIC NAME:	*Corvus corone*
FAMILY:	Corvidae
LENGTH:	47cm (19in)
HABITAT:	Open woodland, grassland, farmland, coastlines, parks, and backyards
DISTRIBUTION:	Europe, Asia, the Nile Valley, and the Middle East
IDENTIFICATION:	Large crow, black overall, with an iridescent green and purple sheen, and a powerful bill

As its name suggests, the Carrion Crow feeds largely on carrion, but it has a highly varied, omnivorous diet, and is something of an opportunistic feeder, consuming invertebrates, small vertebrates such as amphibians, rodents, and young birds, including other members of the crow family, as well as scraps, nuts, seeds, and fruit. It forages mainly on the ground in a wide range of habitats, and is a relatively solitary bird, although it may also be seen in pairs or small flocks. During the breeding season, both male and female Carrion Crows cooperate to construct a large nest of twigs and other plant materials in the fork of a tree, in which the female will lay a clutch of around four or five eggs, incubating them alone for up to three weeks. Following this, both parents will feed the nestlings. The young crows then fledge at approximately five or six weeks of age. Whilst the Carrion Crow is black all over, the Hooded Crow, which was once thought to be a subspecies, *C.c. cornix*, but is now largely accepted as a species in its own right (*Corvus cornix*), has a gray body and a black head, throat, wings, and tail.

ROOK ▼

SCIENTIFIC NAME:	*Corvus frugilegus*
FAMILY:	Corvidae
LENGTH:	46cm (18in)
HABITAT:	Farmland, open woodland, meadows, suburbs, and urban areas
DISTRIBUTION:	Most of Europe, the Middle East, and central and eastern Asia. Also introduced to New Zealand
IDENTIFICATION:	Large crow, black overall, with a reddish tint, long pointed bill with white base, and a high forehead

The Rook is probably the most sociable member of the crow family, and may be found in flocks of up to several hundred or even thousands particularly in winter at communal roosting sites, which are known as rookeries. It is also often found in association with Jackdaws. The Rook is omnivorous, and its diet consists of invertebrates, small vertebrates, birds' eggs, carrion, seeds, fruit, and root crops, with most foraging occurring on the ground. As with most members of the crow family, it will sometimes bury food for later consumption. During the breeding season, both adult birds construct a bulky nest of twigs, earth, bark, and moss, where the female will incubate a clutch of around three to five eggs for about 16 days. Following hatching, both the male and female will care for their young, which fledge at approximately 30 days. However, they will usually remain dependent on their parents for food for a further month, and will not become completely independent for several months. The Rook is a common bird, especially on farmland, but it has often been persecuted as an agricultural pest, and its breast has traditionally been used as a pie filling in Britain.

(COMMON) RAVEN ▲

SCIENTIFIC NAME:	*Corvus corax*
FAMILY:	Corvidae
LENGTH:	60cm (24in)
HABITAT:	Forests, mountains, tundra, coastlines, suburban, and urban areas
DISTRIBUTION:	Throughout the Northern Hemisphere, with the exceptions of Central Africa, Saudi Arabia, and southeast Asia
IDENTIFICATION:	Very large crow-like bird, with long wings, wedge-shaped tail, and massive bill

The largest member of the crow family, the Raven is easily distinguishable from other species by its large size, wedge-shaped tail, and its particularly long, heavy bill. It is relatively common throughout most of the Northern Hemisphere, occurring in a wide range of habitats, although it tends to prefer open areas, especially where there are cliffs for nesting. In towns and cities, however, it will often nest on buildings, telegraph poles, or in similar locations. Pairs of Ravens remain together throughout the year, and are thought often to mate for life. They can often be seen performing aerobatics during the mating season, soaring at great height. Their nests are large untidy constructions of sticks, lined with animal hair, in which the female will lay and incubate four to seven eggs for up to three weeks. Following hatching, the young will be ready to fend for themselves approximately five to six weeks later. The Common Raven feeds on invertebrates, carrion, small birds, reptiles and amphibians, rodents, and even small mammals up to the size of young rabbits. However, they are omnivorous, and will also eat, grain, acorns, fruit and buds, and being opportunistic, will often scavenge at refuse dumps. It is believed to be highly intelligent and adaptable, and capable of learning new behavior when required.

Index of Common Names

Index of Scientific Names

Picture Credits

The publisher would like to thank Photolibrary.com for kindly providing the images listed below.
We would also like to thank the following for their kind permission to reproduce their photographs.

Allen, Doug; Emperor Penguins/Wilson's Storm Petrel Alonso, Sanchez Carlos; black-winged stilt/Great Bustard/ Red Kite /Shore Lark Atkinson, Kathie; Manx Shearwater/Masked Boobies/Australian Magpie / Grey Butcherbird Austermann, Mirian/AA; Californian Condor Bailey, Adrian; Carmine Bee-eaters/Cattle Egrets Bartov, Eyal; Pin Tailed Sand Grouse / Cape Sugarbird Bennett, Bob; Wood Duck Beste, H & J; Wirebird/Southern White Face Benvie, Niall; Jay Birkhead, Mike; Mandarin Duck Birquist, Paul; Verdin Blossom, Joe/SAL; Red Jungle Fowl/ Rothschild's Minah Boag, D; Fieldfare Bollman, Werner; Superb Starling Bomford, Tony; Rough-Legged Buzzard Brooke, Michael; Pied Currawong Brown, Roger; Black-Faced Cuckoo Shrike /Galahs/Mallee Fowl/Striated Pardalote/Mistletoe Bird/Blue-faced Honeyeater /Red-backed Wren/Black-faced Woodswallow Bush, Robin; Australian Brush Turkey/Brown Kiwi/Kea /Superb Lyrebird /Tomtit /Noisy Friarbird Chappell, Mark; Budgerigar/Tufted Puffin Christof, Alain; European Bee-eaters Colbeck, Martyn; Crowned Crane/Secretary Bird Cole, Ken; Black-Capped Chickadee Cordano, Marty; American White Pelican Cook, Peter; Crimson-breasted Shrike Cox, Daniel; Sulphur-crested Cockatoo/ Blue-headed Parrot/Common Loon /Emu/ Great Horned Owl/Japanese Crane/Rhinoceros Hornbill/Sage Grouse/Southern Giant Petrel/White-Throated Sparrow Cushing, Irvine; Shag Day, Kenneth; Guillemot Day, Richard; Northern Cardinal /Blue-Grey Gnatcatcher/ Common Grackle/ Dickcissel /Greater Flamingo/Mountain Bluebird/Yellow Rumped Warbler/Yellowthroat Daybreak Imagery; American Robin /Great Kiskadee/Canada Goose/Chimney Swift De Oliveira, Paulo; Waxbill De Roy, Tui; Vermillion Flycatcher/Harpy Eagle/Red-legged Seriema/Takahe; Degginger, E R; Phainopepla Dermid, Jack; American Bittern/Brown Pelican/Mourning Dove Dick, Michael/AA; Oriental or Asian Bay Owl/Silver-eared Mesia Dinodia Picture Agency; Indian Pitta Downer, John; White Stork Fioratti, Paolo; Hobby Fischer, Berndt; Blue Throat / Montagu's Harrier /Nightjar /Peregrine Falcon/ Red Kite/White-Tailed Tropicbird Fogden, Michael; Green Broadbill /Wire-tailed Manakin / Golden Bowerbird /Common Potoo /Giant Pitta/Weka/Sunbittern /White Tipped Sicklebill Foster Farnetti, Carol; Red-Lored Parrots Franklin, Paul; Olive Chacalaca Furlong, Frances; Common Linnet/Corncrake Gerlach, John; Common Redpoll /American Redstart/ Bobolink/Evening Grosbeak Green, Dennis/SAL; Merlin /Short-eared Owl Grizmek, Christopher /OPAKIA; Ostrich Habicht, Michael; Fox Sparrow Gerlach, John; Bobolink Hallett, Jim; Rook Hamblin, Mark; Swallow /Golden Eagle /Dunnock /Robin / Osprey /Common Dipper/European Greenfinch /Nuthatch /Northern Lapwing /Black Grouse/Black-Legged Kittiwake/ Ringed Plover/ BlueTit/Great Spotted Woodpecker Buzzard /Chaffinch /Coal Tit/Common (Atlantic) Puffin/Crested Tit/Double-Crested Cormorant /Dunlin/Dunnock /Eurasian Goldfinch /Fulmar /Goshawk /Great Crested Grebe /Greylag Goose /Mute Swan /Pintail/ Spoonbill/Water Rail /Yellow

Warbler /Swift/Oystercatcher/Sedge Warbler Hill, Mike; Crested Lark / Red-backed Shrike /Redstart /Bronze Sunbird Howell, N; Tufted Titmouse Jackman, Roger; Caspian Tern Jackson, Tim; Lanner Falcon Jackson, Tim; Shaft-tailed Whydah Jones, Mark; Andean Condor Jones, Adam; Northern bobwhite/Shoebill Kemp, R&J European Serin/Serin Kenney, Brian; Victoria Crowned Pigeon/Wood stork Kent, Breck P.; American Crow/Northern Flicker Knights, Chris; Little Owl/Marsh /Swamp Harrier/Narina / Tufted Duck Korenromp, Jos; Grey Wagtail /Common Redstart/Nightingale/Goldcrest Laidler/K/Survival; Red-billed Toucan Lauber, Lon; Harris hawk/Collared Dove Leach, M; Long-Eared Owl /Crossbill/Tawny Owl Leach, Tom; Arctic Skua/Parasite Jaegar /Greater Yellowlegs/Snow Bunting/Yellow-billed Oxpecker Lubeck, Robert; Black-and-White Warbler Maclean, Gordond; Linnet Mayre, R; Spotted Flycatcher/Green Woodpecker Mills, Stephen; Common Tern Milne, Brian; King Eider Mitchell, John; Himalayan Monal Pheasant Netherton, John; Anhinga Nelson, Alan G.; Hairy Woodpecker Newman, Owen; Grey Heron/Little Auks Osborne, Ben; Wandering Albatross/Magpie OSF; Roadrunner Osolinski, Stan; Double-crested Cormorant/Black Skimmer/Great Egret /Kildeer/Limpkin /Eastern Kingbird/Northern Mockingbird/Purple Gallinule/Rose Ringed Parakeet/Scarlet Ibis/ Smooth-Billed Ani/Straw-Crowned Bulbul /Golden-breasted Starling/Glossy Ibis/ Rock Dove Packwood, Richard; Northern/Winter Wren/Brown-Headed Cowbird/Crested Caracara/Gannet /Common Raven/Marabou Stork/Great Skua Partridge Films; African Skimmer Perrins, Chris; Blue Footed Booby Pfefferle, Manfred; Hawfinch /Andean Cock of the Rock Plage, Mary; Pheasant-Tailed Jacana Photolibrary.com; Lichtenstein's Sandgrouse/Belted Kingfisher/ Diamond Dove/House Sparrow/Pied Flycatcher /New Holland Honeyeater Powles, Mike Eurasian Coot/Bearded Tit Price, Mike; Blue Jay Reinhard, Hans; Wren/European Wryneck Renjifo Juan/AA; Oilbird Reszeter, Jorge; Cetti's Warbler/ Richards, Michale; Snowgoose Ringland, Keith; Pied Wagtail/Capercaillie/Jackdaw Robinson, James, H.; Burrowing Owl Root, Alan/SAL; Little Grebe Rosing, Norbert; Woodpidgeon Rozinski, Bob; Snipe Rue, Len Jnr III; Steller's Jay Saunders, D J; Common Gull /Treecreeper/Kingfisher Schneidermeyer, Frank; Eastern Towhee/Red-Winged Blackbird/Painted Bunting /Sun Concure/Western Meadowlark Senani, Krupakar, Crimson-Breasted Barbet/Coppersmith/Hoopoe/ Red-whiskered Balbul /Paradise Flycatcher Sewell, Michael; Hoatzin/ Great Indian Hornbill/Laughing Kookaburra/ Scarlet Macaw Shahar, Ben, Rafi; Nightjar Sharp, Chris; Song Sparrow Shattil, Wendy; Broad-Tailed Hummingbird Shattil & Rozinski; Bald Eagle/Great Blue Heron/Turkey Vulture Sierra, Jorge; Gryffon Vulture/Golden Oriole Sinha, Vivek; Iora Steelman, C; Rufous Hummingbird/ Wild Turkey TC Nature; Hyacinth Macaw Tibbles, Maurice/SAL; Cuckoo Tilford, Tony; Electus Parrot /Mistle Thrush/ Fairy Bluebird/ Black Cap /Waxwing /African Grey Parrot /Cockatiel/Dark-Eyed Junco/Indigo Bunting/Woodcock/Banded Pitta /Green and Gold Tannager/ Saffron Finch /Great Racket-tailed Drongo /King Bird of Paradise /Magnificent Bird of Paradise/ Purple Grenadier /Gouldian Finch/ Oriental White-eye/Reed Bunting/ Blackbird Tipling, David; Curlew/Common Moorhen/Common Quail/Northern Jacana/ Ptarmigan/Ruff/Teal /Temmincks Tragopan/ Tiwari, Satyendra; Peacock Turner, Steve; Southern/ Double-Wattled Cassowary /Magpie Lark/Common Mynah/Adelie Penguins Ulrich, Tom; Common Poorwill /Forked-tailed Flycatcher/Brown Thrasher /Pine Grosbeak/Pine Siskin/ Red-Eyed Vireo/ Eatern Bluebird/Yellow-bellied Sapsucker /Purple Martin/Black Phoebe Walker, Barry; Yellowhammer Wells, B.&B; Splendid Fairy Wren West, Ian; Whooper Swan/Mallard Willis, G W; Snowy Egret Wisniewski, W/OKAPIA; Great Frigate Bird Woods, Eric; Kestrel/Meadow Pipit Wothe, Konrad; Red-billed Scythbill /Toco Toucan /Pigmy Owl/Long-tailed Broadbill/Black-Capped Donacobius /Longtailed Skua/Jaeger /Southern Red Bishop /White-breasted Nuthatch/ Clark's Nutcracker/Mersenger/Snowy Owl/Roller/Blue-napped Mousebird

We would also like to thank the following Ardea photographers for their kind permission to reproduce the photographs below.

Chapman, G; Crimson Chat, Dunning, J. S; Fasciated Antshrike/ Great Antshrike/Warbling Vireo/Paradise Jacamar Fink, Kenneth W; Bare-throated Bellbird Greensmith, Alan; Asity (Wattled False) Sunbird Hadden, Don; Rifleman Steyn, Peter; Village Weaver Taylor, W; Brown Weebill Trounson, A D & Clampett C; Chestnut-crowned Babbler Watson, M; Redwinged Starling.

Front cover image: Konrad Wothe
Back cover (l-r) Stan Osolinski, Paolo Fioratti, Tony Tilford
Back flap: Tui De Roy
Endpapers: Mark Hamblin

This book would not have been possible without the help of Rebecca Marsden and all the researchers at Photolibrary.com, Sophie Napier at Ardea, T. E. B. Taylor, Richard Betts, Vicki Harris, Jill Dorman and Charlotte de Grey.